HAROLD WILSON AND
EUROPEAN INTEGRATION

CASS SERIES: BRITISH FOREIGN AND COLONIAL POLICY
Series Editor: Peter Catterall
ISSN: 1467-5013

This series provides insights into both the background influences on and the course of policymaking towards Britain's extensive overseas interests during the past 200 years.

Whitehall and the Suez Crisis, Saul Kelly and Anthony Gorst (eds)

Liberals, International Relations and Appeasement: The Liberal Party, 1919–1939, Richard S. Grayson

British Government Policy and Decolonisation, 1945–1963: Scrutinising the Official Mind, Frank Heinlein

Harold Wilson and European Integration: Britain's Second Application to Join the EEC, Oliver Daddow (ed.)

Britain, Israel and the United States, 1955–1958: Beyond Suez, Orna Almog

HAROLD WILSON
and
EUROPEAN INTEGRATION

Britain's Second Application
to Join the EEC

Edited by

OLIVER J. DADDOW

*King's College London at the Joint Services
Command and Staff College*

With a Foreword by

Baroness Williams of Crosby

FRANK CASS
LONDON • PORTLAND, OR

First published in 2003 in Great Britain by
FRANK CASS PUBLISHERS
Crown House, 47 Chase Side,
London N14 5BP

and in the United States of America by
FRANK CASS PUBLISHERS
c/o ISBS, 5824 N.E. Hassalo Street
Portland, Oregon, 97213-3644

Website: www.frankcass.com

British Library Cataloguing in Publication Data

Harold Wilson and European integration: Britain's second
    application to join the EEC. – (Cass series. British
    foreign and colonial policy)
    1. Wilson, Harold, 1916– – Views on European economic
    integration 2. European Economic Community – Great
    Britain 3. Great Britain – Politics and government –
    1964–1979
    I. Daddow, Oliver J.
    327.4′1′04′09046

ISBN 0-7146-5222-9 (cloth)
ISBN 0-7146-8207-1 (paper)
ISSN 1467-5013

Library of Congress Cataloging-in-Publication Data

Harold Wilson and European integration: Britain's second
application to join the EEC / edited by Oliver J. Daddow;
with a foreword by Baroness Williams of Crosby.
        p. cm. – (Cass series – British foreign and colonial policy
    series, ISSN 1456-5013)
    Based on papers presented at a
    conference held Jan. 2000 in association with the Institute
    of Contemporary British History.
        Includes bibliographical references and index.
        ISBN 0-7146-5222-9 (cloth) – ISBN 0-7146-8207-1 (paper)
        1. Wilson, Harold, Sir, 1916– – 2. Great Britain and
    and government. 3. European Union Countries – Politics and
    government. 4. European Union. I. Daddow, Oliver J.,
    1974– II. Institute of Contemporary British History. III. Series.

HC241.25.G7 H36 2002
337.1′42′094109046–dc21

2002024190

Typeset in 10.5/12.5 Zapt Calligraphic by Frank Cass Publishers
Printed in Great Britain by Creative Print and Design, Ebbw Vale, Wales

Contents

Notes on Contributors

Anthony Adamthwaite was educated at the universities of Durham, Leeds and London. He has held several fellowships and visiting professorships, and taught at the University of Salford before moving to the University of California at Berkeley in 1991, where he teaches international history. His most recent book is *Grandeur and Misery: France's Bid for Power in Europe, 1914–1940* (1995). He is currently completing a study of Britain, France and the origins of the European Community.

Philip Alexander completed a PhD entitled 'The Commonwealth and European Integration: Competing Commitments for Britain, 1956–67', at St Catharine's College, Cambridge. He has also contributed a chapter on the second application to Alex May's edited volume *The Commonwealth and Europe* (2001).

Katharina Böhmer studied Neuere/Neueste Geschichte (Modern History), French Literature and Politics in Paris, Saarbrücken, Oxford and Berlin and is currently preparing a Master's thesis on 'Germany and Britain's Second EEC Application' at the Humboldt-Universität zu Berlin, Germany.

Peter Catterall lectures in history and public policy at Queen Mary College, University of London and on European business at City University Business School. He edits the academic journals *Contemporary British History* and *National Identities*. His latest publication (edited with Wolfram Kaiser and Ulrike Walton-Jordan) is *Reforming the Constitution: Debates in Twentieth-Century Britain* (2000). He is currently editing Harold Macmillan's diaries, to be published in two volumes in 2003 and 2004.

Oliver Daddow is Lecturer in the Defence Studies Department, King's College, London at the Joint Services Command and Staff College. He is the author of *Britain and Europe Since 1945: Historiographical Perspectives on Unification* (2003). His major areas of research interest are in post-war British foreign policy, European integration history, historiography and the philosophy of history.

Anne Deighton is Lecturer in European International Politics at the University of Oxford, and a fellow of Wolfson College. She has published extensively on the Cold War, on British foreign policy and Europe, and on European security.

James Ellison is a lecturer in the Department of History, Queen Mary College, University of London. He is the author of *Threatening Europe: Britain and the Creation of the European Community, 1955–1958* (2000).

Piers Ludlow is Lecturer in Modern History at the London School of Economics. He is a specialist on the early decades of the European Community and has published *Dealing with Britain: The Six and the First UK Application to the EEC* (1997) and numerous other articles and chapters on this theme. He is currently preparing a book on the EEC's development during the period 1963–69.

Philip Lynch is a Senior Lecturer in Politics at the University of Leicester. He is author of *The Politics of Nationhood: Sovereignty, Britishness and Conservative Politics* (1999) and co-editor (with Mark Garnett) of *The Conservatives in Crisis* (2003).

Helen Parr teaches history at Queen Mary College, University of London and King's College, London. She is completing her PhD on 'Harold Wilson, Whitehall and British Policy towards the European Community, 1964–1967'.

Neil Rollings is Senior Lecturer in Economic and Social History at Glasgow University. He is currently writing an ESRC-funded handbook on documents in the Public Record Office on economic policy, 1951–64 (with Rodney Lowe, Roger Middleton and Astrid Ringe) and a book on British industry and European integration, 1945–73.

Jane Toomey is a Faculty of Arts Fellow at the National University of Ireland, University College Dublin, where she is completing her doctorate on Britain's second application to join the EEC. Her other areas of research interest include Irish foreign policy, Anglo-Irish relations in the twentieth century and Britain and European integration.

John Young holds the Chair of International History at the University of Nottingham. He is the author of *Winston Churchill's Last Campaign: Britain and the Cold War, 1951–5* (1996), *Britain and the World in the Twentieth Century* (1997) and *Britain and European Unity, 1945–99* (2000), and is currently writing a general study of the international policy of the Wilson governments of 1964–70.

Foreword

For those of us who were members of his government at the time, Harold Wilson's attempt to join the European Economic Community (EEC) seemed motivated above all by the need to hold a fractious Cabinet and a fractious Parliamentary Labour Party together. Indeed, throughout his whole career as Prime Minister, holding his party together remained Harold Wilson's guiding star.

But this exhaustively researched and thorough book shows just how many other factors were at play. One that was very important indeed was the search for ways to maintain Britain's influence in the world, despite a declining share of world trade and a sickly economy. Oliver Daddow, in a subtle introduction, describes the 'missed opportunities' thesis of many historians and commentators on the post-war period. He refers also to those who took the very different view that no one at the time saw 'Europe' as much of an opportunity. The assessment depended to a great extent on whether one was looking forward or looking back. But even hard-headed calculations of Britain's interests were accompanied by a yearning for a global role, and still are. The politicians of the third post-war Labour government, re-elected with a convincing majority in 1966, longed for the power and influence their predecessors had enjoyed during the war and immediate post-war period.

It became painfully clear in the 1960s, as the chapter by Philip Alexander explains, that the member-states of the Commonwealth, the old Dominions as much as the newly independent countries were looking for closer regional associations and new trade opportunities beyond those offered by the erstwhile mother country. This discovery, obvious enough for countries trying to assert their new status in the world, seems to have come as a shock to some ministers, even as a kind of betrayal. So the United Kingdom was driven in self-protection to consider more warmly membership of the EEC. Ironically, it was to the EEC that some of the newer Commonwealth countries, especially in Africa, began to look for investment and markets. The protective shelter of the Lomé convention also had attractions for producers buffeted by the ups and downs of the commodity markets. Harold Wilson could not admit publicly, however, that the United Kingdom was beginning to lose ground in the effort to maintain global influence, not least because his period of office as Prime Minister was peppered with evidence to that effect: the unilateral declaration of independence by Southern Rhodesia, the devaluation of sterling, the withdrawal of British forces from Singapore and Malaysia, the relinquishing of bases east of Suez, and the contemptuous treatment he endured at the hands of President Johnson, especially with regard to his representations on the Vietnam War.

As Helen Parr points out in her chapter on the Foreign and Commonwealth Office, there was a group of Europe enthusiasts in the Foreign Office, some of them in the European Economic Integration Department. They, in turn, were in touch with a group in the US State Department, which saw the United Kingdom as the counter-balance to French ambitions in Europe, and the key to keeping the Federal Republic of Germany within the North Atlantic Treaty Organisation (NATO). Briefed by the Foreign Office for his 'probe' of European capitals, Wilson's enthusiasm for membership of the EEC grew. He began to think that the old Europe might redress the balance of the New World and the new Commonwealth. It was not surprising that, two decades later, Margaret Thatcher came to regard the Foreign Office as the 'wettest' and weakest link in the policy chain.

What is also fascinating about this book is the persistence it reveals of certain policy positions and procedures. The 'probe' of European capitals was a typically Wilsonian ploy for gaining time and putting off debate. Gaining time, because obviously the government was doing *something*; putting off debate, because what was going on was consultation, not the making of a decision. Both ploys have been well learned by Wilson's successors, as the present government's handling of difficult issues like the euro, or, in a different field, missile defence, so clearly demonstrate. There were even 'five conditions' that had to be met if Britain was to join. Perhaps Whitehall keeps tests and conditions on its mantelpiece, as cooks keep jelly moulds, there to be used for any purpose.

The themes, too, keep returning. Is the United Kingdom a committed European member-state, or just an American lackey? Is national sovereignty sacrificed for nothing, or 'pooled' in the interest of having a greater influence over world events? These big questions were largely pushed to one side by the leading British politicians of the day, who saw the EEC very much as just that, a common market integrating for economic and trade purposes, and which played down the political implications. Rightly or wrongly, they believed that the Community was much easier to sell as an economic concept than as a political one. On the other side of the Channel, of course, it was the political that mattered most, the almost miraculous triumph of the Community idea over centuries of hatred and hostility between France and Germany.

No wonder, then, that Germany found the almost mystical meeting on Aachen bridge of Charles de Gaulle and Konrad Adenauer, the great post-war reconciliation, a much richer gift than the rather threadbare attractions of a British-led European technological community which was the tinsel on Wilson's tree. The British, ploddingly pragmatic as ever, could not and did not see that. Their vision was of a United Kingdom helpfully bridging the gap between the United States and Europe. That remains the vision today, though the gap may be widening.

The chapters here by Anne Deighton and Philip Lynch on party attitudes do not so much find resemblances between then and now as contradictions. Edward Heath's Conservative Party was staunchly pro-Europe, although there were signs of dissent around the edges, especially from Enoch Powell. Its votes were available to get the second attempt at entry through the House of Commons; Heath's commitment was too whole-hearted to be the stuff of party-political games. He was rightly critical of Wilson's reluctance to explore defence and foreign policy as potential areas of common ground, once de Gaulle's unflinching opposition to British membership of the Community was again manifested. The history of Europe would have been very different if Wilson had been persuaded. Wilson, on the other hand, played his politics like a fugue, the themes of party unity and deep divisions on Europe being woven together by this master of the art, later to culminate in the melodious solution of a referendum. Clever though that was, not least in holding the Labour Party together, the referendum debate failed to address some of the deepest issues inherent in British membership of the European Community, because those issues had never been properly deliberated in the first or second half-hearted attempts at entry. Until they are, the United Kingdom will never quite know to what it is – or is not – committed.

But it is doubtful whether Wilson had much enthusiasm for the European ideal as such. No British Prime Minister, with the exception of Heath, ever did, though Winston Churchill was briefly inspired by it shortly after the end of the Second World War. Only Heath, forged by his experience of war and the disaster of the Suez expedition, embraced Europe as wholeheartedly as did its founding fathers, Jean Monnet, Paul-Henri Spaak, Robert Schuman, Alcide de Gasperi and Konrad Adenauer. The usual British attitude towards the EEC was cool, pragmatic and guided by economic calculations of the costs and benefits of membership. It was not the stuff of inspiration.

This book charts most aspects of the second attempt to enter the EEC. In particular, it deals in detail with the political and party considerations Wilson had to take into account. Wilson started out on a fairly confident note, setting out the five conditions that would need to be satisfied for Britain to enter, conscious of the need to accept the Treaty of Rome while nevertheless influencing the Community to be open to the world outside, and benefiting, as James Ellison points out, from growing American concern at the divergent path taken by President de Gaulle's France. That concern was exacerbated by the French withdrawal from the integrated military structure of NATO in March 1966, which threatened the cohesion of NATO itself.

The three years from 1964 to 1967, however, were to be an object lesson in Britain's economic weakness. The Confederation of British Industry, though strongly in favour of joining the Community, recognised that the British economy was weak and its manufacturing base uncompetitive. Serious balance-of-payments difficulties culminated in the agonising crisis over devaluation in the summer of 1966, and in the unavoidable decisions of 1967. Paradoxically, that devaluation may have made the United Kingdom less attractive as a potential member of the EEC, but also fortified those in the country who wanted to go in. It was a significant factor in persuading British politicians to recognise how weak their bargaining hand was.

In a fascinating chapter, Katharina Böhmer describes the position of Germany, seen in the United States as the key European country at risk of being seduced from loyalty to NATO by the siren songs of de Gaulle, seen in London as the crucial ally in the new bid for entry. Here again, the United Kingdom had a painful lesson to learn. The Federal Republic found de Gaulle's France a difficult neighbour, and one that challenged the German commitment to an Atlantic alliance. But the bottom line was that a Germany still profoundly grateful to France, and in particular to de Gaulle for his willingness to seek the reconciliation of these two historic enemies, and was not about to abandon its European partner. Certainly, substituting French leadership for British (as George Brown brightly suggested to Germany's Foreign Minister, Willy Brandt) was not a proposal with any great appeal to the German coalition government.

From then to the present day, the prospects for Europe have been blighted by the narrowness of its leaders' vision. Yet the monumental and sometimes monstrous challenges of the new century demand the drive and inspiration of the founding fathers, a drive and an inspiration the United Kingdom has never really understood.

Baroness Williams of Crosby
April 2002

Acknowledgements

This volume is based on the proceedings of a one-day conference, held in association with the Institute of Contemporary British History in January 2000. I would like to thank the Institute of Historical Research for kindly granting us permission to hold the conference in Senate House, and Michael Kandiah, Harriet Jones and Gillian Staerck of the ICBH for all their help in organising the 'London end' of operations in advance of and during the conference. Without their support and backing, this project might never have come off. Thanks are due also to the School of Politics at the University of Nottingham for kindly agreeing to underwrite the cost of the conference. The same goes for my editor at Frank Cass, Andrew Humphrys, who has provided critical support and encouragement throughout the project. Peter Catterall read and commented on the entire manuscript in draft form. I am extremely grateful to him for donating the time to it and for his constructive recommendations throughout. Any errors that remain are, of course, my responsibility.

I would like to express my sincere gratitude to all the contributors, first of all for providing such stimulating papers at the conference, and subsequently for their diligence in putting their chapters together and for putting up with my unfortunate but necessary stream of email correspondence. I would like also to thank the Conservative Party for allowing us to publish extracts from the Conservative Party Archives in the Bodleian Library, Oxford. To the Library itself I would like to extend my gratitude for authorising quotation from the George-Brown Papers.

My longer-term research interest in the history of British European policy flows from my doctoral thesis on the subject, and for their continuing friendship and astute criticism of my work I am deeply indebted to my former supervisors, Richard Aldrich and Anthony Forster. I would like to dedicate this book to Adrienne, for her love and support.

Abbreviations

ABCC	Association of British Chambers of Commerce
AIFTA	Anglo-Irish Free Trade Agreement
AN	Archives Nationales
ANF	Atlantic Nuclear Force
AOT	Associated Overseas Territory
BAOR	British Army of the Rhine
BDI	Bundesverband der Industrie
BEC	British Employers' Confederation
CAP	Common Agricultural Policy
CBI	Confederation of British Industry
CDU	Christian Democratic Party
CERN	European Council for Nuclear Research
CETS	European Conference on Satellite Communications
CIFEFTA	Council of Industrial Federations of the European Free Trade Association
CPA	Conservative Party Archive
CPRS	Central Policy Review Staff
CRD	Conservative Research Department
CRO	Commonwealth Relations Office
CSA	Commonwealth Sugar Agreement
DEA	Department of Economic Affairs
ECSC	European Coal and Steel Community
EDC	European Defence Community
EDM	Early Day Motion
EEC	European Economic Community
EEID	European Economic Integration Department

EEP	External Economic Policy Committee
EFTA	European Free Trade Association
EIU	Economist Intelligence Unit
ELDO	European Launcher Development Organisation
ESRO	European Space Research Organisation
ETC	European Technological Community
EU	European Union
EURM	Ministerial Committee on the Approach to Europe
EURO	Official Committee on the Approach to Europe
FBI	Federation of British Industries
GATT	General Agreement on Tariffs and Trade
GITA	'Going It Alone'
IMF	International Monetary Fund
IRC	Industrial Reorganisation Corporation
LCC	Leader's Consultative Committee
LTP	Long Term Policy Study Group
MAE	Ministère des Affaires Etrangères
Mintech	Ministry of Technology
MLF	Multilateral Force
MRC	Modern Records Centre
NAA	National Archives of Australia
NABM	National Association of British Manufacturers
NAFTA	North Atlantic Free Trade Agreement
NATO	North Atlantic Treaty Organization
NEC	National Executive Committee
NFU	National Farmers' Union
NPG	Nuclear Planning Group
NPT	Non-Proliferation Treaty
NSC	National Security Council

OAU	Organisation of African Unity
OECD	Organisation for Economic Cooperation and Development
OEEC	Organisation for European Economic Cooperation
OPD	Defence and Overseas Policy Committee
PLP	Parliamentary Labour Party
PRO	Public Record Office
R and D	Research and Development
SACEUR	Supreme Allied Commander, Europe
SDP	Social Democratic Party (Britain)
SPD	Social Democratic Party (Germany)
TUC	Trades Union Congress
UDI	Unilateral Declaration of Independence
UN	United Nations
UNCTAD	United Nations Conference on Trade and Development
VAT	Value Added Tax
WEU	Western European Union

—— 1 ——

Introduction: The Historiography of Wilson's Attempt to Take Britain into the EEC

OLIVER J. DADDOW

Foreign policy is developed and projected in a complex domestic and international environment in which 'perception matters as much as reality'.[1] 'Images', remarked Avi Shlaim, 'are a crucial component of the belief system and, therefore, have a decisive effect on foreign policy since decision-makers act in accordance with their perception of reality, not reality itself.'[2] The problems of uncovering the 'objective reality' of foreign policy should alert scholars to the necessary incompleteness of our knowledge about the past, exaggerated by what Richard Immerman refers to as the 'encrustations of interpretation' that inevitably surround historical events.[3] British European policy is no exception. It bears an immense weight of history that shapes policy and is in turn shaped by that policy in a continuous process of interpretation and reinterpretation. Key events have been debated with such intensity that more than one historian has been led to comment that they now possess a 'mythical' quality.[4] Any addition to the growing body of literature on Britain's relationship with the continent must therefore take full account of the historiography to date, because it has provided the backdrop and stimulus to the research contained in this book.[5]

The main argument advanced in this chapter is that interpretations of British European policy have tended to be critical, and Harold Wilson is not a fondly remembered Prime Minister, so it is hardly surprising that his European policy has been poorly received. The highly partisan and personal criticisms that dominate the literature, however, have led to insufficient attention being paid to the particular demands placed upon the Wilson governments charged with constructing and implementing European policy, a lacuna that needs filling. It is usually taken to be just one more strand in Wilson's governance in which personal, party and electoral considerations overrode ideology or ideals, in this case a commitment by the Prime Minister to the European cause. But is this the whole story? Did Wilson launch the second application purely as a response to the series of domestic and international crises besieging the Labour governments in the mid-1960s, or to steal an electoral march on the Conservatives, or to quell threats to his position from within the Labour Cabinet? With the benefit of the official government record for these years, now available in the Public Record Office at Kew, and other as yet unused primary sources abroad, the contributors in this volume offer a corrective and a more sophisticated account of British European policy under the Labour governments of 1964–70. They have not found it possible to redeem Wilson's reputation; nor was that their aim. Rather, they seek to understand the dynamics of the policy process that led to the second application and to investigate the strategy used by British ministers and officials to overcome the suspicion of British intentions, most keenly held by President Charles de Gaulle in Paris. They find that the received wisdom on Wilson's motivation has more than a grain of truth in it, but that setting the second application in a broader historical context highlights an alternative interpretation that this represented a 'successful failure' for the Prime Minister and, indeed, for British European policy. It satisfied a number of personal, domestic and party ends and, by demonstrating Britain's commitment to a European future, prepared the foundations for Britain's entry to the European Economic Community (EEC) in 1973[6].

BRITAIN AND EUROPE: THE CONVENTIONAL WISDOM

Britain's approach to European integration since 1945 has not been well received. The traditional depiction is of an 'awkward' or 'reluctant' country that remained aloof from the process of unification on the continent until joining in 1973, thereafter hampering the efforts of its partners to create ever closer union.[7] Epitomising this interpretation is *The Economist*, a journal that has quite fairly been judged to be one of the 'pillars of Establishment opinion'.[8] It has repeatedly berated British governments for 'missed chances' to lead European integration in the post-war era, citing a number of policy failures.[9] In June 1950, Attlee's Labour government refused to join the European Coal and Steel

Community (ECSC). Between October 1950 and August 1954, Britain stood aloof from efforts to found the European Defence Community (EDC). Finally, in November 1955, Britain withdrew its representative from the Messina process that led to the creation of the European Economic Community (EEC). The longevity of what will be referred to in this chapter as the 'missed opportunities' interpretation of British European policy is testament to its espousal by a transnational collection of politicians, civil servants, academics and journalists. For the purposes of analysis, and allowing for some blurring of the chronological boundaries,[10] it is possible to identify five communities of writers who have given voice to the conventional wisdom on Britain and Europe between the early 1950s and the mid-1980s.

The first group incorporates the 'founding fathers', notably Jean Monnet, Robert Schuman and Paul-Henri Spaak, who set western Europe on the path to supranational integration in the decade after 1945, and who, Wolfram Kaiser explains, stimulated the view that Britain's approach to Europe represents a 'historically unique departure from the apparently normal path of democratic virtue'.[11] As the title of a 1991 study of Monnet suggests, they were convinced that there was a 'path to European unity' from which Britain was wrong to diverge.[12] Why, they asked, were the British 'so resistant to European integration'?[13] The very phrasing of the question has implications for the answer they developed.

As Nigel Ashford has remarked, one of the motor forces of integration and its subsequent historicisation was Monnet and 'his network of friends and colleagues who influenced US policy in favour of supranational European integration'.[14] The American advocates of a united Europe joined with Monnet to form an influential second group that criticised British European policy. Richard Aldrich posits an intelligence connection here, highlighting that supranational integration in Europe was, as early as 1947, perceived in Washington as an important adjunct to America's wider Cold War strategy. His discovery that in the period 1949–60 American 'sources' injected $3 to $4 million into 'European federalist activity',[15] fits into a longer strand to the historiography of post-war Europe which suggests that 'the ultimate purposes of the Marshall Plan were almost entirely political, albeit that its mechanisms were almost entirely economic'.[16] Americans were thus exasperated with Britain's aloofness from Europe, although they could not agree on which missed opportunity was most costly. Secretary of State Dean Acheson's verdict was that Britain's refusal to join the ECSC was 'the greatest mistake of the post-war period'.[17] Ambassador David Bruce, by contrast, thought that the failure to create a European Army – for which Britain is generally blamed – represented 'the greatest lost opportunity in modern European history'.[18]

The third group interpreting British European policy as a series of missed opportunities, Monnet's partners in Britain, is too diverse to examine in depth. However, its influence on the debate about Britain and Europe provides evidence to support Michael Gehler's observation that 'one should not underestimate the influence of the European federalists in setting up different ideas, concepts and programmes on European integration'.[19] It is the historicisation of these ideas and concepts through various channels that is of concern here – first, through the Federal Union and its immediately associated bodies, especially the think tank Federal Trust for Education and Research.[20] Uwe Kitzinger captures the diversity of individuals associated with the federal movements:

> They came from a wide variety of backgrounds: one the son of a peer, another who left school at fourteen, one the son of a small tailor, another the son of a bank clerk, several with family origins on the continent, some candidates or local councillors of the Labour, some of the Liberal and some of the Conservative Party, some full-time trade unionists, some lawyers, some in public relations, one who worked for the British Council of Churches, another for the *Economist*, several at universities or various research institutions.[21]

His words are intensely revealing of the bond between Federal Union and *The Economist*, via the Economist Intelligence Unit (EIU). It has already been noted that this organ was the first to coin the phrase 'missed chances' to describe Britain's post-war approach to Europe, an observation that calls to mind Sean Greenwood's comment that 'until the 1970s the British press tended to be pro-Community'.[22] It is pertinent to speculate on the reasons for this, for it sheds light on the wide-ranging networks of influence that, by the 1960s, had forced missed opportunities discourse to the forefront of the debate. One of *The Economist*'s editorial writers from 1958 was Christopher Layton (son of Walter Layton who had been editor in 1922–38 and a leading figure in the European Movement in the 1950s). He was on the staff after a spell at the EIU and was close to John Pinder,[23] and others,[24] in the EIU 'who had written about the blindness of Britain's negative policy towards European integration'.[25] Federal activists have often worked as and alongside writers for *The Economist*, unsurprisingly placing the same interpretation on British European policy. What makes this detail even more important is that those at the helm of the Federal Trust for over a quarter of a century – Pinder, Richard Mayne and Roy Pryce[26] – have published voluminously on the British approach to European integration,[27] chastising the politicians and civil servants whose 'misjudgements led their European policy so grievously astray'.[28] The historiography of British European policy was driven at first by writers who possessed multiple identities: political activists, journalists, broadcasters and contemporary historians.

The fourth community of writers supporting the missed opportunities approach to British European policy consists of the Europeanists amongst the British political elite, who are equally scathing. Edmund Dell, for instance, wrote of Britain's 'abdication of leadership in Europe'.[29] Roy Jenkins, one-time President of the European Commission, attacked the architect of Britain's first application to join the EEC, Harold Macmillan, for only 'belatedly seeing the light', part of his broader charge that British policy-makers have refused to take the country 'wholeheartedly into Europe'.[30] This viewpoint is echoed in the recollections of many like-minded politicians and civil servants in Britain.[31] The multifarious ways in which 'Europeanism' has been defined in Britain appears to have contributed to the plethora of writers who have interpreted British policy towards European integration as a series of errors,[32] for this group also incorporates those 'Tory Strasbourgers' whose 'European' credentials in the Monnet sense are far less certain but who nonetheless criticise the course of British European policy. Conservative peer Lord Boothby lamented that in 1945 'Britain could and should have taken the undisputed leadership of a united Western Europe … We did nothing.'[33] He was joined by contemporaries David Maxwell Fyfe and Harold Macmillan in a scathing attack on Anthony Eden's policy towards the EDC.[34] What further clouds the debate is that one occasionally discovers self-styled 'sceptics', such as Nicholas Ridley, addressing the Federal Trust in 1969 on the merits of approaching federalism 'through the front door, not the back door'.[35] That the ideological origins of such points of view are not always clear or coherent has not prevented them developing into a formidable critique of Britain's approach to Europe.

The fifth group of commentators voicing the conventional wisdom on Britain and Europe gathers together political scientists and historians, repeating these criticisms that became fashionable between the 1950s and the 1980s. It is almost as if writers were trapped within the discursive framework of missed opportunities. Annette Morgan, reviewing Roger Jowell and Gerald Hoinville's 1976 edited volume on public opinion and the EEC, observes that in the historical introduction to the book 'the joint authors had little scope for originality and little pretension to it'.[36] Theirs followed a line of 'higher' journalistic accounts, notably by Miriam Camps,[37] praised by Mayne and Pinder as 'one of the shrewdest observers of Europe during this period',[38] and several volumes by Kitzinger on Britain's relationship with the EEC.[39] Their ideas appear to have helped shape the texts by Joseph Frankel and Fred Northedge, who penned general studies on British foreign policy.[40] In the 1980s, Michael Charlton's collection of oral evidence from key decision-makers at the time confirmed the dominance of the missed opportunities approach.[41] It was also prevalent in biographic accounts by historians such as Alan Bullock and Richard Lamb.[42] The latter was of the opinion that 'In 1955 Eden could have sailed freely into the still malleable Common Market, and obtained substantial concessions for the Commonwealth. Not for another twenty years was Britain able to negotiate entry and then on worse terms than would have been available under Eden's Prime Ministership.' In the 1990s, the theme of failure continued to be a feature of the academic literature on Britain and the world and, by implication, Britain and Europe.[43]

The missed opportunities interpretation epitomises a generation's sense of tragedy about British foreign policy and is an emotive symbol of their efforts to explain Britain's reduced impact on the world stage. The argument can be made that by the time Wilson came to power, in October 1964, British European policy was being devised and launched in a sceptical domestic and hostile international environment.[44] Of Monnetist outlook or not, the received wisdom was that London placed too much emphasis on the 'special relationship', was hostile to the intentions of the Six, had contributed to its own exclusion from Europe, and that Whitehall policy-makers were short-sighted and reactive rather than visionary and proactive. In short, Britain was forced into short-term arrangements, such as the European Free Trade Association (EFTA), to make up for lost economic and political ground *vis-à-vis* the Community of the Six.[45]

UNDERSTANDING VERSUS EXPLAINING: THE REVOLT AGAINST THE CONVENTIONAL WISDOM

Brian Harrison's view is that missed opportunities discourse was an 'over-personalised, present-oriented "who was to blame and how can we do better next time?" agenda',[46] reflecting the unease that historians began to feel in the 1980s about the tendency to 'accept the continental and North American agendas' when considering British European policy.[47] Both, observes Kaiser, are 'based on the normative assumption that the path taken by the Six in the 1950s was not only successful but natural, and also morally superior to the British preference for intergovernmental institutional structures'.[48] He followed writers such as John Kent and John Young who investigated and found to be false what David Reynolds refers to as 'the anti-reputation of British leaders',[49] leading them to develop a 'new perspective' on British European policy that seeks not to explain failure but to understand what impelled policy-makers to make particular decisions.[50] This led more than one reviewer to comment that they have treated the material in a 'broadly sympathetic way'.[51] The crux of their interpretation is that Britain did not miss any opportunities, chances, boats or buses in the 1950s because, at the time, British leaders did not perceive there were any opportunities to grasp or vehicles to board. As John Charmley expresses it: 'Those who cleave to the "lost opportunities" myth show, by doing so, an inadequate appreciation of the situation in which Britain found herself in 1950–1.'[52] Max Beloff was equally convinced: 'it is hard to see how any British government … could have accepted entering such a venture [as the EEC]'.[53] David Dutton feels likewise:

> … it has become common to suggest that Britain, through a combination of neglect and wilfulness, missed the 'European bus' waiting to transport her to her rightful destiny. But Eden would have wanted to know the precise destiny of such a vehicle.[54]

Jan Melissen and Bert Zeeman summarise with the opinion that 'Britain did not miss the European bus, it just declined to board one that was going in the wrong direction.'[55] Such is the weight of opinion behind Christopher Hill's blunt conclusion that 'it is pointless to spend too much time berating dead or ennobled Prime Ministers for missing the boat'.[56]

The new perspective has developed out of two challenges to the conventional wisdom which, together, bring an alternative interpretation to the fore: 'it is a fallacy to believe that Britain turned her back on continental Europe during the fifteen years or so that followed the Second World War'.[57] The first concerns Britain's *willingness* to 'lead' Europe. Here, key decision-makers are rescued from the charge that they were exceptionally 'anti-European' by the counter-claim that British Prime Ministers and Foreign Secretaries were simply the most ostensible part of a 'broad consensus within Whitehall which recognised the growing importance of Europe to Britain but which was not prepared to narrow its horizons to Europe alone'.[58] In a rare departure from the official norm, John Colville reached to the heart of their argument with these words: 'People now talk as if there were great opportunities missed. I doubt there were those opportunities. Nobody wanted that particular [European] solution.'[59] From the Monnetist perspective there were, notes Greenwood, 'no real "pro-Europeans" in Whitehall in the 1950s, despite their later pleas to the contrary. Few at the time advocated joining integrative efforts in the 1950s; only later did they claim they did.'[60] Hugo Young agrees that the most vocal critics of European policy in the 1950s were hypocritical. Macmillan, he claims, like many of his generation, was a 'European only of his time and place, which is to say a tormented and indecisive one'.[61]

The second challenge made to the orthodoxy has concerned Britain's *ability* to 'lead' Europe. John Young writes:

> The fact is that Britain could not have had the leadership of Europe *on its own terms* because Britain saw no need to abandon its sovereignty to common institutions, whereas the Six saw this as vital. Britain could only have played a leading role in European integration, paradoxically, *if* it had accepted the continentals' terms and embraced supranationalism, but very few people advocated this before 1957.[62]

Moreover, the Six were not waiting idly for Britain to take the lead, bereft of ideas on how to proceed. They were capable of considerable advances exogenous from British input, as the launch of the Messina process and the Spaak negotiations soon after the collapse of the EDC demonstrated. To return to Young:

> The truth of the matter was seen when Britain did try to take the lead in Europe: [Ernest] Bevin tried to 'lead' Europe after 1948, but was unable to prevent the Schuman Plan; Eden tried to establish institutional co-operation with the Six through the 1952 'Eden Plan', yet, as Spaak put it, Europe by this time was in a 'whole hog mood'; British proposals were only 'half-way houses'.[63]

Such attempts to shift the focus away from supposed British failings reflect broader trends in the international historiography of European integration. William Hitchcock, for example, sees a plot to exclude Britain from European affairs:

> Through the means Monnet had devised, France could capture the diplomatic initiative from the Anglo-Americans, subvert British objections to continental unification schemes, and strike a bargain with Germany on a bilateral basis: equality of rights in exchange for a balance of power.[64]

Also on the subversive side, Robin Edmonds and Walter LaFeber saw Paris attempting to exclude Britain and America from European affairs.[65] Young's view of Monnet's intentions is more sanguine: 'The idea of a French "plot" goes too far ... Rather it seems that British membership was not a priority for Monnet.'[66] Monnet's memoirs echo what Young sees as a latent ambiguity in what Monnet ultimately wanted to achieve through the EEC: 'I knew that the essential prize had already been won, irrevocably. Europe was on the move. Whatever the British decided would be their own affair.'[67]

'The uses ... made of history', asserted Morton Kaplan, 'will be no better than the questions put to it.'[68] The historiography of British policy towards European integration provides compelling evidence to support his assertion. Underlying the division between the two interpretations is an epistemological conflict between 'explaining' and 'understanding' international relations.[69] Where the first wave of writers tried to explain Britain's failures in the European arena, recent historians have set themselves the task of understanding the nature of the policy process and the complexities involved in making and delivering a foreign policy strategy, attempting to establish who the major players were and what key assumptions lay behind policy as it emerged in Downing Street and Whitehall. This has involved analysis of shorter periods in the history which, both individually and taken as a whole, amount to a deep critique of the conventional wisdom. The writing of British European policy since 1945 thus provides ample evidence of the essentially contested nature of history. The kind of knowledge one seeks and the era in which one seeks it are formative influences on the kind of knowledge one discovers, because it dictates one's method, sources and style of narrative representation. Turning now to the historiography of Wilson's attempt to take Britain into the EEC, it will be shown that a similarly vitriolic

conventional wisdom – fuelled by the reviling of the Wilson governments in general – has until now been the dominant interpretation of
events.

THE CONVENTIONAL WISDOM ON WILSON AND EUROPE

There is much support for Andrew Thorpe's judgement on the
Wilson era that 'popular memory does not accord these governments a high reputation'.[70] On the personal level, Kenneth Morgan
writes of Wilson's 'long record of deviousness',[71] a commonly held
perception that has prompted Lee Waters to conclude that 'the little
known about this Yorkshireman tends to be negative'.[72] When
Wilson took over the Labour leadership, notes Roy Hattersley, prag-
matism 'was on the point of becoming a major socialist virtue'.[73]
Even before he took up residence in Downing Street, one biographer, the Conservative Member of Parliament Dudley Smith, could
gleefully write that few politicians had 'been accused so regularly of
political untrustworthiness'.[74] On the political level, there are a host
of issues with which one is confronted when attempting to grasp
Wilson's legacy. Among these, three stand out: first, the number
and scale of foreign and defence crises Wilson confronted as
Prime Minister, notably Rhodesia's Unilateral Declaration of
Independence, Indonesia's insurgency against Malaysia, Britain's
withdrawal from 'east of Suez' and the recurrence of the Ulster
problem; second, persistent economic instability which culminated
in the November 1967 devaluation of sterling; and, finally, the attention Wilson received from the British intelligence services.[75]

But there is an additional factor to account for in assessing
Wilson's contribution to British political history: the impression that
'something changed' in British politics during the 1960s. That the
diaries of Richard Crossman, Tony Benn and Barbara Castle quickly
became established readings on British government has helped to
embed the denigration of Wilson deep in the collective British psyche.[76] In addition to their leading argument that the civil service had
a disproportionate and damaging effect on the Labour programmes
of the 1960s, Wilson is also said to have presided over an 'inner cabinet', especially in foreign affairs,[77] and to have relied too much on
unelected advisers such as George Wigg and Marcia Williams.[78]
Furthermore, the Fulton Report on civil service reform, published in
June 1968, making the Prime Minister 'responsible for senior
appointments, the machinery of Government and security matters',

may have had the opposite effect to that intended. Not only were many proposed reforms never implemented,[79] it donated greater powers of patronage to the Prime Minister.[80] 'By the end of the 1960s', remarked Hugh Heclo and Aaron Wildavsky, 'few insiders were particularly happy with the way their machine was working.'[81]

The usual problems of explaining the forces shaping Britain's European policy have thus been exaggerated in Wilson's case by what David Leigh refers to as the 'log of lies, slurs and prejudices which … spun a suffocating web of rumours' around the adminis-tration.[82] Wilson did not help himself, however. His vacillating stance on Europe lends substantial support to the conventional wisdom that here was another story of 'collapsing alternatives',[83] another British Premier committed to traditional roles and goals for Britain, only turning to Europe when it suited him domestically. Wilson made it clear in 1964 that Britain would not seek entry to the Common Market, a policy he reversed with the second application; on losing power, he opposed the terms the Conservatives achieved, but in 1975 secured, through referendum, the country's agreement to remain in the EEC on terms only marginally different from those negotiated by Heath.

From the existing literature, one can distil four main reasons why Wilson sought EEC entry, all of which are highly reminiscent of those conventionally used to explain why Britain first applied to join the Community earlier in the decade.[84] His motivations, argue Dennis Kavanagh and Peter Morris, were 'similar to those of Macmillan; the EEC was a potentially valuable solution to a period of economic and political difficulty'.[85] First, the Wilson application has been taken as a reactive attempt to strengthen Britain's voice on the world stage, a 'change of tactics' in pursuit of traditional power-political goals,[86] another British attempt to retain a semblance of great power status. Clive Ponting recalled the Establishment view under Wilson that Britain should join 'not for the economic benefits … but to preserve Britain's position as an important international power, and keep it involved in the inner circle of diplomatic and strategic affairs'.[87] Wilson's decision to turn decisively to the EEC as a forum for project-ing British influence on the world stage is said to have stemmed from developments in the other two of Winston Churchill's 'three circles' of British foreign policy. Where Macmillan confronted prob-lems within the Commonwealth over the South African question, Wilson contended with the Rhodesian problem, conflict between India and Pakistan and tensions over British immigration policy, which, remarked Robert Lieber, shattered Labour's 'almost mythical devotion to the Commonwealth'.[88] Lyndon Johnson's retention of the White House in 1965 has been seen as Wilson's second external consideration, but the reasons why are somewhat less clear. On one hand, Kitzinger argues that transatlantic relations cooled after 1965 – particularly over Britain's refusal to send a military contingent to Vietnam – so Wilson applied to join the EEC to fill the gap left by the decline in the 'special relationship'.[89] For Elisabeth Barker, on the other, it was a case of transatlantic defence requirements, a reminder of the Cold War context within which European integration continued to take place. Washington, she argues, pressurised London to make an approach to Europe to stabilise the Atlantic Alliance after France withdrew from NATO integrated command structures in March 1966.[90] In the view of twice-Foreign Secretary Michael Stewart, Britain should join to prevent a Charles de Gaulle-led EEC from emerging, to prevent Commonwealth countries drifting into the orbit of the EEC rather than the mother country and to keep the leaders of America, Russia and Japan looking to Britain for diplomatic counsel.[91] Even to a vaunted 'European' like George Brown, Foreign Secretary August 1966–March 1968, the second application boiled down to the 'practical' consideration of 'whether we could afford to stay outside'.[92]

The above remark from Ponting shows his disregard for the economic factors in Wilson's decision, putting him at odds with most other commentators who are in some measure of agreement that economic considerations 'explain Wilson's conversion to the policy of entering the EEC'.[93] 'Wilson's turn to Europe', explains Frankel, 'was rather a resigned acceptance of Britain's growing inability to act in the traditional manner owing to the continuing decline of her economy.'[94] Of prime significance here were the sterling crises that, it is argued, had so enfeebled the British economy by the autumn of 1966 that 'it became clear to a growing number of Labour figures that Britain's economic weakness meant that it must look elsewhere', to the 'more prosperous nations' of the Common Market.[95] Sterling's weakness and the economic imperative for joining was a favourite theme of *The Economist*, which was still campaigning for British EEC membership.[96] Stewart believed that Britain 'would be working at an increasing disadvantage if she stayed out'. Continuing his theme of retaining global influence, he also believed that the Community represented a larger market than Britain could enjoy outside, leading to scale advantages and greater resources for research and development. It threatened to suck American investment away from Britain and the indications were that Commonwealth countries sought trade agreements more vigorously with the EEC than with Britain.[97]

On the economic side, attention has also been drawn to the opinion that EFTA was not proving a viable alternative to membership of the EEC. Some writers even link Labour's change in direction to the tensions caused within EFTA by the government's announcement on 26 October 1964 of a 15 per cent surcharge on all Britain's imports.[98] Though it is tempting to use Britain's policy towards EFTA to elucidate its thinking on EEC matters, the surcharge was imposed on all Britain's imports, causing a 'massive outcry, notably from other European countries' both in and outside EFTA.[99] It is thus problematic to draw conclusions about Wilson's thinking on the EEC from this episode alone. Indeed, Wilson himself argues that in terms of timing and tactics his decision was more affected by the political consequences of remaining inside EFTA, having been told by the Italians in April 1965 that measures to link EFTA and the EEC fell short of what was required to convince de Gaulle of his commitment to a 'European' future for Britain.[100] A further factor in his thinking, but one that has been less widely explored, except by *The Economist*, may have been developments inside the Community, particularly the July 1966 agreement on how to finance the Common Agricultural Policy (CAP). While economic in substance, it seemed to make the Community less inimical to Britain's agricultural interests, and the political overtones were clear. The way in which agreement was reached in the Council of Ministers highlighted how the Community had moved decisively away from supranationalism towards Britain's preferred method of conducting business: intergovernmentally.[101] The way the CAP agreement was negotiated could be taken to underline the primacy of nation-states within the Community, earlier highlighted by the 'empty chair' crisis and the resulting Luxembourg compromise in 1965–66.

As one might expect with Wilson, the personal and party-political dimensions to the bid dominate the historiography. The conventional wisdom has it that the third reason why Wilson applied was as a way of diverting attention from the problems besieging the Labour Party. Even his colleagues did not flinch from depicting it as another Wilson 'gimmick' to unite the Labour Party and hold on to power,[102] or as a reaction to the devaluation crises of 1966, after which the Premier needed 'a device that looked and sounded like business' in the face of mounting troubles for his administration.[103] Through his 'discovery of Europe', wrote Hugh Cudlipp of the *Daily Mirror*, Wilson attempted to 'distract attention from Rhodesia and the economic mess at home'.[104] From across the House of Commons, Edward Heath was of the same mind: 'British policy from 1964 fluctuated greatly with Harold Wilson's capricious nature and tactical initiatives ... in the absence of any conviction, the issue for him was which policy would best serve to hold the Labour Party together.'[105]

This ties in closely with the fourth factor in his decision which appears most regularly in the historiography, his desire to 'dish' the Conservatives 'by pre-empting an issue which Heath had been monopolising',[106] a reminder of the constant interplay between domestic and foreign policy agendas. But it is also alleged that Wilson was using Europe more narrowly, to safeguard his place at the head of government. This was given voice by Peter Shore in one of the first academic articles on Wilson's foreign policy. Though convinced of Wilson's genuine aspirations for a European 'technological community', he argued that the bid served essentially 'un-European' ends:

> There is good reason to believe that Wilson's fateful decision to probe the EEC in 1966 had been motivated not by any shift in personal conviction but by the desire to outwit both ... Heath and, inside his own Cabinet, the 'pro-Marketeers' led by George Brown, by demonstrating that no tolerable conditions of entry were possible.[107]

The plethora of interpretations placed on Wilson's motivation for attempting to take Britain into the EEC is characteristic of the wider historiographic charges against Wilson's handling and leadership of Britain in the 1960s and 1970s. The second application is just one event of many where writers see a betrayal of the socialist cause, insincere policies or narrow personal ambition winning out over the interests of party and country.

Three charges in particular weigh heavily on the historiography of his leadership of the second application, so it is useful to examine them in more detail as a means of setting the context for the contributions in this book which investigate the processes in Downing Street and Whitehall that led to the entry bid. First, argues Castle, the decision was 'ruthlessly stage-managed, under the soothing phrase: "It is, of course, for Cabinet to decide".'[108] The issue that subtly came to dominate Cabinet discussion was not *whether* but *how* to apply: 'Eventually those confronting him found it was too hard to go into reverse, having gone so far.'[109] Second, Wilson 'consistently knocked down arguments against entry and showed himself a convinced pro-EEC figure'.[110] Douglas Jay complains that the 'antis' had difficulty circulating their views,[111] and Ponting claims that 'Wilson was masterminding the production of papers within the Cabinet Office'.[112] Finally, it has been argued that Wilson used his powers of patronage to promote 'Europeanists' to key Cabinet positions, thus artificially tipping the balance in Cabinet in favour of entry. Brown's shift from the Department of Economic Affairs (DEA) to the Foreign Office was, therefore, 'more than a symbol of the change in emphasis from national planning to the attempt to call the old continent in to redress the stagnation of the British isles'.[113]

Other contemporaries were less sure that Wilson's allocation of Cabinet portfolios was his way of 'Europeanising' the debate. Castle noted that Wilson simply 'hated sacking people', finding a suitably important role for Brown for pragmatic reasons.[114] James Callaghan, Jay and Benn, by contrast, argue that Wilson wanted to marginalise this potentially powerful opponent after detecting a plot to oust him.[115] Ben Pimlott agreed that the 1966 reshuffle was designed to 'close the gates to further political manoeuvring'.[116] What further muddies the waters is that Castle reports Brown as saying at the time: 'I hate it. I didn't want it. It was an order: this or I go. He said he couldn't keep me at the DEA after my little bit of business over resigning.'[117] Brown's memoirs add nothing, but Ernest Kay, a personal friend of Wilson, argued that Brown desperately wanted to head the Foreign Office, a fact not lost on Wilson.[118] The missed opportunities interpretation of British European policy has, therefore, incorporated the Wilson years with ease, carrying forward the theme of insular British leaders using Europe for personal and other domestic ends.[119] Wilson is seen as using the second application either to sustain outdated imperial pretensions for Britain, as a solution to economic ills, to keep the Labour Party united or to steal an electoral march on the Conservatives. That he is not a fondly remembered Prime Minister has given the historiography even more of a critical bent, reflecting live political debate at the time about what Wilson was attempting to achieve by turning to Europe in 1967.

What is less commonly reported is that some of his Cabinet colleagues and other contemporaries saw fit to praise his political mastery. Anthony Crosland, for example, judged that 'Harold is a bastard, but he's a genius. He's like Odysseus. Odysseus was also a bastard, but he managed to steer the ship between Scylla and Charybdis.'[120] The last five years have seen the nurturing of what must be considered an alternative interpretation of events, one that pays greater due to both Wilson's handling of the European question and his legacy to British European policy. Given Wilson's predicament, Thorpe diagnoses, his 'solution was, in the short-term, brilliant ... pro-Europeans were appeased because the effort had been made, while the antis were relieved that it had come to nothing'.[121] On the longer-term ramifications of the 'second try', Morgan judges that 'A major positive legacy of the Wilson era was a fundamental and lasting reassessment of Britain's European role.'[122] He also challenges the assumption that Wilson's bid was a knee-jerk reaction to crises in British foreign and economic policy. A reliable indication of Wilson's thinking was, he notes, the March 1966 announcement that Britain was to convert to decimal coinage, a development that 'might well speed on British membership of the European Common Market', but which 'was noticed by relatively few' at the time and, it would appear, since.[123] These approaches echo the process of reinterpretation that has been occurring on single issues, such as Wilson's motivation in proposing a 'European Technological Community' (ETC). It is now only partially accurate to claim that 'most commentators have assumed that there was no real commitment [on Wilson's part] and dismiss it as Wilson's cynical political expediency',[124] a desperate attempt to convince de Gaulle to let Britain into the EEC.[125] Colleagues, biographers and historians of business and scientific communities in Britain in the 1960s are more convinced that Wilson's reorganisation of Whitehall, involving the creation of the Ministry of Technology (Mintech) and the Industrial Reorganisation Corporation (IRC), stemmed from a genuine desire to reorder the scientific basis of British industry and improve competitiveness with America, even if the results were not as planned. As Hattersley put it: 'Nobody who watched Wilson at work during the early years of his Labour government can doubt the sincerity with which he personally believed in the ultimate triumph of technology.'[126] The aim of this book is to use the documentary record to assess the degree to which one can reinterpret other themes in the conduct of European policy under Wilson.

WILSON AND EUROPE: TOWARDS A NEW UNDERSTANDING

The historiography of British European policy since the 1980s has been driven by the desire to interrogate the conventional wisdom about what happened and why. As one might expect, given that the field is dominated by academics and professional historians, part of the revised interpretation has flowed from a belief that understanding contemporary history requires recourse to primary sources, hence the heavy use of archives in the Public Record Office (PRO) in the reconstruction of events. But the revising of the conventional wisdom has also been fuelled by the search for answers to questions left unanswered or, more commonly, unasked by the first wave of writers. In the case of Wilson and Europe, four sets stand out. The first set of questions aims to uncover who made British foreign policy in the period 1964–70. There is a lot of writing on when and why Wilson decided to launch the second application, but less on how it was conceived and fed through the British system of government. What was the process of decision-making and policy-making that led to the second application? What networks of contact and methods of persuasion were used in Downing Street, Whitehall and abroad to secure support for a second attempt to join the Community? Very much linked to this, the second set concerns the broader context of British foreign policy-making: what was the opinion on the European question within the leading political parties, at elite level, in the wider business community and in the country at large? The third set of questions refers to the multilateral context within which that policy evolved. Was British diplomacy towards leading players a help or a hindrance?[127] What input did other powers have to British decision-making? Were Britain's goals helped or hindered by its Continental partners, its ties and obligations to the Commonwealth, or to the United States? What role did the EEC as an international organisation play in Britain's second entry bid? The final set of questions encompasses the alternatives to a second bid for entry: what were the other policies Wilson could have pursued at this time, and how successful might they have been in finding a role for Britain in the 1960s?

By attempting to answer these, and other, questions, this book contributes to the historiography in three main ways. First of all, it provides support for Thorpe's argument that it is possible to interpret 'the second try' in a more nuanced way than has hitherto been the case – that this was another Wilson gimmick, a missed opportunity for the British in Europe, or an insidious manifestation of Wilson's leadership of Britain. Paradoxically, the bid can be seen as a 'successful failure' for the Prime Minister. It satisfied the 'pros' and the 'antis' in the Labour Party and, more importantly, in a deeply divided Cabinet; it helped muffle Conservative criticisms of Labour and satisfied encouragement, however limited, from Britain's diplomatic partners for a renewed assault on 'fortress Europe'. In the longer term, the second application demonstrated Britain's willingness to seek a European solution to its problems, smoothing the way for the UK's accession to the Community in 1973. As Young has pointed out, Britain's official talks with the Six began along lines 'that had been planned under *Wilson*'.[128] The second contribution of this book is that it draws attention to the medium and longer-term consequences of the Wilson bid. The 'second try' satisfied many individuals and agendas, not least those of the Prime Minster himself, who, remarkably, managed to avoid Cabinet resignations over the issue. But its effects were highly damaging in other areas. It did, for example, but paper over the splits within the Labour Party that would simmer throughout the 1970s and result in the breakaway by a 'pro-market' group of MPs, Roy Jenkins, Shirley Williams, David Owen and Bill Rogers, to form the Social Democratic Party (SDP) in 1981. By dodging core issues associated with the political implications of EEC entry, an approach that Macmillan had taken before him, and one that Heath would take after him, Wilson's application bid did nothing for the broader British debate on Europe, which continues to be characterised by a lack of information, misunderstanding and suspicion towards what is perceived as an elite process that is either too remote from, or has no relevance to, everyday life in Britain.

The final contribution of this book is located on the philosophic or historiographic level. It highlights the essentially contested nature of contemporary political history. History writing is an immensely personal process, relying on the sources available, the imaginative powers of the author and, not least, the time of writing, which has a powerful effect on one's attitude to key personalities and events. Ironically, it is only Wilson's cutting of the period of closure on official government sources from 50 to 30 years that now permits this book to be written, such is the link that exists in contemporary British history between the release of documentation to the PRO and academic specialisation in a given area of inquiry. Indeed, this book sustains the argument that the British approach to history remains informed by enlightenment teachings on 'scientific objectivity', the search for hard, traceable 'facts' about the past using sources surviving from the period under scrutiny. Epistemologically, this approach is understandable in the sense that, at the end of the day, originality and evidence are the yardsticks by which historians are judged. But it is also interesting in that the basis on which to develop alternative interpretations seems to exist long before they are actually written. In the case of Wilson and Europe, it has always been possible to interpret his policy more sympathetically than it has conventionally been, but it has taken sociological factors, the passing of time and more practical considerations of the need for evidence to provide the means for a sustained assault on the received wisdom. By asking new questions of the history of British European policy under Wilson and by interrogating the interpretations placed on events in existing literature, this book advances towards a new understanding of the second try.

It is split into two parts. The first analyses the domestic context within which the bid was conceived, concentrating in particular on Wilson's strategy, his relationship with Whitehall policy-makers, his handling of the Labour Party, the impact of Cabinet, commercial and public opinion and the policy of the Conservative Party. In Chapter 2, Anne Deighton analyses Labour Party and public opinion on the question of a second application. She argues that Wilson's policy was not driven by widespread support from within his party, and that his main task was to manage a Cabinet that was deeply divided over the issue of Europe. The 'pros' were characterised by membership of the Labour Committee for Europe, including George Brown and Roy Jenkins, and the Campaign for Democratic Socialism with their links to the Federal Trust and the European Movement. The 'antis' tended to be less well organised, but were associated with membership of the Tribune Group, including Michael Foot, and banded together with the 'global patriots' such as Douglas Jay and Richard Crossman. Wilson himself was thought to belong to the latter group, hence their feeling of betrayal when he launched the second application. She also argues that the second application was not driven by the public, whose support for the second try tended to be shallow and fickle, following trends in support for the Prime Minister personally rather than a course of its own. Despite the methodological problems of extrapolating from opinion polling, the inference can be drawn that European policy in the 1960s remained the preserve of the elite, with the public uninterested and uninformed about the integration process.

In Chapter 3, Philip Lynch continues the party-political theme by considering the policy of Heath's Conservative Party towards the second application. He shows that a confluence of Heath's leadership and the Conservative Policy Review in 1965–67 produced a post-war 'highpoint' in Conservative Europeanism. However, he contends that Wilson's approach caused the Conservatives tactical problems: the leadership did not want to be seen to scupper an application but, given the exigency of the two-party system of government in Britain, did not want to be seen to be falling entirely behind Wilson's policy. The compromise solution was to support the principle of entry, but to oppose the detail, especially the handling and timing of the application. Under the appearance of unity, however, Lynch also finds that the Conservative Party was, like Labour, split over Europe. Dissent from the imperialists on the right of the party fused with ephemeral support from many who were 'pro-entry' but not 'Euro-enthusiasts'.

The inability of British policy-makers to divest themselves of global ambitions is taken up in Chapter 4, in which Helen Parr discusses the role of the Foreign Office in influencing Wilson's policy towards Europe. She focuses on the debate between Downing Street and Whitehall over what tactics to use in pursuit of entry, arguing that although it was a critical turning point for Labour, the July 1966 sterling and balance of payments crises confirmed a long-standing wish to join the EEC on the part of the deeply 'Europeanised' Foreign Office. Its ability to run foreign policy was, however, limited by the haphazard, uncoordinated way in which British foreign policy was developed and projected, characterised by a lack of planning or strategic direction and an innate reactiveness to outside events. The nature of the policy-making machinery allowed Wilson and Brown to wrest the tactical initiative from the Foreign Office after the March 1966 election, stamping their mark via the 'probe' of EEC capitals and other diplomatic moves to outflank de Gaulle. The major area of agreement between them was on the broader implications of British entry for the stability of the Atlantic Alliance and the pursuit of *détente*, but such longer-term Cold War goals had to be eschewed in favour of the more immediate one of entering the Community.

In Chapter 5, John Young explores Wilson's proposals for a technological community in Europe. He suggests primarily that Wilson's policy on technology was more sophisticated than has previously been thought. Wilson's thinking was, moreover, closely in line with, and partly inspired by, European initiatives in the technological arena. However, he argues, there is also a compelling body of evidence to sustain the criticisms of the Europeans that, at the end of the day, Britain was closer to the Americans than to them on technological matters, shown by the replacement of the TSR-2 with the F-111 and by Britain's attempts to distance itself from the European Launcher Development Organisation (ELDO). As Alfred Grosser has observed, the paradox of Wilson's technological policy was that although he 'suddenly declared that Great Britain was on its way to becoming the industrial helot of the United States', he never rejected a single investment application from across the Atlantic.[129] The chances of the European Technological Community proposal succeeding in changing de Gaulle's mind about Britain were, Young contends, also limited by its vagueness, which resulted from the perceived need not to give de Gaulle more grounds on which to attack the British approach to unity and to avoid any entry negotiations being sidetracked by detailed technological discussions.

In Chapter 6, Neil Rollings examines the policy of the Confederation of British Industry (CBI) towards European integration. His central argument is that British industry was more positive about the prospect of EEC membership than it was at the time of the first application, or than it would be subsequently. This was a reflection both of how individual sectors perceived their ability to compete in a European market, voiced in the consultation process of 1967, and of the leadership's ability to manage CBI opinion towards accepting its support for entry. In terms of explaining the CBI's brand of 'Europeanism', Rollings puts it down to more than ideology or an instinctive liking for the integration process, giving greater weight to the CBI's opinion that Britain needed to be on the inside track of embryonic Community economic policy-making and to its dissatisfaction with the *status quo* in Britain. Rollings goes significantly further than earlier writers on the subject by arguing that the CBI had a considerable impact on the formation of Wilson's European policy through its network of informal contacts with key ministers and officials in Whitehall.

The second part of the book concentrates on the global setting of 'the second try', shedding further light on Wilson's motivation for applying and on the diplomatic efforts undertaken to navigate Britain's passage into the EEC. In Chapter 7, Piers Ludlow analyses the EEC's reaction to Britain's second membership bid. While 'the biggest threat to Britain's attempts to gain membership of the Community came from Paris',[130] he points out that the first application had shown that a second battle also needed to be fought at the negotiating table in Brussels: success here might force de Gaulle's hand by removing the basis for another veto. Ludlow charts the increasing polarisation between France on one hand and the Five and the Commission on the other, all of who seemed more sanguine about British entry in 1967 than they had been in 1961–63. He argues that the veto was a defeat for Wilson, but its medium and longer-term

effects were more significant than has hitherto been acknowledged. It
stymied Community development by exacerbating the problems of
agreement on further integrative measures before British entry and,
by putting British membership securely on the EEC agenda, it helped
Edward Heath lead Britain into the EEC six years later.

In Chapter 8, Anthony Adamthwaite explores more deeply the first
of the battles to which Ludlow refers – that with France. He presents
two main arguments: first, the failure of the second application was
not, as some have suggested, inevitable. Wilson could have developed
closer relations with France by redefining Anglo-American relations in
a way that both reflected growing realities in the 'special relationship'
and tempted de Gaulle. Secondly, accounting for the failure to
develop a *rapprochement* relies on an examination of the different leadership styles and personalities in Britain and France, of the different
governmental machineries that, in their unique ways, prevented long-
term strategic planning or innovative thinking and of the rival
conceptions of European unity that hampered cross-Channel diplomacy. Adamthwaite is virulently critical of Britain's efforts to gain
entry to the EEC, blaming clumsy and ill-thought-through diplomatic
efforts on the part of Wilson and his Foreign Secretaries Brown and
Stewart. The dearth of innovative statecraft was, he concedes, partly
a reaction to de Gaulle's persistent negativity and Britain's declining
international position, but more than that, a symptom of poor leadership of Whitehall. Thus, he concludes, one cannot know what would
have happened if Britain had boxed more cleverly with France or
gone the other way and attempted to develop a genuine *entente*, 'but
at least it would gave been worth a try'.[131]

In Chapter 9, James Ellison examines the trilateral relationship
between Britain, France and America, shedding light on the interplay between defence and foreign policy. He argues that the second
application must be understood in the context of the efforts by
Washington to stabilise the Atlantic Alliance during a period of
intense flux, caused by de Gaulle's challenge both to the institutions
of the EEC, to the 'empty chair' crisis and to NATO, by withdrawing
France from the integrated command structure. The narrow aim of
EEC entry must not, he shows, be used as the sole yardstick by
which to judge Wilson's diplomacy. 'The second try' was part of a
broader Anglo-American strategy designed to undermine de
Gaulle's designs for Europe, maintain NATO cohesion and, moreover, keep West Germany harnessed within the Atlantic Alliance. In
the short term, de Gaulle's veto may have represented a failure for

the Wilson government, but in the medium and longer term the very fact that an application was launched in such unfavourable international conditions helped smooth the way for entry when de Gaulle had resigned from power in France and, in wider terms, focused American attention on Britain as its key European partner in NATO, thus strengthening the 'special relationship' which, after Vietnam, had not appeared so 'special' at all.

In Chapter 10, Philip Alexander discusses the interplay between Commonwealth issues and Wilson's European policy. Focusing on defence retrenchment east of Suez, the development of sub-Saharan Africa and South African race relations, he argues that the conventional understanding of the second application is in need of substantial revision. Growing disharmony inside the Commonwealth, far from being only a side issue, presented a quandary for Wilson. On one hand, it stimulated more cogent thinking about how the EEC could provide a new focus for British foreign and commercial policies. On the other, it complicated the diplomatic endeavours to secure membership by selling to the Europeans the idea that Britain had exculpated the last vestiges of its imperial past. Developing a foreign policy is, Alexander shows, hard enough; successfully implementing it in a highly complex, dynamic international environment, in which perceptions of intent constantly change, in which there are lingering national rivalries and where agendas shift swiftly, is extremely difficult.

Katharina Böhmer reinforces this point in Chapter 11 by examining Anglo-German diplomacy and the second application. She shows that, even though the first veto had confirmed that de Gaulle held the key to British membership, Whitehall decision-makers placed much faith in circumventing the General's opposition the second time around by securing Germany's backing for Britain's cause. Ministers and officials thus spent much time attempting to woo their German counterparts, conveniently overlooking or playing down signals from Bonn and elsewhere on the European mainland that France's EEC partners, the so-called 'friendly Five' or just the Five (Belgium, Germany, Italy, Luxembourg and the Netherlands), would not risk another showdown with de Gaulle for Britain's sake. Despite what the British liked to think, in an era of *Ostpolitik* and East–West *détente*, Germany simply did not place Community enlargement high enough on its foreign policy agenda in 1967 to risk damaging its status as a responsible international partner to France by pressuring it about Britain.

In Chapter 12, Jane Toomey explores Ireland's attitude and policy towards the Wilson application. Comparing the British and Irish applications is, she argues, of enormous value. There was a myriad of exchanges both before and during the application process that shed light on a consistent strategy in London and Dublin to secure full membership simultaneously. This joint approach was, however, threatened twice: when it was mooted in the summer of 1967 that Britain might consider joining without Ireland and when, in the wake of de Gaulle's November veto, the Irish flirted with the idea of something less than full membership. That the joint approach survived is down to two reasons. First, Irish fears in 1967 were misplaced, due as much to the tone of Brown's application statement as to developments in British strategy. Second, the 'association' idea was dropped almost as quickly as it was embraced, Irish officials seeing it as a way of driving a wedge between the applicants or undermining their 'European' credentials. The major outcome of the second Anglo-Irish approach to the EEC, Toomey concludes, lay not in the short term but in the longer term. Wilson's refusal to consider alternatives to full membership laid the foundations for Heath, who was able to convince the Six of Britain's growing 'Europeanism'. In this light, the second application can indeed be seen as a 'successful failure'.

There are four leading strands of argument running through the studies in this book, and which Peter Catterall draws out in the concluding chapter. The first is that British foreign policy is not simply 'what the Foreign Office does'; one must account for a whole host of other influences and a porous policy-making machinery in determining how decisions are made. Flowing from that, the second argument is that there was widespread support, if not in the country, then at times from within the Community and, more consistently, within Whitehall and among business elites for a renewed application to join the EEC, a level of support that had not been seen before and would not be seen later. These, together with a series of crises, notably over sterling and defence retrenchment east of Suez, convinced Wilson that Britain would be better off inside the EEC, economically, politically and strategically. The third theme is that the failure to convince de Gaulle of British 'European-ness', already an arduous task, was made all the more difficult by the diplomatic tactics employed by the Prime Minister. Limited by historic suspicion of British policy, an instinctive affinity for the United States, a divided Cabinet and conflicting advice on how to deal with de Gaulle, Wilson had neither the heart nor the political ability to surmount the walls of 'fortress Europe'. Yet, in the final judgement, Wilson's policy can be seen as a 'successful failure'. He managed to appease both the 'pros' and the 'antis' within the Labour Party, to outflank the Conservatives and Liberals on the issue of Europe, and to set the scene for Britain's entry into the Community six years later by restating Britain's ultimate commitment to the Community approach to unity. It is with regard to the longer-term consequences of his policy and tactics that the most damaging critique of Wilson can be made. At the time, however, these were but distant considerations for the Prime Minister.

NOTES

The analysis, opinions and conclusions expressed or implied in this chapter are those of the author and do not necessarily represent the views of the JSCSC, the UK MoD or any other government agency.

1. D. Reynolds, *Britannia Overruled: British Policy and World Power in the Twentieth Century* (London: Longman, 1991), p. 253.
2. A. Shlaim, 'The Foreign Secretary and the Making of Foreign Policy', in A. Shlaim, P. Jones and K. Sainsbury (eds), *British Foreign Secretaries Since 1945* (London: David & Charles, 1977), pp. 13–26 (p. 16).
3. J. E. Dougherty and R. L. Pfaltzgraff, Jr, *Contending Theories of International Relations: A Comprehensive Survey* (New York: Harper & Row, 1981), pp. 468–504; R. H. Immerman, 'In Search of History, and Relevancy: Breaking Through the "Encrustations of Interpretation"', *Diplomatic History*, 12, 2 (1988), pp. 341–56. Their observations are reminiscent of the epistemological questions raised by M. A. Kaplan in *On Historical and Political Knowing* (London: University of Chicago Press, 1971). An equally valuable yet widely misunderstood treatment of these issues is to be found in H. White, *The Content of the Form: Narrative Discourse and Historical Representation* (London: Johns Hopkins University Press, 1992). For a British focus on the problems of what Michael Smith calls the 'control of policy in complex settings' see S. Smith and M. Smith, 'The Analytical Background: Approaches to the Study of Foreign Policy', in M. Smith, S. Smith and B. White (eds), *British Foreign Policy: Tradition, Change and Transformation* (London: Hyman, 1988), pp. 3–23.
4. E. Kane, 'The Myth of Sabotage: British Policy Towards European Integration, 1955–6', in E. du Réau (ed.), *Europe des Élites? Europe des Peuples? La Construction de l'Espace Européen 1945–1960* (Paris: Presses de la Sorbonne Nouvelle, 1999), pp. 291–301; J. Charmley, *Churchill's Grand Alliance: The Anglo-American Special Relationship 1940–57* (London: Hodder and Stoughton, 1995), pp. 247 and 299; P. Catterall's General Editor's Preface to J. Ellison, *Threatening Europe: Britain and the Creation of the European Community, 1955–58* (Basingstoke: Macmillan, 2000), p. 9.
5. A useful way to approach 'historiography' is to view it as the 'history of history-writing'. See Peter Burke's definition in A. Bullock and O. Stallybrass

(eds), *The Fontana Dictionary of Modern Thought* (London: Collins, 1977), p. 286. It involves the scrutiny of the purveyors of historical knowledge, of the processes by which one comes to understand historical events, rather than the events themselves. In short, historiography is the study of what can be labelled the 'history industry', a point well brought out in L. Jordanova, *History in Practice* (London: Arnold, 2000). For an overview of the field see M. Bentley, *Modern Historiography: An Introduction* (London: Routledge, 1999); G. G. Iggers, *Historiography in the Twentieth Century: From Scientific Objectivity to the Postmodern Challenge* (Hanover: Wesleyan University Press, 1997); K. Jenkins, *On 'What is History?' From Carr and Elton to Rorty and White* (London: Routledge, 1995); B. Southgate, *History: What and Why? Ancient, Modern, and Postmodern Perspectives* (London: Routledge, 1996).

6.   The Treaty of Rome, which came into effect on 1 January 1958, established both the European Economic Community (EEC) and the European Atomic Energy Community (Euratom). The first European Community, the European Coal and Steel Community (ECSC), had already been established in April 1951 when the same six states (France, Germany, Italy, Belgium, the Netherlands and Luxembourg) signed the Treaty of Paris. These three groupings remained legally separate entities until 1967 when they were merged, and it became common to speak of the 'European Community' or EC. The focus for Harold Wilson in launching Britain's bid to join the EEC that year, as it had been for his predecessor, Harold Macmillan, in 1961, was mainly on the EEC, so, following the conventional pattern of usage in Britain, this book uses terms such as 'Community' and 'Europe' to refer to the European Economic Community. The use of 'Communities' in some quotations from other sources embraces the two earlier Communities as well as other specialist European organisations.

7.   The most widely acclaimed exposition of this interpretation is M. Camps, *Britain and the European Community 1955–1963* (London: Oxford University Press, 1964). Titles of more recent texts demonstrate the entrenchment of this view. See, for example, S. George, *An Awkward Partner: Britain in the European Community* (New York: Oxford University Press, 1990); D. Gowland and A. Turner, *Reluctant Europeans: Britain and European Integration 1945–1998* (Harlow: Pearson Education, 2000).

8.   R. N. Gardner, 'Sterling–Dollar Diplomacy in Current Perspective', in W. R. Louis and H. Bull (eds), *The Special Relationship: Anglo-American Relations Since 1945* (Oxford: Clarendon Press, 1989), pp. 185–200 (p. 188). It is, notes Christopher Hill, a major 'opinion former'. See his 'Academic International Relations: The Siren Song of Policy Relevance', in C. Hill and P. Beshoff (eds), *Two Worlds of International Relations: Academics, Practitioners and the Trade in Ideas* (London: Routledge, 1994), pp. 3–25 (p. 8). A former editor, Rupert Pennant-Rea, has noted the impact of the 'intelligent' media on politicians that *The Economist* has been quick to exploit, cited in S. Badsey, *Military Operations and the Media* (Camberley: Surrey Strategic and Combat Studies Institute, 1994), p. 16.

9.   *The Economist*, 19 November 1955, pp. 633–4 (p. 633). The paper's internationalist perspective, and thus its aversion to Britain's aloofness from the continent, is set out in the official history by R. D. Edwards, *The Pursuit of Reason: The Economist 1843–1993* (London: Hamish Hamilton, 1993).

10. After the mid-1980s, when this view was first seriously challenged, some writers continued to propagate the conventional wisdom. Others, it is shown below, began to challenge the conventional wisdom in the 1970s. However, in the interests of analytical simplicity, the boundaries may be set as such. A more

detailed examination of the issues raised here is to be found in O. J. Daddow, *Britain and Europe since 1945: Historiographic Perspectives on Unification* (Manchester: Manchester University Press, forthcoming). This builds on ideas first expressed in O. J. Daddow, 'Rhetoric and Reality: The Historiography of British European Policy, 1945–73' (PhD Thesis, University of Nottingham, 2000). A useful reflection on the 'web of influence among journalists, politicians, business leaders, and other professionals and citizens' that critically affects the way in which events are interpreted is to be found in D. Tannen, *The Argument Culture: Changing the Way We Argue and Debate* (New York: Virago Press, 1998), this quote from p. 85.

11. W. Kaiser, *Using Europe, Abusing the Europeans: Britain and European Integration, 1945–63* (London: Macmillan, 1996), introduction, p. 16. Elsewhere in the literature they are referred to more provocatively as the 'Eurosaints' or the 'prophets of a new world order'. These labels are to be found, respectively, in A. Bosco, review of J. Pinder, *European Unity and World Order: Federal Trust 1945–1995*, in *Journal of Common Market Studies*, 35, 2 (1997), p. 325 and A. Milward, *The Reconstruction of Western Europe* (London: Methuen, 1984), p. 17.

12. D. Brinkley and C. Hackett (eds), *Jean Monnet: The Path to European Unity* (Basingstoke: Macmillan, 1991). Other biographic accounts include F. Duchêne, *Jean Monnet: The First Statesman of Interdependence* (London: W. W. Norton, 1991); M. and S. Bromberger, *Jean Monnet and the United States of Europe*, translated by E. P. Halperin (New York: Coward-McCann, 1968). Their memoirs number among them J. Monnet, *Memoirs*, trans. Richard Mayne (London: Collins, 1978) and P. Spaak, *The Continuing Battle: Memoirs of a European* (London: Weidenfeld & Nicolson, 1971).

13. Duchêne, *Jean Monnet*, p. 208.

14. N. Ashford, review of P. Winand, *Eisenhower, Kennedy and the United States of Europe*, in *Journal of Common Market Studies*, 33, 2 (1995), pp. 403–4 (p. 403).

15. R. J. Aldrich, 'European Integration: An American Intelligence Connection', in A. Deighton (ed.), *Building Post-War Europe: National Decision-Makers and European Institutions, 1948–63* (Basingstoke: Macmillan, 1995), pp. 159–79 (p. 159). He concludes on p. 173 as follows: 'A surprising number of the political elite concerned with the emerging European Community in the 1940s and 1950s were also sometime members of the Western intelligence community.'

16. Milward, *The Reconstruction of Western Europe*, p. 5. See also M. J. Hogan, *The Marshall Plan: America, Britain and the Reconstruction of Western Europe, 1947–1952* (Cambridge: Cambridge University Press, 1987), pp. 26–53; M. J. Hogan, *A Cross of Iron: Harry S. Truman and the National Security State, 1945–1954* (Cambridge: Cambridge University Press, 1998), pp. 2–3; A. Milward, *The European Rescue of the Nation-State* (London: Routledge, 1992), p. 348; W. C. Cromwell, *The United States and the European Pillar* (Basingstoke: Macmillan, 1992), p. 1; B. Perkins, 'Unequal Partners: The Truman Administration and Great Britain', in Louis and Bull (eds), *The Special Relationship*, pp. 43–64 (pp. 55–7); D. C. Watt, 'Demythologising the Eisenhower Era', in Louis and Bull (eds), *The Special Relationship*, pp. 65–85 (pp. 80–1). The self-interest at the heart of Washington's aspiration is not lost on William Wallace, who notes that a reconstructed European market 'provided them with the means for national reconstruction'. See William Wallace, reviews of J. Dickie, *Inside the Foreign Office*, and A. Milward, *The European Rescue of the Nation-State*, in *Times Literary Supplement*, 30 April 1993, p. 25.

17. D. Acheson, *Present at the Creation: My Years in the State Department* (New York: Signet, 1969), p. 502. See also pp. 385–7. Acheson was Under-Secretary of State

1945–47 and Secretary of State 1949–53. His plan to use 'material means for immaterial purposes' indicates the interconnection between European unity and American Cold War strategy. T. A. Wilson and R. D. McKinzie, 'Oral History Interview with Dean Acheson, 30 June 1971', Truman Library, <http://www.trumanlibrary.org/oralhist/acheson.htm>, p. 3 (accessed 6 November 2000).

18.   Cited in J. Ramsden, review of N. Lankford, *Aristocrat: The Biography of Ambassador David K. E. Bruce*, in *Contemporary British History*, 11, 2 (1997), pp. 166–8 (p. 168). Bruce was US Ambassador to France, 1949–52, West Germany, 1957–59, and Great Britain, 1961–69.

19.   M. Gehler, review of T. B. Olesen, *Interdependence Versus Integration: Denmark, Scandinavia and Western Europe*, in *Journal of European Integration History*, 3, 2 (1997), pp. 100–2 (p. 102).

20.   A history of Federal Union, founded in 1938, is contained in R. Mayne and J. Pinder, *Federal Union: The Pioneers* (Basingstoke: Macmillan, 1990). The Federal Trust was set up in 1945. Its constitution states that it 'acts as a forum in which the suitability of federal solutions to problems of governance at national, continental and global level can be explored'. See 'A Note for Friends About the Federal Trust', October 1999, p. 1, and its website <http://www.cix.co.uk/~fedtrust>.

21.   U. Kitzinger, *Diplomacy and Persuasion: How Britain Joined the Common Market* (London: Thames & Hudson, 1973), p. 190. Kitzinger was himself part of the federal movement. He worked at the Economic Section of the Council of Europe, 1951–58, at the University of Oxford between 1956 and 1976, taking leave of absence in 1973–75 to work for Christopher Soames, then Vice–President of the European Commission. He sat on the National Council of the European Movement, 1974–76. See *Who's Who 2000* (London: A. & C. Black, 2000), p. 1153.

22.   S. Greenwood, review of D. Baker and D. Seawright (eds), *Britain For and Against Europe: British Politics and European Integration*, in *Journal of Common Market Studies*, 36, 4 (1998), pp. 603–4 (p. 603). Key studies of press and public opinion include R. J. Lieber, *British Politics and European Unity: Parties, Elites, and Pressure Groups* (Berkeley: University of California Press, 1970); R. Jowell and G. Hoinville (eds), *Britain into Europe: Public Opinion and the EEC 1961–75* (London: Croom Helm, 1976); J. Moon, *European Integration in British Politics 1950–1963: A Study of Issue Change* (Aldershot: Gower, 1985).

23.   Pinder has been Chairman of the Federal Trust since 1985. He has been President of the Union of European Federalists, Vice-President of the International European Movement and Board Member of the UK European Movement. He was previously Federal Union press officer, 1950–52, worked at the Economist Intelligence Unit, 1953–54, and as the paper's editorial writer on European affairs, 1954–62. See *Who's Who 2000*, p. 1197.

24.   For instance, Richard Mayne, his friend and colleague, who was 'the first Englishman to sign on to the staff of the Economic Community'. U. Kitzinger, 'New Situations, New Policies', in U. Kitzinger *et al.*, *Britain and the Common Market 1967* (London: BBC, 1967), pp. 8–34 (p. 13). After a period as an official in the ECSC, 1956–58, and in the EEC, 1958–63, he became personal assistant to Monnet and Director of the Documentation Centre of the Action Committee for a United States of Europe, 1963–66, and Director of the Federal Trust, 1971–73. See *Who's Who 2000*, p. 1390.

25.   Mayne and Pinder, *Federal Union*, p. 153.

26.   Pryce was Head of the Information Office of the High Authority of the ECSC,

1957–60, Head of the Joint Information Office of the European Communities, 1960–64, and was Director of the Directorate General for information in the European Commission, 1973–78. He was Director of the Federal Trust, 1983–90. *Who's Who 2000*, p. 1664.

27. Their list of publications includes R. Mayne, *The Recovery of Europe: From Devastation to Unity* (London: Weidenfeld & Nicolson, 1970); R. Mayne, *The Community of Europe* (London: Victor Gollancz, 1982); R. Mayne, *Postwar: The Dawn of Today's Europe* (London: Thames & Hudson, 1983); J. Pinder, *Europe Against De Gaulle* (London: Pall Mall, 1963); J. Pinder, *European Community: The Building of a Union* (Oxford: Opus, 1998); J. Pinder and R. Pryce, *Europe After De Gaulle: Towards the United States of Europe* (Harmondsworth: Penguin, 1969); R. Pryce, *The Political Future of the European Community* (London: John Marshbank, 1962); R. Pryce, *The Dynamics of European Union* (London: Routledge, 1990).

28. Mayne and Pinder, *Federal Union*, p. 98. The implication is that London's preference for the concept of intergovernmentalism 'has a particularly damaging and distorting impact upon the relevance of federalism to the European Community'. See M. Burgess, *Federalism and European Union: Political Ideas, Influences and Strategies in the European Community, 1972–1987* (London: Routledge, 1989), p. 2. One reviewer has remarked on their 'characteristically well-argued appeal to British policy-makers to abjure their intergovernmentalism'. See C. Brewin, review of A. Duff, J. Pinder and R. Pryce, *Maastricht and Beyond: Building the European Union*, in *Journal of Common Market Studies*, 34, 1 (1996), p. 134.

29. E. Dell, *The Schuman Plan and the British Abdication of Leadership in Europe* (Oxford: Oxford University Press, 1995). He was one of the British Labour Party members who rebelled against Party instructions in October 1971 and voted for UK membership of the EEC. See also A. Milward, review of E. Dell, *The Schuman Plan and the British Abdication of Leadership in Europe*, in *Journal of European Integration History*, 3, 2 (1997), pp. 99–100 (p. 99).

30. Lord Jenkins of Hillhead, 'Foreword', in Mayne and Pinder, *Federal Union*, p. 8.

31. Perhaps the most influential has been A. Nutting, *Europe Will Not Wait: A Warning and a Way Out* (London: Hollis & Carter, 1960). Others include R. Denman, *Missed Chances: Britain and Europe in the Twentieth Century* (London: Cassell, 1996); Gladwyn, *The Memoirs of Lord Gladwyn* (London: Weidenfeld & Nicolson, 1972), p. 3; E. Heath, *The Course of My Life: My Autobiography* (London: Hodder & Stoughton, 1998), pp. 355–8. A classic restatement of the missed opportunities approach is to be found in G. Radice, *Offshore: Britain and the European Idea* (London: I. B. Tauris, 1992), particularly pp. 88–117.

32. The ideological diversity of individuals supporting a European future for Britain in the 1960s is nicely highlighted in U. Kitzinger, 'Introduction', in Kitzinger *et al.*, *Britain and the Common Market*, pp. 1–7 (p. 4). On the other side of the coin, Kenneth Morgan has commented on the change in meaning of the term 'Eurosceptic' between the 1960s and today. See K. O. Morgan, *Callaghan: A Life* (Oxford: Oxford University Press, 1997), p. 393.

33. Lord Boothby, *My Yesterday, Your Tomorrow* (London: Hutchinson, 1962), p. 73.

34. Earl of Kilmuir, *Political Adventure: The Memoirs of the Earl of Kilmuir* (London: Weidenfeld & Nicolson, 1964), p. 186; H. Macmillan, *Tides of Fortune, 1945–1955* (London: Macmillan, 1969), pp. 461–3. Virulent criticism of Boothby and Maxwell Fyfe is to be found in D. Carlton, *Anthony Eden: A Biography* (London: Allen Lane, 1981), pp. 309–17.

35. See Mayne and Pinder, *Federal Union*, p. 187. On p. 165 they observe that Max Beloff gave a lecture at the 1961 Easter Seminar of the Cambridge Federal Union Group. He would later contribute an article to M. Holmes (ed.), *The Eurosceptical Reader* (Basingstoke: Macmillan, 1996).
36. A. Morgan, review of *Britain into Europe: Public Opinion and the EEC 1961–75*, edited by R. Jowell and G. Hoinville, in *Journal of Common Market Studies*, 15, 3 (1977), pp. 221–2 (p. 221).
37. Camps, *Britain and the European Community*, especially p. 45. Camps was a foreign affairs officer in the US State Department, 1939–54, specialising in problems relating to European economic cooperation and integration, and was involved in the development and implementation of the Marshall Plan, the Organisation for European Economic Co-operation (later the Organisation for Economic Co-operation and Development) and the ECSC. She was an editor of *The Economist*, 1954–56. This biographic information is taken from 'Mount Holyoke College Archives and Special Collections: Manuscript Register: MS 0627',<http://www/mtholyoke.edu/offices/library/arch/col/ms0627r.htm>. On p. 7 of the Preface she states that her text had been approved by key Whitehall officials such as Frank Lee and Russell Bretherton. See also M. Camps, 'Missing the Boat at Messina and Other Times?', in B. Brivati and H. Jones (eds), *From Reconstruction to Integration: Britain and Europe Since 1945* (Leicester: Leicester University Press, 1993), pp. 134–43 (p. 134). Her other texts include *What Kind of Europe? The Community since De Gaulle's Veto* (London: Oxford University Press, 1965) and *European Unification in the Sixties: From the Veto to the Crisis* (London: Oxford University Press, 1967). For a similar interpretation by two of her contemporaries, see E. Barker, *Britain in a Divided Europe 1945–1970* (London: Weidenfeld & Nicolson, 1971), and N. Beloff, *The General Says No: Britain's Exclusion from Europe* (Harmondsworth: Penguin, 1963).
38. Mayne and Pinder, *Federal Union*, p. 143.
39. U. Kitzinger, *The Challenge of the Common Market*, 4th edn (Oxford: Blackwell, 1962); U. Kitzinger, *Britain, Europe and Beyond: Essays in European Politics* (Leyden: Sythoff, 1964); Kitzinger *et al.*, *Britain and the Common Market*; Kitzinger, *Diplomacy and Persuasion*.
40. J. Frankel, *British Foreign Policy 1945–1973* (London: Oxford University Press, 1975); F. S. Northedge, *Descent from Power: British Foreign Policy 1945–1973* (London: George Allen & Unwin, 1974). This built on his earlier text, F. S. Northedge, *British Foreign Policy: The Process of Readjustment 1945–1961* (London: George Allen & Unwin, 1962).
41. M. Charlton, *The Price of Victory* (London: British Broadcasting Corporation, 1983). His interviews had been serialised two years earlier in *Encounter*. See M. Charlton, 'How and Why Britain Lost the Leadership of Europe (1): "Messina! Messina!" or, the Parting of Ways', *Encounter*, 57, 3 (August 1981), pp. 8–22; M. Charlton, 'How (and Why) Britain Lost the Leadership of Europe (2): A Last Step Sideways', *Encounter*, 57, 3 (September 1981), pp. 22–35; M. Charlton, 'How (and Why) Britain Lost the Leadership of Europe (3): The Channel Crossing', *Encounter*, 57, 3 (October 1981), pp. 22–33.
42. A. Bullock, *Ernest Bevin: Foreign Secretary* (London: Heinemann, 1983), p. 790; R. Lamb, *The Failure of the Eden Government* (London: Sidgwick & Jackson, 1987), p. 101. See also R. Lamb, *The Macmillan Years 1957–1963: The Emerging Truth* (London: John Murray, 1995).
43. See, for example, D. Sanders, *Losing an Empire, Finding a Role: British Foreign Policy Since 1945* (Basingstoke: Macmillan, 1990); S. George (ed.), *Britain and the*

European Community: The Politics of Semi-Detachment (Oxford: Clarendon Press, 1992); A. Sked and C. Cook, *Post-War Britain: A Political History*, 4th edn (London: Penguin, 1993); P. Clarke, *Hope and Glory: Britain and the World 1900–1990* (London: Penguin, 1996), p. 236.

44. This observation has also been made about the literature on Britain's first application to join the EEC. G. Wilkes, 'The First Failure to Steer Britain into the European Communities: An Introduction', in G. Wilkes (ed.), *Britain's Failure to Enter the European Community 1961–63: The Enlargement Negotiations and Crises in European, Atlantic and Commonwealth Relations* (London: Frank Cass, 1997), pp. 1–32 (pp. 3–10).

45. For an economic perspective on British decline, see N. Crafts, *Britain's Relative Economic Decline 1870–1995: A Quantitative Perspective* (London: Social Market Foundation, 1997), pp. 43–62.

46. B. Harrison, review of R. Coopey, S. Fielding and N. Tiratsoo (eds), *The Wilson Governments 1964–1970*, in *Contemporary Record*, 7, 2 (1993), pp. 490–1 (p. 490); S. Croft, 'British Policy towards Western Europe: The Best of Possible Worlds?', *International Affairs*, 64, 4 (1988), pp. 617–29 (p. 618).

47. Texts which stimulated this approach include A. Seldon, *Churchill's Indian Summer: The Conservative Government, 1951–55* (London: Hodder & Stoughton, 1981); D. C. Watt, *Succeeding John Bull: America in Britain's Place 1900–1975* (Cambridge: Cambridge University Press, 1984); G. Warner, 'The Labour Governments and the Unity of Western Europe, 1945–51', in R. Ovendale (ed.), *The Foreign Policy of the British Labour Governments, 1945–1951* (Leicester: Leicester University Press, 1984), pp. 61–82; J. Melissen and B. Zeeman, 'Britain and Western Europe, 1945–51: Opportunities Lost?', *International Affairs*, 63, 1 (1987), pp. 81–95; J. Kent, 'Bevin's Imperialism and the Idea of Euro-Africa, 1945–49', in M. Dockrill and J. W. Young (eds), *British Foreign Policy, 1945–56* (Basingstoke: Macmillan, 1989), pp. 47–76; A. Deighton, 'Missing the Boat: Britain and Europe 1945–61', *Contemporary Record*, 4, 1 (1990), pp. 15–17; S. Greenwood, *Britain and European Co-operation Since 1945* (Oxford: Blackwell, 1992); J. W. Young, *Britain and European Unity 1945–1992* (Basingstoke: Macmillan, 1993), now in its 2nd edn, *Britain and European Unity, 1945–1999* (Basingstoke: Macmillan, 2000). See also Lord Beloff, *Britain and European Union: Dialogue of the Deaf* (Basingstoke: Macmillan, 1996); N. P. Ludlow, *Dealing With Britain: The Six and the First UK Application to the EEC* (Cambridge: Cambridge University Press, 1997).

48. Kaiser, *Using Europe*, p. 16.

49. D. Reynolds, review of J. W. Young (ed.), *The Foreign Policy of Churchill's Peacetime Administration, 1951–55*, in *International Affairs*, 65, 1 (1989), p. 144.

50. J. Kent and J. W. Young, 'British Policy Overseas: The "Third Force" and the Origins of NATO – In Search of a New Perspective', in B. Heuser and R. O'Neill (eds), *Securing Peace in Europe, 1945–62: Thoughts for the Post Cold War Era* (Basingstoke: Macmillan, 1989), pp. 41–61.

51. M. Hopkins, review of J. W. Young, *Britain and European Unity 1945–1992*, in *International Affairs*, 70, 4 (1994), p. 811. Nicholas Rees uses the same terminology in his review of S. Greenwood, *Britain and European Co-operation since 1945*, in *International Affairs*, 69, 4 (1993), pp. 792–3 (p. 792).

52. Charmley, *Churchill's Grand Alliance*, p. 247.

53. Beloff, *Britain and European Union*, p. 55.

54. D. Dutton, *Anthony Eden: A Life and Reputation* (London: Edward Arnold, 1997), p. 302.

55. Melissen and Zeeman, 'Britain and Western Europe', p. 93.

56. C. Hill, 'The Historical Background', in Smith, Smith and White (eds), *British Foreign Policy*, pp. 24–49 (p. 45). See also D. Watt, 'Introduction: Anglo-American Relations', in Louis and Bull (eds), *The Special Relationship*, pp. 1–14 (p. 7).

57. Deighton, 'Missing the Boat', p. 15.

58. J. Barnes, 'From Eden to Macmillan, 1955–59', in P. Hennessy and A. Seldon (eds), *Ruling Performance: British Governments from Attlee to Thatcher* (Oxford: Basil Blackwell, 1987), pp. 98–149 (p. 131). His view is supported in S. Burgess and G. Edwards, 'The Six Plus One: British Policy-Making and the Question of European Economic Integration, 1955', *International Affairs*, 64, 3 (1988), pp. 393–413 (p. 413), and in Dutton, *Anthony Eden*, p. 307. See also Kaiser, *Using Europe*, pp. 43–4.

59. Quoted in Charlton, *The Price of Victory*, p. 23. It has also been put as follows: 'Britain was not psychologically ready to "enter Europe" in 1955 ... This was certainly the general view at the time.' K. Sainsbury, 'Selwyn Lloyd', in Shlaim, Jones and Sainsbury (eds), *British Foreign Secretaries*, pp. 117–43 (p. 124).

60. Greenwood, *Britain and European Co-operation*, p. 78.

61. Young, *This Blessed Plot*, p. 115.

62. Young, *Britain and European Unity*, 2nd edn, pp. 49–50. Emphasis in original.

63. Ibid., p. 49.

64. W. I. Hitchcock, 'France, the Western Alliance and the Origins of the Schuman Plan, 1948–1950', *Diplomatic History*, 21, 4 (1997), pp. 603–30 (p. 628).

65. R. Edmonds, *Setting the Mould: The United States and Britain, 1945–1950* (Oxford: Oxford University Press, 1986), pp. 210–11; W. LaFeber, *America, Russia, and the Cold War 1945–1992*, 7th edn (New York: McGraw-Hill, 1993), p. 86. See also R. Aron, 'The Historical Sketch of the Great Debate', in D. Lerner and R. Aron (eds), *France Defeats EDC* (London: Thames & Hudson, 1957), pp. 2–21 (p. 3); Winand, *Eisenhower, Kennedy*, p. 23.

66. Young, *Britain and European Unity*, p. 30.

67. Monnet, *Memoirs*, p. 306. And as he reportedly told Chancellor Stafford Cripps: 'I hope with all my heart that you will join in this from the start. But if you don't, we shall go ahead without you.' Cited Bullock, *Ernest Bevin*, p. 778.

68. Kaplan, *On Historical and Political Knowing*, p. 99.

69. M. Hollis and S. Smith, *Explaining and Understanding International Relations* (Oxford: Clarendon Press, 1991). Wilkes implied just such a philosophical division between the two communities of writers when he identified the reasons for historians' dissatisfaction with the conventional wisdom: 'The weight given to the UK's mistakes in historical accounts has had some unfortunate side-effects: [writers] have tended to pass quickly over important episodes in British–Six relations which did not involve conflict, and have often been more concerned to explain the inadequacy of the motivation or vision behind European policies than to analyse their causes and effects thoroughly.' Wilkes, 'The First Failure', p. 4.

70. A. Thorpe, *A History of the British Labour Party* (Basingstoke: Macmillan, 1997), p. 157. For an incisive review of the debate by someone who met regularly with the leading figures of the Wilson administrations in his time at the *Guardian* see John Cole's memoirs, *As it Seemed to Me: Political Memoirs* (London: Phoenix, 1996), pp. 58–72.

71. Morgan, *Callaghan*, p. 181.

72. L. Waters, 'Harold Wilson', <http://www.ukpol.co.uk/wilsonhtml>, p. 1. Two exceptions to this trend are E. Short, *Whip to Wilson: The Crucial Years of Labour Government* (London: Macdonald, 1989) and E. Kay, *Pragmatic Premier: An*

Intimate Portrait of Harold Wilson (London: Leslie Frewin, 1967).

73. R. Hattersley, *Fifty Years On: A Prejudiced History of Britain Since 1945* (London: Abacus, 1997), p. 153.

74. D. Smith, *Harold Wilson: A Critical Biography* (London: Robert Hale, 1964), pp. 11–12. See also P. Foot, *The Politics of Harold Wilson* (London: Penguin, 1968).

75. Although this came to a head during his 1974–76 administrations it has surely had a deleterious effect on his reputation. Peter Wright charted the reasons for the intelligence interest: Wilson's promotion of East–West trade, his visits to Russia and his propensity as Premier to 'surround himself with other East European émigré businessmen'. These were published in *Spycatcher* (Australia: William Heinemann, 1987), pp. 362–74. This quote is from p. 364. A critical analysis of MI5's investigations can be found in D. Leigh, *The Wilson Plot: The Intelligence Services and the Discrediting of a Prime Minister* (London: Heinemann, 1988). See also G. Weidenfeld, *Remembering My Good Friends: An Autobiography* (London: HarperCollins, 1995), pp. 351–3.

76. T. Benn, *Out of the Wilderness: Diaries 1963–67* (London: Hutchinson, 1987); B. Castle, *The Castle Diaries 1964–70* (London: Weidenfeld & Nicolson, 1984); R. Crossman, *The Diaries of a Cabinet Minister: Vol. I, Minister of Housing, 1964–66* (London: Hamish Hamilton/Jonathan Cape, 1977); R. Crossman, *The Diaries of a Cabinet Minister: Vol. II, Lord President of the Council and Leader of the House of Commons, 1966–68* (London: Hamish Hamilton/Jonathan Cape, 1976).

77. Kevin Jefferys defines the 'inner cabinet' as follows: 'a shifting group of up to ten senior ministers who met informally in order to take a broad view of government policy and to suggest new initiatives'. K. Jefferys, *Anthony Crosland: A New Biography* (London: Richard Cohen, 1999), p. 132. For other contemporary critiques of the policy process under Wilson – especially the opinion that he presided over a 'kitchen cabinet' which ran counter to 'Cabinet government' – see J. Haines, *The Politics of Power* (London: Jonathan Cape, 1977), p. 157; D. Jay, *Change and Fortune: A Political Record* (London: Hutchinson, 1980), p. 378; C. Ponting, *Breach of Promise: Labour in Power 1964–1970* (London: Hamish Hamilton, 1989), pp. 33–5. These have fed the recent history. See, for example, K. O. Morgan, *Labour People: Leaders and Lieutenants: Hardie to Kinnock* (Oxford: Oxford University Press, 1989), p. 256; A. Morgan, *Harold Wilson* (London: Pluto, 1992), p. 390.

78. Wigg was Paymaster-General, 1964–67, Williams his Private Secretary.

79. Those on the left of the Party believed that Fulton confirmed 'the existing social order' in Whitehall. A. Birch, *The British System of Government* (London: Routledge, 1998), pp. 144–5.

80. Earl Jellicoe, 'Lord Edward Arthur Alexander Shackleton', *Biographic Memoirs of Fellows of the Royal Society*, 45 (1999), pp. 485–505 (p. 494).

81. H. Heclo and A. Wildavsky, *The Private Government of Public Money: Community and Policy Inside British Politics* (Basingstoke: Macmillan, 1974), p. 266.

82. Leigh, *The Wilson Plot*, front cover précis, hardback edition.

83. Lieber, *British Politics and European Unity*, p. 261. See also N. Ashford, 'The Political Parties' in George (ed.), *Britain and the European Community*, pp. 119–48 (p. 126).

84. For Wilson's own account, unfortunately thinner on the subject of his motivation than on the process by which he achieved Cabinet agreement, see H. Wilson, *The Labour Government 1964–1970: A Personal Record* (London: Weidenfeld & Nicolson/Michael Joseph, 1971), especially pp. 386–91.

85. D. Kavanagh and P. Morris, *Consensus Politics From Attlee to Major*, 2nd edn (Oxford: Blackwell, 1994), p. 106.

86. George, *An Awkward Partner*, p. 44. See also Kaiser, *Using Europe*, Chapters 5 and 6, and Reynolds, *Britannia Overruled*, p. 242.
87. Ponting, *Breach of Promise*, p. 205.
88. Lieber, *British Politics and European Unity*, pp. 261–3.
89. Kitzinger, *The Second Try*, p. 12. For a more subtle appraisal of Anglo-American relations in this period see Morgan, *Callaghan*, pp. 223–6. The tensions created by Vietnam are also explored in A. Dobson, 'The Years of Transition: Anglo-American Relations 1961–1967', *Review of International Studies*, 16 (1990), pp. 239–58 (p. 249).
90. Barker, *Britain in a Divided Europe*, p. 219.
91. M. Stewart, *Life and Labour: An Autobiography* (London: Sidgwick & Jackson, 1980), pp. 162–3, 199. He headed the Foreign Office from January 1965 to August 1966 and from March 1968 to June 1970, sandwiching the stint by George Brown.
92. G. Brown, *In My Way: The Political Memoirs of Lord George-Brown* (London: Victor Gollancz, 1971), p. 212.
93. M. Proudfoot, *British Politics and Government 1951–1970: A Study of an Affluent Society* (London: Faber & Faber, 1974), p. 208.
94. Frankel, *British Foreign Policy*, pp. 165–6.
95. Morgan, *Callaghan*, p. 253.
96. Its opinion can be traced through *The Economist*, 24 October 1964, p. 334; *The Economist*, 13 February 1965, p. 642; *The Economist*, 20 February 1965, pp. 745–7; *The Economist*, 27 March 1965, p. 1410; *The Economist*, 24 July 1965, p. 325; *The Economist*, 5 February 1966, pp. 487–8; *The Economist*, 19 March 1966, pp. 1096–7; *The Economist*, 2 April 1966, pp. 17–18.
97. Stewart, *Life and Labour*, p. 199.
98. P. Ziegler, *Wilson: The Authorised Life of Lord Wilson of Rievaulx* (London: Wiedenfeld & Nicolson, 1993), p. 240; Denman, *Missed Chances*, p. 227.
99. Morgan, *Callaghan*, pp. 213–14.
100. Wilson, *The Labour Government*, p. 98.
101. *The Economist*, 30 July 1966, pp. 419–20. See also Proudfoot, *British Politics*, p. 213.
102. Crossman, *The Diaries of a Cabinet Minister, Vol. II*, p. 283 (11 December 1966).
103. Cited Kitzinger, *Diplomacy and Persuasion*, p. 280. On Wilson's party and personal concerns see also Morgan, *Callaghan*, p. 254; Ponting, *Breach of Promise*, pp. 213–15.
104. Quoted in B. Pimlott, *Harold Wilson* (London: HarperCollins, 1993), p. 435. See also D. Healey, *The Time of My Life* (London: W. W. Norton, 1990), p. 333; Denman, *Missed Chances*, p. 228.
105. Heath, *The Course of My Life*, p. 355.
106. Lieber, *British Politics and European Unity*, p. 263. See also Frankel, *British Foreign Policy*, p. 35.
107. C. Wrigley, 'Now You See It, Now You Don't: Harold Wilson and Labour's Foreign Policy 1964–70', in R. Coopey, S. Fielding and N. Tiratsoo (eds), *The Wilson Governments 1964–1970* (London: Pinter, 1993), pp. 123–35 (p. 123).
108. Castle, *The Castle Diaries*, p. 247 (27 April 1967).
109. Wrigley, 'Now You See It', p. 130.
110. Ponting, *Breach of Promise*, p. 210. See also Lieber, *British Politics and European Unity*, pp. 253–4.
111. He notes, for example, that the Prime Minister prevented him from airing his March 1967 paper on the economic costs and benefits of joining the EEC. Jay, *Change and Fortune*, p. 384. See also Birch, *The British System*, p. 132 and Chap-

ter 2 in this volume.

112. Ponting, *Breach of Promise*, p. 210. Reynolds supports their claims in *Britannia Overruled*, pp. 231–2.

113. Kitzinger, *The Second Try*, p. 13. See also D. Owen, *Time to Declare* (London: Michael Joseph, 1991), p. 99; P. Jones, 'George Brown', in Shlaim, Jones and Sainsbury (eds), *British Foreign Secretaries*, pp. 205–20 (p. 205). This aspect of Wilson's strategy is also discussed in Pimlott, *Harold Wilson*, pp. 435–6; Morgan, *Harold Wilson*, p. 291; Morgan, *Callaghan*, p. 254.

114. Castle, *The Castle Diaries*, p. 208 (6 January 1967). Williams also attempts to exonerate Wilson in *Inside Number Ten* (London: Weidenfeld & Nicolson 1972), pp. 130–1.

115. J. Callaghan, *Time and Chance* (London: Collins, 1987), pp. 184–5; Jay, *Change and Fortune*, pp. 363–4; Benn, *Out of the Wilderness*, p. 477 (23 September 1966).

116. Pimlott, *Harold Wilson*, p. 437. See also Sked and Cook, *Post-War Britain*, pp. 222–3.

117. Cited Castle, *The Castle Diaries*, p. 165 (8 September 1966).

118. Kay, *Pragmatic Premier*, p. 221.

119. J. Grigg, 'Policies of Impotence', *International Affairs*, 48, 1 (1972), pp. 72–6 (p. 75).

120. Tony Crosland's words are quoted by his wife in S. Crosland, *Tony Crosland* (London: Jonathan Cape, 1982), p. 173. He was Minister of State at the DEA from October 1964, then Secretary of State for Education and Science, January 1965–August 1967, when he moved to become President of the Board of Trade.

121. Thorpe, *A History of the British Labour Party*, p. 170.

122. From the title of U. Kitzinger, *The Second Try: Labour and the EEC* (Oxford: Pergamon, 1968); K. O. Morgan, 'The Wilson Years: 1964–1970', in N. Tiratsoo (ed.), *From Blitz to Blair: A New History of Britain Since 1939* (London: Phoenix, 1998), pp. 132–62 (p. 149).

123. Ibid., p. 235.

124. R. Coopey, S. Fielding and N. Tiratsoo, 'Introduction', in Coopey, Fielding and Tiratsoo (eds), *The Wilson Governments*, pp. 1–9 (p. 5).

125. For example, A. Grosser, *The Western Alliance: European–American Relations Since 1945*, translated by Michael Shaw (New York: Continuum, 1980), p. 224. From the Department of Education and Science, Crosland judged: 'Good diversionary tactics when the economy is sinking round us. But nonsense, utter nonsense.' Quoted in Crosland, *Tony Crosland*, p. 185.

126. Hattersley, *Fifty Years On*, p. 168. See also the verdict of the Secretary of State for Economic Affairs, 1967–69, P. Shore, *Leading the Left* (London: Jonathan Cape, 1993), pp. 88–90; Morgan, *Harold Wilson*, p. 246; Pimlott, *Harold Wilson*, p. 274; D. Horner, 'The Road to Scarborough: Wilson, Labour and the Scientific Revolution', in Coopey, Fielding and Tiratsoo (eds), *The Wilson Governments*, pp. 48–71 (p. 49); P. Mottershead, 'Industrial Policy', in F. T. Blackaby (ed.), *British Economic Policy 1960–74* (Cambridge: Cambridge University Press, 1978), pp. 418–83 (p. 432); R. Hamilton, 'Despite Best Intentions: The Evolution of the British Microcomputer Industry', *Business History*, 38, 2 (1995), pp. 81–104 (p. 89); Barker, *Britain in a Divided Europe*, p. 221; G. Owen, *From Empire to Europe: The Decline and Revival of British Industry Since the Second World War* (London: HarperCollins, 1999), pp. 72, 193 and 452–3.

127. An important question given James Ellison's discovery that, just a decade earlier, British diplomacy severely damaged its cause in the Free Trade Area negotiations. Ellison, *Threatening Europe*, especially pp. 210–14. Similar diplomatic threats appear to have been the order of the day during the second

application; see P. Paterson, *Tired and Emotional: The Life of Lord George Brown* (London: Chatto & Windus, 1993), p. 198.

128. Young, *Britain and European Unity*, 2nd edn, p. 101.
129. Original emphasis. Grosser, *The Western Alliance*, p. 224.
130. See p. 135 below.
131. See p. 169 below.

PART I:

THE DOMESTIC CONTEXT

The Labour Party, Public Opinion and 'the Second Try' in 1967

ANNE DEIGHTON

Foreign policy actions are the result both of pressures from the international environment and of those at work within the nation-state.[1] This chapter will consider some of the domestic pressures by assessing the impact of opinion in the Parliamentary Labour Party (PLP) and the Cabinet, and the impact of the application upon public opinion as expressed through opinion polling. This chapter does not deal with elite opinion: at the level of elite activity, peak groups, business and commercial interests were generally in favour of Britain's membership of the Communities.[2] Key industrial and commercial players were kept informed of developments during this period, and it is clear that Wilson was under considerable pressure from them to put in an application, with the Confederation of British Industry (CBI) reporting that 'virtually everyone in the City was in favour'.[3] The enthusiasm for a second application on the business side serves to throw into sharper focus the contradictory signals emanating from the Labour Party, the Cabinet and public opinion within the country as a whole. In many respects, the most potent challenges Harold Wilson faced in guiding Britain towards a second application came variously from sources closer to him (within the Party and Cabinet) and from the harder to measure, yet nonetheless significant, body of public opinion on the 'European question'.

The evidence presented in this chapter suggests that the 1967 application was not driven by widespread pressure from across the Labour Party. Wilson had to secure and sustain parliamentary party unity as he moved his party away from its 1962 rejection of Britain's membership application. While he knew that there was a clear element of support within the Party for membership, management of a Cabinet that was divided on the issue was one of his major tasks. The application was not, furthermore, driven by public demand, and contemporary polls reveal that support for the application was largely determined by support for Wilson himself as leader, and indeed, that this support proved to be rather shallow and fickle. Further, as the second application and its rejection took place over such a short period, there was not very much scope either to manage and shape opinion within the Labour Party, or in the country. In practice, the Prime Minister took for granted the support of the general public, as he held a comfortable majority after the 1966 general election which he could count on to get him through parliamentary votes. Like Macmillan before him, and Heath after 1970, Wilson failed to explain the full significance of the potential consequences of membership of the European Economic Community (EEC): it was presented as being largely about economics and economic change. This tactical decision was to have long-term negative consequences for his party, public opinion and the wider British debate on Europe. The question of winning hearts and minds was never seriously addressed in 1967.

This topic is therefore of more than intrinsic academic interest and importance, as both party politics and public opinion have acquired great significance for an understanding of Britain's uneasy attitude to European integration. It was in part the EEC issue that split the Labour Party open: by 1983, it had a manifesto commitment to withdraw from the Community without a further referendum. The snapshot of public attitudes and priorities provided by contemporary polling reveals the ambivalence of general public opinion at a time when Britain's role as a world power was drawing to a close. Public opinion was, and has remained resistant to any great enthusiasm about European supranational integration, although those polled in the 1960s were probably more prepared to give a popular leader in power the benefit of the doubt on the EEC than was to be the case subsequently. As is well known, over time these party divisions and continued public antipathy came to threaten the support for Britain's membership and its participation in the European enterprise, whichever party was in power. Major debates on European unity have normally been cross-cutting issues, characterised by divisions in both parties in House of Commons votes. While there has been only one referendum on the EEC, public opinion as expressed through a referendum still remains on the table as a decisive but unpredictable tool in Britain's decision-making about its role in the European Union (EU).[4] If 'Europe' was an elite enterprise in the 1960s, British politicians can no longer entertain such comfortable assumptions. Wilson's management of his party and of public opinion contributed to these difficulties: at best, his lack of clarity confused the issues, and contributed to the increasingly antipathetic, if not hostile, climate towards the EEC in subsequent decades.[5]

THE LABOUR PARTY AND THE CABINET

During the first Wilson administration of 1964–66, the Prime Minister made it clear that there was no question whatever of Britain either seeking or being asked to seek, entry into the EEC in the immediately foreseeable future.[6] Perhaps exaggerated by a slender parliamentary majority and no particular feeling in Cabinet towards membership, his position was consistent with the stance taken by Labour when in Opposition during the early 1960s. For, in September 1962, as the negotiations between the British and the six members of the EEC were nearing their climax, the Party's National Executive Committee (NEC) had issued a document setting out five broad conditions which would have to be satisfied if there was to be Labour Party support for the attempt to join the EEC.[7] Then, at the Labour Party conference the following month, leader Hugh Gaitskell led his party to a popular condemnation of the Conservative government's application:[8]

> ... it does mean, if this is the idea, the end of Britain as an independent European state. I make no apology of repeating it. It means the end of a thousand years of history ... It is sheer nonsense.[9]

Labour's 1966 election manifesto reveals a more sympathetic stance towards the Community, and stated that Britain, in consultation with its European Free Trade Association (EFTA) partners, should be ready to enter the EEC, provided that essential British and Commonwealth interests were safeguarded. But it made no particular commitment to a quick application.[10] Indeed, on 18 March 1966, in an election speech in Bristol, Wilson described the Conservative Party leader Heath, who was always an enthusiastic supporter of Britain's Community membership, as a biddable spaniel who would happily lay down to have his tummy tickled by Charles de Gaulle. However, he also talked about the challenging adventure for Labour if Britain did make a 'probe' to investigate the feasibility of membership.[11] Given such ambiguities, it is hardly surprising that controversy still surrounds Wilson's precise motivations for the 1967 application, although it is clear that he was faced by an enormously complex decision on the application, and was armed only, it seemed, with 'collapsing alternatives' to the EEC.[12] The considerations were both economic and political. Economic competitiveness was not considered to be a great issue; more important was the need for new markets. Exports to the Commonwealth had fallen from 50 per cent to 25 per cent of the British total since 1955, while those to the Six had risen from 12 per cent to 25 per cent.[13]

How to sustain Britain's political and diplomatic position in a rapidly changing world was the really demanding question, and it was here that domestic opinion on membership became a further complicating factor in an already difficult decision-making process. In Whitehall, opinion by 1966 was swinging behind membership of the EEC, particularly within sections of the Foreign Office.[14] The Conservative Party, which had been pro-application since 1965, echoed this largely positive approach to the EEC. Indeed, the knowledge that he would not face fundamental opposition from the Conservatives was important for Wilson. The press was, with the notable exception of the *Express*, 'generally pro-Community' and hence supportive of the application.[15] But there appeared to be no strong, broadly based Labour Party pressure for membership in 1966–67, and this was combined with a lack of understanding of the issues involved.[16] 'Europe' seemed of minor importance compared, for example, to the Vietnam War. There was only a handful of resolutions on Europe presented by constituency parties for consideration by the Party conference in 1967, and local parties only began to take an interest after Wilson's May 1967 House of Commons speech.[17]

The Party was not well prepared for this application, and Wilson's decision was certainly not driven from pressures across the Party as a whole. Pro-membership pressure came largely from the Campaign for Democratic Socialism and the Labour Committee for Europe. This latter elite group was very well funded through the European Movement. It also received help from the Federal Trust and the Britain in Europe group. These pro-European groups were not specifically tied to Labour Party membership and were issue rather than party-based, and are evidence of the proliferation of Europeanist interest groups working to influence government opinion in the 1960s. Members who were in the Labour Party were also well placed, and tended to be middle-class intellectuals or, like Roy Jenkins and George Brown, had access to power and the media. In 1964, 53 Members of Parliament (MPs) were members, by the following year there were 60, and by March 1967, 104.[18] Of course, such a grouping would be a natural home for ambitious Labour MPs when it was known that Wilson was actively considering an application, which may help to explain the rise in membership. The new intake of Labour MPs in 1966, which brought an increased parliamentary majority for Wilson, was also significant here.

The influence of the pro-Community groups was tempered considerably by dissenting voices within the Labour Party. Some of the groups that resisted an application were identifiable by ideology. Left-wing opposition was focused around the Tribune Group, which had also benefited from new members in 1966. In general, the left-wingers deplored the EEC as a capitalist organisation that did not promote the interests of labour. Membership, they said, would undermine the dynamism and values of British socialism, while also taking away the capacity of the state to plan the economy. MPs such as the Tribunite leader, Michael Foot, argued passionately not only that the Commonwealth remained more important, but that a rise in food prices was unacceptable and that the EEC was inward-looking and contrary both to Labour's planning and its socialist traditions.[19] Hostility to American values and American dominance played a powerful role in the hostility to the EEC among many on the left.[20] One of the high points of Tribune activity during this period was a parliamentary Early Day Motion, which labelled the EEC first as a capitalist institution which would weaken freedom to plan the British economy, and second as little more than an economic counterpart to the North Atlantic Treaty Organisation (NATO). This collected 100 signatures in February 1967 and was followed in April 1967 by the production of a manifesto which attracted the signatures of 74 Labour MPs.[21] Peter Shore, who served at the Department of Economic Affairs before becoming Minister Without Portfolio, later noted, 'deep in Labour's psyche is … a policy based on the belief that capitalism itself is the main cause of national rivalry and war'.[22] According to this interpretation, the EEC would not even do the job of bringing peace to Europe, as European federalists claimed.

Shore, together with the President of the Board of Trade, Douglas Jay, represented the 'global patriots' in the Labour Party. Their ideas were not ideological in a party-political sense, and were shared by opponents to the EEC on both the right and the left of the Party: they represented the idea of Britain's role as being rightfully in the wider world beyond Europe. This ideal had been reinforced during the first post-war Labour government by the development of the concept of the Commonwealth, and held enormous sway during the early 1960s when it was espoused by Gaitskell, James Callaghan, Richard Crossman and many others, including Wilson himself. It was generally coupled with a belief in free trade, and depicted the EEC as a closed economic trading bloc that would handicap prospects for economic development across the wider world.[23] However, events since Labour had returned to power in 1964 undermined the saliency of so-called 'global' arguments, as white Commonwealth countries in particular worked to find new markets and build new strategic alliances. Such long-standing opposition to the EEC on the left of the Labour Party calls into question Wilson's room for manoeuvre with respect to European policy. Any application which threatened to alienate large sections of his party was probably inconceivable before 1966. And, even with a sizeable majority after 1966, Wilson was hampered from showing his hand or declaring his intent too brazenly, because the most prominent opposition groups had also gained in size and voice.

The intense contradictions in the PLP were reflected in Cabinet arguments over the second application. The divisions in the Cabinet were profound. Given that his personal commitment to the EEC was weak, what were Wilson's tactics?[24] On 22 October 1966, after preliminary discussions with the Six, the Cabinet was convened for a day-long meeting in Chequers, the Prime Minister's country house, to discuss the possibility of moving forward towards an application, given that the NEC conditions of September 1962 had apparently now largely been met.[25] During the summer of 1966, Crossman, Lord President of the Council, warned that the priority was the balance of trade. He found an ally in Jay, who argued that an application would be premature, leading Michael Stewart, Secretary of State for Economic Affairs, to insist that the time for big arguments about any policy shift had not arrived.[26] Barbara Castle wrote that the Cabinet meetings were a battle between the economists who were unenchanted by the prospect of membership and who were backed by herself, Denis Healey, Minister of Defence, Crossman, Jay, Fred Peart, Minister of Agriculture, Herbert Bowden, Secretary of State for Commonwealth Affairs, Richard Marsh, Minister of Power and Callaghan (who was 'wobbling'), against the Europeanists, led by Brown and Stewart.[27]

It was Brown who put forward the strongest pro-entry case in Cabinet. He allowed Wilson to trim his arguments and offer a more moderate approach, thus edging his way, step by step, towards his goal, without committing himself too openly to his colleagues. He was extremely skilled at guiding the Cabinet into many sessions with lengthy discussions on details, which was an effective way of avoiding the issues of principle. Castle thought that Britain would go into Europe 'on a wave of exhaustion', 'just boring our way in', as Benn put it.[28] As Wilson himself admitted wryly, 'if anyone had asked for a document on the effect of entry into the Common Market on British pigeon-fancying, he would have got it'.[29]

In part because of these divisions within the Cabinet, the management of the 'approach to Europe' was firmly controlled from Number Ten. All requests for press interviews with Cabinet ministers, junior ministers and even Parliamentary Private Secretaries had to be cleared by Downing Street; departmental problems were not to be exposed or exaggerated to the press. Turf wars between the Foreign Office and Number Ten were frequent, leading to accusations that the Foreign Office was, on occasion, 'less than frank' with the Cabinet Office. To deal with this, some officials decided there were certain matters with which the Foreign Secretary should not be troubled.[30] The records also reveal that reports from the Ministry of Agriculture, which was broadly opposed to entry, were read and edited by the Cabinet Office.[31]

The Chequers meeting was followed up by more Cabinet meetings, after which it was finally agreed to let Wilson and Brown go on a European tour to try and assess the chances of a new application.[32] The debate had ranged widely over issues concerning the balance of payments, agriculture, competitiveness, control of the British economy and foreign policy, and constitutional issues. Hostility in the Cabinet was still widespread, although that of its most politically ambitious members became more muted.[33] On 16 November 1966 Wilson told the House of Commons that, with their approval, a new, high-level approach would now be made to 'see whether the conditions exist – or do not exist – for fruitful negotiations … We mean business.'[34] No vote was taken in the House on this occasion. The Wilson–Brown probe of the capitals of the six EEC members took place between January and March 1967. The Cabinet then agreed that Wilson would announce to the House of Commons Britain's intention to apply for membership.[35] Both the United States and the Soviet Union were reported to be in favour, as were the 'friendly five' (Belgium, Germany, Italy, Luxembourg and the Netherlands). Conditional support from the Commonwealth and EFTA had already been secured.[36] Castle noted that Wilson actually called his statement an 'unconditional application for negotiations about the conditions for entry'. She added that only she and Marsh came out against an application and that Peart and Jay said it depended on the conditions achieved. Unfortunately, however, the voting is not recorded in the minutes and accounts differ.[37] The 'best bet now is to get the Cabinet committed to conditions that will endure failure', she gloomily concluded. Jay made alarmist speeches while Wilson and Brown were in Bonn assessing German reactions to any application, claiming that membership would cost £2 billion a year. He also tried unsuccessfully to get mass Cabinet resignations to stop Wilson. These public utterances forced Wilson to remind the Cabinet of the need for personal discretion, and the obligations of collective Cabinet responsibility.[38] In August, Jay was retired from his post as President of the Board of Trade and from the Cabinet.[39]

Between 8 and 10 May, Wilson reported to the House of Commons on the results of the probe, and recommended a new application for membership of the EEC. It was admitted that food prices might rise by 10–14 per cent and the cost of living by 3.5 per cent, so no immediate nirvana was promised. In the vote, in which a three-line whip was imposed upon both Labour and Conservative MPs in favour of the motion, the voting was 488 to 62 in favour. Whilst this looks an imposing victory, 36 Labour MPs defied the whip and voted against the motion and 50 abstained. So, whilst the 10 May vote could be interpreted as the largest majority that Labour had ever had for a foreign policy issue, such a view overlooks the fact that the majority was only secured because of the three-line whip applied on both parties in favour of the application. Such was the depth of feeling on this issue, that seven Labour Parliamentary Private Secretaries lost their jobs afterwards.[40] Of the Conservatives, 26 voted against the government's motion. The level of defections and abstentions was a clear sign that it would not be easy to take entry through without cross-party consensus.

How personally committed to the application was the Party leader and head of the government? This question is important, not least because management of his Cabinet was to prove a difficult task. Wilson is recorded in just about every analysis of his premiership as being ambiguous, devious and unclear to his Cabinet, to the Party and to the country. His biographer, Ben Pimlott, finds that his 'position on Europe, about which he had no strong feelings, was designed more for Labour party consumption than for the electorate'.[41] To keep what all the memoir accounts reveal as a fractious and quarrelsome party together was the first requirement of his leadership.[42] He is thus not a leader who has attracted the plaudits of later writers. Hugo Young writes of 'his fascination with tactics, his professional vanity, his impressionable mind, the grandeur of his self-confidence, his refusal to acknowledge the realities of international power. It was at times comical, at others almost calamitous.'[43] Castle talks of the effects of the 'insidious pull of office' on him and his high popularity ratings until the end of 1966, which no doubt boosted this self-image.[44]

Managing dissension in the PLP and Cabinet presented a formidable challenge to Wilson. Three major debates were held within the

PLP, on 6, 20 and 27 April 1967, Wilson addressing them personally on the last occasion. The discussions were vigorous and often critical; however, Wilson felt that expressed opinion had largely swung behind him before the House of Commons debate of May. Moreover, those who opposed the application had no convincing response to the question of alternatives, particularly after the failure of the National Plan between 1964–66. Foot's rousing speech in the Commons debate between 8–10 May is full of analysis, but weak on solutions. Three alternatives were discussed: the 'Going-It-Alone' option (GITA), an Atlantic free trade area into which studies were made in 1966–67 (the Javits plan) and association with the EEC under Article 238. The lack of a viable alternative agenda for the opposition groups, and the ideological oppositionists in particular, is reflected in the writings of Paul Foot, in the stance of the Young Socialists and, on the continent, by Ernest Mandel.[45] By insinuating the prospect of a new application in the autumn of 1966, and then by undertaking the probe, Wilson had cleverly shifted the prospect of an application up the national political agenda, and created a situation in which it would no longer be possible simply to do nothing more about it, despite the warnings of the Secretary to the Cabinet, Burke Trend, to avoid such a step.[46]

Wilson was clearly aware in 1966–67 that keeping the Party together would be a mammoth task: earlier tensions had only been resolved by Gaitskell's clarion call against British membership of the EEC at the conference in 1962 (and then, of course, by de Gaulle's veto of 1963). After the 1967 probe, when he became far more personally enthusiastic about membership, Wilson appears to have thought that, by guile and persuasion, he could perhaps circumnavigate French hostility to a renewed British application. Like Macmillan before him he was tempted by the prospect of personal, prime ministerial diplomacy with the General. Wilson had to rely on his personal popularity, and to depend on the lure of power and position to keep his unruly and opinionated Cabinet under control – and indeed, none of them did resign on the issue in 1966–67. How far the whole application was actually 'subordinated to other considerations of party policy and party management', as Lord Beloff argued, remains an open question, although it does seem that there was a genuine element of 'conversion' after the probe.[47] Wilson was deeply committed to maintaining the value of sterling, and this issue became closely meshed into the arguments among his Cabinet colleagues between the summer of 1966 and November 1967. He long opposed devaluation for emotional and economic reasons going back to his days at the Board of Trade during the devaluation crisis of 1949, which resulted in many public pronouncements against devaluation and its costs. This commitment led him into embarrassment with the Americans over their support for sterling and Britain's support for the war in Vietnam. Although the full story of Wilson and sterling between 1966 and 1967 has yet to be told, the EEC application may have been partially stimulated by his desire to leave sterling's value unchanged whilst appeasing Europeanist pro-devaluers, like Jenkins and Brown, with the prospect of an application.

The TUC's economic committee also voted in favour of the application, which was duly deposited in Brussels on 11 May 1967.[48] On 16 May, de Gaulle effectively tried to stall the application, referring to its potential to bring 'destructive upheavals' to the Community.[49] However, having got so far, the Labour government clearly could not yet take France's third *Non* as a final no. Wilson had now to force Britain's way into the EEC.[50] The gloves were off, and the diplomacy of the following months involved pressures, threats and cajoling. The struggle for the application was reflected in the difficulties that officials had in ensuring that Cabinet members were kept in line, while they were themselves under considerable pressure to act very quickly.[51] Meanwhile, in Brussels, French pressure upon heads of government to delay consideration of the application meant that it was not even acknowledged until 5 June. The Belgian Foreign Minister suggested that Brown make his case through the Western European Union Council, which he did on 4 July.

The Labour Party conference of October 1967 moved behind the Wilson application (but only by 3,359,000 votes to 2,697,000, with voting on a block-voting system), but in mid-November Wilson was forced to devalue sterling, which dropped by 14.3 per cent to $2.40, and his own personal popularity, already weakened after the autumn 1966 squeeze, plummeted. This must surely have had an adverse effect on the public's enthusiasm for the EEC. Fear of sterling's weakness and the impact that an application might have on its strength had been a preoccupation since the beginning of the year, but its position had been made worse by the Six Day War in the Middle East. The following week, de Gaulle dealt his *coup de grâce* in another press conference, which has been described by John Newhouse as 'his most boisterous ever', in which he asserted that Britain was still not ready for membership. Wilson could only respond by meeting each criticism point by point, and by insisting that the application should be left on the agenda for later discussion.[52]

PUBLIC OPINION

In 1964, Kenneth Younger, a former Labour Party Minister of State and then Director of the Royal Institute of International Affairs, wrote a much-quoted article on public opinion and British foreign policy. Although his article appeared nearly three years before a second application was made for British membership of the EEC, Younger's analysis would remain acutely relevant to the issue of public opinion and the EEC in 1967.[53] In it, he reflected with regret on the remoteness of the ordinary citizen from foreign policy, and on the public's lack of interest in world events in the intervals between crises. He argued that public opinion rarely makes itself decisively felt as a separate force of which governments consciously have to take account, but that it nevertheless does set limits on what a prudent government might attempt. He noted that, during the first application of 1961–63, Macmillan's government did not engage openly and directly with public opinion as it feared, on the one hand, that this might constrain its overseas diplomacy and, on the other, that if the application failed, then it would have to answer to its voters. He concluded his article by arguing that parliament had a duty to play a more effective mediating role between the electorate and the government in power.

Assessing public opinion presents methodological problems for the historian, not least because the questions asked by pollsters during this period dealt both with EEC membership and with the alternative relationships which formed a traditional dimension of British opinion on international affairs, in particular those with the United States and the Commonwealth. The questions asked may also have skewed the responses – for example, presenting the EEC as an alternative to the United States.[54] Public opinion is notoriously affected by rapid swings in mood, by personalities, by major events such as wars, as well as by longer-term factors such as norms and values, and by political bias. Furthermore, it is hard to disentangle cause from effect when measuring public opinion: is government policy a function of, or reaction to, public opinion or vice versa? Even if one does uncover decisive public attitudes towards given issues, measuring its practical impact on government policy remains a hazardous exercise.

By mid-1965, the relevant poll figures from Gallup were showing a sustained interest in the possibility of British membership of the EEC, reaching a peak of around 70 per cent approval of moving closer to the European mainland in the summer of 1966. This enthusiasm was, though, to decline as the application progressed, not least because, as the prospect of membership got closer, it appeared to look less attractive. By June 1967, only 25 per cent approved, while 56 per cent disapproved, if membership meant breaking the relationship with the United States. Further, on what was called a 'trust factor', by December 1967, the USA scored highest with 57 per cent, Australia followed with 44 per cent, Canada 38 per cent, and only then do the European countries appear on the returns, headed by Scandinavia.[55]

TABLE 2.1
ON THE PROSPECTS OF MOVING CLOSER TOWARDS
MEMBERSHIP OF THE EEC

	Approval	*Disapproval*	*Don't know*
June 1965	55	21	24
Dec. 1965	60	17	23
March 1966	59	18	23
May 1966	70	10	20
Aug. 1966	71	12	17
Nov. 1966	65	14	21
Feb. 1967	61	20	19
March 1967	57	27	16
May 1967	43	30	27
July 1967	40	45	15
Nov. 1967	37	44	19

Source: Polling extrapolated from Gallup polls, in R. J. Shepherd, *Public Opinion and European Integration* (New York: Saxon House, 1975).

That the leaders of all three parties favoured entry to the EEC probably affected polling positively. But it was Wilson's personal popularity, and his personal interest in the idea, that most strongly affected positive general support for the application amongst Labour supporters. James Spence argues that, coupled with evidence that the public had only the haziest idea about what membership actually involved, the sense of a deepening economic crisis and apprehension about rising food prices then came to influence polling statistics as well. By the time of the November devaluation, support for membership had been badly eroded; although it must be added that it was well-known by then that de Gaulle had never spoken out in favour of the application.[56]

The Conservative Party commissioned a major poll on the application, with fieldwork covering the period from March to April 1967. The 'somewhat confusing picture' of their results noted that Labour supporters based approval for entry upon party loyalty, rather than attachment to the EEC. Likewise, they found that there were more Conservative voters who were hostile to membership, and, worryingly, that the leader of the Conservative Party, Heath, who was personally strongly in favour of entry, did not generate the enthusiasm of

Conservative voters in the way that Wilson did for Labour supporters. This poll also found very little support for 'ever closer union', as well as a very limited understanding of the issues involved beyond an appreciation that food prices would rise and a hope that personal prosperity would be improved by membership. Loyalty to America ran higher than that towards the EEC. In general, the poll further reflected declining support for membership as the prospects of a firm application being lodged grew more likely. Only 51 per cent remained in favour by 1967, as opposed to 66 per cent in June 1966.[57]

TABLE 2.2
IN FAVOUR OF THE APPLICATION (%)

	All parties	June 1966	Cons.	Labour	Lib.
In Favour					
Very strongly	18	28	18	24	23
Fairly strongly	23	30	23	24	23
Not very strongly	11	9	8	12	10
All in favour	52	67	49	60	56
Against					
Very strongly	13	7	15	8	8
Fairly strongly	11	8	12	9	14
Not very strongly	8	5	11	7	6
All against	32	20	38	24	28
Don't know	16	13	13	15	16

Source: 'Attitudes to Europe and the Common Market', Opinion Research Centre, 1967, CPA: CC0 180/13/1/1.

CONCLUSION

This chapter has shown that Wilson's Labour Party, his Cabinet and the country at large were divided over the question of Britain's entry to the EEC. In 1962, Gaitskell had led Labour away from support, meaning that Wilson's key task was to convince his followers that the experience of power had proved to him the inevitability of a new application. Among the party elites, support or opposition turned on questions of ideology, of Britain's rightful role in the world or on the defence of sterling. Many doubted whether de Gaulle could be persuaded in any case. These divisions were reflected in Wilson's Cabinet. Here his tactic was to allow opponents of entry to talk themselves out, knowing that they lacked clear and persuasive alternatives to British membership, and that resignations by ambitious politicians were unlikely so early in the life of the second administration. Wilson did manage to keep control of dissenters in 1966–67, and indeed managed in 1975 to secure a referendum result which enabled him to say that Britain was in the EEC on its own terms. But the divisions and bitterness that accompanied the debate on the EEC were effectively to destroy the Party for nearly two decades.

The problem with the general public was rather different. Support for the application appears to have been determined by support for Wilson personally. Ignorance about and indifference to the EEC was widespread. It was seen as an economic enterprise that might give a chance for greater prosperity as long as food prices did not rise too far. However, as the prospect of entry grew closer, even the support of Labour voters died away. Wilson had not tackled the political implications of entry during the election campaign, and played these down in his addresses to the House of Commons and the PLP. Thus, the public opinion polling data reflects the widely held perception of the EEC issue as one that affected elites, rather than publics. National parties, and indeed, individual personalities, were of the greatest importance to those polled, and economic issues that had a direct bearing on day-to-day life were more important than political ideals. The polls thus reflect a misunderstanding about the long-term implications of the EEC as an international organisation.

It is only since the Maastricht Treaty that the extent of the penetration of the European Communities into national systems has been realised as an issue for the managers of public opinion. Arguments about the impact of membership on Britain's constitutional practices and procedures were not as widely debated during this period as later. The sovereignty and constitutional considerations were always played down by British Prime Ministers, frequently with a comforting verbal blurring between losing and merging sovereignty, but this issue has refused to go away. By the early 1970s, this theme was to capture the attention of such people as the previously pro-EEC Benn, who was to become a prime mover in the referendum of 1975. Constitutional questions were later also to engage those on the right of the political spectrum, notably Enoch Powell. To the wider public, these issues were to remain a largely closed book. In the 1960s, the questions surrounding membership of the EEC were generally considered to be questions for elites. Thirty years on, this view has proved to be untenable.

NOTES

1. See further, A. Deighton, 'Foreign Policy-Making: The Macmillan Years', in W. Kaiser and G. Staerck (eds), *British Foreign Policy, 1955–64: Contracting Options* (London: Macmillan, 2000), pp. 1–18.
2. For a penetrating overview of elites, see L. Ruano, 'Elites, Public Opinion and Pressure Groups: The British Position in Agriculture during Negotiations for Accession to the EC, 1961–1975', *Journal of European Integration History*, 5, 1 (1999), pp. 7–22, as well as Chapter 6 in this volume. For a clear and recent account of Britain's applications to the EEC see A. May, *Britain and Europe since 1945* (London: Longman, 1999), Chs 4–6.
3. Public Record Office (PRO): PREM 13/1481. There were meetings with CBI representatives and the economic committee of the TUC. See PRO: PREM 13/2164. *The Economist* conducted a comprehensive survey of business and commercial attitudes, *The Economist*, 19 November 1966, pp. 828–38. Over 100 British firms had already acquired subsidiaries in the EEC. N. Beloff, 'What Happened in Britain after the General Said No', in P. Uri (ed.), *From Commonwealth to Common Market* (London: Penguin, 1968), pp. 50–61 (p. 54). It was reported to the Cabinet that the CBI thought that, as talks had proceeded so far, not to apply would now have an economically depressing effect. See PRO: CAB 128/42, CC(67)22nd, 20 April 1967.
4. J. Smith, 'The 1975 Referendum', *Journal of European Integration History*, 5, 1 (1999), pp. 41–56.
5. General surveys of these issues over time can be found in N. Ashford, 'The Political Parties', A. B. Philip, 'British Pressure Groups and the European Community', and N. Nugent, 'British Public Opinion and the European Community', all in S. George (ed.), *Britain and the European Community: The Politics of Semi-Detachment* (Oxford: Clarendon Press, 1992), pp. 119–48, 149–71, 172–201 respectively.
6. In 1964, relations with Britain showed a 'drift away from the foreground of Community thinking'; see the Foreign Office's 'Annual Report on the European Communities for 1964', PRO: FO 371/182299.
7. The conditions were: strong and binding safeguards for trade and other interests of friends and partners in the Commonwealth, freedom to pursue an independent foreign policy, fulfilment of the government's pledge to other members of EFTA, the right to plan the economy and guarantees to safeguard British agriculture.
8. National Executive Committee, 29 September 1962, quoted in U. Kitzinger, *The European Common Market and Community* (London: Routledge & Kegan Paul, 1967), pp. 168–76. For an account of Gaitskell's motivations see B. Brivati, *Hugh Gaitskell* (London: Richard Cohen, 1997), Ch. 17.
9. Quoted in Brivati, *Hugh Gaitskell*, p. 414.
10. *Labour Party Election Manifesto, 1966*, Part 6, Section 4, <www.ukpol.co.uk/man.shtml>.
11. *The Times*, 19 March 1966. Nora Beloff, 'What Happened in Britain', pp. 63–4.
12. R. J. Lieber, *British Politics and European Unity: Parties, Elites and Pressure Groups* (London: University of California Press, 1970), p. 374.
13. P. Oppenheimer, 'Europe and the Common Market', *National Westminster Bank Quarterly Review*, pp. 5–21. Oppenheimer was personally hostile to the application, and wrote that the current was trying to 'bamboozle the public'.
14. H. Young, *This Blessed Plot: Britain and Europe from Churchill to Blair* (London: Macmillan, 1998), Ch. 6. However, there were grave doubts among senior civil servants that an immediate application could succeed. For an early warning, see Reilly note, 4 July 1966, in which Jean Monnet's verdict that de Gaulle had not changed, and that the time was not ripe for an application, was relayed to the Prime Minister, PRO: PREM 13/907. See also PRO: FCO 30/82, Gore-Booth to Brown, 23 February 1967, Nield to Brown, 17 March 1967; private papers of the British Ambassador to Paris, Patrick Reilly (to be made available in the Bodleian Library, Oxford, when catalogued); A. Cairncross, *The Wilson Years: A Treasury Diary, 1964–1969* (London: Historians' Press, 1997); P. Gore-Booth, *With Great Truth and Respect* (London: Constable, 1974).

15. G. Wilkes and D. Wring, 'The British Press and European Integration: 1948–1996', in D. Baker and D. Seawright (eds), *Britain For and Against Europe: British Politics and the Question of European Integration* (Oxford: Clarendon Press, 1998), pp. 185–205 (p. 192).

16. PRO: FCO 30/252, Foreign Office discussions on the domestic context of the Approach to Europe.

17. Labour Party, fiches 261/48, 270/157, 862. On the Young Socialists' lack of clarity, see Labour Party, NEC, fiche 859, Bodleian Library, University of Oxford.

18. The Labour Committee for Europe could count among their number Lord Chalfont, Edmund Dell, Roy Hattersley, David Marquand, Robert Maxwell, Christopher Mayhew, David Owen, Giles Radice, Shirley Williams, Geoffrey de Freitas and Ivor Richard, to name but a few of the public figures, PRO: FCO 30/50.

19. Other leading Tribune members included the campaigner Konni Zilliacus.

20. This thread of the argument was to emerge even more powerfully by the end of the decade with the appearance of the immensely influential book by J. Servan-Schreiber, *The American Challenge*, trans. by R. Steel (London: Hamish Hamilton, 1968), although the very French argument here was that the EEC should be developed to act as a counterweight to American capitalism and hegemony.

21. N. H. Twitchell, *The Tribune Group: Factional Conflict in the Labour Party, 1964–1970* (London: Rabbit Press, 1998), p. 62. Tribunites also abstained on the Defence White Paper in 1967, on the grounds that it was not radical enough. However, as the case of Eric Heffer showed, not all Tribune members were necessarily anti-EEC.

22. P. Shore, *Leading the Left* (London: Weidenfeld & Nicolson, 1993), p. 8. Shore's ideas were a combination of nationalism and ideological hostility to the EEC.

23. D. Jay, *The European Economic Community* (Manchester: Manchester Statistical Society, 1970), and *Change and Fortune: A Political Record* (London: Hutchinson, 1980).

24. As opposed to his strategy.

25. See note 7 above for list of conditions.

26. PRO: PREM 13/907, 4 and 5 July 1966.

27. PRO: CAB 128/41, CC(66), 22 October 1966; B. Castle, *The Castle Diaries* (London: Weidenfeld & Nicolson, 1984), pp. 177–9 (22 October 1966), 183 (9 November 1966), 249 (30 April 1967).

28. Castle, *The Castle Diaries*, pp. 236 (21 March 1967), 242 (13 April 1967); P. Hennessy, *The Prime Minister: The Office and its Holders since 1945* (London: Allen Lane, 2000), pp. 312, 289. Hennessy notes that there were no fewer than seven meetings between April and May 1967, and remarks on Wilson's penchant for letting the Cabinet ramble, talking itself out, to no firm conclusion.

29. H. Wilson, *The Labour Government, 1964–1970: A Personal Record* (London: Weidenfeld & Nicolson/Michael Joseph, 1971), p. 387.

30. PRO: PREM 13/1482, notes by Trend, May 1967; see also PRO: PREM 13/908.

31. PRO: PREM 13/1632, February to April 1967.

32. PRO: CAB 128/41, CC(66)53, 1 November 1966, CC(66)54, 3 November 1966, CC(66)55, 9 November 1966; 10 November 1966; Wilson, *The Labour Government*, pp. 296, 299.

33. Lord Beloff, *Britain and European Union: Dialogue of the Deaf* (London: Macmillan, 1996), pp. 71–3; K. O. Morgan, *Callaghan: A Life* (Oxford: Oxford University Press, 1997), p. 254. Healey barely mentions the second application, except to point out that he thought that de Gaulle would never admit Britain into the Common Market; that he supported Jay's determined campaign against a second application; that he was himself a pragmatist; that he found the Euro-fanatics intellectually disreputable and the anti-Europeanists' extremism distasteful: D. Healey, *The Time of My Life* (London: Michael Joseph, 1989), pp. 211–12, 329–30; A. Benn, *Out of the Wilderness: Diaries 1963–67* (London: Hutchinson, 1987); J. Callaghan, *Time and Chance* (London: Collins, 1987).

34. *Hansard: House of Commons Debates*, column 1540, 10 November 1966; PRO: CAB 128/41, CC(66)64th, 6 December 1966.

35. PRO: CAB 128/42, CC(67)27, 2 May 1967; Castle, *Diaries*, pp. 241–2 (13 April 1967); Wilson, *The Labour Government*, pp. 388–9. A consultative committee of top indus-

trialists was also kept closely informed, PRO: PREM 13/1475.

36. PRO: CAB 128/42, CC(67)22, 20 April 1967. The reason given for Soviet support was fear that a 'resurgent Germany might dominate Western Europe' after de Gaulle left office.

37. Castle, *The Castle Diaries*, pp. 250–1 (2 May 1967); Beloff, *Britain and European Union*, p. 75; Young, *This Blessed Plot*, pp. 194–5. George Brown refers to his 'suspicious' Cabinet colleagues on the Europe issue in *In My Way: The Political Memoirs of Lord George-Brown* (London: Victor Gollancz, 1971), p. 219.

38. F. Nicolson and R. East, *From the Six to the Twelve: The Enlargement of the European Communities* (London: Longman, 1987), p. 47.

39. Having been reprimanded for his speech, PRO: PREM 13/1638; Castle, *The Castle Diaries*, p. 244 (25 April 1967).

40. There had been extensive discussion about whether the 1961 application should be revived or a new application made. On voting statistics, see P. Norton, *Dissension in the House of Commons: Intra-party Dissent in the House of Commons Division Lobbies, 1945–1974* (London: Macmillan, 1975), pp. 269–72; Hansard: *House of Commons Debates*, 8–10 May, 1967; M. Newman, *Socialism and European Unity: The Dilemma of the Left in Britain and France* (London: Junction, 1983), p. 228; L. J. Robins, *The Reluctant Party: Labour and the EEC 1961–75* (Ormskirk: G.W. Hesketh, 1979).

41. B. Pimlott, *Harold Wilson* (London: HarperCollins, 1992), p. 397.

42. Wilson was 'first and last a party man', argued Peter Hennessy on Radio 4, 24 May 1995, on the occasion of the death of Wilson. See also Hennessy, *The Prime Minister*, p. 289.

43. Young, *This Blessed Plot*, p. 191.

44. Castle, *The Castle Diaries*, p. 237 (21 March 1967).

45. P. Foot, *The Politics of Harold Wilson* (London: Penguin, 1968); E. Mandel, *Europe Versus America? Contradictions of Imperialism* (London: New Left Books, 1970), especially Ch. 11.

46. PRO: PREM 12/1475, Trend to Wilson, 16 December, 1966. John Robinson, a Foreign Office enthusiast for entry, thought that anti-marketeers were not a problem for Labour. See Conservative Party Archive (CPA): CRD 3/10/10, letter from Hurd to Heath, 22 September 1967, Bodleian Library, Oxford.

47. Beloff, *Britain and the European Union*, p. 75.

48. The TUC was anxious about an influx of foreign labour into Britain. See PRO: CAB 128/42, CC(67)20, 13 April 1967.

49. *Le Monde*, 17 May 1967. De Gaulle told the American Ambassador to France that he considered his press conference amounted to a veto, PRO: PREM 13/1482, O'Neill to Private Secretary, 18 May 1967.

50. U. Kitzinger, *The Second Try: Labour and the EEC* (Oxford: Pergamon, 1968).

51. Thomas Balogh, one of Wilson's economic advisers, and hostile to the application, noted that decision-makers were under a 'torrent of paper', and that officials were giving the impression that issues had been better considered than was the case, PRO: PREM 13/1475, 16 December 1966, 4 July 1967.

52. J. Newhouse, *De Gaulle and the Anglo-Saxons* (London: Deutsch, 1970), p. 309; *Le Monde*, 28 November 1967.

53. K. Younger, 'Public Opinion and British Foreign Policy', *International Affairs*, 40, 1, (1964), pp. 22–33.

54. On polling, see *Gallup International Public Opinion Polls: Great Britain, 1937–1975* (New York: Random House); R. J. Shepherd, *Public Opinion and European Integration* (New York: Saxon House, 1975); J. Spence, 'Movements in the Public Mood: 1961–75', in R. Jowell and G. Hoinville (eds), *Britain into Europe: Public Opinion and the EEC, 1961–75* (London: Croom Helm, 1976), Ch. 2. On methodological and analytical problems associated with studying public opinion, see Nugent, 'Public Opinion', pp. 172–5.

55. Gallup polls as quoted in Shepherd, *Public Opinion*, pp. 60, 93.

56. Spence, 'Movements', pp. 23–5. Greater hostility to membership among women, the old and working-class groups remained consistent.

57. 'Attitudes to Europe and the Common Market', Opinion Research Centre, 1967, CPA: CC0 180/13/1/1.

—3—

The Conservatives and the Wilson Application

PHILIP LYNCH

By 1966, the Conservative Party had recovered from the setback of Charles de Gaulle's 1963 veto of Harold Macmillan's application to take Britain into the European Economic Community (EEC). Under the leadership of Edward Heath,[1] the internal divisions on Europe evident during Macmillan's application appeared to have largely healed; early EEC entry was confirmed as a central pillar of Conservative policy and a dynamic vision of further integration developed. The pro-entry message featured prominently in that year's general election. Labour's launch of a 'probe' to ascertain the views of Britain's EEC neighbours in November 1966, followed by its membership application in May 1967, therefore posed a number of political problems for the Conservatives. The change in policy threatened to rob the Conservatives of their distinctive message and, if the bid proved successful, to deny them the expected electoral benefits. If the bid failed, EEC membership would seem an unrealistic and unpopular goal. The Conservatives therefore supported the entry bid, imposing a three-line whip for the key vote in the House of Commons. But they distanced themselves from the timing and conduct of the bid, engaging in limited political skirmishing without landing the blows that could scupper the application and leave the Tories accused of sabotaging the 'second try'. Political calculations were complicated by unease in the party over the leadership's tactics and by Heath's private expectation that the application would fail. However, what emerges most clearly is that, in terms of launching the second application, the domestic political climate was generally more favourable for Harold Wilson than it had been earlier or would be later.

This chapter explores in three parts the Conservative Party's reaction to Wilson's attempt to take Britain into the EEC. The first examines the strengthening 'pro-Europeanism' inside the Conservative Party, brought about by the confluence of Heath winning of the Party leadership contest in 1965 and the broader support for joining the EEC engendered by the Conservative Policy Review of 1965–67. The second part analyses the change in Conservative tactics necessitated by Wilson's application to join the EEC. It explains that, despite broadly supporting the second bid, the Conservatives felt compelled to oppose Wilson on policy detail. This was underpinned by Heath's personal attacks on the Prime Minister's refusal to explore the possibility of defence and foreign policy cooperation with the EEC. The final part searches under the veneer of unity to find that, undermining its 'party of Europe' image, the Conservative Party remained divided over the question of Europe during the Wilson application. The entrenchment of divergent views between Heath, Enoch Powell and their followers would, it suggests, have repercussions for the unity of the Conservative Party in later decades.

EUROPE AND THE CONSERVATIVE POLICY REVIEW

Support for EEC entry had remained Conservative Party policy after the 1963 veto, but appeared as a long-term objective only in the 1964 election manifesto, which stated that the conditions for early entry were not in place. A year later, leader Alec Douglas-Home reiterated Conservative support for European unity, stating that a future agreement between Britain, the Six and the European Free Trade Association (EFTA) states 'will have to cover the economy, the politics and in due course the security' of those countries.[2] The following month, the Shadow Cabinet (officially known as the Leader's Consultative Committee) considered two papers on Europe prepared by Reginald Maudling and Duncan Sandys.[3] They envisaged the rapid development of the EEC, highlighted a political case for membership and feared the effects of exclusion. The Shadow Cabinet decided to reiterate 'constantly' the party's intention to seek early entry and to 'educate' the party, public opinion, the farming community and the Commonwealth to this end. Although now accepting the Treaty of Rome as it stood, rather than seeking renegotiation of the Treaty ahead of entry, it was deemed unwise to emphasise this.[4]

Europe had little impact on the party's essentially non-ideological leadership contest in 1965, although Heath, as Macmillan's chief negotiator, was identified as an advocate of entry while his main rival,

Maudling, had been wary of moves towards Europe.[5] Ironically, given
his relatively poor parliamentary performance as leader, Heath's victory owed much to perceptions that he was the more effective and
pugnacious of the candidates. However, his coordinating role in the
party's policy review and his leadership election victory boosted the
Tory case for entry. The Policy Committee on Foreign Affairs, chaired
by Lord Carrington, examined the European aspect of this review.
This was established in early 1965 and reported in August of that year.[6]
Compared with other groups, the Committee was concerned with
reaffirming existing policy rather than challenging its fundamental
tenets.[7] In its final report, the Committee recommended that the manifesto should state that early British membership of the EEC would be
in the best interests of Britain, Europe and the Commonwealth. It
highlighted the political case for entry, confirmed the need to accept
the Treaty of Rome and avoid setting 'unrealistic conditions', and
warned against an 'outdated conception of nationalism'. Although
significant structural reforms would be required before entry, the
Committee felt that the economy and the agricultural sector could
benefit from membership and be competitive in the EEC. It urged
enhanced practical cooperation with European states (for example, in
space exploration and the Blue Streak project) before entry and
advised further defence integration, although there were differences
within the group on this issue. Finally, the Committee rejected 'piece-
meal cooperation' with the EEC (closer EEC–EFTA links were seen as
a 'blind alley') and dismissed suggestions that stronger Commonwealth and Atlantic alliance ties could substitute for entry.[8]

Following the winding down of the Policy Committee on Foreign
Affairs, a number of parliamentary party committees examined EEC
entry in 1966–67.[9] The Parliamentary Foreign Affairs Committee
served as a forum for non-specialist general discussions on foreign
policy. The Committee on Europe (Policy Research), a sub-committee
of the above, was established in May 1966 and chaired by Lord Robin
Balniel, the front-bench spokesman on Europe. Its reports tackled topics such as the EEC and social policy, taxation, industry, agriculture,
Australia and EFTA. One of the more interesting papers to emerge
was that by Sir Anthony Meyer proposing closer European cooperation in high technology, which bore similarities to Wilson's proposal
for a Technological Community, but was rejected by Heath.[10] A short-
lived Tactics Committee was created in May 1967 to place
parliamentary questions on the negotiations, its key players being
Sandys and the then pro-EEC Nicholas Ridley. Finally, the
Coordinating Committee on Europe sought to coordinate activity in

the parliamentary party during the period, but was of limited importance. In the wider party, the Foreign Affairs Forum sounded out non-parliamentary opinion on the EEC, and the Conservative Commonwealth and Overseas Council (Europe Group) examined relations with the Commonwealth. The Conservative Research Department (CRD), which included pro-entry figures such as Brendon Sewill, Gordon Pears, Guy Hadley and Douglas Hurd, prepared a number of reports on the EEC.

What can be seen from these initiatives is that in the build up to the second application 'Europe' came to form an important element of Conservative policy and political strategy. During its spell in Opposition, the Conservative Party's status as the 'party of Europe' was consolidated, with the period from 1965 to 1967 marking a high-water point of Conservative pro-Europeanism. Support for early entry into the EEC was a core policy goal, viewed by Heath as essential to his programme for the modernisation of Britain. The Conservative leadership was now prepared to accept the Treaty of Rome, customs union and Common Agricultural Policy (CAP), focusing on achieving appropriate transitional arrangements for the British economy. Membership was linked to domestic policy reform, the Tories proposing change to the agricultural support system, the introduction of a Value Added Tax (VAT) system and economic reforms to prepare Britain for entry. Heath also espoused a dynamic perspective on the EEC, supporting further economic and political integration plus European defence cooperation. These developments were to have a strong impact on Wilson's conduct of the second application.

POLITICAL STRATEGY AND TACTICS

Before the launch of the probe, the issue of EEC membership fitted neatly into the adversarial political structure of the British two-party system. Early entry was a key plank of the Conservative Party's political and electoral strategy, it being viewed as a positive message likely to play well with target voters and a pro-Common Market press.[11] It also showed Wilson in a negative light and exposed divisions in the Labour Party. The Conservative's 1966 general election manifesto declared an intention to 'work energetically for entry into the European Common Market at the first favourable opportunity' and to 'prepare for entry by relating the development of our own policies to those of the Common Market, wherever appropriate'.[12] Half of all Conservative candidates highlighted the importance of EEC entry during the campaign. Heath contrasted the Tory position with

Labour's insistence on entry conditions that would prove unacceptable to the Six, concentrating in particular on Wilson's adherence to
the five conditions of entry laid down by the Labour Party in 1962.[13]
Playing on Heath's role in the 1961–63 Brussels negotiations, the
Conservatives claimed to have greater experience and understanding
of the requirements of EEC entry than a Labour Party whose leader
was primarily motivated by tactical expediency, had a record of hostility to the EEC and who led a Cabinet and party that were divided
on the issue.[14]

Suggestions that the French were favourable to British entry
appeared to add credibility to the Conservative case, but in a keynote
speech at Bristol, Wilson claimed that with 'one encouraging gesture
from the French … the Conservative leader rolls on his back like a
spaniel'.[15] In their eagerness to join 'without any conditions or safeguards', the Tories were depicted as ignoring the concerns of farmers,
housewives, EFTA and the Commonwealth. Conservative policy, he
went on, would increase the cost of living, undermine the balance of
payments and disrupt Commonwealth trade. Wilson also castigated
the Conservative record on Europe, infuriating Heath by accusing
Macmillan of failing to deal straight with de Gaulle and thereby jeopardising EEC entry. Yet Wilson also claimed that if essential conditions
were met, Britain would be ready to join the EEC under a Labour government. Significantly, a contemporary study of the election lamented
that it was 'hard to disentangle where the advantage lay' on the issue
of membership, noting that it fell down the agenda after Wilson's
speech.[16]

The Wilson government's decision in November 1966 to launch
the probe exploring the prospects for entry necessitated a change in
Conservative tactics. Senior Conservatives feared that the policy
change would adversely affect their political fortunes. Heath told the
Shadow Cabinet that a successful Labour application would 'remove
from us the advantage of being the pro-Europe party'. If the application failed, Wilson could claim that, after serious investigations, it had
proved impossible to gain entry while safeguarding Britain's interests,
allowing Labour to portray a Conservative commitment to entry as
'unpatriotic'.[17] A second failure might fatally damage the prospects of
membership, would turn public opinion against Europe and drive
sections of the party to embrace alternatives to the EEC. The Director
of the Conservative Research Department, Sewill, warned that should
negotiations with the Six prove unsuccessful (as some were already
predicting), it would be difficult to criticise the government, having
supported it earlier, thus handing Wilson 'another glorious failure'. Sir

Michael Fraser's 1967 paper, entitled 'Some Thoughts on Strategy and Tactics', depicted EEC entry as the most important element of Conservative strategy, but the 'hardest to see clearly'. He saw the outcome of the application as playing a major role in the next election, but warned that 'the government will be in a strong position whether the negotiations succeed or fail'. A successful outcome could lead Wilson to call a snap election before Britain formally joined the EEC, when the costs of membership would become more apparent. If the negotiations failed, the Conservatives might be blamed for undermining them. If there was a second veto, 'our best card will have gone: no one would seriously believe that a Conservative Government could get into Europe'.[18]

During 1966–67, the Party maintained its commitment to entry but did not automatically approve of Labour's conduct of the application, thereby allowing the Conservatives to save face as and when the negotiations floundered. Heath was critical of Labour's preconditions for entry and questioned Wilson's commitment to Europe, but shrank away from an overtly adversarial approach for fear of being accused of undermining the application. As a second veto began to appear likely, the leadership sanctioned a limited reappraisal of alternatives to entry though this was largely designed to quell dissent among the Tory backbenchers and counter a Wilson U-turn on Europe. Although the Conservative approach to the 'second try' exhibited some tactical shifts, six core themes ran through policy in 1966–67.

The first was to maintain support for entry in principle. During the probe and application period, the Conservatives maintained their official position of support for early EEC entry and publicly welcomed Labour's moves towards membership. Most significant, both politically and symbolically, was the imposition of a three-line whip on support for the application. Despite this, the leadership ensured that there would be limits to their support; as Heath put it, 'it was important to stress that while we supported the application to join, we did not approve everything in the White Paper and in the Government's handling and timing'.[19] 'For both national and party reasons', he felt that the Conservatives should set out the case for entry but contrast their genuine commitment with the limitations and weaknesses of Labour's case.[20] In November 1966, the Conservative front bench supported Labour's decision to conduct discussions with the six EEC member states and promised support for 'any genuine attempt' to achieve entry. Comparisons were drawn between the favourable political and parliamentary circumstances facing the government and those of Macmillan's application, which Labour had opposed. In May

1967, Heath claimed that the decision to seek membership was 'a plea-surable occasion for me personally' and offered to 'do everything in our power' to ensure that entry negotiations were successful, while carefully examining their progress.[21]

Heath claims that he resisted the temptation to make party politi-cal capital from Labour's application because of the overriding importance of achieving membership. Successful membership required a broad political consensus: 'if the Opposition plays party politics on this question, it can raise a serious doubt in the minds of our partners as to whether the UK will deliver on its obligations under the Treaties, because the Opposition of today may be the government of tomorrow'.[22] But more mundane party political considerations surely played a part. By emphasising its interest in the conduct of any negotiations that took place, the Conservative leadership was at pains to ensure that it was not too tightly bound to the details or conduct of Labour policy. Though offering constructive advice to the govern-ment and eschewing an openly adversarial approach, the Conserva-tives were not averse to scoring political points off Labour on the issue. They were, however, mindful of the dangers of appearing unprincipled or of being accused of sabotaging Labour's bid. The Shadow Cabinet 'felt it most important that we should at no point be seen to be resenting' Labour's application.[23] Although the Conserva-tives were unlikely to reap much political reward from a successful application, they might be damaged if they 'played the issue cynical-ly for party advantage'.[24]

The second theme was to question Labour's commitment to 'Europe'. Throughout the period of the probe, Conservatives tried to portray Heath as a pro-European man of principle and Wilson as a manipulative tactician without a sincere commitment to entry. Heath felt that the Prime Minister wanted the probe to succeed, but was motivated by short-term political calculations. Heath reminded MPs of Wilson's earlier anti-EEC position, noting that 'what five years ago was about to be abject surrender has become at least a merchant adventure'. A lack of genuine commitment and political will, plus a failure to 'think European', would jeopardise the success of any appli-cation.[25] Doubts were also cast on whether the Cabinet appreciated the nature of the EEC as a developing political community. Fraser's paper on tactics concluded by suggesting that the Conservatives should 'privately cast doubts on the unity of the Labour Cabinet', blaming any failed application on Labour divisions and stressing the need for a united government if it were to succeed.[26] The Conser-vative Party thus did much to propagate the conventional wisdom that Wilson was using Europe for narrow personal and party ends.[27]

The third theme running through Conservative policy in 1966–67 was to criticise Labour's entry conditions. The Conservatives spelled out their approach to entry during the probe, offering what they claimed were constructive suggestions, but also tackling Wilson on his insistence that 'essential British and Commonwealth interests' must be safeguarded. Heath argued in November 1966 that negotiations could not begin until the government had accepted the Treaty of Rome 'unequivocally'. The common external tariff, the emerging CAP and economic union were, he claimed, fundamental, non-negotiable elements of the EEC. The length of the transition period, supplements to the CAP for new members and selected arrangements for Commonwealth trade were, though, areas in which the government could legitimately seek negotiations. In May 1967, Wilson publicly accepted the Treaty and the CAP, allowing the Conservatives to claim some influence over the application but removing a key distinction between the two parties. As will be discussed below, Heath also argued from an early stage that the government must signal its support for further political and defence integration. The Conservatives also pointed out that domestic obstacles to entry, such as Labour's opposition to an agricultural levies scheme, would need to be tackled if the bid was to succeed. Moreover, they said, the performance of Britain's economy would have to improve and there would also need to be a viable balance-of-payments surplus, a stable exchange rate for sterling and a solution to International Monetary Fund (IMF) indebtedness. However, the Tory front bench failed to effectively tackle the government on the economic situation in general and devaluation in particular.[28] Heath had opposed devaluation during the 1967 sterling crisis, arguing that it was not a remedy for the country's economic ills and would further damage Britain's reputation, focusing his post-devaluation criticisms on government deceit.

The Conservatives, fourthly, questioned the timing of the probe and subsequent application. One of the paradoxes of the adversarial system of government in Britain is that Heath did not want to inflict fatal wounds on Labour's bid, yet felt compelled to point out that Opposition support for entry did not mean *carte blanche* approval of government actions. By concentrating on the mechanisms of the 'second try', Conservative spokesmen criticised the conduct of negotiations and the timing of the application It has been shown above how Heath claimed that Labour did not appreciate the complexities or difficulties involved in negotiating EEC entry. Tory strategists compared Labour's inexperience and negotiating problems with Heath's experience, his pro-European record and knowledge of the Six. While Wilson claimed that the bid would enter 'uncharted waters', Heath argued that he was sufficiently familiar with the charts to advise on how best to steer through the difficult waters ahead. In addition, by early 1967, Heath believed that the application had been made at the wrong time, particularly given the poor economic situation, and without adequate preparation. He privately felt that the probe had been 'a complete waste of time' and predicted that negotiations would drag on before ultimately failing.[29]

Meanwhile, the Committee on Europe (Policy Research) recommended that Tory MPs engage in 'a continuous bombardment of small specific matters revealing incompetence, inactivity and lack of foresight' during the probe period. Such criticism would dissociate the Party from the execution of the probe and application, and from its probable failure.[30] The 'continuous bombardment' proved something of a damp squib, though the Conservatives did find their target with their criticisms of George Brown's and Lord Chalfont's diplomacy. Heath initially criticised Wilson's handling of relations with France, warning that any expectations that the 'friendly five' (Belgium, Germany, Italy, Luxembourg and the Netherlands) could successfully pressure de Gaulle into admitting the UK would be dashed and could be counter-productive. He believed that strengthened Anglo-French cooperation was essential for British entry, meeting with de Gaulle in 1965 to emphasise Conservative commitment to entry. But Wilson taunted Heath that he was closer to the French position than that of the Five. As the application floundered, Tory MPs and the Conservative-supporting press continued to criticise the government for the poor timing and conduct of the bid.

Aside from specifics, the fifth theme of Conservative policy was to develop the case for further integration. The policy review had confirmed Conservative support for early membership of the EEC, but also developed a dynamic perspective on further integration that went beyond what Labour envisaged. In particular, Heath advocated defence integration in Europe, urging the government to seize the initiative in this area. Wilson demurred, pointing out that the Treaty of Rome said nothing about supranational authority in either foreign or defence policy. In his March 1967 Godkin lectures at Harvard and again in May 1967, Heath proposed that the British and French nuclear deterrents be held in trust by the two states for the EEC as a whole:

> I propose that France and Britain, each with its own nuclear deterrent, should say that we are prepared to have, for example,

some sort of committee as there is in NATO [North Atlantic Treaty Organisation] – the Macnamara Committee or something of the sort … we would hold the deterrent in trust for these countries.[31]

In language highly reminiscent of the 'Third Force' concept of unity espoused by a significant number of policy-makers in both Britain and France since 1945, Heath wanted the EEC to build from economic union to common defence and foreign policies to form a European 'counter-balance to the other side of the Atlantic'.[32] The EEC was more that just a common market, he argued: Community law would extend into many areas of national economic life and economic integration would ultimately go beyond the imminent customs union – 'the logical conclusion in a complete market is to move over *de jure* or *de facto* to a common currency'.[33] He was less convinced about the prospects in the technological arena. Though supporting some *ad hoc* cooperation between European industries, Heath had rejected Meyer's proposals on technological cooperation and felt that Wilson's proposal for a European Technological Community (ETC) would gain little support from the Six.[34] The idea of a firmer defence identity for the EEC was, however, more a reflection of Heath's personal views both on the future development of Europe and the importance of Anglo-French cooperation rather than official Conservative policy. They were viewed with considerable suspicion in the parliamentary party and were not widely supported in the Shadow Cabinet, which decided that 'it would be a mistake for us to overstress the defence aspect of Europe at this stage, or go into details on the possibilities'.[35] The Policy Committee on Foreign Affairs had earlier expressed 'serious doubts' about defence cooperation and warned there was no evidence that de Gaulle would support such a scheme.[36]

The final theme to emerge from Conservative policy in the years 1966–67 was the party's willingness to consider, internally at least, potential alternatives to EEC membership. It appears that privately, Heath relatively quickly came to believe that any application for membership by the Wilson government would fail. Nigel Ashford reports that a meeting of Heath, Pears, Hadley and Hurd in December 1966 concluded that a veto was likely.[37] On 25 January 1967, Heath told the Shadow Cabinet that de Gaulle was likely to veto entry on the grounds that Britain would change the EEC beyond all recognition. He feared that de Gaulle would then propose the formation of a new European organisation, turning the Five against Britain.[38] This view was vindicated when, soon after Labour's application was announced, the bid visibly ran aground. At a press conference in May

1967, de Gaulle outlined significant objections to British entry before announcing a second veto in November of that year. Despite government pronouncements that efforts would continue, the Council of Ministers effectively brought a halt to negotiations in December 1967. In May, Heath told the Commons that the 'main alternative is to go on as we are, as a member of EFTA and of the Commonwealth preferential area'.[39]

Hence, Labour's application forced the Conservatives, albeit in a limited and half-hearted fashion, to consider long-term alternatives to membership of the EEC. That senior Conservatives felt a second veto would effectively end hopes of British membership of the EEC had already put this on the agenda, and alternatives to entry were being considered within the Conservative Party. The Shadow Cabinet agreed that the party 'must be ready with alternative ideas for Britain' if the application failed while being careful to avoid 'predicting failure or appearing wise after the event'.[40] The two main alternatives examined were a North Atlantic Free Trade Agreement (NAFTA) and 'Association' with the EEC. Closer economic and political relations with the Commonwealth were not generally regarded as a viable alternative, given its declining significance and status together with the problems with Rhodesia.[41] The NAFTA idea, by contrast, won support on the Conservative back benches as the likelihood of a French veto increased, and gained additional impetus with the publication of a letter on the matter by US Senator Jacob Javits in *The Times*.[42] Peter Blaker's April 1967 paper, entitled 'The Case for an Atlantic Free Trade Area', claimed that an Atlantic alternative would have real economic and political benefits.[43] But the chances of an Atlantic alternative being endorsed by the Conservative Party were virtually nil. A month before Blaker's paper was circulated to its members, the Committee on Europe (Policy Research) had unanimously agreed that any alternative to EEC entry would have to be European.[44] An Atlantic alternative was declared a non-starter: there was no evidence that US policy-makers would be interested in such a scheme. Hurd feared that Britain would be a backwater 'gradually reduced to a whisky–tweeds–Wedgwood china economy'.[45]

European alternatives to EEC entry received more serious attention. In May 1967 a paper by Pears of the CRD on 'Other Ways into Europe' was distributed to members of the Committee on Europe (Policy Research).[46] This suggested that Association under Article 238 of the Treaty of Rome would have some benefits if the conditions were right and it marked a clear step towards full membership. But Association was always going to be a problematic second best –

especially given the institutional and financial problems it posed for the EEC and the likelihood that France would oppose favourable treatment for the UK. Within months, Pears claimed that 'any form of Association which could ever be acceptable to us would be essentially a fiction designed to cover the *de facto* admission of the UK to full membership over a period and lacking only full political and financial participation until this transition period has been completed'.[47] He recommended *ad hoc* cooperation and closer links between the EEC and EFTA, with full membership as the longer-term objective.

The re-examination of these alternatives was pursued for primarily tactical reasons, rather than out of any sustained conviction that the commitment to EEC entry was fundamentally flawed.[48] The leadership was keen to quell internal dissent, to limit the chances of the party being saddled with an unpopular and unworkable policy and to discredit alternatives to EEC entry – especially important if Wilson were to embrace another option. A revived Committee on Europe (Policy Research), including a sprinkling of anti-marketeers, met in February 1968. A 'large majority' of the Committee did not wish to question the party's commitment to Europe, but accepted that further consideration of interim relationships was required while Britain was in 'parking orbit'.[49] The evidence that, within a year, the tone of Conservative policy had changed, suggests that this was only a half-hearted exercise. The 1968 'Make Life Better' policy paper departed from the 1966 election manifesto's pledge to seek early entry, committing the party only to negotiations on future membership. This reflected concerns in the party about the rationale and profile of the Conservative commitment to the EEC, the decline in public support for entry and fears that Labour would highlight the Tories' supposed unconditional commitment to entry. The 1970 manifesto committed the party only 'to negotiate – no more, no less'. Iain Macleod's suggestion that the party hold a referendum on EEC entry was rejected.[50]

DIVISIONS IN THE CONSERVATIVE PARTY

The development of Conservative policy on Europe and the party's support for Wilson's application marks out the period 1965–67 as a high point of Conservative 'pro-Europeanism', hence the claims that it was the Conservatives who were the 'party of Europe' by the mid-1960s. At the party's annual conference in 1966, a ballot on EEC membership saw 1,452 votes for and 475 against. The Young Conservatives, the Conservative Political Centre and the CRD all broadly supported entry. Elsewhere, the One Nation Group's 1965 pamphlet 'One Europe' set out a case for economic, political and defence integration.[51] Pro-entry Tories were also active in the Campaign for European Political Unity and later the European Forum. However, support for EEC entry in the party was characterised by breadth rather than depth. A majority of Conservative MPs supported entry, but were not necessarily committed Euro-enthusiasts. Some, such as Peter Walker, who had been wary of entry in 1961, now accepted it, though this was often born not from a positive endorsement of the EEC but an acceptance that entry was the most practical option and was settled party policy. It has been estimated that at the time of the first application, some 40 Conservative MPs were convinced opponents of entry with around 100 harbouring some anxieties.[52] Such opposition is also to be found in the statistics that in July 1961, 49 Conservatives signed an Early Day Motion (EDM) expressing concerns about the sovereignty implications of entry; in December 1962, 47 signed an EDM urging the government to remain firm in the negotiations even if this meant breaking them off; and in the August 1961 Commons' votes on EEC entry, while only one Conservative MP, Anthony Fell, voted against, up to 29 abstained. De Gaulle's first veto may well have prevented a larger Conservative rebellion on the terms of entry. Opposition to membership within the party was still largely confined to the traditional right, but the anti-marketeers did not form a coherent faction or voting bloc.[53]

Heath thus recalls that the decision to support Wilson's application 'caused some disquiet in the party'.[54] A letter from Sewill to Pears on 23 November 1967 spoke of 'widespread unease in the parliamentary party'. However, save for a small group of committed opponents of entry, disquiet tended to focus on the leadership's tactical response to the application rather than to the principle of membership itself. Nonetheless, potential embarrassment was countered when the Shadow Cabinet agreed to impose a three-line whip requiring Conservative MPs to support the bid.[55] It was then approved by 488 votes to 62, with 216 Conservative MPs voting in favour, including some who would later become prominent anti-marketeers. A total of 26 Conservative and Ulster Unionist MPs voted against the application, along with 36 Labour MPs; 50 abstained.[56] The Tory rebels aired a range of anti-EEC arguments, including the loss of sovereignty, the economic costs of entry, the impact on British agriculture and the effect on the Commonwealth. Of the Conservative rebels, six had abstained in the 1961 entry vote, while 16 would subsequently vote against membership in 1971. Dissent on the EEC entry issue continued to come disproportionately from the traditional Tory right: 13 of the rebels opposed the imposition of sanctions on Rhodesia in 1965, 11 would later vote against the third reading of the 1968 Race Relations Bill. The anti-marketeers had failed to significantly broaden their base in the parliamentary party or to enlist the support of political heavy-weights. One study suggested that the rebels tended to have fewer career constraints (in terms of aspirations to office or group loyalty) than the parliamentary party as a whole.[57]

Unease with the party's commitment to EEC entry increased after the 1967 veto. An Atlantic free trade area, which might include some combination of the United States, the EFTA members and selected Commonwealth states, emerged as the favoured option of the Anti-Common Market League. In 1968, there were 12 pro-North American Free Trade Agreement resolutions at the party's annual conference, but the following year's conference brought a decisive vote for Europe. Among the party leadership, Ashford cites Maudling, Quinton Hogg and Balniel as concerned about a continued emphasis on entry after the veto.[58] But the Shadow Cabinet did not actively pursue alternatives to entry, instead scaling back its enthusiasm for a commitment to entry in favour of a more cautious stance. Enoch Powell did not dissent during discussions on EEC entry in Macmillan's Cabinet, subsequently claiming that membership had been presented as a matter of free trade.[59] He supported entry in the 1964 election and voted in favour in 1967. Powell's public statement of opposition to entry in March 1969 marked an important stage in the development of Conservative anti-EEC opinion, though his proto-Eurosceptic analysis would not attract large-scale support from the neo-liberal right until the late 1980s.

Importantly, however, the divisions examined above resulted by the late 1960s in the entrenchment within the party of two different visions of Conservative statecraft and 'politics of nationhood'.[60] For Heath, on the one hand, sovereignty was a resource to be pooled in the EEC in order to increase British influence and underpin the modernisation of the state and the economy. As Leader of the Opposition, he also supported Scottish devolution and committed his party to improving race relations while curbing secondary immigration. Powell, on the other hand, aimed to safeguard parliamentary sovereignty and national identity from perceived threats at home and abroad, opposing EEC membership, demanding strict immigration and repatriation measures, and developing an integrationist perspective on Northern Ireland. The crystallisation of these views was to have important consequences for the wider 'European' debate in Britain in subsequent decades.

CONCLUSION

Wilson's application meant that the Conservatives lost their distinctive pro-European message at a time when the Tory leadership saw this as the cornerstone of its programme for government and a key weapon in its electoral armoury. Labour's bid raised a critical problem for a Conservative leadership already facing criticism over its political direction and effectiveness as an Opposition. On one hand, Heath was keen that the Conservatives looked like a principled, pro-entry 'government in waiting', and thus offered support for the application. On the other, faced with murmurings of discontent in his party and personally doubting the success of the entry bid, Heath sought to distance the Conservatives from the handling of the application. He realised the long-term benefits of elite consensus on entry, but suspected that tactical considerations shaped Wilson's position and feared the short-term political consequences of both a successful and a failed Labour bid.

The promise of an elite consensus on Europe which might pave the way for smooth entry and then effective membership proved illusory, as de Gaulle's second veto forced Labour, and to a lesser extent the Conservatives, to rethink their position and further fostered anti-EEC sentiment in both parties. In the early 1970s, the domestic political debate on the EEC saw the return of inter-party adversarial politics and an escalation of intra-party dissent. The peak of the Conservatives' 'party of Europe' self-identification had passed. The Tories were now officially committed only 'to negotiate – no more, no less', while more organised and coherent opposition to the EEC was emerging within their ranks. Wilson's main focus during the Heath government's entry bid was on finding a formula to hold the Labour Party together, opposing 'Tory terms' for entry. Anti-EEC dissent in the Conservative Party, and in particular Powell's high-profile critique, made for a difficult political climate, as did opinion polls showing a sharp decline in public support for entry after 1967.[61]

Heath was, moreover, aware of the possible impact of the 'sovereignty' issue in 1967:

> When we surrender some sovereignty, we shall have a share in the sovereignty of the Community as a whole, and of other members of it. It is not, as is sometimes thought, an abandonment of sovereignty to other countries; it is a sharing of other people's sovereignty as well as a pooling of our own.[62]

But, as was the case with the Macmillan application, the implications of EEC membership for national sovereignty were somewhat disguised, and rarely fully spelled out by either government or opposition. The Conservative leadership made limited comment on the 1967 White Paper's verdict on the constitutional implications of joining the EEC. Heath felt that arguments on federalism and political unity were sterile, believing that 'the unity of Europe will in the end be achieved by European governments forming the habit of working together'.[63] He did not thus set out a coherent vision of European unity, preferring to point out that, inside the EEC, Britain could better influence the ongoing debate on the balance between intergovernmental and supranational elements. Putting such limits on the public debate appears to have stored up trouble for the Conservative Party, now that the 'sovereignty' question has come to dominate the European agenda in the UK. Although the failure of the 'second try' contributed to a more difficult domestic political environment for pro-EEC Conservatives, circumstances within the EEC were to prove more favourable in the early 1970s than they had been in the late 1960s. Labour's membership application remained on the table and was reactivated by the Heath government at a time, post-de Gaulle, when Britain was in a stronger position to pursue negotiations to a successful conclusion.[64] The long-sought prize of EEC membership was within Heath's grasp, but the repercussions of two failed applications helped deny his government the 'full-hearted consent' of the Conservative Party and the British people, and contributed to Britain's 'awkward partner' status within the Community.

NOTES

The author would like to thank the staff at the Conservative Party Archive in the Bodleian Library, Oxford, for their help.

1. Macmillan's chief negotiator in 1961–63.
2. A. Douglas-Home, speech to the Young Conservatives Conference, Scarborough, 13 February 1965.
3. Conservative Party Archive (CPA): Leader's Consultative Committee (LCC) (65) 24, 25 March 1965, Maudling, 'The Conservative Party in Europe'; CPA: LCC (65) 25, 25 March 1965, Sandys, 'Britain and Europe'; LCC (65) 37th meeting, 30 March 1965.
4. CPA: LCC (65) 37th meeting, 30 March 1965. See also Policy Committee on Foreign Affairs, 26 March 1965, PC/7/65/9.
5. Peter Walker, Heath's campaign manager, was then opposed to EEC membership. See P. Walker, *Staying Power* (London: Bloomsbury, 1996), p. 53.

6. The members of the Committee were: Carrington (Chair), Michael Alison, Sir Tufton Beamish, John Biggs-Davison, Jock Bruce-Gardyne, Douglas Dodds-Parker, Sir Anthony Meyer, Norman St John Stevas, Peter Thomas, Paul Williams and Sir Philip de Zulueta.
7. J. Ramsden, *The Making of Conservative Party Policy* (London: Longman, 1980), p. 247.
8. CPA: PG/7/65/17, 6 August 1965, Report of the Policy Group on Foreign Affairs.
9. CPA: CRD3/10/11, letter from Pears to Wood, 9 November 1967; N. Ashford, 'The Conservative Party and European Integration, 1945–75' (unpublished PhD Thesis, University of Warwick, 1985), pp. 219–21.
10. A. Meyer, 'Industrial Cooperation with Europe', 15 November 1966, Committee on Europe (Policy Research); Ashford, 'The Conservative Party', pp. 220, 234.
11. See Chapter 2 in this book by Anne Deighton.
12. *Action Not Words*, Conservative Party Election Manifesto, 1966. See also *General Election 1966: Daily Notes 1* (London: Conservative Research Department, 1966), p. 11.
13. These were: Commonwealth safeguards, freedom to pursue one's own foreign policy, EFTA pledges, right to plan one's own economy, guarantees on British agriculture.
14. *General Election 1966: Daily Notes 2* (London: Conservative Research Department, 1966), p. 40, urged Conservative activists to taunt pro-Market Labour candidates with Wilson's lack of enthusiasm for entry 'on every possible occasion'.
15. Reprinted in U. Kitzinger, *The Second Try: Labour and the EEC* (Oxford: Pergamon, 1968), pp. 108–12.
16. D. Butler and A. King, *The British General Election of 1966* (London: Macmillan, 1966), p. 114.
17. CPA: LCC (66) 135th meeting, 14 November 1966.
18. CPA: LCC (67) 145, M. Fraser, 'Some Thoughts on Strategy and Tactics'. Fraser was deputy chairman of the party with special responsibility for the Research Department.
19. CPA: LCC (67) 172nd meeting, 3 May 1967.
20. CPA: LCC (66) 135th meeting, 14 November 1966.
21. *Hansard: House of Commons Debates*, 746, column 1283, 9 May 1967.
22. E. Heath, *The Course of My Life: My Autobiography* (London: Hodder & Stoughton, 1998), p. 358.
23. CPA: LCC (66) 135th meeting, 14 November 1966.
24. Heath, *The Course of My Life*, p. 358.
25. *Hansard: House of Commons Debates*, 736, column 652, 17 November 1966.
26. CPA: LCC (67) 145, Fraser, 'Some Thoughts on Strategy and Tactics'.
27. For more on this, see Chapter 1 in this volume.
28. See, for example, J. Prior, *A Balance of Power* (London: Hamish Hamilton, 1986), p. 45.
29. CPA: CRD 3/10/10, Sewill to Pears, 5 June 1967.
30. Minutes of 5th meeting, Committee on Europe (Policy Research), 21 February 1967.
31. *Hansard: House of Commons Debates*, 746, column 1300, 9 May 1967.
32. *Hansard: House of Commons Debates*, 736, column 667, 17 November 1966. On Heath's views, see his *Old World, New Horizons: Britain, the Common Market and the Atlantic Alliance* (London: Oxford University Press, 1970) and 'Realism in British Foreign Policy', *Foreign Affairs*, 48, 1, (1969), pp. 39–50.
33. *Hansard: House of Commons Debates*, 746, column 1290, 9 May 1967.

34. Heath, *Old World, New Horizons*, p. 43; *Hansard: House of Commons Debates*, 743, columns 709–11, 16 March 1967.
35. CPA: LCC (66) 135th meeting, 14 November 1966.
36. CPA: PC/7/65/9, Policy Committee on Foreign Affairs, 'Britain and Europe – A Note on the Main Issues', 26 March 1965. See also Kitzinger, *The Second Try*, p. 7.
37. Ashford, 'The Conservative Party', pp. 211, 234.
38. CPA: LCC (67) 150th meeting, 25 January 1967.
39. *Hansard: House of Commons Debates*, 746, column 1295, 9 May 1967.
40. CPA: LCC (67) 174th meeting, 31 May 1967.
41. CPA: CRD 3/10/9, Conservative Commonwealth and Overseas Committee; W. Gorrell-Barnes, 'Britain, the EEC and the Commonwealth', April 1966.
42. See Kitzinger, *The Second Try*, pp. 156–64.
43. CPA: CRD 3/10/10, P. Blaker, 'The Case for an Atlantic Free Trade Area', 25 April 1967.
44. Committee on Europe (Policy Research), 6th meeting, 8 March 1967.
45. CPA: CRD 3/10/8, letter from Hurd to Heath, 16 January 1967.
46. CPA: CRD 3/10/9, G. Pears, 'Other Ways into Europe (if Early Entry to the EEC is not Available)', 2 May 1967. See also 'Alternatives to Membership of the EEC – Association under Article 238 of the Treaty of Rome', Conservative Commonwealth and Overseas Council (Europe Group), 11 December 1967.
47. Letter from Pears to Gorrell-Barnes, 7 August 1967, CCOC.
48. CPA: CRD 3/10/4, Committee on Europe (Policy Research), minutes of 6th meeting, 8 March 1967; CPA: CRD 3/10/60, G. Pears, 'Relationships to be Explored if Full Membership of the EEC is Denied Us', 8 December 1967.
49. CPA: CRD 3/10/5.Committee on Europe (Policy Research), minutes of meeting of 7 February 1968.
50. R. Shepherd, *Iain Macleod* (London: Hutchinson, 1994), pp. 514–15.
51. One Nation Group, *One Europe* (London: Conservative Political Centre).
52. R. Butt, 'The Common Market and Conservative Party Politics, 1961–2', *Government and Opposition*, 2 (1967), pp. 372–86.
53. Ashford, 'The Conservative Party', pp. 218–19. See also D. Dutton, 'Anticipating Maastricht: The Conservative Party and Britain's First Application to Join the European Community', *Contemporary Record*, 7, 3 (1993), pp. 522–40.
54. Heath, *The Course of My Life*, p. 358.
55. CPA: LCC (67) 172nd meeting, 3 May 1967; LCC (67) 173rd meeting, 8 May 1967.
56. The Conservative and Unionist MPs voting against the 1967 application were: R. Bell; Sir C. Black; Sir E. Brown; Sir E. Bullus; F. Burden; Sir B. Craddock; Sir S. Cunningham; G. Currie; J. Farr; G. Forrest; R. Harris; M. Hutchison; J. Jennings; Sir D. Kaberry; H. Kerby; Sir S. McAdden; S. McMaster; J. Maginnis; N. Marten; Sir H. Nicholls; L. Orr; Sir R. Russell; E. Taylor; Sir W. Teeling; R. Turton and Sir D. Walker-Smith. The same 26 MPs voted for Turton's Motion condemning the application. See P. Norton, *Dissension in the House of Commons: Intra-Party Dissent in the House of Commons Division Lobbies, 1945–74* (London: Macmillan, 1975), pp. 271–2.
57. J. Schwarz and G. Lambert, 'The Voting Behaviour of British Conservative Backbenchers', in S. Patterson and J. Walker (eds), *Comparative Legislative Behaviour: Frontiers of Research* (London: Wiley, 1972), pp. 79-80.
58. Ashford, 'The Conservative Party', pp. 214–15.
59. S. Heffer, *Like the Roman: The Life of Enoch Powell* (London: Phoenix Press, 1999), pp. 304, 517.
60. P. Lynch, *The Politics of Nationhood: Sovereignty, Britishness and Conservative Politics* (London: Macmillan, 1999), pp. 28–47.

61. See Chapter 2 in this volume for more on opinion polling at the time of the second application.
62. *Hansard: House of Commons Debates*, 736, columns 653–4, 17 November 1966.
63. Heath, 'Realism in British Foreign Policy', p. 42.
64. J. W. Young, *Britain and European Unity 1945–99* (London: Macmillan, 2000), pp. 101–2; H. Young, *This Blessed Plot: Britain and Europe from Churchill to Blair* (London: Macmillan, 1998), pp. 223–4.

— 4 —

Gone Native: The Foreign Office and Harold Wilson's Policy Towards the EEC, 1964–67

HELEN PARR

The late 1960s marked a turning point in Britain's post-war foreign policy, as the Labour Cabinet agreed to seek membership of the European Economic Community (EEC) and accepted withdrawal from Britain's military role east of Suez.[1] The Foreign Office was the leading Whitehall department on European tactics and strategy,[2] within which the European Economic Organisations Department, after 1967 the European Economic Integration Department (EEID), headed by Con O'Neill and assisted by officials such as John Robinson, developed an expertise on the workings of the European Economic Community that introduced a new Community-led focus to European policy-making.[3]

This chapter assesses the role of the Foreign Office in influencing Harold Wilson's policy towards the EEC from 1964 until the Cabinet's decision to apply in 1967. It opens by examining the interplay between Wilson and the Foreign Office on the question of Europe during his first term in office, moving on to analyse the impact of the 1966 sterling crisis on the membership decision. The final section shows how at this point Wilson began to seize the initiative from the Foreign Office, giving a firmer lead from Downing Street. What emerges most strongly is the uncoordinated, almost haphazard, way in which Wilson's foreign policy was developed. Incrementalism, not planning, was the order of the day. What also emerges is the role played by the sterling crisis in prompting a radical rethink of Britain's world role. Paradoxically, however, while it hurried the 'second try' on to the foreign policy agenda, neither Whitehall nor the Labour goverment could bring themselves to let go of Britain's great-power aspirations.

THE INFLUENCE OF THE FOREIGN OFFICE ON WILSON'S EUROPEAN POLICY, OCTOBER 1964–MARCH 1966

The Foreign Office's reaction to the failure of the 1961–63 Brussels negotiations was to review Britain's approach to the EEC. Leading officials in the Foreign Office, Commonwealth Relations Office, Treasury, Board of Trade and Ministry of Agriculture accepted the imperatives for moving towards Europe that had originally been forwarded in the planning staff's review of policy in 1959.[4] Politically, it was deemed essential to secure as much influence as possible over the development of the Community and on American policy and to use this influence to promote an 'outward looking' European entity against Gaullist or German nationalist tendencies.[5] Economically, the benefits of membership would be less in trade than economies of scale, 'becoming part of a larger market and a larger economy'.[6] In contrast to the continuity in the assessments of why Britain should seek membership, judgements on the tactics required to achieve membership underwent considerable change. Officials felt that another political initiative to get into the Community was not possible, at least until the end of the Community's transitional period in 1970. Moreover, de Gaulle's veto ruled out the tactic, used by Harold Macmillan, of seeking to make adjustments to the Community in advance of membership in order to bring Europe more into line with Britain's 'essential interests'.[7] To get into the Community, it was now said, Britain would have to accept fully the Treaty of Rome and the arrangements made under it and adapt to its provisions during transitional periods.[8] Interim policy would have to demonstrate Britain's intention to accept the Treaty in order to continue to encourage the 'friendly five' (Belgium, Germany, Italy, Luxembourg and the Netherlands) to champion Britain's cause.[9] Demonstrating intent to accept the Treaty of Rome implied acceptance of the Community's supranational provisions, as well as yielding ground on Britain's 'essential interests'. The incoming Labour government, however, based policy towards Europe on satisfaction of the five conditions prior to membership and in so far as they wanted membership at all, considered the French conception of a non-supranational European Community as more satisfactory than the Five's preference for a 'Europe de la Commission'.[10]

The official record suggests Wilson's European policy was more than just a knee-jerk reaction to events in 1966. The Vienna initiative in May 1965 to build bridges in commercial policy between the European Free Trade Association (EFTA) and the EEC was his first move.[11] Pressure to 'take a fresh look' at Britain's relations with the EEC came from the Foreign Office and bypassed the interdepartmental External Economic Policy Committee (EEP) in which the 'pro-European' First Secretary George Brown had ordered analysis of Britain's relationship with the EEC.[12] The immediate spur to action was the danger that President Charles de Gaulle of France could, following the settlement of the level for cereals prices in December 1964, tempt the West German Chancellor, Ludwig Erhard to form a political and defence union among the Six. Britain's unsympathetic stance to American proposals for a mixed-manned multilateral force (MLF) in Europe, which Erhard supported, gave force to de Gaulle's arguments that only France offered a 'European' defence solution to Germany's security problems.[13] The Foreign Office's planning staff concluded that lack of British interest in Europe increased the risk that Germany would turn even more to France than it had already in signing the Elysée Treaty in January 1963. It also felt that it might undermine the resolve of the Dutch and the Belgians, who since 1961 had agreed not to move to political union without British membership.[14] It could also enforce tendencies in Washington to isolationism: 'the average American is at present bored and irritated with foreigners of all kinds and is in a dangerously introspective mood'.[15] The bridge-building initiative was therefore a pragmatic response to specific circumstances on the continent. At the same time, it was hoped an initiative would give EFTA some direction, following its members' dissatisfaction at Britain's unilateral imposition of an import surcharge in November 1964.[16]

As well as a pragmatic reaction, the Foreign Office saw a European initiative as a way of demonstrating interest in eventual membership.[17] Wilson also showed understanding of the need to develop such a position:

> The ultimate solution [to the division in Europe] seems only feasible in terms which it is still difficult to envisage – a solution based on the inclusion of the UK and other EFTA countries (some of the latter as associates) in a Community based on the Treaty of Rome but developing and adapting policies acceptable to us. There can be no question of our trying to deal with this problem

by seeking immediate entry to the Community, if only because of
the General's veto on us. Thus the problem is keeping hope and
direction at a time when it is not possible to merge the two
groups.[18]

Wilson therefore accepted at this point that he would eventually
have to take Britain into some sort of European Community. But with
a parliamentary majority of only three and with over half the Cabinet
opposed to membership, now was not the time for an initiative.[19]
Some officials were certainly under the impression that Wilson was
thinking of eventual membership: 'we understand that the Prime
Minister wants to play this along ministerially'.[20] However, tactically,
Wilson was fundamentally at odds with the Foreign Office. While the
Foreign Office envisaged paying the economic price for the political
benefits of membership, Wilson did not:

> What is the right sort of Europe? Unless it is outward looking and
> not autarchic it must be inimical to Atlantic and Commonwealth
> links. The real test is agricultural policy, which in its present form
> is autarchic and would deal a death blow to Commonwealth
> trade.[21]

From the Foreign Office's perspective, the Prime Minister's analysis
was not practical diplomacy: Wilson's tactical requirements in fact
ruled out a bid for membership with any hope of success.

However, Foreign Office pressure did lead to Wilson's agreement,
in January 1966, that secret studies should begin in Whitehall on
Britain's future relations with Europe, geared towards making an
'early initiative' after the March election.[22] The stimulus this time was
the longevity of the Community's 'empty chair' crisis,[23] combined
with indications that the French intended to withdraw from the military command structure of the North Atlantic Treaty Organisation
(NATO). In response to de Gaulle's challenge to the supranationalism
of the EEC, the Foreign Office made it clear that Britain should support the Five's hopes of achieving a 'Europe de la Commission'
against French aspirations of promoting a greater degree of intergovernmentalism within the Community.[24] The Department of Economic
Affairs (DEA), created by the Labour government to encourage
growth through planning and led by Brown, did not agree.
Permanent Under-Secretary Eric Roll argued instead that weakening
the supranational element of integration made it easier for the politi-

cal elite to accept British membership.[25] Harold Wilson certainly favoured the settlement of the crisis on French terms:

> There is a lot here I find hard to swallow. Why should we find the acceptance of the French conditions dangerous since they reject supranationality, play down the Commission and oppose majority voting. These ought to help us and also minimise the dangers of an exclusively European foreign policy and an ultimately European deterrent. On agriculture and the Commonwealth there seems to be no analysis of the cost to our balance of payments. All the figures I have seen would seem to be ruinous to our already vulnerable balance of payments. It is still a recipe for high prices therefore high wages and high industrial costs. On planning I am sure that had we been in the EEC last year we would have had to accept full deflation [sic], as Italy was forced by the EEC to do.[26]

The judgement by Miriam Camps that the government missed an opportunity to join the EEC during the 'empty chair' crisis is thus too harsh, overlooking as it does three crucial factors.[27] First, paralysis in the Community had not changed the fact that de Gaulle did not want Britain in and that British accession would require a unanimous decision in the Council of Ministers. Second, it was only after suggestions from the Five that if the deadlock persisted they would invite Britain to join, that the Foreign Office suggested an initiative.[28] Finally, and most significantly, the gravity of the crisis deepened as it became clear that de Gaulle intended to remove France from the integrated command structure of NATO. Indications were that he was willing to take on simultaneous crises in the EEC and in NATO,[29] and in that event the whole basis of European unity could unravel. The new Foreign Secretary, Michael Stewart, argued that if the future of the European Community was under threat, the Germans would be much more likely to follow the French nationalist example and team up with them in a political and defence union. He went on that it was essential to demonstrate Britain's readiness to join the European Communities (that is, the EEC and its associated organisations) by declaring acceptance of the Rome Treaty and by showing that the five conditions could now be met. Britain's interest in participating in a supranational European Community would demonstrate to the Five, and in particular the Germans, the longer-term benefits of the path to west European unity within an Atlantic framework. Stewart concluded: 'It is a turning point. We must do what we can to make a French victory less probable.'[30]

Wilson agreed to instigate studies, but refused on domestic political grounds to make a declaration of intent to accept the Treaty of Rome, making clear his unwillingness to embrace the 'political repercussions' of such a 'precise commitment to a new policy'.[31] Instead, he suggested a 'probe' of the countries of the Six by a prominent person to demonstrate interest in eventual membership.[32] Studies began with a view to the possibility of an 'early initiative' after the March election. However, fundamental tactical differences ruled out an initiative that had any hope of success. Wilson was opposed to supranationality, to loss of preferences for Commonwealth trade and to the Common Agricultural Policy (CAP). Moreover, he saw the Treaty of Rome as incompatible with Labour's economic policies. This dilemma was unresolved when the Six settled their differences at Luxembourg on 30 January and removed the immediate need for an initiative. In words reminiscent of the conventional wisdom about British European policy in the 1960s, Stewart said that an approach would now look as if 'we had missed the bus and were sending someone to see where it had gone'.[33]

THE INFLUENCE OF THE FOREIGN OFFICE ON HAROLD WILSON'S DECISION TO TURN TO EUROPE, MARCH–OCTOBER 1966

The studies commissioned in January were formalised in the creation of four new Europe Committees, official and ministerial, after the March election.[34] Brown wanted to take control of European policy, with the objective of embarking on an initiative to Europe.[35] In keeping with the DEA's reaction to the 'empty chair' crisis, he saw that the French challenge to supranationality could be a way of removing one of the main obstacles to membership and so convincing the government to advance.[36] Brown did not accept all the Foreign Office's tactics, but was willing to embrace its suggestions, advocating a declaration of intent to accept the Treaty of Rome and a move away from strict adherence to the five conditions.[37] Nevertheless, he maintained great faith in Britain's ability to take the lead in the Community, and so to negotiate changes to the Treaty, as well as to 'outflank' de Gaulle.[38] The Foreign Office was therefore sidelined in terms of what the government wanted to do. Nor did they have immediate influence on Wilson's announcement at a meeting at Chequers on 22 October, that he and Brown would embark on a probe of the countries of the Six to see if the conditions existed for membership.

The Foreign Office's anxiety was that Wilson's attitude to the Treaty of Rome could dangerously undermine NATO policy. The Prime Minister was clearly seeking ways of moving closer to Europe, and suggested that discussions in NATO could be used as 'a cover also for probing on the EEC'.[39] He agreed to investigate the text of the Treaty of Rome, as opposed to the working rules and practices, in an attempt to find a way around making a declaration.[40] However, de Gaulle's withdrawal from NATO's command structure strengthened the Foreign Office's belief that they would have to demonstrate interest in joining a supranational Community. Supranationalism was essential to keep Germany enmeshed in the Atlantic security structure and, without the French, Germany loomed 'proportionately larger' in NATO.[41] To attempt to team up with the General on supranationality would undermine the basis of the Western Alliance and so ruled out this approach to the Community:

> For us to take sides with him against the Five about the economic and political future of Europe would certainly be to put at risk not only our relations with the USA and our other NATO allies, but also our longer term relationship with Europe as a whole.[42]

O'Neill's European Economic Organisations Department also felt that the government's position on the conditions of membership ruled out an immediate initiative. An attempt to determine Britain's position on the conditions of membership could bring conclusions that made reconciliation with the Six even less likely than it was already. In particular, the President of the Board of Trade, Douglas Jay, held views that were entirely incompatible with a successful bid, insisting on the precedence of Commonwealth trade.[43] The Ministry of Agriculture had objections to acceptance of the CAP, a position strengthened by the settlement of the financing arrangements in May and further pricing arrangements in July.[44] Pressure from both these departments prevented the Foreign Office pursuing suggestions from the Germans and the Dutch for an in-depth study of the problems posed by the agricultural arrangements for this section of British industry.[45] To compound these difficulties, Britain's balance-of-payments problems also raised serious questions about an immediate initiative. The government's economic advisers, Thomas Balogh and Nicholas Kaldor, argued that Britain's manufacturing industry was too weak to cope with the trading liberalisation inherent in the 'cold douche' of competition.[46] Furthermore, the Treasury also came to the view that the liberalisation of restrictions on the movement of capital would lead to an anticipatory outflow of sterling in advance of membership. William Armstrong, Permanent Under-Secretary at the Treasury, shocked ministers at the Chequers meeting on Europe by arguing that 1968 would be too early to contemplate membership without devaluation.[47] Balogh and Kaldor both believed membership to be impossible for at least five years, while, from O'Neill's point of view, no initiative at all was better than an initiative confirming the advisers' prognosis.[48]

The timing of the initiative thus points to the 1966 July sterling crisis as Wilson's main source of motivation. Events that month are well documented and its centrality in existing historiography points to its impact.[49] This was 'Labour's Suez': it fundamentally altered what the Party's leading figures thought they could do as a government.[50] Above all, it illustrated the government's lack of alternatives. The acceptance of a stringent deflation finished the prospects for growth under Labour's flagship policy, the National Plan.[51] The evidence of the contraction of the government's power forced Wilson from his former position of agreeing to demonstrate interest in 'eventual membership'. After July, Wilson accepted that it was necessary to make the sacrifices outlined by the Foreign Office's tactical position in order genuinely to seek 'eventual membership'. Through economic failure, the tactical impasse was overcome.

THE INFLUENCE OF THE FOREIGN OFFICE ON THE 'PROBE' AND THE DECISION TO APPLY FOR MEMBERSHIP OF THE EEC, NOVEMBER 1966–APRIL 1967

The influence of the European Economic Integration Department (EEID) was absolutely central to the conduct of the probe and therefore to the government's ability to make the application. Through their expertise in the workings of the European Community, EEID officials were able to dominate the agenda, assisted by the complicity of the Cabinet Office. The probe and application could therefore be used in the pursuit of the Foreign Office's goals of eventual membership of the European Communities and of increasing influence in Europe to develop Cold War strategy. For the EEID, the significance of the probe and application was the Prime Minister's demonstration of interest in eventual membership. There was no alternative for Britain, it felt, but membership of the EEC, a conclusion accepted throughout the Foreign Office and in Whitehall. In addition, the EEID's more radical conclusion was that European membership could be a vehicle to disengage from Britain's world commitments rather than a means of boosting Britain's strength. This perspective, however, was not so widely accepted.

Control over the machinery to administer the process of the probe and application now passed to the centre of government. The Cabinet Office's William Neild chaired the Official Committee on the Approach to Europe (EURO), set up to coordinate preparation for the probe.[52] After the application, the Ministerial Committee on the Approach to Europe (EURM) was established to supervise negotiations, but this time under Brown's chairmanship.[53] This centralised approach handed the Cabinet Office a high degree of control, but the agenda was dominated by the Foreign Office. Specialisation in the EEID left it as the only Whitehall department with a strong knowledge of the workings of the Community. Officials' expertise was rooted in the work done earlier in the decade during the Brussels negotiations earlier in the decade, which had forced an understanding of the Six and the Community and left this as the obvious area on which the EEID could concentrate. Development of an understanding of the Community was assisted because several officials in the EEID, including O'Neill at its head and Robinson, had worked on Europe for many years.[54] They put their expertise into considering how to overcome de Gaulle's opposition to British membership. The key to outflanking de Gaulle was, they believed, the treatment of the conditions of membership. While de Gaulle would not let Britain into Europe, he was reluctant to issue a second overt political veto. Minimising Britain's emphasis on the conditions of membership would thus rob de Gaulle of his most credible counter-argument to British entry and would at least shift blame for Britain's exclusion on to him:

> Avoid giving the General any chance to represent plausibly to the Five and to French public opinion that the UK could not be regarded as an acceptable candidate for entry because she cannot yet subscribe to the basic rules of the club.[55]

Foreign Office tactical thought was once again fundamentally at odds with the tenor of Wilson and Brown's starting position. To the Cabinet, Wilson and Brown emphasised that they would seek accommodation with de Gaulle on supranationality, negotiate changes to the CAP, controls on portfolio investment, regional policies and on safeguarding New Zealand's trade.[56] However, Wilson complied with Foreign Office advice to minimise the emphasis on these difficulties. After 9 November, when the decision to make the probe was taken in Cabinet, Wilson denied substantive collective discussion on what conditions the government could accept. Some ministers were consulted once in the Economic Policy (Steering) Committee, but the details of what Wilson and Brown would say in Europe were not debated in Cabinet.[57] Furthermore, the exploratory nature of the probe was used as an argument to avert the pressure for consultations from industry, agriculture, EFTA and the Commonwealth.[58] Whitehall departments were dealt with in the same way. O'Neill in the EURO Committee deflected the Commonwealth Relations Office from an inflexible adherence to a detailed list of provisions required for Commonwealth trade, arguing that it was too early to agree a rigid negotiating position.[59]

The Foreign Office had an almost complete dominance over the political arguments *vis-à-vis* the probe, constructing its case around the possibility of getting round de Gaulle. In the short term, it was necessary to prevent a Gaullist veto by playing down the conditions of membership. In the longer term, the probe and application could be used to build support in France and in the Five for eventual membership of a post-de Gaulle Europe.[60] This approach might also undermine support for de Gaulle's policies in the interim by bringing home to French public opinion and to the Five the implications of de Gaulle's actions.[61] The goal of this policy was to make further action against NATO (there were indications that de Gaulle intended to withdraw completely from the Atlantic Alliance) more difficult for him.[62] These policies were not directly advocated through the committee structure. Foreign Office influence on the Prime Minister came principally through Wilson's Private Secretary, ex-Foreign Office man Michael Palliser, who advised on the main lines of Wilson's political approach. Palliser wanted to 'play the German card' in France.[63] This would expose the contradictions in de Gaulle's policy towards German reunification, by playing on fears among the French public and political elite that France would be unable to control alone the reunified Germany de Gaulle claimed to want.[64] In addition, focus on the enlargement of the Community to include Britain and EFTA countries would serve to demonstrate that France did not have a monopoly over the promotion of *détente*, for only with British and EFTA membership would Europe be able to influence the decisions of the superpowers in world affairs.[65] This approach was pursued in direct discussion with the General and was allied with threatening diplomacy towards the Germans. Focusing on the Social Democrat Foreign Secretary Willy Brandt, rather than the Chancellor Kurt Kiesinger, Wilson argued that, if rebuffed, Britain would turn away from Europe. Germany would be left alone with only the French for security in defence and international finance.[66] In this way, the probe could be used to further the pursuit of European unity in the Atlantic framework: vying with de Gaulle for influence in Germany.

During the probe, Wilson and Brown adopted 'European'-sounding political arguments and progressively played down the conditions of membership. This marked a significant advance in Britain's approach to the EEC and was entirely the result of longer-term Foreign Office pressure. Politically, Wilson argued that Britain could accept the Treaty of Rome 'subject to the necessary adjustments consequent on the accession of a new member, provided that HMG [Her Majesty's Government] receives satisfaction on the points on which they saw difficulty'.[67] He then outlined the advantages British and EFTA membership would bring to the European Communities. Britain would provide technological expertise for the Community, enabling the Europeans to stand up to American dominance. Politically, Britain and EFTA would strengthen Europe and provide Europe with a voice in world affairs:

> Europe had an even wider role to play in the world at large, but she would not be able to play it unless she were powerful, and that meant economically powerful. The task of the great European powers, of France and of Britain, was not to be mere messenger boys between the two great powers. They had a bigger role to play – and other nations wished them to play it – than merely waiting in the ante-rooms while the two great powers settled everything direct between themselves.[68]

Wilson did, however, equivocate on the question of majority voting, stating that Britain could accept it only as much as the Community could.[69]

Wilson and Brown gradually became more relaxed as to the problems posed by the conditions of membership. It would therefore seem as if the conduct of the probe influenced their perceptions of what could realistically be achieved in negotiation with the Five. They quickly acknowledged that there would be no difficulties in regard to regional policy resulting from membership.[70] By the end of the probe, the problems were considered mainly to result from Britain's inequitable contribution to the Common Agricultural Fund and the requirement to lift restrictions on portfolio investment flows. Wilson stated that Britain would not seek to make fundamental changes to the CAP in advance of membership.[71] The Five and the Commission had sympathy with Britain's position towards New Zealand trade. They also recognised that the levy system was unfairly weighted against Britain's contribution. The Dutch and the Vice-President of the Commission, Sicco Mansholt, suggested that Britain could participate in the scheduled 1969 renegotiation of the agricultural arrangements.[72] But sterling posed the most intractable obstacle. The French questioned Britain's ability to cope with membership because of the weakness of sterling.[73] Furthermore, the Germans were concerned that Article 108 of the Treaty, which ruled out devaluation and offered help to member states in the event of balance-of-payments difficulties, could be used excessively by Britain.[74] Thus Britain could effectively hold the Community to ransom over the maintenance of its world role. Wilson did suggest that Britain could be interested in developing a single currency in Europe,[75] but this was not pursued. His principal response to interrogation about sterling was the bland one that Britain would not enter the Community until the economy was strong.[76]

Wilson's approach was greeted with sympathy by the Five and the Commission for the main reason that they felt it had more consideration for Community affairs than had Macmillan's approach in 1961, leading them to remark on Britain's 'sincerity' and 'determination' to enter the Community.[77] Furthermore, the probe denied de Gaulle the opportunity to obstruct an application. By contrast, de Gaulle was induced to say that Britain was clearly 'mooring alongside' the Continent,[78] a change from his comments in January 1963, when he had portrayed Britain as moving towards the European mainland, but still attached to America. He had been forced to admit that Britain was more of a viable candidate for membership, something the Foreign Office saw as a considerable success.[79] However, there was still no prospect of a successful application while de Gaulle was in power. The Germans told the French that they would not force the French to let Britain in and certainly none of the Five would contemplate breaking up the Community, which in any case the Foreign Office would not want.[80] By February 1967, the EEID was divided as to the wisdom of continuing with the application. O'Neill and Brown felt that it would be impossible to continue because the Cabinet would not agree to the conditions necessary to conduct successful negotiations.[81] Robinson, however, identified by Hugo Young as the 'man of fire' in contrast to

O'Neill's 'restraining force', argued that the government must continue with the application in order to retain the momentum gained by the probe.[82] Palliser agreed with this approach:

> This is all a war of nerves – to see whether your nerve is as strong as the General's. My money is confidently on yours! ... My advice is 'bash on, regardless', and I give it because it is just what he does not want you to do.[83]

Failure to continue, he felt, would only give victory to the opponents of Britain's entry domestically and abroad. Wilson agreed that he had to continue to shift the Cabinet towards a European application.[84]

CONCLUSION

Wilson therefore embarked on an application that was likely to fail in the short term. But this was no 'gimmick'. His pragmatic response to Foreign Office pressure prior to 1966 indicates his willingness to consider 'eventual membership' of the Community. However, the contraction of options illustrated by the July crisis forced him to accept the sacrifices to sovereignty demanded by membership and led him to make a genuine attempt to seek membership. The eight Cabinet discussions in 1967 at which the application bid was discussed reveal the seriousness of his initiative. The Prime Minister argued that even if the application failed, the Labour government would have to accept membership in the long term: 'if rebuffed, we should not rule out the possibility of joining Europe later'.[85] His assessment accepted the Foreign Office conclusion that there was absolutely no alternative for Britain. Abstention from joining any group and the possibility of joining the North Atlantic Free Trade Agreement (NAFTA) had been studied and ruled out. Failure to seek membership would lead Britain into dependency on the United States, and a forced association with American policies in Singapore, Malaysia and Vietnam.[86] To retain independence and to pursue Britain's interests, he concluded, Britain had absolutely no choice but to join the EEC.[87] Assessment of Britain's decline had reached new depths, and this marked a change in thinking about EEC membership in Britain. The Foreign Office's advice to accept the provisions of the Treaty of Rome was also a radical change in thinking about the nature of Britain's relationship with the European Community. However, in order to pursue short-term Foreign Office tactics, Wilson avoided Cabinet discussion of whether or not Britain could relinquish the conditions of membership. By the time de Gaulle's veto was confirmed in December 1967, the Cabinet had not agreed a negotiating position.

Despite these unprecedented conclusions, there was no coordinated political direction to foreign policy at this time. April 1967 saw two of the most radical decisions in post-war policy-making. On 4 April, the Cabinet agreed to withdraw from Singapore and Malaysia by 1974–75 and to present this as a major change in foreign policy.[88] On 30 April, it accepted an application to the EEC, formally attaching no settlement of prior conditions to Britain's accession.[89] These decisions had been reached entirely separately, both in their own ways the result of the July 1966 sterling crisis. In part, the disjointed approach was because the machinery dealing with the successive defence reviews made long-term planning difficult. The Cabinet's Defence and Overseas Policy Committee (OPD), chaired by Burke Trend, dealt overwhelmingly with the supplementary defence review in early 1967.[90] There was no attempt to link this to the European application. Similarly, in the Foreign Office, the Permanent Under-Secretary's Department's planning staff, responsible for strategic thinking, devoted time predominantly to the defence review.[91] In terms of Cold War and NATO policy, the European application was not integrated into strategy. Eventual European membership was the cornerstone of policy, as it would increase Britain's influence in Washington and Bonn and so facilitate the pursuit of *détente*.[92] But the application was not incorporated into planning for policy towards Europe. Other goals, such as nuclear non-proliferation and the strengthening of Britain's defence commitment to Europe, had to be subordinated to the short-term attempt to get into the Community.[93]

The lack of political direction also reflected Wilson's concentration on the management of the Cabinet, which was deeply divided on all the central issues: membership of the EEC, withdrawal from east of Suez and devaluation of the pound. This mix of opinions meant that there was no overall agreement as to the purpose of the European membership bid. In a radical break with post-war foreign policy, however, officials in the EEID now saw European membership as a vehicle to disengage from wider commitments, rather than a means of bolstering Britain's ability to carry out these obligations. The ambiguous expression reflected the broader lack of support for such ideas:

> It can be held that, ever since the war, we have tried to play the part of a world power without a sufficient economic and military

foundation; that, in fact, we have tried to live beyond our political means. Given this premise, a desire to join the EEC can be seen as either one of two things. It can be seen as a realisation on our part that we must abandon dreams of a world role ... Alternatively, our desire to join the EEC can be seen as an effort to strengthen the base from which we exert world influence, so that we can exert that influence more effectively.[94]

O'Neill also saw European membership as a means of leading the British public away from an imperial understanding of Britain's place in the world:

> For the last twenty years this country has been adrift. On the whole it has been a period of decline in our international standing and power. This has helped to produce a national mood of frustration and uncertainty. We do not know where we are going and have begun to lose confidence in ourselves. Perhaps a point has now been reached when the acceptance of a new goal and a new commitment could give the country as a whole a focus around which to crystallise its hopes and energies. Entry into Europe might provide the stimulus and the target we require.[95]

But his conclusions were not widely accepted. Cabinet Secretary Trend clearly saw the prestige afforded by the Commonwealth as more important than the influence provided by European membership.[96] In the Cabinet in April, the politico-military implications of Britain's membership were not fully discussed. Brown seemed willing to present the European membership bid in these terms and the argument was made in Cabinet that 'a new role of political leadership would provide the political stimulus formerly given by our imperial role'.[97]

Foreign Office influence on Harold Wilson's European policy was therefore mixed. It had considerable influence from 1964–66, but the Prime Minister did not accept its tactical conclusions on how to achieve membership. Wilson's decision to embark on the initiative was not the result of Foreign Office pressure, but of the shock of the 1966 July sterling crisis. The Foreign Office dominated the tactical approach to the Community, both in terms of the treatment of the conditions of membership and of the political arguments. In a more proactive approach to policy, it was also able to use the probe and application to further Cold War goals. The tactical approach and the assessments of Britain's political decline were unprecedented, and the conclusion that European membership could be used to disengage from Britain's world role a radical break. However, these ideas were not fully accepted in Whitehall or by the Cabinet.

NOTES

The author would like to thank James Ellison for his comments on earlier drafts of this chapter.

1. G. Wyn Rees, 'British Strategic Thinking and Europe, 1964–1970', *Journal of European Integration History*, 5, 1 (1999), pp. 57–71 (p. 57); M. Carver, *Tightrope Walking: British Defence Policy since 1945* (London: Hutchinson, 1992), p. 80.
2. H. Wallace, 'The Domestic Policy-Making Implications of the Labour Government's Application to the EEC, 1964–1970' (unpublished PhD thesis, Manchester University, 1976), p. 200.
3. Wallace, 'Domestic Policy-Making', pp. 208–10; H. Young, *This Blessed Plot: Britain and Europe from Churchill to Blair* (London: Macmillan, 1998), pp. 172–81.
4. J. Ellison, *Threatening Europe: Britain and the Creation of the European Community, 1955–58* (London: Macmillan, 2000), pp. 228–9; W. Kaiser, *Using Europe, Abusing the Europeans: Britain and European Integration, 1945–63* (London: Macmillan, 1996), p. 124; Public Record Office (PRO): T 312/1011, Pitblado Report, 'The UK and the EEC', 11 September 1964. See also T 312/1010, Keeble to Owen, 5 June 1964.
5. PRO: T 312/1010, 'Political Implications of UK Remaining Outside the EEC', Hood to Pitblado, 4 June 1964.
6. PRO: T 312/1011, Pitblado Report, 'The UK and the EEC', 11 September 1964.
7. On Macmillan's tactical approach, see A. Deighton and P. Ludlow, 'A Conditional Application: British Management of the First Attempt to Seek Membership of the EEC', in A. Deighton (ed.), *Building Post-War Europe: National Decision Makers and European Institutions, 1948–1963* (London: Macmillan, 1995), pp. 107–23 (p. 108).
8. PRO: T 312/1012, SC(64)24, 'Britain and the European Economic Community', July 1964.
9. PRO: T 312/1011, Pitblado Report, 'The UK and the EEC', 11 September 1964.
10. The conditions were: strong and binding safeguards for the trade and interests of friends and partners in the Commonwealth; freedom to pursue an independent foreign policy; fulfilment of the government's pledges to the other members of EFTA; the right to plan the economy; and guarantees to safeguard British agriculture. L. J. Robins, *The Reluctant Party: Labour and the EEC, 1961–1975* (Ormskirk: G.W. Hesketh, 1979), pp. 39, 46; R. Pearce (ed.), *Patrick Gordon Walker Diaries* (London: Historian's Press, 1991), p. 301 (August 1964).
11. H. Wilson, *The Labour Government, 1964–70: A Personal Record* (London: Weidenfeld & Nicolson/Michael Joseph, 1971), pp. 96–8.
12. PRO: PREM 13/306, PM/65/26, Stewart to Wilson, 12 February 1965; PRO: CAB 134/1771, EEP(65) 3rd, 29 January 1965.
13. PRO: PREM 13/27, Dixon to FO, telegram 893, 3 December 1964. See also M. Camps, *European Unification in the Sixties: From the Veto to the Crisis* (London: Oxford University Press, 1967), p. 19; A. Buchan, 'The Multilateral Force: A Study in Alliance Politics', *International Affairs*, 40, 4 (1964), pp. 619–37 (p. 630); PRO: PREM 13/27, Roberts to FO, telegram 1220, 1 December 1964; PRO: FO 953/2215,

Roberts to FO, telegram 29, 12 January 1965; PRO: FO 953/2215, Roberts to FO, telegram 29, 12 January 1965.

14. PRO: FO 371/184288/W6/12, Palliser to Nicholls, 9 February 1965; P. Gerbert, 'The Fouchet Negotiations for Political Union and the British Application', in G. Wilkes (ed.), *Britain's Failure to Enter the European Communities 1961–1963: The Enlargement Negotiations and Crises in European, Atlantic and Commonwealth Relations* (London: Frank Cass, 1997), pp. 135–42 (p. 140).

15. PRO: FO 371/184288/W6/12, Palliser to Nicholls, 9 February 1965.

16. PRO: PREM 13/307, Trend to Wilson, 11 May 1965.

17. PRO: FO 371/184288/W6/13, Nicholls to Caccia, 26 February 1965.

18. PRO: CAB 130/227, MISC48/2, Wilson, 'Linking EEC–EFTA', 7 May 1965.

19. For an example of ministerial views, see D. Jay, *Change and Fortune: A Political Record* (London: Hutchinson, 1980), pp. 349–55; PRO: PREM 13/904, Jay paper, 15 June 1965. For O'Neill's own account, see C. O'Neill, *Britain's Entry into the European Community: Report on the Negotiations of 1970–1972* (London: Frank Cass, 2000).

20. PRO: T 312/1014, Pitblado to Rickett, 1 June 1965.

21. PRO: PREM 13/306, Wilson comments on Stewart to Wilson, 3 March 1965.

22. PRO: T 312/1016, Meeting Permanent Secretaries, 26 January 1966; PRO: PREM 13/908, Trend to Wilson, 21 October 1966: 'studies commissioned on May 9, when an early initiative seemed a possibility'; PREM 13/905, Report of Officials led by Roll, 5 April 1966.

23. The French had withdrawn participation from Community institutions following failure to reach agreement on methods for payments into the Common Agricultural Fund and had turned the deadlock into a battle about the future supranational character of the Community. See Camps, *European Unification*, pp. 60–70; N. P. Ludlow, 'Challenging French Leadership in Europe: Germany, Italy, the Netherlands and the Outbreak of the Empty Chair Crisis of 1965–1966', *Contemporary European History*, 8, 2 (1999), pp. 231–48 (pp. 231–3).

24. PRO: T 312/1015, Statham to Owen, 'Contingency Planning', 20 September 1965.

25. PRO: T 312/1014, Charles to Owen, 30 July 1967; PRO: T 312/1015, Roll to Gore-Booth, 20 October 1965; PRO: FO 371/188327, Roll to Gore-Booth and reply, 12 January 1966.

26. PRO: PREM 13/904, Stewart to Wilson and Wilson's comments, 10 December 1965.

27. Camps, *European Unification*, pp. 176–7.

28. PRO: T 312/1016, Gore-Booth, 'Possible Approach by the Five', 25 January 1966; PRO: FO 371/188328/M10810/24, draft paper by Statham, comments by Palliser and Barnes, 21 January 1966.

29. PRO: T 312/1015, Reilly to Stewart, 23 November 1965.

30. PRO: PREM 13/904, Stewart to Wilson, 10 December 1965.

31. PRO: PREM 13/905, Stewart to Wilson, 21 January 1966.

32. PRO: PREM 13/905, Stewart to Wilson, 21 January 1966.

33. PRO: PREM 13/905, Stewart to Wilson, 2 February 1966.

34. PRO: CAB 134/2705, E(66)1, 9 May 1966; CAB 134/2757, EO(66)1st, 13 July 1966; CAB 134/2757, Economic Sub-Committee; CAB 134/2759, Legal and Constitutional Sub-Committee.

35. PRO: PREM 13/906, Brown to Wilson, 16 May 1966, 23 June 1966 and 29 June 1966.

36. See Wallace, 'Domestic Policy-Making', pp. 140–2.

37. PRO: PREM 13/906, Brown to Wilson, 16 May 1965; PRO: PREM 13/907, guidance telegram 188, 29 June 1966.

38. G. Brown, *In My Way: The Political Memoirs of Lord George-Brown* (London: Victor Gollancz, 1971), pp. 205, 209; PRO: FO 371/188346/M10810/458, Fenn to Gore-

Booth, 28 August 1966, and Brown comments on 'How to Get into the Common Market', Foreign Office paper, 18 August 1966.

39. PRO: PREM 13/1044, Wilson comments on FO to Brussels, telegram 478, 20 April 1966; PRO: FO 371/188336/M10810/198, Barnes to Hancock, 5 May 1966; PRO: PREM 13/905, MacLehose to Palliser, 5 May 1966; PRO: PREM 13/1044, meeting between Wilson, Stewart, Thomson and Palliser, 6 May 1966.
40. PRO: PREM 13/906, Wilson to Brown, 19 May 1966.
41. PRO: FO 371/190534/W6/3, Barnes comment on Thomson to Barnes, 13 April 1966.
42. PRO: FO 371/189108, OPD(66)44, 'The International Consequences of General de Gaulle's Policy', Chair of the DOPC Official Committee, 31 March 1966. See also PRO: CAB 134/2705, E(66)8, 'The Politico-Military Implications of UK entry into the European Communities', EEOD, 23 August 1966.
43. PRO: CAB 134/2705, E(66)6, 'Economic Implications of Membership of the European Communities', President of the Board of Trade, 5 July 1966.
44. See PRO: FO 371/188343/M10810/388, O'Neill comment, 26 July 1966, and PRO: FO 371/188341/10840/120, Marjoribanks to FO, telegram 33, 4 August 1966.
45. PRO: FO 371/188344/M10810/405, Statham memo, 1 August 1966.
46. PRO: CAB 134/2757, EO(E)(66)6th, 14 July 1966.
47. PRO: CAB 130/298, MISC126(66)1st, 22 October 1966.
48. PRO: FO 371/188340/M10810/308, meeting between Brown, Roll, Thomson and O'Neill, comments by O'Neill, 30 June 1966.
49. B. Pimlott, *Harold Wilson* (London: HarperCollins, 1993), pp. 408–37; J. Callaghan, *Time and Chance* (London: Collins, 1987), pp. 193–205; P. Ziegler, *Wilson: The Authorised Life of Lord Wilson of Rievaulx* (London: Wiedenfeld & Nicolson, 1993), pp. 252–60; E. Dell, *The Chancellors: A History of the Chancellors of the Exchequer, 1945–1990* (London: HarperCollins, 1997), pp. 334–9.
50. R. Crossman, 'Britain and Europe: A Personal History', *The Round Table*, October 1971, p. 511, cited in Kitzinger, *Diplomacy*, p. 282.
51. PRO: PREM 13/827, Stewart to Wilson, 17 October 1966; see also P. Hennessy, *Prime Minister: The Office and its Holders since 1945* (London: Penguin, 2000), pp. 311–12.
52. PRO: CAB 134/2811, EURO(66)1, 14 November 1966.
53. PRO: CAB 134/2803, EURM(67)1, 24 May 1967.
54. Young, *This Blessed Plot*, pp. 173–97.
55. PRO: CAB 134/2814, EURO(67)12, Foreign Office, Steering Brief for Paris, 16 January 1967.
56. PRO: CAB 129/127, C(66)149, Brown, Europe: Memorandum, 7 November 1966.
57. PRO: CAB 128/41, CC(66)55th, 9 November 1966; PRO: CAB 134/3196, SEP(67)1st, 9 January 1967; PRO: CAB 128/42, CC(67)1st, 12 January 1967.
58. PRO: EW5/21, Casey to Mitchell, record of meeting of Industrial Consultative Committee, 9 December 1966; PRO: CAB 134/2811, EURO(66)1st, 14 November 1966; PRO: CAB 134/2811, EURO(66)3rd, 24 November 1966.
59. PRO: CAB 134/2811, EURO(66)6th, 16 December 1966; see also PRO: CAB 134/2811, EURO(66)7th, 21 December 1966 on agricultural policy.
60. PRO: FO 371/189108, OPD(O)(66)44, 'The International Consequences of General de Gaulle's Foreign Policy', DOPC, 31 March 1966.
61. See, for example, PRO: PREM 13/897, Wright to Palliser, 18 October 1966 and Palliser's response, 21 October 1966. See also PRO: FO 371/189106/RF1022/23, Reilly despatch number 42, 22 June 1966.
62. PRO: FCO 30/82, Reilly to Gore-Booth, 21 February 1967.
63. For further discussion of Anglo-German diplomacy see Chapter 11 in this book.
64. PRO: PREM 13/897, Wright to Palliser, 18 October 1966 and Palliser's response, 21 October 1966. See also PRO: FO 371/189106/RF1022/23, Reilly despatch number 42, 22 June 1966.

65. PRO: FCO 30/169, Robinson to Statham, 14 March 1967; PRO: FCO 33/44, Simpson-Orlebar comments, 24 April 1967; PRO: CAB 134/2814, EURO(67)12, Foreign Office, Steering Brief for Paris, 16 January 1967.
66. PRO: PREM 13/1479, Wilson–Brandt conversation, 13 April 1967.
67. PRO: CAB 129/127, C(66)149, Brown, Europe: Memorandum, 7 November 1966; PRO: PREM 13/1477, Probe, Germany, 15 February 1967, 10am.
68. PRO: PREM 13/1475, Probe, France: 24 January 1967, 10am; PRO: CAB 134/2814, EURO(67)12, Foreign Office, Steering Brief for Paris, 16 January 1967. See also PRO: PREM 13/1475, Probe, Italy: 16 January 1967, 10am; PRO: PREM 13/1477, Probe, Germany: 15 February 1967, 10am.
69. PRO: PREM 13/1477, Probe, Germany: 15 February 1967, 3.30pm.
70. PRO: PREM 13/1477, Probe, Germany: 15 February 1967, 10am.
71. PRO: PREM 13/1478, Probe, Luxembourg: 8 March 1967, 10am.
72. PRO: PREM 13/1476, Probe, Commission: 1 February 1967, 2.30pm; PRO: PREM 13/1477, Probe, Netherlands: 27 February 1967, 10am.
73. PRO: PREM 13/1476, Probe, France: 24 January 1967, 10am.
74. PRO: FCO 30/187, German working party paper on monetary questions in connection with British accession to the EEC, Galsworthy to Statham, 20 January 1967.
75. PRO: PREM 13/1476, Probe, Belgium: 1 February 1967.
76. PRO: PREM 13/1477, Probe, Germany: 15 February 1967, 3.30pm.
77. See, for example, PRO: PREM 13/1475, Probe, Rome: 16 January 1967, 10am; PRO: PREM 13/1476, Probe, Belgium: 1 February 1967, 9.30am.
78. PRO: PREM 13/1476, Probe, France: 25 January 1967, 4.25pm.
79. PRO: PREM 13/1477, O'Neill to Pilcher, 3 February 1967.
80. J. W. Young, *Britain and European Unity, 1945–1999*, 2nd edn (Basingstoke: Macmillan, 2000), pp. 92–3; PRO: FCO 30/186, Brussels to FO, telegram 14, 19 January 1967; Brussels to FO, telegram 16, 19 January 1967. See also PRO: FCO 30/188, O'Neill to Gore-Booth, 28 February 1967; Roberts to O'Neill, 9 March 1967; PRO: FCO 30/189, Galsworthy to Statham, 14 March 1967.
81. PRO: FCO 30/82, O'Neill to MacLehose, 24 February 1967; meeting Brown and Mulley, 24 February 1967.
82. PRO: FCO 30/82, Robinson to O'Neill, 28 February 1967; Young, *This Blessed Plot*, p. 178.
83. PRO: PREM 13/1482, Palliser to Wilson, 20 May 1967.
84. PRO: FCO 30/82, Wilson to Trend, undated, early March 1967.
85. PRO: CAB 128/42, CC(67)22nd, 20 April 1967.
86. PRO: CAB 128/42, CC(67)25th, 30 April 1967.
87. See also Young, *Britain and European Unity*, p. 96.
88. PRO: CAB 128/42, CC(67)16th, 4 April 1967.
89. PRO: CAB 128/42, CC(67)26th, 30 April 1967.
90. PRO: CAB 148/52-60: Defence Review Working Party; PRO: CAB 148/73: Working Party on Overseas Expenditure OPD(O)(E); and PRO: CAB 148/74: Working Party on Offset OPD(O)(GC).
91. See the index for PRO: FCO 49: Planning Staff and Commonwealth Policy and Planning Department (including Z: PUSD) which confirms the predomination of the Defence Review.
92. PRO: CAB 148/68, OPD(OD)(66)16th, 13 July 1966.
93. PRO: FCO 30/82, O'Neill to MacLehose, 23 February 1967.
94. PRO: CAB 134/2705, E(66)8, 'Whether Membership of the Community would involve us in long-term political and military commitments and whether this should be publicly declared', 23 August 1966.

95. PRO: FO 371/188347/M10810/475, O'Neill to Thomson and Gore-Booth, 21 October 1966. See also Young, *This Blessed Plot*, p. 190.
96. PRO: PREM 13/908, Trend to Wilson, 21 October 1966.
97. PRO: CAB 128/42, CC(67)25th, 30 April 1967.

5

Technological Cooperation in Wilson's Strategy for EEC Entry

JOHN W. YOUNG

Since the second British application to join the European Economic Community (EEC) always faced an expected veto from Charles de Gaulle, Harold Wilson devoted considerable attention to winning the French President over. One feature of his strategy was the 'European Technological Community' (ETC), first proposed in late 1966. Wilson was already identified with a policy of building Britain's technological strength and believed he could offer much to Europe in this field, perhaps tempting de Gaulle into conceding EEC enlargement. The high point of Wilson's campaign came on 13 November 1967, when his annual Guildhall speech was largely devoted to technology. Alongside multilateral talks about an ETC, he urged the creation of a 'European Institute of Technology', more Europe-wide industrial groups and the harmonisation of European practices in such areas as patents and restrictive practices. The speech received widespread international coverage.[1]

This chapter seeks to illuminate this under-studied feature of the 'second try' in four sections: the first focuses on the roots of Wilson's interest in technological cooperation, which came to the fore after Labour was returned to power in 1964; the second explores the crucial months of September–December 1966 when Wilson officially launched his technological strategy; the third examines how Wilson played on the technological dimension of his thinking during his 'probe' of EEC capitals at the beginning of 1967; the final section assesses the impact of de Gaulle's 1967 veto on British membership on Wilson's plans in the technological arena. The evidence presented below provides compelling reasons to reassess the conventional wisdom that Wilson played the technology card for purely rhetorical reasons. His strategy was, in fact, more sophisticated than has hither-to been thought and his ideas were in line with, and partly inspired by, European initiatives on the technological front. His unwillingness to put flesh on the bones of his various proposals was indicative of his fear that France would attack his plans, jeopardising British EEC entry and creating a rift between Britain and Europe on what 'technological cooperation' implied in practice. On a more critical note, Britain pos-sessed a preference for working with the Americans in many key fields, which drew de Gaulle's attention to a constancy in British pol-icy: London could not, in his opinion, offer enough in the technological arena.

LABOUR, TECHNOLOGY AND EUROPE, 1964–66

When Labour entered office, it was understood that the only coun-tries with which Britain could cooperate equally on technological projects were in western Europe. They could provide industrial activities and financial support on a level comparable to Britain's, and offered the chance to compete with the United States.[2] The need to compete with the United States in advanced technologies was seen as a pressing one in Europe in the 1960s. In Britain this was reflected in the fears, widely discussed in the media and govern-ment, of a 'brain drain' of educated individuals across the Atlantic. But significantly, from the perspective of EEC entry, France was especially concerned by US predominance, as reflected in the suc-cess of Jean-Jacques Servan-Schreiber's 1967 book, *Le Défi Americain*. It pointed out that, in 1965 alone, the USA invested $4 billion in Europe and predicted that, by 1980, European-based American industry would be the third largest industrial force in the world, after the two superpowers.[3] Europe had only a few large multina-tional companies, such as Philips and Unilever, and the Labour government, through the Industrial Reorganisation Corporation (IRC), encouraged structural changes in industry towards larger-scale units, which were believed – under the fashionable logic of 'big is beautiful' – to be more competitive. Wilson talked of reinvigorat-ing British industry through the 'white heat' of a 'scientific revolution', whereby the improved application of technology, along-side better government planning, expanded higher education and an end to restrictive practices, would improve Britain's economic prospects. This was the theme of his most famous speech as Opposition leader, during the 1963 party conference.[4] Once in office he set up a Ministry of Technology (soon known as 'Mintech'), which in 1966 was led by a dynamic young minister, Anthony Wedgwood Benn. Recent research has suggested that Britain's political and business leaders were far from being the anti-scientific traditionalists depicted by critics: previous Conservative administrations had already encouraged large-scale technological projects, and only the superpowers significantly outspent Britain on research and development (R and D). Furthermore, the Labour government soon recognised that a concentration on technology was no guarantee of economic growth, and policy developed in directions different from those suggested by the rhetoric of 'white heat'. R and D in the defence field was deemed wasteful and was cut back, with a greater emphasis on private enterprise and a commercial return, whilst Mintech focused its efforts less on technology, more on questions of efficient industrial organisation.[5]

Wilson's technological enthusing, wedded to the belief that Britain was stronger than Europe in this field and could help match American power, fostered the conviction that London had something to offer that de Gaulle would find hard to resist. However, it is equally important to understand that Labour's policy in 1964–66 included developments that undermined the potential for close cooperation with the EEC. Three changes in the aerospace field are worth particular note. First, within months of assuming power, the government not only cancelled a number of British aircraft projects, but also decided to replace these with American-manufactured alternatives. The most famous cancellation was TSR-2, a long-range fighter-bomber, which was to be replaced by the US F-111. Other victims were the P-1154 fighter and the HS-681 transport. One element in these cancellations was the fact that, whereas defence took up 40 per cent of R and D expenditure, it only accounted for a 2.5 per cent of exports; another was the lower cost of American aircraft. However, the Aviation Minister, Roy Jenkins, warned Wilson that 'The massive scale on which we are proposing to "go American" in our immediate purchases will not improve our relations with France.' There were several Anglo-French defence projects underway, including the variable-geometry AFVGA fighter. Jenkins's warning was treated seriously and, when Wilson visited de Gaulle in April 1965, the significance of American purchases was carefully played down.[6]

The need to tread warily was made doubly necessary by British questioning of the most famous Anglo-French aerospace project, Concorde. This expensive airliner, though revolutionary, was never likely to pay for itself and Labour ministers hoped to abandon it. But it was subject to a 1962 Anglo-French treaty, which made it essential to negotiate cancellation with the French. They proved unwilling to cancel and hinted that, if London acted unilaterally, the issue would be taken to the International Court of Justice. Jenkins was given legal advice that, if France did this, 'we ... might well have damages of the order of two hundred million pounds awarded against us' and in January 1965 ministers reluctantly decided the project must proceed.[7] The decision was not final, however, and in June to July 1966, when the country faced a severe balance-of-payments crisis, a divided Cabinet again looked at cancellation. The Foreign Secretary, Michael Stewart, was keen to retain Concorde because Anglo-French relations were currently troubled, not least because de Gaulle had recently taken France out of the North Atlantic Treaty Organisation's (NATO) military structure; but George Brown, head of the Department of Economic Affairs (DEA), complained that Britain was trying 'at a disproportionate economic and financial cost, to appease the consequences of a tough political stance' towards Paris. The best that London could secure was the creation of an Anglo-French committee to examine the aircraft's financial prospects.[8]

The third development that called into question Britain's European credentials was the European Launcher Development Organisation (ELDO). This was another expensive, prestige project begun in 1962 and encouraged by the Conservative government, whose Blue Streak rocket was to be the bedrock of European efforts to enter the 'space race'. Britain's partners in the scheme were Australia (needed for launch sites) and all the members of the EEC except Luxembourg. Once again costs overran earlier estimates and Labour looked at cancellation. Whitehall officials reported in January 1965 that a rocket based on Blue Streak would be inferior to US launchers; but they also recognised that a withdrawal by Britain would upset the other governments.[9] By 1966 the Cabinet had decided to extricate themselves from ELDO as soon as was practicable but, in order to minimise criticism, they successfully proposed a European review of space projects, hoping that other countries would see the wisdom of changing policy.[10] Again, Stewart argued that the termination of Britain's role in ELDO would damage its position in Europe, but strength of feeling was such that, in January 1966, Cabinet decided to restrict spending on ELDO to £8 million.[11] In May, they went beyond this and agreed to terminate the project. However, two developments prevented this decision from coming into effect. First, there was a press leak, which sparked off criticism on the continent; then, there was legal advice which suggested that (as with Concorde) Britain could be sued by its partners if it acted unilaterally. London therefore backtracked and asked ELDO to reduce Britain's contribution, while securing safeguards against any future commitment to meet escalating costs. As a result, Britain's share of ELDO expenditure fell to about a quarter, a similar level to France and Germany.[12]

Three points stand out from the above cases. First, they show that the British were reluctant to maintain high spending on 'prestige projects', ready to upset European partners if joint ventures became too costly, and willing to cooperate with the Americans when this better suited national needs. Wilson was aware of all this and, in the 1967 Guildhall speech stated: 'I do not have in mind further costly Government finance ventures, whether in space or elsewhere.' Instead, he argued, 'effective European cooperation' required 'industrial partnership and industrial integration based on pooling ... research and development in ... viable strategic economic enterprises'.[13] This fitted Labour's general policy on technology, based on commercial value rather than status, but it was clear, on ELDO in particular, that EEC states might not share Britain's approach: they entertained hopes of matching the United States even in highly advanced technologies. The second point also raises questions about whether an ETC with Britain was necessarily tempting to continental states: for Concorde and ELDO showed it was quite possible to develop Anglo-European projects without creating an overarching transnational structure. Other examples were the European Space Research Organisation (ESRO) and the European Council for Nuclear Research (CERN), both of which had British membership. Yet, in the Guildhall speech, Wilson argued that joint technological endeavours were 'not a substitute for British membership of the EEC'.[14] It is thus significant that, before Labour's bid to enter the EEC had been tabled, the question of technological cooperation already impacted on British relations with EEC members. The Foreign Office was particularly concerned about the detrimental impact of a negative attitude towards existing technological ventures, yet even a leading 'pro-European' like Brown was counted on the other side of the debate. Once the 'second try' got underway, contradictions in Britain's position made technology an uncertain field for winning over de Gaulle to British membership.

LAUNCHING THE ETC, SEPTEMBER–DECEMBER 1966

The first serious proposal for European technological cooperation in 1966 came not from Britain, but Italy. There was already considerable debate in the European press about the so-called 'technological gap' with the United States,[15] and Belgium had earlier proposed a conference on the subject.[16] The Italian proposal, published on 16 September, would have worked through NATO and had American support: the United States would provide technological know-how to European governments, who would share the costs of developing joint projects to exploit this. Wilson's Private Secretary, Michael Palliser, suggested that Britain should be interested in the subject in the light of a possible EEC entry bid, a suggestion with which the Prime Minister agreed.[17] Wilson may at this point also have been influenced by the debate in the press and, what is more, British policy towards the EEC was undergoing significant change.[18] In July there had been a severe balance-of-payments crisis, strengthening the case of those who argued that the country's future would be more secure in the EEC. Brown's transfer to the Foreign Office, in August, solidified the 'pro-market' lobby. A special weekend of talks was held by the Cabinet in late October and, on 10 November, Wilson announced publicly that he and Brown would make a 'probe' – a tour of EEC capitals – in the New Year, to test the waters for EEC entry.[19] European technological cooperation did not feature much in the discussions of October, although one leading 'anti-marketeer' complained that, at a key meeting, 'Benn disappointed me by acquiescing in an application on obscure, if fashionable grounds, of technology.'[20] In part, this low profile at ministerial level was because technology had not yet been studied sufficiently by civil servants: Mintech officials only got a general paper together on the subject on 1 December, intending this to form the basis of interdepartmental discussion, which got underway later that month.[21] Also, technological cooperation, rather than being something from which Britain would gain (and thus a factor in internal arguments over EEC membership), was primarily seen as offering gains to the EEC (and so became most useful when entry talks got underway).

Certainly, following the probe announcement, Wilson lost little time in launching the ETC. He did so on 14 November, in the annual Guildhall speech, traditionally devoted to foreign policy. After discussing the Cabinet's decision, Wilson then pressed for 'a new technological community to pool ... the enormous technological inventiveness of Britain and other European countries', making the EEC competitive with the United States. 'I can think of nothing that would make a greater reality of the whole European concept.' The Prime Minister had little to say on the details of the ETC, how it would be negotiated or the form it would take, but he declared that 'in this field ... no-one has more to contribute than Britain ... '.[22] As Benn noted, the ETC section of the speech 'was extremely vague from beginning to end but it was Harold's way of keeping the pressure going on Europe'.[23] This indeed was the whole point: as Wilson told Brown, when reminded of the Italian proposal on technological cooperation, 'they'll get nowt thro' NATO and must support our entry to EEC when we will really talk business'.[24] According to Solly Zuckerman, the government's Chief Scientific Advisor, Wilson 'said that he had put the finishing touches to the speech in the car on his way to the Guildhall, and that it was up to officials to add substance to his proposals'. Yet Zuckerman also adds that, in conversation with him, Wilson seemed serious about EEC action: 'British manufacturing industry was not competitive in world markets. The industries of fragmented Europe undercut each other ... Europe was totally overshadowed by the American giant.'[25] This situation 'had to be changed'. Zuckerman shared this outlook and told Richard 'Otto' Clarke, the Permanent Secretary of Mintech, that industrial cooperation on technology in Europe must take a market-oriented approach, focusing on ventures that promised substantial commercial rewards.[26]

As to the Italian proposal on technological cooperation, that had been discussed on 2 November at a meeting of the ministerial Science and Technology Committee, chaired by Wilson, where a report was received from officials criticising Italian arguments as misconceived. Zuckerman's summary of this report is revealing about the government's approach to European technological cooperation:

> The basic problem ... was not the relative technological backwardness of Europe but the inability ... to match the advantages which United States industry derived from ... a very large domestic market ... Even if the 'technological gap' could be eliminated wherever it existed ... European industry would still be handicapped because it could not at present operate on the same scale and therefore could not match the level of expenditure on research and development by ... United States firms.

In the ensuing discussion, there was general support for this key argument, the logic of which suggested Britain *must* work with Europe if American technological prowess was to be matched. As a result, officials were asked to draft a memorandum on the possibilities for multilateral cooperation on technology in Europe. But the Italian proposal was rejected, ministers deciding that, 'while not supporting the ... initiative, we should for political reasons avoid taking the lead in opposition to it'. As Wilson said in conclusion, the British 'should ensure that discussions on the [Italian] proposal should not go too fast and ... give time for the Government to bring forward alternative proposals of its own'.[27]

London thus avoided a direct attack on the Italians, who were one of the 'friendly five' EEC countries – along with Belgium, Germany, Luxembourg and the Netherlands – favourable to British entry, and relied on the scepticism of other NATO countries to prevent progress on their proposal.[28] At the NATO Council in mid-December, Brown pressed the Italian Foreign Minister, Amintore Fanfani, on the need to look away from NATO to EEC-based technological cooperation, and the British were relieved when the Italian scheme was simply put forward for further study.[29] The Foreign Office expressed the hope that discussion of it had 'whet European appetites for technological cooperation with us',[30] but Britain's delegation to NATO was told to avoid discussion of the substance of Italian ideas in the further studies of it.[31] Yet, even at this juncture, Britain's desire to focus technological cooperation on Europe was inconsistent. At its 2 November meeting, the Science and Technology Committee rejected a proposal for further cooperation with the European Conference on Satellite Communications (CETS) on a television relay satellite, because of scarce resources and a lack of commercial benefits.[32] Yet at the same time the British were interested in working with Washington on satellites, especially in the military field. Brown warned Wilson afterwards that any announcement of this position would 'look a bit odd' in light of the Guildhall speech and the British did not make their decision public as yet.[33]

During the following year the policy remained a potential time bomb for the ETC. Zuckerman warned Wilson in May that existing policy could harm the EEC entry bid and, in July, Palliser told the Prime Minister that the satellite issue could prove 'of exceptional importance' because it appeared to symbolise Britain's choice of a 'US option' over a European one.[34] Nonetheless, ministers refused to shift in a European direction and the Science and Technology Committee decided to explain Britain's doubts about a satellite programme to CETS, as a step towards withdrawal. The only reason this decision was not carried out was because it was discovered that Britain could 'play for time' and keep a design team in CETS for a mere £17,500.[35] A similar episode was recorded by Benn in late 1966, when Peter Shore, Wilson's Parliamentary Private Secretary, argued that the ETC should mean Britain procuring only from European sources, 'this was turned down contemptuously' by civil servants, who preferred 'to buy American'.[36] Even Otto Clarke, whose ministry was central to the pursuit of the ETC, was keen to preserve cooperation with the Americans in the military and aerospace spheres.[37] Some civil servants were quite cynical about the way the ETC should be used. A Foreign Office Assistant Under-Secretary, Terence Garvey, saw the idea 'mainly from the card-playing angle' of 'how we can use the concern in Europe about technological competitiveness to further the government's primary objective of getting into the EEC. For this purpose ... it fortunately does not matter if we are a bit vague about what ... we have in mind.' According to Garvey, Britain should avoid precipitate concessions on technology and 'keep the carrot dangling, at least until we are safely in the EEC', at which point, thanks to the country's technological lead, 'our firms ought to be able to ... eat up their less efficient European opposite numbers' in 'a series of amalgamations with the British coming out on top'. It would be wrong to make too much of one letter, especially since Garvey admitted his views were largely personal.[38]

Elsewhere there were more positive views in Whitehall, not least from Gordon Bowen, the Under-Secretary who took charge of drafting Mintech's initial position paper and who, at an interdepartmental meeting in mid-December, pointedly objected to Garvey's arguments. At the same meeting, Clarke argued that Britain should be clear about the meaning of ETC from the start.[39] But, in a telegram to its European posts soon afterwards, the Foreign Office said that 'our immediate aim ... is to make the best possible use of European anxieties about technological backwardness ... as a lever in support of our approach to Europe'.[40] And, when the British negotiating position for the probe was defined, it was this narrow tactical approach that triumphed over pressures to define a detailed policy on technology.

THE PROBE, JANUARY–MARCH 1967

Wilson wrote of the ETC: 'Nothing did more in Europe, as we found on our visits there, to convince opinion that we ... were ready to provide ... a fresh, characteristically British, driving force to the European economic idea.'[41] This obscures the fact that, although technology was discussed during the probe of EEC capitals, the British avoided concrete offers of cooperation and refused to give precision to the ETC. The only detail to emerge in early 1967 was that there was no wish for a separate 'technological community' in an institutional sense.[42] The steering brief, which guided Wilson and Brown in their discussions, was based on ST(67)1, which came before the Science and Technology Committee on 9 January. But a draft brief, together with speaking notes, was discussed three days earlier by the Official Committee on the Approach to Europe (EURO), chaired by the Treasury's William Neild, which supervised the approach to the EEC.[43] This earlier discussion confirmed that the significance of technology was likely to be tactical; the brief

> should be drawn up with regard to the specific requirements of the probing operation; and Ministers should ... make clear ... that the Community would not be able to enjoy the benefit of full technological cooperation with Britain unless Britain was a member of the [EEC].[44]

Ministerial discussion took a similar line. Benn opened with a sketch of his ministry's thinking on the issue and outlined four kinds of technological cooperation that might be pursued inside the EEC: intergovernmental action on large politically significant projects, such as space research; action by governments on important schemes that were not economically viable, such as the development of water resources; legal measures to encourage European technological growth; and, most importantly, cooperation between private firms. Benn's exposition showed it was quite possible for the British to produce detailed ideas on an ETC, but, as he said, 'we needed to be clear ... whether the proposals for a technological community related to our political objectives or whether we regarded them as an important objective in their own right'. The answer he got was that political aims were paramount. A number of interesting and tellingly frank points were made in discussion that suggested it could not be otherwise. First, an ETC 'which would give Europe wider access to our technological expertise would be disadvantageous ... unless ... we had access to a wider European market through membership of the EEC'. Second, the extent of Britain's technological lead over the rest of western Europe 'has been somewhat exaggerated in many quarters' (a particularly damning admission). Finally, Britain must always set its own national priorities, 'pursuing those branches of technology in which we could foresee the most economic advantage to ourselves'. In summing up, Wilson 'said it was agreed that we should not be over-optimistic' about the economic benefits of a technological community, but the ETC could nonetheless 'be used in the forthcoming discussions in Europe to our political advantage'.[45] There was no need to decide the details of how technological cooperation would work in practice, simply because these might take the focus away from the need for British entry. But, there was also the consideration that, if Britain did outline its technology plans in detail, this could make them easier for the French to attack.[46]

The timing of the probe could hardly have been better from the point of public interest in the 'technology gap'. As an American diplomat remarked, it was difficult to avoid the subject in the European press, for whom it had become an obsession.[47] The 'friendly five' leaders were interested to hear Wilson's ideas, but he did no more than underline what Britain might contribute in technology once EEC entry was attained. The pattern was established with the opening visit of the probe, to Italy, where he stuck rigidly to the lines of ST(67)1 in talks with Prime Minister Aldo Moro.[48] As the probe progressed it was possible to sense scepticism about the ETC even among the 'friendly' countries. Thus, in Brussels, the Belgian Prime Minister raised Britain's reticence about European cooperation on space satellites.[49] Wilson continued to make his case regardless.[50] But whatever the views of the Five, the key visit of the probe was to Paris, in late January. The Ambassador to France, Sir Patrick Reilly, believed technological cooperation was a field that might genuinely move de Gaulle and Palliser agreed: if the General could be convinced that an Anglo-French combination would make Europe technologically powerful, matching the United States, this might be a significant lever for enlargement.[51] However, in the head-to-head between Wilson and the General, such optimism proved ill-founded. When the former spoke of the scope for Anglo-European technological cooperation de Gaulle agreed, but pointed out that such cooperation was possible through bilateral arrangements. Wilson's argument that valuable opportunities would be lost if Britain were kept out of the EEC, fell on deaf ears.[52]

Undeterred, the Paris embassy persisted in the belief that technology might yet win de Gaulle over. One embassy official urged that Britain should clarify its policy on technology, or risk seeing the General 'trumping one of the best cards we have'.[53] In March, Reilly suggested a number of practical ideas for developing technological cooperation, not on a Community-wide scale, but on a bilateral or trilateral basis – which he believed the French would prefer because it was more efficient and cost-effective – and he argued that the worst policy in current circumstances was to do nothing practical.[54] Reilly's arguments stirred up some debate in Mintech about Britain's best tactics and data was collected on British technological achievements, so as to be ready to respond to European requests for details on the ETC.[55] The Foreign Office, however, firmly believed that new initiatives in Anglo-French cooperation were out of the question before de Gaulle agreed to enlargement.[56]

APPLICATION AND VETO, APRIL–OCTOBER 1967

During April there was a series of Cabinet meetings about EEC entry, culminating in a decision, on 2 May, to apply. A few weeks later de Gaulle declared, in a press conference, that British membership would upset the Community. But he stopped short of a veto and Palliser recommended that Wilson should 'bash on, regardless'.[57] Apart from the debate over Reilly's arguments, the ETC barely figured in London's deliberations during this time, even if it was not forgotten. In mid-March, Wilson said that policy-making on existing European technological cooperation must be better coordinated in Whitehall, but also dismissed ELDO and ESRO as 'relics of the past'.[58] In May he said he wanted more thought to be given to organising the ETC, but only 'to display the extent of the contribution Britain can make in the technological field, *once we are in the Community* as inducement to our negotiating partners to hasten our entry'.[59] Benn made a speech on 6 June, saying: 'Technology can be the major factor uniting Europe.'[60] And in July the Foreign Office produced a memorandum outlining a possible structure for the ETC, clearly based on earlier Mintech ideas, with a common policy on standards and patents, a focus on aerospace and computers, and the inclusion of nuclear cooperation.[61] But the slow pace in defining British policy was underlined at a meeting between Wilson and Zuckerman in August, when they agreed that an interdepartmental study was still required to look at how to establish the ETC, how to dovetail it with the entry talks and the steps that might be taken ahead of entry.[62]

Perhaps the lack of progress was unsurprising, since British tactics still revolved around holding out the prospect of technological cooperation in order to gain entry to the EEC, without giving much in the way of concrete promises.[63] Wilson's own focus until mid-1967 was on winning de Gaulle over by personal persuasion, the last attempt being made at Versailles on 19–20 June. Here technology again featured as a major 'carrot' to tempt the President. Reilly still believed this cause was not hopeless and even suggested an offer to help France build a hydrogen bomb (though he also pointed out the danger in this: de Gaulle could leak word of the offer and thereby embarrass Wilson).[64] The idea of Anglo-French nuclear sharing between Britain and France had been a feature of the first EEC application in 1961–63 and Michael Michaels, head of the Atomic Energy Division, told Benn that the ETC 'cannot be resolved unless there is some sort of an understanding about nuclear sharing which would … break our special relationship with the United States …'.[65] But such a revolution in British foreign policy was never likely. In the key session at Versailles, Wilson deployed his usual argument that, with British help, Europe could build up its 'technological and industrial strength ... to compete on equal terms with the US and the Soviet Union'. He laid particular emphasis on computers and aerospace. Reilly's idea of cooperation on a hydrogen bomb was not pursued, but Wilson did talk of Anglo-French cooperation on the civil side of the nuclear issue, where they might jointly produce nuclear fuel. Even on the military side there were hints of a shift in Wilson's policy: Britain, he said, would not buy Poseidon, the American-made successor to the Polaris missile. De Gaulle was unimpressed with all this, pointing out that Anglo-French technological cooperation was already possible (on Concorde, for example) and arguing that Britain was still heavily dependent on Washington in the foreign and defence fields, even if the Poseidon decision were to be welcomed. If Britain, with its pro-American policies in Vietnam and NATO joined the EEC, he continued, it would work with Germany and Holland to subsume the Community in an Atlantic group.[66]

After Versailles, Reilly advised against any attempt to back the General into a corner: 'I fear that if a decision were forced on him in, say, the next six months, it ... would be one to prevent ... negotiations.'[67] Ignoring such advice, Wilson's tactics shifted from winning the President by persuasion to uniting the Five against him, in the hope of pressuring him into accepting British membership. British policy became crudely threatening in October when the Foreign Office Minister of State, Alun Chalfont, threatened to reconsider the commitment to European defence if the road to Europe was blocked.[68] Where ETC was concerned, in late July Mintech asked the Science and Technology Committee whether Britain should 'drag its feet' on technological projects with France, raising the spectre that such cooperation would be endangered if Britain were kept out of the EEC. The Cabinet Secretary, Burke Trend, believed it was 'clearly right in present circumstances' to avoid further technological cooperation with France and the Committee duly endorsed this line. But, as Wilson said in his summing up, there were limits to what Britain could do: it was difficult to put existing projects in danger, especially projects where Britain gained as much benefit as France. The essential aim, after all, was to win de Gaulle to EEC enlargement, not completely alienate him.[69] Nevertheless, Wilson continued to want France to 'be confronted with a certain dilemma': they could not expect greater technological cooperation unless Britain was allowed into the EEC.[70]

The decision to make technology the centrepiece of the Guildhall speech was itself a reflection of the desire to pressurise de Gaulle and perhaps forestall the veto that was now being predicted. By late October Wilson was ready to propose formal talks on an ETC, even if this was not formed until after enlargement, and meetings were held to convince key ministers that the speech should relaunch the campaign for an ETC.[71] Neild and the EURO Committee had their doubts about this, arguing that if Wilson emphasised technology in this way, he would be expected to follow it with practical suggestions, otherwise the proposal's emptiness would be exposed and interest would quickly dry up.[72] Wilson met Neild, Trend and Zuckerman on 2 November and decided, nonetheless, to proceed. He did, however, subsequently agree that a European conference on the ETC should be avoided, partly because this could give France a chance to sabotage things, but also because Britain still lacked concrete ideas to put forward.[73] Preparations for the speech included consultations with the Trades Union Congress (TUC) and the Confederation of British Industry (CBI). It was John Davies of the CBI who suggested that a European 'Institute of Technology' should be included.[74]

'Rarely could a prime minister have had a more difficult task in making the principal speech', Wilson later recalled about the events of 13 November. But by then his troubles had nothing to do with technology. Instead, the occasion coincided with a major currency crisis that led, within days, to the devaluation of sterling.[75] Some Cabinet ministers, unaware of the preparations for the address, even dismissed its technological content as an attempt to distract attention from the pound.[76] The payments crisis swamped the EEC application, with de Gaulle seizing on devaluation as proof that Britain was unfit for membership and vetoing the attempt. Surprisingly, this did not kill off work on the ETC in Whitehall. On 27 November, five days after the veto, Wilson told Benn there should be an 'effective follow-up' to the Guildhall speech and within days Mintech completed a memorandum on a 'European Technological Institute', designed to encourage the restructuring of European industry in ways that could best exploit technology.[77] Zuckerman felt this was too general an approach and, with Wilson's consent, devised a scheme for a 'European Technological Organisation', to bring together those industries which could best share technology and could develop joint plans to match US competition.[78]

Two Cabinet memoranda were drawn up, embodying a combination of the Mintech and Zuckerman approaches, but while Wilson described these as 'rattling good papers' and although they formed part of a Cabinet debate about Europe on 27 February, it was impossible to make progress on them.[79] Neither had the CBI and TUC shown much enthusiasm for government ideas.[80] More importantly, Britain's policy was in an impasse following the veto. The Dutch, the most 'friendly' of the Five, were currently blocking progress in the EEC in protest at de Gaulle's behaviour, but this policy also prevented EEC discussion of technology.[81] By mid-April there was renewed concern in Downing Street over progress,[82] but this was partly because the Cabinet, exasperated by the continuing costs of European space projects, now decided to announce Britain's intention to pull out of ELDO and CETS. On this occasion Stewart (back at the Foreign Office) argued in vain that the decision could have a disastrous effect in Europe unless it was accompanied by some concrete British ideas on a European technological body.[83] Some ministers of the Five suggested that Britain and the EEC should try to make progress on technological cooperation ahead of British entry,[84] but the Foreign Office and Wilson felt this was undesirable, because their aim was to secure full membership not some halfway house.[85]

CONCLUSION

It is easy to list reasons why the ETC failed to provide Britain with a gateway to Europe. The scheme was only launched in late 1966 because the 'second try' was in the offing and in reaction to an Italian initiative. De Gaulle gave two main reasons why the French government was not tempted by it: Anglo-European technological cooperation was possible without an ETC, and Britain was too close to the Americans in areas like nuclear weapons and aerospace for its European commitment to be certain. It was difficult to refute these arguments because they were largely true. That it was possible to cooperate on technology without an ETC was confirmed, for example, by a visit Wilson made to Bonn in February 1969 when space research, the European airbus project and British, German and Dutch collaboration on centrifuge were all discussed. 'More than on any previous European visit we spent a greater part of our time discussing problems of technological cooperation', Wilson later recalled.[86] As to the argument that Britain was too close to America, that was amply demonstrated by its nuclear weapons policy. 'The problem', Zuckerman later wrote, 'was that, when it came to action, it always seemed impossible to cut through the coils that bound us to the United States, particularly in the nuclear field.' The corollary of this was a reluctance to commit to European ventures. At a meeting in 1970 to discuss aircraft projects, Zuckerman found 'Benn was surrounded by … officials, of whom only one spoke up in favour of the British aviation industry "getting into bed" with the French.' Zuckerman felt that the centrifuge project, with Germany and Holland, was the only significant new example of British enthusiasm for multilateral technological coopera- tion in Europe in the later 1960s.[87] Here, at least, was an example of Britain looking away from the USA for partners on a nuclear project, even if rather late in the day.

De Gaulle's doubts were the most vital problem for the British. But even apart from them, Wilson's policy was crippled by internal weak- nesses, particularly the reluctance to give details about the ETC, because this would provide a target for France to attack, it could lead to Britain's entry bid becoming bogged down in detailed talks on technology, and because Britain did not actually have as much to offer as was generally believed. There was, however, another important dimension to the problems of ETC, and that was the way in which the entry bid cut across the shift of direction in Britain's own technology policy. As Wilson explained to Germany's Chancellor, Kurt Kiesinger: 'There had been a tendency in the past for technological cooperation in Europe to consist of somewhat platonic meetings of scientists or of costly intergovernmental projects in space. He hoped that in future there could be much more direct cooperation between business firms on more practical projects.'[88] In recent years, Britain's R and D effort had been too devoted to prestige projects and Labour was attempting a new approach in which profit, private enterprise and industrial mergers were the vital elements. From private remarks, it seems Wilson did have a genuine interest in developing European technol- ogy. But he also had a deep personal commitment to ending expensive multilateral projects: in August 1967, for example, he asked whether a failed ELDO rocket launch provided an opportunity to re- examine British participation.[89] It was a commitment other ministers shared. Thus, in July 1967 the Science and Technology Committee again debated the cancellation of Concorde because of rising costs, while in December there was discussion about 'the tactics of disen- gagement' from CERN.[90]

In 1966–67, then, Wilson not only tried to use Britain's supposed technological prowess to win British membership; he also tried to sell the EEC a new approach to technological efforts, based on British experience. Tackling this two-fold challenge was difficult enough when he was unwilling to reveal specifics. It was well-nigh impossi- ble when the Europeans, even the Five, showed themselves loyal to the established approach, keen to match the Americans in prestige areas and disappointed with Britain's indifference towards ELDO, CERN and similar projects. Yet the British persisted in the belief that their policy was 'right'. As Benn told an April 1968 meeting of ministers: 'We know that the only way to compete with the Americans is on the basis of technological projects launched for sound commercial reasons. In this respect our thinking is well in advance of the Europeans and we can't afford to pander to them.'[91] This may have been so, but, as the Rome embassy pointed out, Britain was doing nothing practical to impress the Five; instead it had shown no interest in the 1966 Italian proposal and had distanced itself from ELDO.[92] That the ETC should be held out as a kind of carrot to tempt the EEC into letting Britain inside was a consistent line in Wilson's policy.[93] But on closer examination the carrot turned into a hologram: an impressive image, impossible to grasp. As Stewart remarked to the Prime Minister in July 1968, 'the trouble with the technological initiative was that it always seemed to change its shape when one tried to grapple with it'.[94]

NOTES

I am grateful to the British Academy for providing funding for my research at the Public Record Office.

1. Reproduced in U. Kitzinger, *The Second Try: Labour and the EEC* (Oxford: Pergamon, 1968), pp. 307–10; and on publicity see Public Record Office (PRO): PREM 13/1728, *passim*.
2. PRO: PREM 13/1177, Palliser to Wilson, 13 January 1965.
3. Published in Britain as *The American Challenge*, trans. R. Steel (London: Hamish Hamilton, 1968).
4. Labour Party: Report of the Sixty-Second Annual Conference, Scarborough, 1963 (London: Transport House, 1964).
5. D. Edgerton, 'The "White Heat" Revisited: The British Government and Technology in the 1960s', *Twentieth Century British History*, 7, 1 (1996), pp. 53–82.
6. S. Straw and J. W. Young, 'The Wilson Government and the Demise of TSR-2', *Journal of Strategic Studies*, 20, 4 (1997), pp. 18–44 (p. 32).
7. R. Jenkins, *A Life at the Centre* (New York: Random House, 1991), pp. 154–9 (p. 159).
8. PRO: CAB 128/41, CC 33(66), 30 June, and CC 39(66), 21 July; PRO: PREM 13/1308, Stewart to Wilson, 21 June, and Brown to Wilson, 24 June 1966.
9. PRO: PREM 13/1177, Rogers to Wilson, 14 January 1965.
10. PRO: CAB 128/39, CC 71(65), 16 December 1965.
11. PRO: CAB 128/41, CC 2(66), 20 January 1966.
12. PRO: CAB 128/41, CC 26, 27 and 33(66), 26 May, 9 and 30 June 1966; documents *passim* in PRO: PREM 13/1177, 1178 and 1780; and see R. Crossman, *The Diaries of a Cabinet Minister: Vol. I, Minister of Housing, 1964–66* (London: Hamish Hamilton/Jonathan Cape, 1977), pp. 530, 537 (26 May and 14 June 1966

respectively).
13. Quoted in Kitzinger, *The Second Try*, p. 308.
14. Ibid., p. 307.
15. See press cuttings, *passim*, PRO: HF 2/20 and 21.
16. PRO: HF 2/20, Voysey to Willan, 29 August 1966.
17. PRO: PREM 13/1850, FO to Rome (22 September 1966), Palliser to Wilson (23 September 1966), and Wilson's handwritten 'Yes'.
18. T. Benn, *Out of the Wilderness: Diaries 1963–67* (London: Hutchinson, 1987), p. 481 (16 November 1966).
19. See J. W. Young, *Britain and European Unity, 1945–99* (London: Macmillan, 2000), pp. 88–91.
20. D. Jay, *Change and Fortune: A Political Record* (London: Hutchinson, 1980), p. 388.
21. PRO: HF 2/20, Bowen to Secretary, 1 December 1966. See 13 December for a redraft of this paper.
22. H. Wilson, *The Labour Government, 1964–70: A Personal Record* (London: Weidenfeld & Nicolson/Michael Joseph, 1971), p. 300.
23. Benn, *Out of the Wilderness*, pp. 481–2 (16 November 1966).
24. PRO: PREM 13/1850, Brown to Wilson, 24 November 1966; and reply, no date.
25. S. Zuckerman, *Monkeys, Men and Missiles* (London: Collins, 1988), p. 438.
26. PRO: HF 2/20, Zuckerman to Clarke, 7 December 1966.
27. PRO: CAB 134/3308, ST(66)2nd, 2 November 1966.
28. PRO: HF 2/21, brief for NATO Ministerial Meeting, 14–16 December 1966; and see PRO: PREM 13/1850, Trend to Wilson, 1 November 1966, Brown to Wilson, 24 November 1966, and Callaghan to Wilson, 12 December 1966.
29. PRO: PREM 13/1850, record of Brown–Fanfani meeting, 14 December 1966, and telegram, UKDEL NATO (Paris) to Foreign Office, 16 December 1966.
30. PRO: HF 2/20, FO outward telegram, 23 December 1966.
31. London had also concluded that if technological cooperation were to be tackled on a transatlantic scale this was best done by the Organisation for Economic Cooperation and Development (OECD). See PRO: HF 2/21, FO to UKDEL, 7 February 1967.
32. PRO: CAB 134/3308, ST(66)2nd, 2 November 1966.
33. PRO: PREM 13/1780, Brown to Wilson, 17 November 1966, and Palliser to MacLehose, 21 November 1966.
34. PRO: PREM 13/1780, Zuckerman to Wilson, 15 May 1967, and Palliser to Wilson, 4 July 1967.
35. PRO: CAB 134/3309, ST(67)3rd, 5 July 1967; PREM 13/1780, documents 4 to 14 July 1967, especially Trend to Wilson, 10 July.
36. Benn, *Out of the Wilderness*, p. 482 (16 November 1966).
37. PRO: HF 2/20, Clarke's statement, meeting of 9 December 1966.
38. PRO: HF 2/20, Garvey to Jenkyns, 7 December 1966.
39. PRO: HF 2/20, record of meeting, 9 December 1966.
40. PRO: HF 2/20, FO outward telegram, 23 December 1966.
41. Wilson, *The Labour Government*, p. 300.
42. There was general agreement on this point at the interdepartmental meeting on 9 December 1966 (see PRO: HF 2/20).
43. On administrative arrangements, see PRO: HF 2/20, Wilson to Benn, 12 December 1966.
44. PRO: CAB 134/2813, EURO(67)2nd, item 2, 6 January 1967; and see PRO: HF 2/21, Bowen to Neild, 4 January 1967, for the draft brief and speaking notes.
45. PRO: CAB 134/3309, ST(67)1st, 9 January 1967; PRO: PREM 13/1850, Trend to Wilson, 5 January 1967.
46. PRO: PREM 13/1510, Palliser to Tickell, 23 February 1967.
47. PRO: HF 2/21, address by Ambassador Robert Schaetzel, 15 February 1967.

48. PRO: PREM 13/1850, record of Wilson–Moro meeting, 16 January 1967.
49. PRO: PREM 13/1476, London to Bonn, 3 February 1967.
50. PRO: PREM 13/1850, records of meetings with Boeynants of Belgium, 1 February 1967, and Zijlistra of Holland, 27 February 1967; PREM 13/1477, London to Rome, 17 February 1967 (summarising the Bonn talks).
51. PRO: PREM 13/1475, Reilly to Brown, 4 January 1967, and Palliser to Wilson, 6 January 1967.
52. For a summary of the main points, see PRO: PREM 13/1476, London to Bonn, 26 January 1967.
53. PRO: PREM 13/1510, Tickell to Lush and Palliser, 13 February 1967.
54. PRO: HF 2/21, Reilly to Jackling, 28 March 1967.
55. PRO: HF 2/21, Stewart to Bowen and Slater, 20 and 26 April 1967.
56. PRO: HF 2/21, Jackling to Reilly, 7 April 1967.
57. PRO: PREM 13/1482, 20 May 1967.
58. PRO: PREM 13/1850, note of Wilson–Zuckerman meeting, 17 March 1967.
59. PRO: PREM 13/1851, Palliser to Trend, 15 May 1967. Emphasis in original.
60. Copy in PRO: HF 2/21.
61. PRO: PREM 13/1851, Buxton to Palliser, 12 July 1967.
62. PRO: PREM 13/1851, record of Wilson–Zuckerman meeting, 1 August 1967.
63. But on the ways in which Britain and France already cooperated, see PRO: HF 2/21, Bowen to Knighton, 14 June 1967.
64. PRO: PREM 13/1479, Reilly to Mulley, 20 April 1967.
65. Benn, *Out of the Wilderness*, p. 503 (7 June 1967).
66. PRO: PREM 13/1731, record of meeting, 19 June 1967; and see PRO: HF 2/21, Benn to Wilson, 13 June 1967, for briefing of Wilson ahead of the summit.
67. PRO: PREM 13/1483, Reilly to Gore-Booth, 28 June 1967.
68. Young, *Britain and European Unity*, pp. 94–5.
69. PRO: PREM 13/1851, Trend to Wilson, 24 July 1967; PRO: CAB 134/3309, ST(67)5th, 25 July 1967.
70. PRO: PREM 13/1851, Palliser to Maitland, 10 November 1967.
71. PRO: PREM 13/1851, Palliser to Knighton, 25 October 1967.
72. PRO: PREM 13/1851, Neild to Jackling, and attached memorandum on ETC, 1 November 1967.
73. PRO: PREM 13/1851, records of meetings, 2 and 3 November, and Neild to O'Neill, 3 November 1967.
74. PRO: PREM 13/1851, record of meetings, 7 and 8 November 1967.
75. Wilson, *The Labour Government*, p. 454.
76. R. Crossman, *The Diaries of a Cabinet Minister: Vol. II, Lord President of the Council and Leader of the House of Commons, 1966–68* (London: Hamish Hamilton/Jonathan Cape, 1976), p. 570 (14 November 1967); Susan Crosland, *Tony Crosland* (London: Jonathan Cape, 1982), p. 185.
77. PRO: PREM 13/2416, Wilson to Benn, 27 November, and Benn to Wilson, 1 December 1967.
78. PRO: PREM 13/2416, record of Wilson–Zuckerman meeting, 11 December 1967, and Zuckerman to Wilson, 9 February 1968.
79. PRO: PREM 13/2416, Halls to Benn, 26 February 1968 (includes quote from Wilson); PRO: CAB 128/43, CC(68)15th, 27 February 1968; CAB 129/136, C(68)40 and 41; B. Castle, *The Castle Diaries, 1964–70* (London: Weidenfeld & Nicolson, 1984), pp. 382–3.
80. PRO: PREM 13/2416, records of meetings, 12 and 13 February 1968, and Wilson to Benn, 10 April 1968.
81. PRO: PREM 13/2416, Trend to Wilson, 26 February 1968.
82. PRO: PREM 13/2416, record of Wilson–Zuckerman meeting, 8 April 1968, and Wilson to Benn, 10 April 1968.
83. PRO: CAB 128/43, CC(68)27th (11 April 1968); and see *Hansard: House of Commons*

Debates, 763, columns 40–2, for Benn's announcement. Stewart agreed, however, that Britain's purpose was to pursue viable industrial activity rather than 'prestige' projects. See Michael Stewart Papers, Churchill College, Cambridge, STWT 8/1/5, diary, 7 May 1968.

84. PRO: PREM 13/2112, record of Stewart–Brandt meeting, 24 May 1968, and PRO: PREM 13/2113, Harmel to Stewart, 12 September 1968.
85. PRO: PREM 13/2113, Hancock to Permanent Under-Secretary, 10 July 1968, and Palliser to Maitland, 12 September 1968.
86. Wilson, *The Labour Government*, p. 612.
87. Zuckerman, *Monkeys*, pp. 436, 439–40, 443.
88. PRO: PREM 13/1851, record of Wilson–Kiesinger meeting, 25 October 1967 (misdated November).
89. PRO: PREM 13/1780, Palliser to Maitland, 4 August 1967.
90. PRO: CAB 134/3309, ST(67)5th, 25 July 1967, and ST(67)7th, 11 December 1967.
91. Crossman, *The Diaries of a Cabinet Minister, Vol. II*, p. 762 (4 April 1968).
92. PRO: PREM 13/2113, Ford to Robinson, 9 August 1968.
93. For example, PRO: PREM 13/1780, Wilson to Zuckerman, 4 August 1967.
94. PRO: PREM 13/2113, Palliser to Maitland, giving account of Wilson–Stewart meeting, 22 July 1968.

6

The Confederation of British Industry and European Integration in the 1960s

NEIL ROLLINGS

In the summer of 1999 the Confederation of British Industry (CBI) commissioned the opinion pollsters MORI to conduct a survey of the CBI's members on their attitudes to various aspects of economic and monetary union. When five complaints were made, it was left to the Professional Standards Committee of the Market Research Society to adjudicate that the questionnaire wording was fair. All of this information is available on the CBI's web page as part of a lengthy justification and explanation of the methodology adopted in reaching the survey results.[1] The need for such a detailed explanation illustrates how careful the CBI leadership feels it has to be to show that it has not 'cooked the books' in favour of support for closer European integration. This reflects not only the extent to which the CBI is currently regarded with suspicion by parts of business, notably anti-euro pressure groups such as 'Business for Sterling', but also how it cannot now speak as the single authoritative voice of business on the issue of Europe.

In the 1960s the situation was completely different. After the formation of the CBI,[2] only the Association of British Chambers of Commerce (ABCC) remained separate from the previous main representative associations of business.[3] Thus, in the mid-1960s the CBI spoke with considerable authority and with little dissent from within industry. Similarly, the methodology adopted for its 1966–67 survey of its members' opinions on European integration provides a stark contrast with that followed in 1999. The questionnaire had to be answered in the light of reading a report written by the CBI's Europe Steering Committee, which supported British membership of the

Common Market.[4] In short, the CBI leadership was able to point the membership towards the desired response. This is just one example of the considerable freedom of manoeuvre available to the leadership of the CBI at the time of Britain's second application to join the EEC. It was able to push the cause of European integration with little internal or external criticism. Indeed, British industry was apparently more positive about joining the EEC at this time than when Britain first applied in 1961 and when it finally gained membership in the early 1970s. The emergence of this position will be considered in the first part of this chapter, which deals with the development of the CBI's thinking from 1963 to 1968. The second part will explain the reasons for the CBI's strong support for EEC entry, given the contemporary belief that the economic arguments for and against membership were finely balanced.[5] While it is common to present the CBI as one of the strongest and most consistent supporters of closer links between Britain and the rest of Europe, it will be argued here that there were particular reasons why the second application was viewed as so important, relating to its timing and to industry's perception of the meaning of European integration.[6] The final part will reinterpret the CBI's impact on government policy, which was dismissed as non-existent in the most detailed study of the CBI's role.[7] It will be shown, by contrast, that there were areas where the CBI clearly felt it impacted upon Britain's second attempt to gain entry to the EEC.

THE CBI AND EUROPEAN INTEGRATION, 1963–68

All three of the predecessor associations of the CBI were, with varying degrees of enthusiasm, in favour of Britain's application to join the Common Market in 1961, maintaining that stance during the ultimately doomed Brussels negotiations on Britain's first entry bid.[8] The ending of these negotiations stimulated a significant shift away from outright support for British entry into the EEC on the part of the Federation of British Industries (FBI), towards giving preference to global considerations over regional ones. However, it was also a response to changed circumstances. Given that membership of the EEC was discounted for the foreseeable future, global trade liberalisation offered, among other things, the best alternative route to gaining freer access to the markets of the Six. Fear of exclusion from these markets remained a potent concern and made the successful conclusion of the Kennedy Round of the General Agreement on Tariffs and Trade (GATT) negotiations all the more imperative.[9]

FIGURE 6.1
VALUE OF BRITISH EXPORTS (£ MILLION) 1960-68

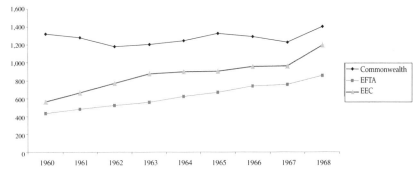

Source: Annual Abstract of Statistics (London, HMSO)

Once it became clear that the Kennedy Round offered no quick and easy solution and the growth in exports to the Six began to slow in 1964, as illustrated in Figure 6.1, it was always likely that the issue of European integration would re-emerge.[10] For business, this became clear in January 1965. As a forerunner to the possibility of merger, the FBI, the British Employers' Confederation (BEC) and the National Association of British Manufacturers (NABM) organised a joint conference in Eastbourne to consider 'The Next Five Years', much on the lines of the FBI's 1960 Brighton conference. One of the conclusions of the conference was that:

> British industry has for many years actively wished to see an economically integrated Europe. We greatly regret the continued division. While we see no early prospect of an end to the division we think its implications for industry must continually be subjected to critical scrutiny. Equally the objective of healing the breach must remain in the forefront of policy.[11]

Little immediately followed from the conference because of the merger of the three associations into the CBI during the course of 1965: new staff had to be appointed and new administrative machinery established. However, once the CBI was up and running, the issue of Europe came to the fore again. John Davies, the new Director-General and 'a passionate European', raised the issue in his inaugural address to the CBI Council in September.[12] As he told the press, one of the new body's six 'points of attack' would be that: 'The CBI will carry on the FBI torch that Britain should seek every opportunity of moving closer to Europe with the objective of Common Market membership.'[13] A month later the Council approved the proposal for a study of the European Communities.[14] By the end of 1965 the CBI's Europe Steering Committee had already met and agreed its terms of reference:

> To examine the past and prospective development of the European Communities within the EEC, ECSC and Euratom Treaties and their implementation in law and practice, with a view to assessing the practical implications for British industry of closer relationships with the Communities and to make recommendations for future CBI policy and action in this regard.[15]

Although the 24 members of the Steering Committee met only 11 times before producing their report, their influence on the CBI's position on Europe was crucial because it was their report, published in December 1966, which formed the basis of the wider consultation of its membership, referred to above.[16] One key decision taken by the Steering Committee was that 'closer relationships' were assumed to mean full membership of the EEC, not only for Britain, but also for most other European Free Trade Association (EFTA) countries. This removed one of the major potential obstacles to support for Britain's entry into the Common Market before the study had even started. Thus, while the CBI's overseas director could tell members that the study was not prejudging the issue and might even conclude that EEC membership was not appropriate, this was not likely to be the case.[17] Having set this framework, the Steering Committee devolved the detailed studies to the relevant standing committees of the CBI and other bodies. It gave them common terms of reference of considering developments in Community law and practice, identifying and commenting on the practical implications of any substantial differences between Britain and the EEC, defining areas where substantial advantages or disadvantages might be expected, and considering the form of any necessary transitional arrangements.[18] In addition, a Europe Panel was established to give advice to the CBI staff on the subjects requiring study, to coordinate the papers, iron out inconsistencies and advise the Steering Committee.[19]

The detailed studies were extensive, with the majority published as supporting papers to the Steering Committee's report.[20] They were all, with the exception of that on agriculture by the National Farmers' Union (NFU), broadly positive in their conclusions about the balance of advantage from closer association and certainly saw few insuperable problems even when it was thought that there would be increased costs for British industry, for example on equal pay. The Steering Committee's report was, if anything, even more positive, 'fudging' or ignoring a number of difficulties and sensitive issues associated with British entry into the EEC. The Committee conceded that the draft paper on monetary implications was too optimistic, and should rather refer to the balance of advantage between the sterling area becoming a responsibility of the EEC and European countries getting free access to the London capital market.[21] Nevertheless, on the crucial issue of devaluation prior to entry, the paper, following Bank of England advice, said nothing, despite the Europe Panel believing that this would have to be broached if the balance-of-payments costs were found to outweigh the benefits.[22]

A number of other substantive alterations were made, all of which created a more positive picture of the balance of advantages and disadvantages of British entry into the EEC. For example, a sentence was deleted from the section on general economic policy which advocated urgent consultation on the problems of redundancy and redeployment, following the rationalisation of British industry expected to result from membership.[23] The qualifications and reservations made at the start of the very first paragraph were also removed.[24] Most significant, however, was the way the Steering Committee dealt with the fundamental issue of the cost of the Common Agricultural Policy (CAP) to Britain's cost of living and balance of payments. The NFU had supplied the supporting paper on agriculture in which the various concerns of British farmers were set out. In addition, they supplied a paper estimating the costs at £685 million to the cost of living, and £350–400 million to the balance of payments. At first, the Steering Committee agreed that any figures of the costs in their report had to have been produced from within the committee rather than from outside sources.[25] But within a couple of weeks, at their final meeting prior to the report's publication, they considered a paper on the costs prepared by Unilever. This put the respective costs at £500 million and £165 million. The Steering Committee, acknowledging its lack of expertise, agreed to publish both papers as appendices to the report but still felt able to state in the report, itself that: 'It seems a reasonable assumption for industry to make that the true outcome may lie somewhere between the two, with the long term trend probably in the direction of the lower estimate', that is, Unilever's.[26]

The Times summarised the Steering Committee's report, published in December 1966, as follows: 'British industry has given an emphatic yes to joining the Common Market'.[27] Its main conclusions were set out boldly in the opening paragraph, which read:

This Committee is firmly convinced that, from an industrial point of view

(1) there would be a clear and progressive balance of advantage to British industry from membership of an enlarged European Economic Community,

(2) the Treaty of Rome and the Community's method of operation are acceptable given reasonable transitional arrangements, and

(3) entry should be negotiated as soon as possible.[28]

It was these three points on which attention has always focused, in part because they formed the basis of the ensuing consultation process.[29] Consultation took four forms: a survey questionnaire to the 1,700 firms used in the CBI's Industrial Trends Survey; the views of the CBI's 12 regional councils and its Small Firms Steering Group; submissions by member trade associations and employers' organisations; and by means of enquiries among other bodies related in their activities to manufacturing industry, such as transport, distribution and the City.[30] The survey questionnaire was the first to be completed. It asked for consideration of the effects of British membership of an enlarged EEC on various aspects of the individual company's operations, its markets, its need to adapt, and the balance of advantage with regard to costs, profitability and growth. Turning to the perceived effect on

TABLE 6.1
REPRESENTATIVENESS OF THE 1967 CBI SAMPLE SURVEY

Industry	% of national industrial output	% of CBI response
Mechanical engineering	14.14	24
Electrical engineering	9.04	11
Metals and metal manufacture	13.33	12
Vehicles	13.03	6
Textiles, clothing, footwear and leather	11.59	13
Food, drink and tobacco	11.22	7
Chemicals	10.78	8
Building materials, pottery and glass, timber and wooden furniture	6.63	6
Paper and printing	7.76	5
Other industries	2.49	10
Size of company		
(by no. of employees)		
0–199	17.8	29
200–499	13.8	19
500–4,999	30.2	39
5,000 +	38.1	13

Source: MRC: MSS200/C/1/2/O, Norman to members, 7 March 1967, appendix to press release.

the whole of industry, the questionnaire then asked whether the respondent agreed with the three conclusions set out in the opening paragraph of the Steering Committee's report.

Eight hundred and sixty-five replies were received from individual companies, representing just over 50 per cent of the sample.[31] These companies were in general positive about the effect of membership on them or saw little effect; few expected a detrimental effect. There was an astonishing degree of support for the conclusions of the Steering Committee: 91 per cent believed there would be a clear and progressive balance of advantage to British industry as a whole from membership, 90 per cent thought the Treaty of Rome and the Community's method of operation acceptable given reasonable transitional arrangements, and 89 per cent agreed that entry should be negotiated as soon as possible.[32] The Europe Steering Committee found the results 'too good to be true' and agreed that their presentation to the press should be 'dead-pan', as 'there was a danger of appearing too euphoric about the degree of support by industry for entry'.[33] They were aware that views could change, had probably not been worked out in detail, and that the consultation process was still in progress. Nevertheless, the resulting press release has been seen as the 'most important single CBI announcement' on Europe in this period.[34] The rest of the consultation process merely reiterated these conclusions: there was 'virtually unanimous support' (with the notable exception of the NFU) for the conclusions of the Steering Committee report.[35] The only note of caution was the tendency of trade associations to highlight the likelihood of short-term difficulties: it was again agreed not to publish a detailed analysis by industry.[36] Given such support for British entry into the Common Market, the centrepiece of the third and final volume of the CBI's study, published on 4 July 1967, was not the report on consultation but 'a programme for action' drawn up by the Steering Committee itself. This set out a series of recommendations on the steps which industry and the government needed to take to ease any transitional difficulties and to make the most of entry once it occurred.[37]

Thus, the CBI had as good as completed its consultation process on Britain and Europe prior to the Labour government's formal announcement of a second application. The CBI's position from 1965 onwards constituted clear support for entry into the Common Market, even after de Gaulle's rejection in November 1967. This position was also different from that taken by the FBI during and after the first application. The caution so apparent earlier seems to have disappeared with the ringing endorsement of the Steering Committee's report in the consultation process of 1967. Thereafter the focus of its attention, in terms of its policy position, was the programme of action. In 1968 the Steering Committee reviewed the situation in the light of the successful completion of the Kennedy Round, sterling devaluation and the rejection of Britain's second application. The review reaffirmed their 1966 position in favour of entry even if the effect of exclusion had been mitigated by the Kennedy Round and devaluation: the need was to intensify efforts on the lines of the programme of action.[38] To this end, the Steering Committee recommended the publication of a CBI statement of policy on Europe which would make these points and urge the continued building of closer links with the EEC. This was approved by the CBI Council.[39] Hence, the evolution of the CBI's policy towards British membership of the EEC is relatively clear: while it in no way started from a position of ambivalence, the CBI moved rapidly between the first and second applications to being strongly in favour of Britain joining the EEC. The second part of the chapter explores the reasons why the CBI was so strongly in favour of British entry into the EEC by the time of the second application.

EXPLAINING THE CBI'S POSITIVE ATTITUDE

There are four possible factors in the CBI's strong embrace of a European role for Britain in the mid-1960s. The first lies in the creation of the CBI itself in 1965, Michael Newman arguing that it was more representative of large-scale industry than the FBI had been.[40] But this view is hard to substantiate. The FBI had a reputation of being primarily concerned with large firms, and it was to avoid this criticism that the CBI established its Small Firms Steering Group.[41] The position of small firms was considered specifically with regard to European integration, and the questionnaire results, while illustrating more caution in small firms than larger ones, still showed support for the Steering Committee's conclusions running at a level above 80 per cent.[42] It does, however, raise the possibility of a second factor relating to the creation of the CBI. As the results of the survey show, there was remarkably little opposition to the Steering Committee's position. There was a complaint about the representativeness of the views of 800 firms out of 14,000 members, but the director-general brushed this aside by pointing to the other forms of consultation that were also taking place.[43] Given that the CBI had been created to be the representative voice of industry, its leadership and officials were in an extremely strong position compared to their predecessors. Companies and trade associations could leave the CBI, but there was no other organisation offering them a mouthpiece for their discontent to which they could turn. This gave the leadership considerable freedom of manoeuvre to develop what they considered to be appropriate policy positions for British industry.

The third factor focuses on the leaders of the CBI, not only John Davies, who were 'pro-European', just like their predecessors at the FBI. The ability of the leadership of the CBI to create business opinion on Europe was one factor in explaining why British industry was apparently so strongly in favour of entry into the Common Market.[44] Led by the Europe Steering Committee, it was able to set a clear agenda arguing in favour of membership of the EEC. It was always likely that this would result in a more positive response from a consultation exercise based on their report, than if a more neutral approach had been adopted. The CBI leadership was able to lead its members to the conclusions the leadership wanted. This is not to say that its members were completely subservient or that they were hoodwinked, simply that they were pointed towards the advantages of membership. Finally, the CBI leadership and, from the evidence of the sample survey, much of the membership too, were confident of the ability of British industry to compete. The Steering Committee's report made clear that it was felt that Britain would be able to compete in Europe and, in response to the questionnaire, only 17 per cent felt that entry would lead to a drop in profitability, as opposed to 41 per cent who expected an increase and 35 per cent who saw no effect either way on their profits.[45] This might well have been a mixture of rhetoric and lack of realism, but on a number of occasions CBI representatives took their European counterparts to task for believing in the widespread failings of British industry and the underlying weaknesses of the British economy.[46] Whether this confidence in British industry was justified is irrelevant here, it simply provided further support for the case for entry and access to European markets.

Yet these factors do not in themselves provide a full account of why the CBI was so clearly in favour of joining the EEC. One additionally needs to consider what membership of the EEC meant for British industry in the mid-1960s. It is common to focus on the tariff issue. This was dealt with in the first and longest of the supporting papers published in *Britain and Europe Volume II*. *Volume I*, the Steering Committee's report, also noted that 'For industry the principal argument of entering the European Economic Community has always been that it would offer unimpeded access by British exporters to one of the largest and most dynamic trading areas in the world.'[47] Even here, however, it was the dynamic effects through economies of scale which were often highlighted, rather than simply access to markets.[48] Furthermore, the CBI's 1968 policy statement argued that there were 'compelling reasons' for joining the EEC other than tariff reductions.[49] Nor was this the case only after the successful completion of the Kennedy Round in 1967. Earlier, in 1966, the Steering Committee's report had noted that:

> At least as important [as tariffs] would be the gradual assimilation of the economies of the Member States. ... Tariffs are merely one group among the complex factors, tangible and intangible, that would influence the scope and direction of British industrial thought and action.[50]

What were these 'complex factors'? The Bundesverband der Industrie (BDI), the CBI's German equivalent, had given some indication when its representatives told the CBI that a customs union was not enough in their eyes and that key issues on which they wanted action were the CAP, taxation, monopoly policy, economic policy and monetary policy.[51] The range of topics covered by the supporting papers to the Europe Steering Committee's report gives some further indication, dealing with, among other things, equal pay, social security harmonisation, vocational training, transport, capital movements, monetary implications, restrictive practices and monopolies, and taxation. It was recognised that the whole institutional framework in which British industry operated could change with Common Market membership.[52]

That the CBI's attitude to membership was so positive reveals much about the extent to which it disliked elements of the existing domestic institutional framework. It was this, and in particular government policy, which was frequently highlighted as the cause of British industry's problems. For example, the 1967 programme of action, set out in *Britain and Europe, Volume III*, assigned responsibility for action on each of its proposals. The government appeared in the list 29 times, 12 more times than the CBI, while companies and trade associations were only referred to on 11 and ten occasions respectively.[53] The cases of restrictive practices and monopolies and taxation are particularly illustrative. In both cases, the CBI felt that British industry was disadvantaged by the framework in which it had to operate and that membership of the EEC would offer a way out of these difficulties. In 1965 the Labour government introduced the Monopolies and Mergers Act. The critique of this piece of legislation provided by the CBI's Trade Practices Policy Committee is informative, as it stressed that none of the EEC member countries had similar legislation and that the Commission wanted to encourage mergers.[54]

Similarly, the CBI looked at the tax systems in place across the Channel with envy. For many years it had complained about the tax burden imposed on British industry, and demanded a shift in the tax base away from profits and direct taxation in general to a greater emphasis on indirect taxation. As the Steering Committee's report put it:

> The present heavy incidence of direct taxation on company earnings and dividends operates as a severe check to the accumulation of capital necessary for rapid growth. If British industry is to compete on level terms with its European neighbours it is essential that the more liberal tax treatment accorded company profits on the Continent is reflected in the structure of British taxation …
>
> [Taxation] is … an area where it will be particularly important that the implications of possible membership should be given due weight in the evolution of British policy.[55]

In other words, the CBI was urging moves towards the introduction of a Value Added Tax (VAT) and the consequent reduction in direct taxation even before Common Market entry, suggesting that it adopted a broad perspective on the implications of British entry to the Common Market. This was related to seeing EEC entry as an external solution to domestic problems and dissatisfactions.

It links to a further consideration which underpinned the CBI's desire to join the Common Market at this particular time. As the Steering Committee's third conclusion made clear, Britain's speedy entry was desirable 'Because so much of Community policy is still in embryo, the quicker Britain can share in the decision-making process the better.'[56] In the eyes of the CBI, the mid-1960s offered a window of opportunity. Institutional structures were appearing in the EEC, some of which seemed preferable to those in Britain, but the advantages which these were seen to offer could be mitigated as the EEC continued to develop with Britain on the outside. The longer before Britain became a member the more it would be forced to accept the existing policies and commitments, which would not have been formulated with Britain in mind.[57] The urgency attached to achieving entry at this time was a final pressure acting to make the CBI so clear and positive in its support for entry into the EEC in the mid-1960s. This factor, allied to the desire to reform the domestic framework in which industry operated, and a strong CBI leadership which remained confident of

British industry's abilities to compete, explains why the CBI, and its members, were more positive about membership of the Common Market at this time than before or since.

THE IMPACT OF THE CBI'S VIEWS

The conventional wisdom is that British business, represented by the CBI, formed part of a growing body of pro-European opinion which served to build up pressure on the Labour government to embark on negotiations.[58] Nevertheless, the most detailed study of the impact of the CBI on government policy on Europe came to the conclusion that while the Labour government was in close consultation with the CBI and Trades Union Congress (TUC) over domestic policy, these bodies 'found themselves in a position of unprecedented weakness when it came to influencing Britain's European policy'.[59] The CBI had little influence, Robert Lieber argues, because 'the content and fervour of industry's position thus committed it so overwhelmingly to Common Market entry that the government had little compulsion for seeking to bargain in detail'.[60] He then illustrates the weakness of the CBI and other interest groups by showing how the Industrial Consultative Committee on the Approach to Europe, set up in November 1966, ultimately proved meaningless in policy terms. It met infrequently and was a forum for one-way briefings by government rather than two-way consultation.

Without wishing to overemphasise the role of the CBI and its impact on government policy, Lieber's analysis seems to be too dismissive. His focus on formal consultation underplays informal influence. Consultation between the CBI and government was a continuous process throughout this period. Thus, when the CBI informed Whitehall of its decision to embark on a study of relations with Europe, it received encouragement and support from officials in both the Board of Trade and the Foreign Office.[61] In January 1966 the CBI met for an informal dinner with Con O'Neill and John Robinson from the Foreign Office, Frank Figgures from the Treasury, Eric Roll from the Department of Economic Affairs (DEA) and Bill Hughes from the Board of Trade, beginning a considerable period of informal consultation. The impact of such consultation and the close relations between the CBI and the Board of Trade should not, however, be overstated. The CBI Overseas Committee acknowledged this:

> While it is well adapted to consultation on tactical issues it is less satisfactory where questions of broad strategy are involved.

There is no mechanism whereby on a continuing basis ministers and officials of the Board of Trade can be brought face to face with the thinking of leaders of industry on matters of long-term commercial strategy. Inevitably this tends to result in the government taking the initiative very often and industries being consulted afterwards.[62]

As a result, the CBI leadership made a conscious effort to bring the results of the CBI study to the attention of ministers. The study was discussed with the head of the Department of Economic Affairs (DEA), George Brown, and Minister of State at the Foreign Office George Thomson at a CBI lunch in June 1966, although Brown at first questioned the timing of the study.[63] Similarly, *Britain and Europe, Volume III* was presented to the Prime Minister, accompanied by the Foreign Secretary, Michael Stewart, and the Joint Minister of State at the Foreign Office, Fred Mulley, in July 1967. It was agreed that joint meetings between government departments and the CBI were to be held and that 'the CBI and government should work together to maintain the momentum, both at home and abroad, in the approach to Europe'.[64] Such meetings may not seem particularly significant, but they need to be put into the context of the web of relations between the CBI and the Labour government. At the start of the Labour administration relations between the CBI and the government were good, but began to deteriorate as policy differences emerged. Government action to freeze laundry prices in October 1966 enraged the CBI and put the 'entire relationship with government in jeopardy'.[65] The CBI called a special meeting in November to review this relationship. Although things were patched up following a government apology, the CBI's trust and cooperation never returned and the relationship became increasingly bitter. Given that there was this growing tension over domestic policy, the relationship over Europe appears extremely harmonious by comparison. This agreement was to provide the opportunity for the CBI to influence government policy.

Nor is Lieber correct in assuming that the CBI had nothing with which to bargain in its relationship with government. If nothing else, that the CBI was so positive about European integration at this time proved a stick with which to beat those members of Wilson's Cabinet who were opposed to membership.[66] More directly, the CBI had regular contact with its counterparts around Europe, and often with these countries' civil servants. This was not only a useful source of information on attitudes on the European mainland, but was also a way of raising issues in Europe which highlighted the contribution Britain could make.[67] This proved to be particularly the case with Wilson's desire for a European technology community. He specifically sought advice on how the CBI's contacts could be used to further this idea. More than this, the CBI Council was told in confidence that the Director-General 'had made a significant contribution to the Prime Minister's thinking: the specific suggestion of a[n] [European Institute of Technology] had been his'.[68] None of this is to say that the CBI was the formative influence on government policy on Europe, merely that to argue that it had no impact is too sweeping. There was constant consultation with officials and, even with ministers, and there was some direct influence. This is significant given the increasingly frosty relationship that was developing between the two bodies over domestic economic policy.

CONCLUSION

This chapter has shown that the CBI was strongly in favour of entry into the Common Market in the 1960s. This is not a particularly profound finding in itself. However, in tracing the development of the CBI's position in the first section of the paper, substance and nuance has been added to the existing picture. After 1963 the FBI adopted a global perspective, but once the CBI was established in the summer of 1965 its leadership came out firmly in support of EEC entry. Moreover, the CBI did have some influence on government policy formulation beyond consultation on detail with civil servants, most notably on Wilson's idea of a technology community. The chapter has also attempted to explain the factors which led the CBI to adopt such a positive position.

There are two main conclusions that can be drawn from the preceding analysis. First, as noted in the introduction and in contrast to the current situation, the CBI did speak authoritatively as the voice of British industry. Dissent within industry was much more muted and isolated. This allowed the leadership to adopt a methodology which led its membership in the direction of confirming the leadership's goal of British entry into the EEC. Second, the attraction of the EEC to British industry was not related solely to access to European markets and the achievement of economies of scale. Rather, the CBI adopted a wider perspective, stressing that membership of the EEC offered the prospect of a new institutional framework in which British business could operate. Clearly, there were potential risks, but these would be minimised by early entry, explaining the urgency which the CBI attached to the issue. Indeed, that the CBI was so positive about the advantages of this new working environment for British business points to considerable dissatisfaction with the situation at home, particularly over taxation. In this sense, British industry's desire to be a part of the EEC was not driven by European idealism, nor by a detailed calculation of the costs and benefits, but by a degree of envy and dissatisfaction with the *status quo* in Britain.

NOTES

The research for this paper was funded by the Leverhulme Trust as part of a project on British industry and Europe 1945–73. I would like to thank Alan McKinlay, Helen Mercer and Robbie Guerrero Wilson for their respective contributions to that project.

1. See <http://www.cbi.org.uk/atwork/emures1.html> and related pages.
2. The CBI was formed in the summer of 1965 as a result of the merger of the Federation of British Industries (FBI), the British Employers' Confederation (BEC) and the National Association of British Manufacturers (NABM).
3. There was also the Institute of Directors. At this time it was strongly in favour of British entry into the EEC.
4. CBI, *Britain and Europe Vol. I: An Industrial Appraisal* (London, 1966).
5. U. Kitzinger, *The Second Try: Labour and the EEC* (Oxford: Pergamon, 1968), p. 189, and J. W. Young, *Britain and European Unity, 1945–1999*, 2nd edn (Basingstoke: Macmillan, 2000), p. 99.
6. See, for example, J. Greenwood and L. Stanich, 'British Business: Managing Complexity', in D. Baker and D. Seawright (eds), *Britain For and Against Europe: British Politics and the Question of European Integration* (Oxford: Clarendon Press, 1998), pp. 148–64 (p. 151).
7. For a very clear example see, R. J. Lieber, *British Politics and European Unity: Parties, Elites, and Pressure Groups* (Berkeley: University of California Press, 1970), pp. 265–70.
8. For more on business opinion at the time of the first application, see A. McKinlay, H. Mercer and N. Rollings, 'Reluctant Europeans?: The Federation of British Industries and European Integration 1945–63', *Business History*, 42, 4 (2000), pp. 91–116. See also FBI, *British Industry and Europe* (London, 1961); *The Times*, 21 July 1961, pp. 14–15.
9. Public Record Office (PRO): BT 278/27, Noble to Reilly, 28 March 1963, and PRO: BT 11/6168, 'British Trade Policy: Notes on European Aspects', unsigned and undated but *c.* July 1964.
10. M. Camps, *European Unification in the Sixties: From the Veto to the Crisis* (London: Oxford University Press, 1967), pp. 157-8.
11. Modern Records Centre, University of Warwick (MRC): MSS200/C/1/1, CC 16.65, Proposed CBI study of the European communities: 'Report of the Eastbourne Conference', October 1965. See also FBI, *Britain's Economic Problems and Policies: The Next Five Years* (London, 1965) and S. Blank, *Industry and Government in Britain* (Farnborough: Saxon House, 1973), pp. 224–5, and N. Kipping, *Summing Up* (London: Hutchinson, 1972), pp. 102–3.

12. MRC: MSS200/C/1/1, CC 16.65.
13. *The Times*, 15 September 1965, p. 15.
14. MRC: MSS200/C/1/1, Council meeting, 20 October 1965.
15. MRC: MSS200/C/1/2/O, CO.55.65, first meeting of the Europe Steering Committee, 2 December 1965.
16. Ibid.
17. MRC: MSS200/C/1/2/O, CO.45.65, 'Overseas Director's Newsletter No. 19', 11 November 1965. See also *The Times*, 21 October 1965, p. 18.
18. CBI, *Britain and Europe, Vol. II: Supporting Papers* (London, 1967), p. 1.
19. MRC: MSS200/C/1/1/2, panel meeting, 2 March 1966.
20. Those published covered the common external tariff and common commercial policy, agriculture, free movement of workers, vocational training and the European Social Fund, equal pay, harmonisation of social security, energy, coal, iron and steel, transport, liberalisation of capital movements, taxation, restrictive practices and monopolies, and monetary implications of EEC membership. The first of these had a further 13 papers appended which dealt with various trading and tariff issues. See CBI, *Britain and Europe, Vol. II*.
21. MRC: MSS200/C/1/2/O, O.130.66, 4th meeting of the Europe Steering Committee. The paper was E.298.66.
22. MRC: MSS200/C/1/1/2, European Panel meetings, 16 June 1966 and 22 July 1966. Gerry Norman, its chairman, argued against the need for devaluation when meeting Swedish industrialists and civil servants, MRC: MSS200/C/1/2/O, O.152.66, note of a visit to Sweden 12–13 September 1966 by Norman and Felgate.
23. MRC: MSS200/C/1/2/O, O.170.66, 9th meeting of the Europe Steering Committee, 12 October 1966.
24. Ibid., O.173.66, 10th meeting of the Europe Steering Committee, 20 October 1966.
25. Ibid.
26. Ibid., 11th meeting of the Europe Steering Committee, 8 November 1966; and CBI, *Britain and Europe, Vol. I*, p. 15.
27. *The Times*, 22 December 1966, p. 17.
28. CBI, *Britain and Europe Vol. I*, p. 3.
29. U. Kitzinger, *Diplomacy and Persuasion: How Britain Joined the Common Market* (London: Thames & Hudson, 1973), p. 259, and C. W. Frey, 'Meaning Business: The British Application to Join the Common Market, November 1966–October 1967', *Journal of Common Market Studies*, 6, 3 (1967–68), pp. 197–230 (p. 218).
30. CBI, *Britain and Europe, Vol. III: A Programme of Action* (London, 1967), p. 3.
31. Interestingly, in terms of size of firm, small companies, usually more cautious about EEC membership, were over-represented, while large companies, generally vigorous supporters of Britain joining the Common Market, were significantly under-represented.
32. See *The Times*, 8 March 1967, and Kitzinger, *Second Try*, pp. 168–70, for the results of the survey.
33. MRC: MSS200/C/3/IA/1/14, Melville to Davies, 2 March 1967, and MRC: MSS200/C/1/2/O, O.26A.67, 12th meeting of the Europe Steering Committee, 2 March 1967.
34. Frey, 'Meaning Business', p. 218.
35. CBI, *Britain and Europe, Vol. III*, p. 15.
36. MRC: MSS200/C/1/2/O, O.44A.67, 13th meeting of the Europe Steering Committee, 10 May 1967.
37. CBI, *Britain and Europe, Vol. III*, pp. 5–13.
38. MRC: MSS200/C/1/1, C.21.68, 'Britain and Europe: The Way Ahead' by the

Europe Steering Committee, undated but *c.* March 1968, and CBI Council, 20 March 1968.

39. MRC: MSS200/C/1/1, C.21.68, CBI Council, 20 March 1968.
40. M. Newman, *Socialism and European Unity: The Dilemma of the Left in Britain and France* (London: Junction, 1983), p. 206.
41. MRC: MSS200/C/1/2/R, R.34.66, Sir Nutcombe Hume, the chair of the steering group at its first meeting, 12 October 1966.
42. MRC: MSS200/C/1/1, C.59.67, CBI Council meeting, 21 June 1967; CBI, *Britain and Europe, Vol. III*, p. 22; MRC: MSS200/C/1/2/O, Norman to members, 7 March 1967, covering press release.
43. MRC: MSS200/C/3/IA/1/14, Wilmott to Davies, 16 March 1967, and reply, 21 March 1967.
44. Kitzinger, *Diplomacy and Persuasion*, p. 259. On the FBI's leadership see McKinlay, Mercer and Rollings, 'Reluctant Europeans?'.
45. CBI, *Britain and Europe, Vol. I*, pp. 2 and 24; MRC: MSS200/C/1/2/O, Norman to members, 7 March 1967.
46. One report on a visit to Denmark noted that British industry's own propaganda against itself had been all too effective, and that it had been necessary to correct familiar misapprehensions about the failure of British exports and Britain's strike proneness. See MRC: MSS200/C/1/2/O, O.179.66, note of a visit to Denmark, 31 October–1 November, by Norman, Threlfall and Whitehorn, November 1966, and O.152.66, note of a visit to Sweden 12–13 September, by Norman and Felgate, September 1966.
47. CBI, *Britain and Europe, Vol. I*, p. 7.
48. MRC: MSS200/C/1/1, CBI Council meeting, 21 June 1967.
49. Ibid., C.21A.68, March 1968.
50. CBI, *Britain and Europe, Vol. I*, p. 8.
51. MRC: MSS200/C/1/2/O, O.82.66, note of a visit to Germany, 4 April 1966, by Norman and Whitehorn, May 1966.
52. For further consideration of this issue, see N. Rollings, 'British Industry and European Integration 1961–73: From First Application to Final Membership', *Business and Economic History*, 27, 2 (1998), pp. 444–54.
53. CBI, *Britain and Europe, Vol. III*, pp. 7–13.
54. MRC: MSS200/C/1/1, C.62.66, 'UK Anti-Trust Legislation: Reasons for Seeking Changes', September 1966.
55. CBI, *Britain and Europe, Vol. I*, pp. 20–1.
56. CBI, *Britain and Europe, Vol. I*, p. 3.
57. Ibid., p. 6.
58. Camps, *European Unification*, p. 182; H. Young, *This Blessed Plot: Britain and Europe from Churchill to Blair* (London: Macmillan, 1998), p. 195; Young, *Britain and European Unity*, p. 91; Frey, 'Meaning Business', pp. 215–19.
59. Lieber, *British Politics*, p. 265.
60. Ibid., p. 269.
61. MRC: MSS200/C/3/IA/1/9, Phillips (Board of Trade) to Whitehorn, 7 October 1965, and O'Neill to Whitehorn, 15 October 1965.
62. MRC: MSS200/C/1/2/O, CO.10.66, 'Methods of Consultation Between Government and Industry on Overseas Trade Policy', undated but *c.* January 1966.
63. Ibid., O.102.66A, 27 June 1966.
64. MRC: MSS200/C/1/1, C.61.67, Director-General's report to Council, July 1967.
65. W. Grant and D. Marsh, *The CBI* (London: Hodder & Stoughton, 1977), pp. 188–90.
66. PRO: CAB 128/42, CC(67)17, item 4, 6 April 1967.

67. MRC: MSS200/C/1/2/O, O.32.67, Record of Council of Industrial Federations of the European Free Trade Association (CIFEFTA) conference, 20 March 1967.
68. MRC: MSS200/C/1/1, C.96.67, CBI Council meeting, 15 November 1967. For more on the technological community dimension to Wilson's entry bid, see Chapter 5 in this book.

PART II:

THE EXTERNAL CONTEXT

7

A Short-Term Defeat: The Community Institutions and the Second British Application to Join the EEC

N. PIERS LUDLOW

Charles de Gaulle's veto of Harold Macmillan's application to join the European Economic Community (EEC) in January 1963 made it clear that the biggest threat to Britain's attempts to gain membership of the Community came from Paris. The experience of Britain's first membership bid, however, had also taught London that ultimate success could only be reached by means of a lengthy and fraught negotiation with the EEC 'Six' in Brussels. Bilateral diplomacy towards the French designed to avert another veto would therefore have to be flanked by a multilateral effort to sell Britain's membership claims at a Commu-nity level. In so doing, it would have to hope to fare better than in 1961–63, when it is arguably the case that the mis-management of the Brussels dimension of the negotiations had not only cost Macmillan and his government much time and energy, but also proved a necessary precondition for the General's veto.[1]

In 1967, it quickly became apparent that any further negotiations in Brussels possessed additional importance in the light of the renewed hostility of the French, signalled most clearly by de Gaulle's so-called 'velvet veto' of 16 May. For, if Britain was to have any hope of 'not taking "no" for an answer' and outflanking the French leader, it could only hope to do so by means of recruiting the 'friendly five' EEC member states to its cause (Belgium, Germany, Italy, Luxembourg and the Netherlands). In a sense, there were two diplomatic battles to be won: one in Paris, the other in Brussels. This chapter will focus on the sustained efforts of the British and their numerous continental allies to win the latter. The first part explores France's continued opposition to British EEC membership, determined by President de Gaulle and voiced by his Foreign Minister Maurice Couve de Murville. That France's objections were seen as increasingly untenable is suggested by the second part, which concentrates on the broader Community response to Harold Wilson's application. It sheds light on the solidarity of the Five behind the second application, support echoed by the European Commission as it developed its own response through 1967. The longer-term repercussions of de Gaulle's second veto are the subject of the final part of the chapter. Here it is argued that France's unilateral action in blocking the Wilson application stymied Community development by exacerbating tensions among the Six, and by putting Britain's accession so high on the EEC agenda that France's partners were wary of taking further integrative steps ahead of Britain joining. Paradoxically, the failure of the 'second try' seemed to make the expansion of the EEC a more likely medium-term project.

This chapter will thus demonstrate how traumatic an experience for the EEC the second British application proved to be, and how the wounds which it had caused, far from healing over in the wake of Britain's retreat at the end of 1967, in fact festered and were to poison the atmosphere in Brussels throughout the remainder of the 1960s. The row over Wilson's membership bid helped create a consensus among Community members that a solution to the question of enlargement was a vital prerequisite for any further advance in Brussels – a sentiment which was greatly to assist Edward Heath when he began his negotiations with the EEC in 1970. Throughout, the chapter will be based on the archives of the Community institutions themselves, augmented where necessary by references to British and French official papers.

THE FRENCH CASE AGAINST ENLARGEMENT

Wilson's letter applying for membership of the EEC arrived in Brussels on 11 May 1967; de Gaulle's unenthusiastic response was made public only five days later. The French President could not, however, prevent the Community institutions from debating the issue. Indeed in his press conference, the General had explicitly rejected the use of a veto.[2] The French case against enlargement thus had to be set out repeatedly in Brussels, first and most extensively in July, when the Council of Ministers met to consider the issue, and then on several more occasions in the autumn. It is worthwhile examining the arguments advanced by the French in a little more detail, if only to identify what the case was that Britain and its allies amongst the Six had to try to rebut.

At the heart of the French critique of enlargement lay the claim that any expansion of Community membership would alter the EEC and divert it from the course upon which it was set. Admitting Britain, and with it also Denmark, Ireland and Norway, all of whom had also applied or were expected to apply in the near future, would, in French eyes, have a dramatic and detrimental impact on the Community in three respects: on its international position, its internal functioning and its ability to devise more effective common policies. Internationally, the French feared that an enlarged Community would loom so large in global trade relations that the United States would have to respond, initiating commercial negotiations designed to create a colossal Atlantic free trade area. This in turn, while perhaps economically attractive to some, could not fail to subvert the political purposes that underpinned European integration. Within an Atlantic framework, and deprived of the solidarity which sprang from their exclusive commercial ties, the Community member states would stand no chance of being able to move towards political union or a more coordinated foreign policy. The economic consolidation of the Western bloc foreseen by the French, would also have baleful effects on East–West relations. Confronted by an enlarged EEC, and by an emerging Atlantic community, the Soviet Union would inevitably be obliged to retaliate, turning its back on *détente* and moving to consolidate its own Eastern sphere.

The French believed that enlargement would be equally damaging to the Community's internal development. The inclusion of new members, with divergent traditions and different national interests, would make it much harder to create the type of consensus about the EEC's development which had underpinned the successes of the Six. Nor would the Community's institutional structure be able to cope with an increase in membership from half a dozen to ten or more. If the membership of the EEC were allowed to grow to a point where it resembled that of the now-defunct Organisation for European Economic Co-operation (OEEC), the body created in 1948 to distribute Marshall Aid, but which had become a byword in European circles for institutional ineffectiveness, did it not also follow that the enlarged Community would be no more capable of reaching agreement and consensus than the OEEC had been? In short, enlargement would undermine the achievements and structures of the Community and prevent the realisation of that true European unity envisaged by the founders.[3]

To make matters worse, British membership in particular would, according to France, pose a number of more specific challenges and threats to the EEC's development. Two particular difficulties stood out. The first was the continuing uncertainty over whether Britain would be either willing or able to accept the Common Agricultural Policy (CAP) as it currently existed. For Britain, the adoption of the CAP would require the abandonment of trading patterns and food consumption habits in place since the era of Cobden, and the acceptance of a system of CAP finance which was likely to result in the British paying an extremely large amount of money into Community coffers. Whether Britain would be able to do this could, moreover, be questioned in light of the second major issue fastened onto by the French, namely, the state of Britain's economy and in particular the chronic weakness of sterling. According to Couve, the man primarily responsible for advancing the French case in the Council of Ministers, the pound had been a fragile currency throughout the post-war period and was unlikely to escape from its current predicament unless the British were to cast off entirely their extensive (and expensive) responsibilities towards the sterling area. As a result, a Community which welcomed British membership before the sterling problem had been resolved, would soon find itself obliged to intervene in support of the beleaguered currency and, most probably, having to free Britain from some of the more painful aspects of EEC membership so as to avert a major balance-of-payments crisis.[4]

The sheer length and ferocity of the French denunciation of enlargement clearly surprised the five other member states of the EEC. According to the Commission report on the July ministerial meeting, there was an unusual period of silence after Couve had finished speaking, while his fellow ministers absorbed the profusion of claims which the French representative had made.[5] He had presented his country's arguments with all the eloquence and forcefulness for which he had become renowned. Only a few days earlier, Jean Rey, the new President of the European Commission, had commented to George Brown, the British Foreign Secretary, that de Gaulle was fortunate in having in Couve 'someone who could put an indefensible foreign policy in presentable clothes', and the Frenchmen's performance on 10 July only confirmed this impression.[6]

But, looked at in more detail, both the length of the French case, and the doom-mongering nature of so many of its predictions, reveal more about the weakness of the French position in 1967 than they do about its strength. This is particularly striking when Couve's 1967 performance is contrasted with his own interventions in the course of the

1961–63 negotiations. During the earlier membership talks, the strength of the French case had resulted from the near impossibility of distinguishing between maliciously conceived arguments designed to thwart Britain's approach and perfectly legitimate arguments intended to safeguard the Community's fabric and structure. French anxieties about the CAP, or the way in which the common external tariff would survive if the numerous exceptions which Britain sought were granted, were all too plausible and hence usually won at least some sympathy from either the European Commission or some other member states. In 1961 and 1962 at least, the French were thus rarely isolated, and even on those comparatively infrequent occasions when they did find themselves on their own, were nearly always perceived by their Community partners to be doing no more than mounting a tough but fair defence of their interests.[7] In 1967 this veneer of respectability was almost entirely missing from Couve's case.

Part of the change was attributable to Britain's more wholehearted approach to the Community. Britain, it should be remembered, had not decided to join the EEC in 1961; it had merely submitted a formal application so that the terms of membership could be determined and only intended to make a decision for or against on the basis of these terms. The highly conditional nature of Macmillan's membership bid had meant that many of the Six had harboured question marks about Britain's sincerity. They had approached negotiations as determined to resist Britain's attempts to change the Community as they had been to smooth Britain's path to membership. This had created an ideal environment for French procrastination and delay. In 1967, by contrast, no formal conditions had been attached to Britain's membership bid. The enthusiastically pro-European sentiments of Brown's speech to the Western European Union (WEU), in July 1967, were weighed down with a far shorter list of practical difficulties ahead than those that Edward Heath had been obliged to mention when opening Britain's first membership bid in October 1961. To make the application still more convincing, the 1967 bid had enjoyed bipartisan support in the House of Commons,[8] whereas in 1961 Labour had merely abstained. Britain, it appeared, had finally shed its doubts about European unity. There were hence far fewer misgivings amongst the Five upon which the French were able to play.

THE 'FRIENDLY FIVE'

In the 1967 negotiations the French found themselves more isolated than they had ever been prior to January 1963. The Germans, the

Italians and the Belgians did periodically acknowledge that a few of the arguments put forward by the French had some foundation. Willy Brandt conceded, for instance, that British membership would alter the Community and somewhat change its evolutionary course. But the German Foreign Minister went on to point out that the argument that British involvement would make it harder for the Community to develop a true political union alongside its economic union would only have carried weight had the Six been far advanced in their own pursuit of this aim. As it was, however, the Six had failed to make any significant progress towards even the most basic aspects of political union. British membership could scarcely make matters worse.[9] Likewise, Joseph Luns, the Dutch Foreign Minister, admitted that the weakness of sterling did indeed pose a potential problem to the EEC. But had not France too faced problems of monetary weakness when the Treaty of Rome had first been signed, problems which its partners had trusted that Paris would solve and which had been successfully overcome? He felt that the Six should extend to Britain the trust which the Five had shown to France in 1958.[10]

The wider French objections against Britain joining were dismissed in four ways. First, there was no likelihood, Luns asserted, of the United States pressurising the Community into far-reaching further liberalisation; Washington's appetite for freer trade had been largely satisfied by the recently concluded Kennedy Round of General Agreement on Tariffs and Trade (GATT) negotiations. Second, according to Pierre Harmel, the Belgian Foreign Minister, the enlarged Community was not likely to lapse into OEEC-like institutional paralysis: the OEEC had lacked either the Community's technical or political objectives, it had not had an institution like the Commission to drive integration forward, nor had it enjoyed the EEC's political dynamism. Third, in the light of Brown's statement to the WEU, it was also impossible, Harmel noted, to question Britain's commitment to the objectives and goals that the Six had set themselves. The final and perhaps most fundamental challenge to the French position was made by Amintore Fanfani, the Italian Foreign Minister, who pointed out that his French counterpart had entirely overlooked the multiple advantages, political and economic, which British membership, in particular, would bring. Once these were taken into account, it became clear that the current opportunity could not be missed. The representatives of Germany, Italy, Belgium, the Netherlands and Luxembourg therefore called for the enlargement procedure set out in Article 237 of the Treaty of Rome to be set in motion as soon as possible, and for British membership to be approached in a favourable spirit.[11]

The five-to-one split within the Council was thus more blatant than it had ever been during Britain's first approach to the Community. Retrospectively, French participants liked to argue that they had been confronted with a clear five-to-one split even in the earlier negotiations.[12] This gave credibility to their claim that de Gaulle's veto had then rescued the Community from internal dissolution. But in reality, such polarisation had seldom occurred. The means by which the first application had been brought to its premature conclusion ensured, however, that the French were all but entirely isolated from the very beginning of the 1967 discussions. De Gaulle's success in blocking Britain's first approach to the Community, and his apparent determination to do the same to its second try, had pushed the Five into a type of unified Anglophile bloc which differed radically from the much more fluid coalitions of views that had characterised the 1961–63 negotiations. Couve's eloquence could do little to bridge the gulf that existed between France and its Community partners.

French isolation was further accentuated by the clear volte-face of the European Commission on the issue of enlargement. When the British had first sought to join the EEC, the Commission had been somewhat muted in its enthusiasm. In a formal sense, it had given a rhetorical welcome to Macmillan's application and had played an active and largely constructive role during the Brussels negotiations. Some of its members, notably the Dutch Vice-President, Sicco Mansholt, had genuinely wished to see the British take their place within the EEC. And all of the Commission's leaders had been sincere in their condemnation of the manner in which the 1961–63 discussion of enlargement had been brought to its abrupt and premature end. But, from the President, Walter Hallstein, down, many of those involved with the European Commission in the early years had never entirely overcome their doubts about Britain's sincerity, had resented the number and complexity of changes to the Community which Heath and his fellow negotiators had requested, and had feared for the way in which the complex task of widening the Community might delay or even obstruct progress towards the ambitious goals that the Six had set themselves. In 1961–63, the tacit consensus among the leaders and staff of the European Commission seemed to be that enlargement was an unwelcome distraction from the more pressing task of implementing the Treaty of Rome.[13]

Four years later the basic Commission attitude appeared to have undergone a near 180 degree turn. Rather than a somewhat disagreeable development, to be coped with but not really to be welcomed, the approach of Britain and its fellow applicants was regarded as an important event which, if skilfully used, could be turned to the Community's, and the Commission's, advantage. Widening was no longer perceived to be a potential obstruction to deepening, but instead as something which could actually make it easier to press ahead with the EEC's development. The difference in sentiment was apparent from the very first discussion among the members of the Commission about Britain's new bid. Whereas in 1961 the corresponding meeting had ended with a formal decision to welcome the applicants, the 1967 Commission had to remind itself that too enthusiastic a corporate response was likely to serve as a red rag to the French, and resolved to limit itself to personal statements by individual Commissioners.[14] Even this self-denying ordinance turned out to be insufficient, Vice-President Lionello Levi-Sandri's welcome of British membership proving sufficiently fulsome to earn a formal complaint from the French.[15] That close and effective alliance between the European Commission and the French which had characterised the 1961–63 negotiations, and which had been compared by one eye-witness to that between the Pope and the Holy Roman Emperor, appeared unlikely to reappear in a second round of enlargement discussions.[16]

The overwhelming goodwill with which the new British approach was received in all of the Community capitals, other than Paris, was quickly translated into practical assistance and advice. To a large extent this replicated the offers of help and information with which London had been showered during the first entry bid.[17] But what was new was the extremely effective, if discreet, collaboration which was to emerge between the British and the European Commission. Such contacts were officially sanctioned in the course of Brown's meeting with Rey in early July and were to become a notable feature of the months during which the Commission worked to prepare its *avis* – the official assessment of enlargement which it is required by the Treaty to make, and which the Council of Ministers had requested for late September 1967.[18] In order to avoid French complaints, meetings between Commission officials and their British counterparts were kept as low profile as possible. On many occasions they took place at the home of Sir James Marjoribanks, the British Head of Mission to the European Communities, who arranged lunch parties where senior British civil servants working on the British bid 'just happened' to sit next to Commission officials preparing the relevant sections of the *avis*. So it is almost certainly the case that the British were able to influence the Commission's thinking throughout the summer months.[19] Certainly, the Commission's *avis*, when complete, contained only one section (that on monetary affairs) to which the British objected, and was generally in line with British hopes.[20] And there was particular satisfaction in London at the report's principal conclusion:

> It is the Commission's Opinion that, in order to dispel the uncertainty which still attaches in particular to certain fundamental points, negotiations should be opened in the most appropriate forms with the States which have applied for membership, in order to examine in more detail, as is indeed necessary, the problems brought out in this document and to see whether arrangements can be made under which the indispensable cohesion and dynamism will be maintained in an enlarged Community.[21]

The Commission, in other words, had thrown its weight fully behind the Five in its belief that full membership negotiations between the Community and the various applicants, including Britain, should begin as soon as possible. The pressure on France to allow this to happen had greatly increased.

A PYRRHIC VICTORY

Despite their near total isolation, however, the French did not buckle. At the 23–24 October meeting of the Council of Ministers, at which discussions of enlargement resumed in the light of the Commission's *avis*, Couve showed the same readiness to defy the majority opinion which he had demonstrated in July.[22] Indeed, he seemed totally undeterred by the fact that the Commission's report had largely contradicted most of the alarmist predictions he had made earlier in the year, reiterating much of the same case and adding a few new lines of argument, some of which were even less convincing than those advanced in the summer. It may have been somewhat demeaning for the Council's foremost debater to be reduced to claiming, for instance, that it would be much harder for an enlarged Community to devise the planned common transport policy since none of the new member states would share a direct interest in river transport on the Rhine, but there could be no doubting the French Foreign Minister's dogged determination to hold firm to his position and prevent full membership negotiations from opening.[23]

French defiance was, of course, nothing new in a Community context. For much of the mid-1960s, Gaullist France had found itself in a minority position over Community affairs, hence Couve was well accustomed to stubborn rearguard fights. But in the case of the discussions about enlargement, the French could draw solace from at least two factors. The first was that both the opening and the completion of any accession negotiations were clearly matters on which unanimous agreement amongst the member states had to be reached. Legally, therefore, the French were well within their rights to block the process, however objectionable this appeared to their EEC partners and to the candidate states. Second, the French were very aware that none of their partners wished to engage in another major confrontation. The six month stand-off between the Five and the French, known as the 'empty chair' crisis, was still much too fresh in the memories of all those involved in the Brussels discussions (the crisis had only been resolved in January 1966) for anybody in the Community to wish a further large-scale dispute.[24] The Council debates about enlargement, while polarised, were therefore characterised by a remarkable degree of restraint in the language used by both sides; the type of threat discourse which had become rife as the Community headed towards crisis in 1965 was notable by its absence in 1967. The Commission report on the July 1967 debate, for instance, commented that it 'was conducted with seriousness and vigour, but without bitterness'.[25]

Until late 1967 the French appear to have been hoping that the enlargement issue might just go away. Either the Five would conclude that, in the light of the Council impasse, the continuation of discussions was worse than useless and allow the issue to be quietly shelved, or the British themselves would decide that they were unlikely to progress in Brussels and therefore withdraw their candidacy. Unfortunately for Paris, such calculations underestimated the determination of both the British and their allies among the Five. In Brussels, and especially Bonn, the hope remained alive that if some procedural method could be found to allow the discussions between the British and the Community to begin, the logic of events might draw the French into a position where their objections to enlargement would become unsustainable.[26] In London, Wilson had attached too much of his own credibility to the application for a meek withdrawal to be a feasible option. Hence, like two wary but determined fencers, the French and the Five circled each other, neither daring to launch a full-scale attack, nor willing or able to retreat. Britain meanwhile could only stand and watch the two duellists, urging the Five onwards, but unable to enter the fray itself. A stalemate appeared to have been established which could last indefinitely.

In these tense and frustrating circumstances for both sides, the devaluation of the pound on 18 November 1967, appeared to offer the

French an opportunity to break the impasse. Just as the Nassau deal in December 1962 had provided de Gaulle with a wonderful pretext to bring the first membership negotiations to an end, so the devaluation of sterling seemed to vindicate many of the French concerns about the state of the British economy and justify their sceptical stance towards the second British application. The Five were at pains to deny that this was the case. At a Council meeting on 20 November, minister after minister lined up to praise Britain's 'courageous' decision and to argue that the fall of the pound would make it easier rather than harder for Britain to cope with the challenge of Community membership.[27] But de Gaulle was not to be deterred; on 27 November, he convened another of his celebrated press conferences, and told the assembled journalists that:

> To let Britain enter, and to this end to start a negotiation, would be … to agree in advance to … the destruction of an edifice [the Community] which has been built at the cost of so much effort and amid so many hopes.

France, he went on to make clear, was not ready to allow this to happen.[28] Having chosen to ignore the 'velvet' veto of May 1967, Britain and its allies had now been confronted with the iron fist.

To most British observers, both at the time and since, this second intervention by de Gaulle appeared to confirm that it was futile to continue pressing a second application on the Community. Many had always harboured severe doubts about whether it would prove possible to overcome Gaullist hesitations about British membership;[29] in light of this new, and all too clear, *prise de position* by the French President, there was little point in continuing to pursue an unattainable target. The 'Great Debate' about Britain's role in Europe would continue, and both main political parties remained committed to taking Britain into the EEC, but it was generally recognised that such a development would only be possible once de Gaulle had left office. In Whitehall, the preparations for membership negotiations were put on the back burner. But among Britain's allies on the continent, reactions were rather more heated. Although privately most governments resigned themselves to having to wait further for Community enlargement, there was a strong sense that de Gaulle should not be allowed to get away with his second veto unchallenged. Such views were to become very apparent at the Council meeting in Brussels on 18–19 December. At first, admittedly, this meeting seemed to be dominated by no more than a reiteration of well-established views.

Indeed, the only noticeable change in the early stages of the meeting was that the French case had been significantly strengthened by sterling's woes, and that even the most Anglophile of delegations was obliged to admit that immediate entry in such circumstances was not a viable option. But none of the Five was prepared to accept the French claim that British economic difficulties should be resolved before the start of negotiations; on the contrary, they maintained that Britain's own efforts to strengthen its economy should proceed in parallel with the membership negotiations in Brussels, which were anyway expected to be prolonged. The prospect of imminent entry into the Community would, moreover, help the recovery of the British economy and provide the government with an additional incentive to make the necessary short-term sacrifices.[30]

Aware of the need to resolve the issue, one way or the other, and keen to avoid an outright Community crisis, the German Presidency encouraged the members of the Council to agree to a written document, setting out clearly the five-to-one divergence of opinion. This text would concede that in the circumstances the start of membership negotiations was impossible, but state openly that five member states and the Commission would have wished otherwise. As such, it would have drawn a partial line under the affair. But while the final textual amendments to this document were being discussed, the Commission, the Dutch, the Belgians and the Italians launched an almost unprecedented protest against the unsatisfactory nature of this conclusion. As a result, while a text was eventually agreed, it was accompanied by unilateral statements by the three disgruntled member states, deploring France's unilateral campaign to block enlargement and reserving the right to revive the issue at any time in the future. Symbolically, the British application (and those of the other three applicants) would continue to feature on the Council agenda.[31]

As would become clear over the following months, this rebellion was not just a momentary flash of anger. Instead, it was an early sign that de Gaulle's 1967 veto had failed to end Community discussions of enlargement as his 1963 veto had done. On the earlier occasion, the French President's press conference had sparked angry reactions from most of the Five. The Dutch and the Italians had even, though briefly and somewhat half-heartedly, flirted with retaliatory measures designed to obstruct French EEC priorities.[32] But such countermeasures had proved short-lived, and within months the Community had edged itself back into normal operation. The success of Gerhard Schröder's so-called action plan of mid-1963 had underlined the extent to which the Six had put behind them their disagreement over

British membership.[33] But in 1967 the Five did not allow the issue of enlargement to be shelved in the same fashion. Their short-term anger may have subsided somewhat, but throughout the ensuing two years, enlargement was repeatedly discussed. Council debates of the issue, which had been entirely absent from the period between January 1963 and May 1967, became a regular occurrence during 1968 and 1969, repeatedly drawing to Brussels heavyweight figures like Brandt, Luns and Couve, who might otherwise have dispatched subordinates to 'normal' Council sessions. Furthermore, virtually all attempts to debate the Community's future development – a priority in the late 1960s, given the fact that the original EEC agenda was all but complete – were stymied by the unresolved 'British question'. Even suggestions as seemingly innocuous as the French desire to introduce a European patent scheme, were hijacked by the Dutch, Italians and Belgians who insisted that no such step could be taken in a grouping which did not include Britain and the Scandinavians.[34] As de Gaulle's successor, Georges Pompidou, was wearily to acknowledge to Georg Kiesinger, the German Chancellor, Britain had haunted virtually every Council meeting of the preceding two years and would continue to do so until the issue of Community enlargement was satisfactorily resolved.[35]

CONCLUSION

De Gaulle's apparent success in barring Britain's route once more was always likely to be a Pyrrhic victory. Although of scant immediate comfort to disappointed British negotiators, the 1967 bid had actually served to make the expansion of Community membership seem a much more likely prospect in the medium term. After all, the strength of the pro-enlargement consensus amongst the Five had seemingly grown considerably since 1963. Few of those uncomfortable doubts about Britain's own commitment, which had persisted after the first de Gaulle veto, were allowed to survive a second. Instead, the conviction grew still firmer that it was only the ageing French leader who stood between Britain and the EEC. It was no longer worth asking 'if' the Community would widen; the only real uncertainty was 'when'.

That this was so appeared even more unquestionable in the light of the ineffectiveness of the French case in 1967. Anger at the 1963 veto, while real, had always been somewhat mitigated by the belief that there might well have been a legitimate French case behind the General's intervention. In other words, the method taken to end the negotiations had been unfair, but the harbouring of doubts about enlargement was legitimate. Nowhere had such views been more apparent than in the European Commission.[36] But by 1967 the Commission's volte-face on British membership was indicative of a more general weakening of the anti-enlargement case. This was confirmed by the deeply unconvincing performance of Couve in the Council discussions. Of all the French Foreign Minister's plethora of arguments thrown against the case for immediate enlargement, only those centring on the weakness of the British economy gave any sign of having hit the mark. The rest were largely ignored by the Five or brushed aside with comparative ease. The prospects of France being able to mount an effective assault on enlargement without having to resort to a Presidential veto had never looked so poor, particularly if the short-term problems of the British economy were resolved.

Furthermore, the extent to which even France would remain opposed to enlargement became much more questionable as a result of the lingering tensions over British membership which so complicated the Community's operations during 1968 and 1969. Although the Community continued to function with just six member states, and as such to fulfil the multiple French national interests which were served by European integration, Paris came increasingly to recognise that no significant forward movement would be possible until the impasse over enlargement had been resolved. The French governmental consensus in favour of barring Britain's path thus began to disintegrate even before de Gaulle resigned from the Presidency. Once he had gone, however, a softening of the French line on British membership was almost inevitable. Pompidou, of course, was too shrewd a politician to give way on enlargement without obtaining the maximum possible *quid pro quo* from his Community partners and before having pushed British negotiators almost to breaking point.[37] But having observed at first hand the disruption which de Gaulle's two vetoes had caused, Pompidou went into the enlargement negotiations of 1970–72 resolved not to resort to a third Presidential intervention. The prospects of success of Heath's negotiators were considerably improved as a result. The 1967 failure should therefore be seen as much as a staging post *en route* to the success of 1973, as it was a reprise of the 1961–63 debacle.

NOTES

1. N. P. Ludlow, *Dealing with Britain: The Six and the First UK Application to the EEC* (Cambridge: Cambridge University Press, 1997), pp. 244–9.
2. For the text of de Gaulle's press conference, see C. de Gaulle, *Discours et Messages, Volume V* (Paris: Plon, 1970), pp. 168–74.

3. Council of Ministers Archives, Brussels (CMA): I/4/67 (GB2), extrait de procès-verbal de la réunion restreinte tenue à l'occasion de la deuxième session du conseil, 10–11 July 1967.
4. Ibid.; Richard Cobden, laissez-faire economist of the Manchester school.
5. European Commission Historical Archives, Brussels (ECHA): BDT 144/92, carton 179, G(67)207, compte rendu de la deuxième réunion du conseil, 11 July 1967.
6. Public Record Office (PRO): FCO 30/102, record of a conversation between the Foreign Secretary and the President of the Commission of the European Communities at the British Embassy, The Hague, 4 July 1967.
7. For a detailed discussion of French negotiating tactics during the first application, see Ludlow, *Dealing With Britain*, pp. 157–61, 238–40.
8. For more on the evolution of Conservative Party policy on Europe during the Wilson years, see Chapter 3 in this volume.
9. CMA: I/4/67 (GB2), extrait de procès-verbal de la réunion restreinte tenue à l'occasion de la deuxième session du conseil, 10 and 11 July 1967.
10. Ibid.
11. Ibid.
12. M. Couve de Murville, *Un Politique Etrangère, 1958–1969* (Paris: Plon, 1971), p. 405.
13. For a more detailed discussion of the Commission and the first British application, see N. P. Ludlow, 'Influence and Vulnerability: The Role of the European Commission', in R. Griffiths and S. Ward (eds), *Courting the Common Market: The First Attempt to Enlarge the EEC, 1961–3* (London: Lothian Foundation Press, 1996), pp. 139–55, and Ludlow, *Dealing With Britain*, pp. 165–6, 240–1.
14. ECHA: COM(61) PV 155 final, deuxième partie, 26 July 1961, and COM(67) PV 401 final, deuxième partie, 3 May 1967.
15. ECHA: COM(61) PVs 402 and 403, 10 and 17 May 1967.
16. N. Beloff, *The General Says No: Britain's Exclusion from Europe* (Harmondsworth: Penguin, 1963), p. 123.
17. See A. Varsori, 'The Art of Mediation: Italy and Britain's Attempt to Join the EEC, 1960–3', S. Lee, 'Germany and the First Enlargement Negotiations, 1961–3', and R. Dingemans and A. Boekestijn, 'The Netherlands and the Enlargement Proposals', all in A. Deighton and A. S. Milward (eds), *Widening, Deepening and Acceleration: The European Economic Community 1957–1963* (Brussels: Nomos-Verlag, 1999), pp. 241–56, 211–24, 225–41 respectively.
18. PRO: FCO 30/102, Record of a conversation between the Foreign Secretary and the President of the Commission of the European Communities at the British Embassy, The Hague, 4 July 1967.
19. PRO: FCO 30/102, Marjoribanks to Foreign Office, 3 July 1967.
20. PRO: FCO 30/103, Marjoribanks to Foreign Office, 30 September 1967.
21. ECHA: COM(67)750, 'Opinion on the Applications for Membership received from the United Kingdom, Ireland, Denmark and Norway', 29 September 1967.
22. CMA: I/14/67 (GB10), extrait du procès-verbal de la réunion restreinte tenue à l'occasion de la neuvième session du conseil, 23–24 October 1967.
23. Ibid.
24. For details about the crisis, see J. Newhouse, *Collision in Brussels: The Common Market Crisis of 30 June 1965* (London: Faber & Faber, 1967).
25. ECHA: BDT 144/92; Carton 179; G(67)207, compte rendu de la deuxième réunion du conseil, 11 July 1967.
26. See PRO: FCO 30/102, Marjoribanks to Foreign Office, 27 September 1967, for one such suggestion from the Commission.
27. CMA: I/15/67 (GB11), extrait du procès-verbal de la réunion restreinte tenue à l'occasion de la treizième session du conseil, 20 November 1967.
28. De Gaulle, *Discours et Messages*, pp. 243–4.
29. B. Pimlott, *Harold Wilson* (London: HarperCollins, 1993), p. 438.
30. CMA: I/8/68 (GB5), extrait de procès-verbal de la réunion restreinte tenue à

l'occasion de la dix-huitième session du conseil, 18 and 19 December 1967.

31. Ibid. For the indignant French reaction to these events, see Service Générale de Coopération Interministérille archives (Fontainebleau), Versement 900639.
32. Ludlow, *Dealing With Britain*, pp. 213–19, 227–8.
33. For details of the action plan, see O. Bange, 'Picking Up the Pieces: Schröder's Working Programme for the European Communities and the Solution to the 1963 Crisis' (unpublished PhD thesis, University of London, 1997).
34. CMA: R/2111/68 (PV/CONS/R 10), procès-verbal de la réunion restreinte tenue à l'occasion de la 51ième session du conseil, 4 and 5 November 1968.
35. Pompidou papers, 5AG2/1010, entretien en tête à tête entre le Chancelier Kiesinger et le Président Pompidou.
36. See, for instance, R. Marjolin, *Architect of European Unity: Memoirs 1911–1986* (London: Weidenfeld & Nicolson, 1989), p. 338.
37. To appreciate just how hard the French did push Britain in 1970–72, see U. Kitzinger, *Diplomacy and Persuasion: How Britain Joined the Common Market* (London: Thames & Hudson, 1973) and C. O'Neill, *Britain's Entry into the European Community: Report on the Negotiations of 1970–1972* (London: Frank Cass, 2000).

8

John Bull v. Marianne, Round Two: Anglo-French Relations and Britain's Second EEC Membership Bid

ANTHONY ADAMTHWAITE

In November 1967 Charles de Gaulle vetoed Britain's second application for membership of the European Economic Community (EEC). The veto came as no surprise: from the summer of 1966 the French government had made it clear that it would oppose a renewed application, and accounts of the episode have consequently treated the failure of the second bid as a foregone conclusion. Scholarly interest has tended to focus on the motivation of the Labour leadership, which swung from opposing membership in 1962 to advocacy in 1967.[1] As a result, the dynamics of the Anglo-French relationship have received remarkably little attention, a gap in the historiography which has been exacerbated by the relatively poor quality of French archival material on this period. Having discussed in more detail the nature of the sources, this chapter concentrates on three main issues. It opens by highlighting the limited state of foreign policy innovation and planning in Paris and London, which led to a distinct lack of strategic thinking on major foreign policy issues under both de Gaulle and Harold Wilson. Together with their historic rivalry for the leadership of Europe, it might seem inevitable that they could not develop closer relations in the EEC context. The second part speculates on Wilson's decision to apply for membership at a time when Anglo-French relations had hit a nadir during bilateral discussions in the summer of 1966. The final part continues to unravel Wilson's motives in light of the 'probe' of EEC capitals at the beginning of 1967. Paradoxically, the Prime Minister seems to have become more energised the more frosty Britain's relations with France became, and the more the 'friendly five' (Belgium, Germany, Italy, Luxembourg and the Netherlands) made it plain they would not support Britain at the risk of upsetting France. It points to vanity, a dearth of alternatives and opportunism as the main factors in Wilson's approach to Europe.

Two contentions flow from this analysis. The first is that the failure of the 1967 bid was not inevitable. True, the roadblocks were formidable, but they might have been cleared. In de Gaulle's own words, 'there were no mountains between England and France'.[2] Missing from the Anglo-French exchanges was any sense of a real *entente*. Harold Macmillan's ability to play the nuclear card had been stymied by President John Kennedy in 1961. But Wilson in 1966 might have played the alliance card: trying to develop a strategy that included a redefinition of Anglo-American relations might have tempted de Gaulle. The second contention is that the 1960s offered a major opportunity to reposition western Europe in world politics, an opportunity that would not reoccur until the 1990s. Arguably, an effective Anglo-French alliance powering the European Community might have successfully accomplished what France was incapable of creating single-handedly: a 'European Europe', partner rather than client of the United States, with the potential to broker East–West *détente*. In sum, more imaginative statecraft in 1966–67 would have promoted a European rescue of national foreign policies.

SOURCES

Analysing French foreign policy poses particular methodological problems. Before attempting to reconstruct the Anglo-French relationship under Wilson and de Gaulle, it is therefore useful to identify a major impediment to this exercise: the nature of the source material. Far more is available on the British side than on the French. In the Fifth Republic, foreign affairs and defence were General de Gaulle's domain, yet comparatively little is known about his day-to-day decision-making. *Memoires d'Espoir*, like all memoirs, is selective and misleading.[3] Conversations reported tend to be retrospective reconstructions rather than accurate summaries from the archives. The only personal papers available are those published in *Lettres, Notes et Carnets*, of which a mere handful relate directly to international affairs.[4] Cabinet minutes and the main presidential files, with a few exceptions, remain closed. The main archival source for the General's conduct of policy is thus the official record of discussions and meetings with foreign leaders and ambassadors. This series, *Entretiens et*

Messages, forms the backbone of Maurice Vaïsse's masterly overview of Gaullist foreign policy. However, as Vaïsse warns, great caution is needed, because the official record does not necessarily convey the President's true opinions and may mislead as much as it informs. The General carefully courted his interlocutors, for example telling the British how bad the Germans were and vice versa. More seriously, comparisons reveal significant differences of content between the French text and the British and German versions of the same conversation, discrepancies that result from the casualness of Elysée record-keeping procedures. Sometimes de Gaulle relied on his interpreter's notes, sometimes he gave a verbal summary to an aide.[5] Alas, Quai d'Orsay (Ministry of Foreign Affairs) files do not fill the large gaps. Predictably, since high policy was made by the President in the Elysée, the published collection, *Documents Diplomatiques Français*, has little to say about policy-making, nor has it yet reached 1964. The foreign ministry records contain masses of incoming cables and dispatches, but few traces of strategic discussions.

British Foreign Office papers are, by contrast, much more illuminating about internal office thinking. The contrast reflects a fundamental difference in record-keeping practice. In London, incoming traffic moved up the hierarchical ladder, gathering minutes and recommendations. Consequently, on major issues, file annotations provide the type of insights into official opinion that Paris almost totally lacks. Of course, the record usually needs fleshing out from private papers, letters and diaries, but here again the French paper trail is thinner than the British. For example, three members of the second Wilson government published diaries, compared to only one French minister. Although Wilson's papers remain closed, the authorised biography makes extensive use of them.[6] It is important to bear the primary source limitations in mind because they hamper one's ability to uncover precisely what the General was thinking at a particular time. Nonetheless, it is possible to identify the main obstacles to a closer Anglo-French relationship in the period 1964–67.

RIVAL DECISION-MAKING

Analysis of decision-making in London and Paris is important because it helps to explain the lack of constructive solutions to the Anglo-French quarrel over the EEC. On the French side, there were severe limitations on the development of a foreign policy that would promote *entente* with Britain. The major reason is that de Gaulle was responsible for foreign and defence matters, leaving the Quai to carry out his wishes. American Secretary of State Dean Rusk recalled visiting the Elysée:

> the French prime minister and foreign minister came in after we had arrived and I watched with amazement as the prime minister walked up to de Gaulle, gave a little schoolboy bow, clicked his heels and presented himself much like a cadet at St Cyr. The foreign minister did the same.[7]

The Cabinet was virtually a rubber stamp to policy already set out by de Gaulle. No general discussion took place, a situation exacerbated by the General rarely disclosing his intentions in Cabinet or elsewhere. Typically, Foreign Minister Maurice Couve de Murville would make a statement on current issues, followed by the next item on the agenda. On key issues such as British entry into the Community, de Gaulle would go round the table asking each minister for his opinion, but it was not an invitation to debate. Following de Gaulle's 1963 veto on British entry, American Ambassador Charles Bohlen talked with 'at least ten Cabinet officers … I received widely different interpretations and concluded that de Gaulle kept them in ignorance of what he was doing'.[8] Naturally, de Gaulle consulted ministers and leading officials, but it was done on a one-on-one basis and through *ad hoc* meetings of senior ministers. Such tight presidential control of defence and foreign policy tended to minimise or exclude wide-ranging reviews and discussions.

There were three other restraints on policy debates. First, the character of the Fifth Republic and de Gaulle's own eminence as leader of the Free French movement in 1940 and saviour of the state in 1958 inhibited the opening up of major policy issues. Unlike British ministers jockeying for position, the French were staunch Gaullists eager to serve. Key players such as Prime Minister Georges Pompidou and his predecessor Michel Debré may well have wanted British membership of the EEC as a counterweight to growing German power, but they were too loyal to challenge their master. The regime's strength thus seems to have acted as a restraint on new policy initiatives. Second, there was a fusion of political and administrative elites: one-third of ministers were senior civil servants compared with 12 per cent under the Fourth Republic. This gave strength and cohesion to the regime. Finally, there was a remarkable continuity of Foreign Ministry leadership which led to a certain inflexibility, a natural reluctance to rethink policies. Couve was Foreign Minister during 1958–68, Olivier Wormser, Director of Economic and Financial Affairs from 1954–66.

Such continuity of expertise gave France a distinct advantage over British elites. Couve, for instance, saw five British Foreign Secretaries come and go during his decade of office.

By contrast, Whitehall had several prime movers. Downing Street, the Foreign Office, the Cabinet, Cabinet Office and Treasury each contained their own groups of 'pro-marketeers' and 'anti-marketeers'. Officials and ministers continually wrestled with the question of whether Britain should reapply, rather than asking how French support could be secured for a new application. It can therefore be argued that the failure to address the crucial issue of Anglo-French relations in an enlarged Community resulted partly from Wilson's leadership style, partly from the deficiencies of the Whitehall policy-making machine and partly from the crisis-ridden climate of the mid-1960s. The Prime Minister was a superb tactician, not a strategist with long-term vision. Natural secrecy and taciturnity were reinforced by a calculated ambiguity, designed to promote constructive tension among those around him. Whereas de Gaulle was cocooned by a loyal and committed machine, Wilson had to run the gauntlet of ambitious rivals and sceptical colleagues and advisors. In Cabinet, Douglas Jay and Barbara Castle headed a sizeable group of anti-marketeers; at Number Ten, the strong scepticism of Political Secretary Marcia Williams and Economics Advisor Thomas Balogh was balanced by the EEC enthusiasm of Private Secretary Michael Palliser. At the Cabinet Office, Cabinet Secretary Burke Trend and William Neild favoured entry, perhaps explaining why Wilson put Neild in charge of a special unit in the Cabinet Office on Community membership. Wilson's was a brilliant tightrope act that avoided open splits and resignations, but the excessive secrecy and ambiguity kept everyone guessing and inhibited full and timely debate. Even the Chancellor, James Callaghan, was left asking in November 1966, 'what's Harold playing at?'.[9]

Ironically, given Wilson's electoral hype about 'technological revolution', the performance of the two governmental machines was like the difference between a French TGV and a British local train, slowly bumping its way along. The pragmatic, short-termist civil service culture did not encourage long-range thinking. There was an overwhelming case for a stronger Cabinet Office with a think-tank, in order to coordinate the competing claims of major Whitehall departments. The example of Macmillan's Future Policy Committee of 1959 which had essayed a ten-year overview was not followed, and the Central Policy Review Staff (CPRS) was a creation of Edward Heath's government in 1971. To make matters worse, Whitehall was in the throes of modernisation: the Plowden Report of 1963 led to the merger of the Foreign Office and Commonwealth Relations Office in 1968, coinciding with the Fulton Report that same year which called for an overhaul of the civil service.[10] Modernisation came at the worst moment for British politics. Buffeted by economic and financial storms, oppressed by devaluation pressures, beset by international challenges in Rhodesia, Vietnam, Indonesia, Aden and Nigeria, Wilson and his colleagues seem to have been unable to think or plan more than a few days ahead. Wilson's memoirs, wittingly or unwittingly, capture the feeling of an administration living from one crisis to the next. 'Drift without due consideration of consequences seems to be the order of the day', Balogh complained.[11]

Different leadership styles and government machines are only part of the explanation for the failure to promote a new entente; competing European agendas also presented a major obstacle. London and Paris projected rival visions of Europe: an 'Atlanticist Europe', allowing Britain to dominate western Europe and keeping close ties with the United States, versus a French-led 'European Europe', as far as possible independent, armed with its own nuclear deterrent and acting as a 'Third Force' between the superpowers. 'We believe General de Gaulle's concept of European unity and of the future relationship between Europe and the United States to be fundamentally opposed to our own', declared Foreign Secretary Michael Stewart.[12] De Gaulle accused Britain of wanting an American Europe:

> A Europe which in its economy and still more in its defence and in its politics would be placed under an inexorable American hegemony. A Europe in which every European country, starting with our own, would lose its soul.[13]

Opposing agendas expressed historic national rivalry and enmity reaching back to the Hundred Years' War. The perception of policymakers was that Britain and France were contending for the leadership of Europe. De Gaulle's Agriculture Minister Edgar Pisani had explained the January 1963 veto to his British counterpart, Christopher Soames, in those very terms: 'My friend, it's very simple. Now, with the six [*sic*], there are five hens and a cock. If you join (with other countries) there will be perhaps seven or eight hens but with two cocks. So it won't be as pleasant.'[14] Paul Reynaud, Prime Minister in 1940, claimed that when he protested about de Gaulle's 1963 veto he received an empty envelope in the General's handwriting with the sentence 'if undelivered please forward to Waterloo, Belgium'.[15]

Yet too much can be made of historical and cultural differences. De Gaulle's attitude towards Britain was ambivalent: the efforts of Winston Churchill and Franklin Roosevelt to oust him as Free French leader were bitterly resented, yet he was also grateful for Churchill's welcome in June 1940. Indeed, the different visions of Europe were overridden when London and Paris judged agreement both necessary and desirable, so despite the war of words in the wake of the 1963 veto, fences were mended. Several important bilateral technological projects were promoted, including Channel Tunnel feasibility studies, the supersonic airliner Concorde and joint military aircraft projects.[16] Significantly, de Gaulle did not allow the past to stand in his way when in February 1969 he offered Britain political partnership.

MENDING FENCES, 1964–65

Conditions for a Franco-British rapprochement did not look favourable in 1964. The Wilson Cabinet of October 1964 with its miniscule parliamentary majority of four was not in the best position to launch major initiatives on Europe. Party and Cabinet were split on Community membership, so, predictably, the new government asserted its Atlanticist and Commonwealth sympathies. What was new, however, was the desire to repair Anglo-French relations, the Prime Minister approving an American suggestion for Anglo-French talks on Africa and signalling his wish to meet de Gaulle. But it did not appear that mistrust of Britain across the Channel had dissipated: although the General expressed a readiness to welcome the new British leader, privately he was full of misgivings about the Labour government and Britain's role in the world. As a nation, he said, Britain seemed in free fall, drained by the sacrifices of the Second World War and now virtually an American colony. Good leaders, he lamented, were lacking: 'They have only wimps leading them, starting with the Socialists. And they are under America's heel.' As for Wilson: 'I will perhaps receive him, but there will be no negotiations. I cannot stop him coming to see me … he's a madcap … wants to make mischief … he beats on every drum … pound sterling, the multilateral force, Concorde, anything.' However, de Gaulle was optimistic for Britain's future. The British, he confided to Information Minister Alain Peyrefitte, had too much energy and vitality to accept an American empire. Revival would come, 'but no one can say when'. And, significantly, he did not wish to add to Britain's troubles, instructing Peyrefitte, 'above all, don't say anything which might seem to overwhelm them. You can see that they are down on their luck. When we were in a worse state after the collapse they still supported us.'[17]

Churchill's funeral on 30 January 1965 brought the two leaders together sooner than anticipated. In style and appearance they seemed poles apart: the tall, aloof, monarchical President speaking a pure classical French, the shorter pipe-smoking Prime Minister in his new Gannex raincoat, cultivating a Yorkshire accent. A 50-minute talk at the French embassy served as an icebreaker, and de Gaulle 'let the press know that we had made an extremely good start in our relationship'.[18] But such top-level niceties papered over fundamental tensions in the relationship. Preparing for Wilson's visit to Paris in early April the Quai d'Orsay took stock of British policy. The principal voice in formulating Quai views was Olivier Wormser, Director of Economic and Financial Affairs since 1954, influential in shaping the Quai's response to Macmillan's entry bid in 1961. Wormser's analysis overflowed with scepticism and suspicion. Britain, he argued, after trying to make France the scapegoat for the failure of its first entry bid, had adopted a more nuanced approach, combining a strong presence in European institutions like the Council of Europe with efforts to reinvigorate the European Free Trade Association (EFTA). Notwithstanding Wilson's friendly words to de Gaulle at Churchill's funeral, and signs of renewed public interest in the Community, the Foreign Office wanted 'to find a way of meddling in the affairs of the Six, doubtless to paralyse them'. It had consistently sought to minimise cooperation between the Six while highlighting similar arrangements among the seven EFTA states, as well as denying the importance of Franco-German cooperation by organising Franco-British and Anglo-German consultations.[19]

The April meeting generated agreements on Concorde, the Jaguar military aircraft, the Channel Tunnel and high-level discussions on Africa and the Middle East. But the opportunity to explore French thinking on a renewed membership bid and perhaps seek a common position on European cooperation was missed. At the first meeting on 2 April, de Gaulle offered a cue, wondering 'whether the Prime Minister wished to talk about Europe, the Common Market was making progress'. Being both unprepared and unwilling, Wilson did not respond, talking instead about East–West relations and Vietnam. The next day he took the lead, asking 'How de Gaulle viewed developments in Europe', carefully closing off the membership issue: 'Britain would always be prepared to talk about joining on terms which would reconcile her national and Commonwealth interests, taking a realistic view it could not be said that that situation obtained today.'[20] Overnight Wilson had got his lines together, but Stewart was caught out. At a separate Foreign Ministers' meeting Couve skilfully took the lead, opening the conversation with a direct question: did Britain intend to enter the Common Market? Astonishingly, Stewart had not been briefed for a membership question and improvised.[21] The outcome was an increasingly acerbic exchange about the responsibilities for failure in 1963. Stewart implied that the French had changed their tune, blaming at the time the 'special relationship' and now saying that agricultural policy had been the problem. The Paris talks confirmed that neither Downing Street nor the Foreign Office wanted to reopen the membership issue. France's London Ambassador, Geoffrey de Courcel, recalled Wilson saying: 'Personally the Common Market is of no interest to me. What we must do is set up Anglo-French cooperation.'[22] Nor were officials pushing for a new initiative, otherwise Stewart would surely have been adequately briefed. Con O'Neill, Ambassador to the EEC and a leading 'Europhile', concluded that for the present Britain could do nothing.[23] Yet if the British had made an overture the French might have been receptive. The Community tensions that climaxed in the 'empty chair' crisis of July 1965 were already palpable, as indeed was France's disappointment with the fruits of the 1963 Franco-German treaty.

Within months of the April meeting Wilson edged towards a new EEC application, and by October 1966 the Cabinet had authorised the Prime Minister and new Foreign Secretary, George Brown, to conduct a 'probe' in the capitals of the Six. Why and when did Wilson decide on a second bid? Had he reason to believe that de Gaulle would now allow British entry? The why is much easier to answer than the when. Wilson's secretive, taciturn and opportunistic personality made him hard to fathom. With his Cabinet and party divided on Europe, he played his cards close to his chest. Two dates have been suggested for the decision to make a second membership bid: either after the landslide electoral victory of March 1966 or after the July sterling crisis. The decision was not the outcome of a long and hard policy review, nor a Pauline conversion on the flight to Brussels, but, as Robert Lieber suggests, a case of 'collapsing alternatives'.[24] Although there were hints in the spring of 1966 that Paris might welcome another bid, French signals were ambiguous and certainly did not drive the new approach. One can indeed point to several other proximate causes of the revival of interest in the EEC. On the political side, in the early 1960s Labour scepticism about the EEC sprang partly from the belief that the balancing of Churchill's 'three circles' of the Commonwealth, the English-speaking world and Europe was still the best formula for Britain's external policy. However, by 1965–66 two of the circles, the Commonwealth and the English-speaking world, were looking much the worse for wear. Successive crises in South Africa, Aden, Rhodesia, Cyprus and Malaysia overwhelmed the former; junior partnership with the United States had been replaced by military and economic dependence. Wilson's determination to avoid devaluation made sterling dependent on American backing but, paradoxically, support for American intervention in Vietnam exposed the government to increasing criticism. External political forces also helped to make up Wilson's mind. EEC strength, especially West Germany's, was perceived as a threat to the 'special relationship'. Joining, it was believed, would confirm Britain as America's gateway to Europe. On the economic side, as Britain sank deeper into the financial mire, the EEC, with its high growth rate, began to seem like a lifeboat which would rescue the economy and stave off devaluation until Britain was safely inside. Moreover, with public opinion polls surging in favour of EEC membership, it was obvious that if Wilson did not take a new initiative, Heath's Conservatives would play the 'Europe' card at the next election. These combined with internal pressures from industry, and within Whitehall, to launch a second application.[25]

France was not a passive player in the decision-making process. It inadvertently gave encouragement to Wilson through its unilateral action on the EEC and North Atlantic Treaty Organisation (NATO) fronts. Two events in particular highlight this point: the EEC 'empty chair' crisis and France's departure from NATO's integrated command structure in March 1966. Confirmation that France would oppose a supranational federal Europe was reassuring and suggested that once inside the Community Britain would have opportunities to wrest the initiative from France. However, in terms of direct encouragement, little was forthcoming. The visit of Prime Minister Georges Pompidou and Foreign Minister Couve on 6–7 July 1966 was the first high-level Anglo-French exchange since Wilson's Paris trip the previous year. How did the Quai d'Orsay now evaluate the evolution of British policy towards Europe? Wormser's was still the main voice and, unfortunately for Wilson, to describe his advice as negative would be an understatement. London, he warned, as in 1961–63, was seeking to distort the issues:

> It is said that Britain wants to know whether France will lift its veto on British membership. But for us what matters is to know whether Britain will be able to accept the rules of the Rome Treaty and the arrangements concluded since 1963. The British government wishes to become a member of the EEC but since it questions the essential characteristics one no longer knows for sure

whether it is a case of bringing the UK into the Common Market or, on the contrary, of bringing the Common Market into the Commonwealth and Efta [*sic*]. Having reversed the givens of the problem the British government hopes once again to make us a scapegoat and put us in the position of an accused before the negotiation has even opened ... people are speculating in London on the difficulty the French government will have in 'blocking' for a second time a British initiative. Moreover the Nato [*sic*] crisis in separating us from our allies facilitates a manoeuvre whose object is clearly to isolate us from the outset ... unless the British make a serious mistake our isolation will increase in the course of negotiations. These will take place between the Six and the British government, the commission [*sic*] giving only an opinion since it does not have a mandated role. So two things can happen: either the Six will negotiate separately – and very quickly it will be one against Six; or else as in 61–63 [*sic*] the Six decide to find first a common position. In this case France will be negotiating with England through intermediaries and its concerns will be challenged in two successive stages.

His conclusion was firm and unequivocal:

It is in the light of these considerations that the French government should define its position, keeping in mind that negotiations cannot lead to the British accepting our theses and thus the enlargement of the Community must by definition lead to a free trade zone, probably global.[26]

On the eve of the visit Wormser sharpened his advice:

A Community enlarged by the addition of Great Britain and its friends will be subject necessarily to centrifugal forces and liable to dissolution for political as well as economic reasons. This dissolution will take the form of an expanding free trade area, something which, rightly or wrongly, we have until now opposed. The Government, if it accepts Britain into the Common market, should have no illusions on this evolution.[27]

The Quai's economic expert argued that Britain had disabled itself in advance, by declaring its political will to enter the Community 'provided satisfactory conditions are obtained'. In other words, contended Wormser, Britain 'is not ready to accept the treaty arrangements ... notably the CAP but asks for the rules to be changed'. An analysis of Anglo-American relations completed the Foreign Ministry's assessment. Washington, which had striven to secure membership in 1961–63, still wanted Britain in the Community. However, an American-backed Britain posed a financial and political threat to France and its partners. The United States wanted to transfer British debts and deficits to the Community and Washington hoped that within a few years the federal potential of the EEC would be reasserted.[28] Much more than a Wilson charm offensive would have been required to neutralise the Quai d'Orsay's outlook. Britain's dire economic straits confirmed one of the main French arguments against entry: economic and financial unpreparedness. As Pompidou and Couve arrived, the prospects were already looking bleak, as sharp raids on sterling signalled the start of one of the worst sterling crises since 1945. And for much of May and June a seamen's strike paralysed the ports. One of the few skills the Wilson Cabinet displayed in their European policy was the knack of making a difficult situation worse, and the atmosphere was not improved by Defence Secretary Denis Healey's attack on de Gaulle 'as a bad ally in Nato [sic] and a bad partner in the Common Market'.[29]

The French had taken the measure of their hosts. At a pre-trip briefing the French delegation spoke 'with scarcely veiled contempt' about Wilson. Quizzed about First Secretary George Brown's support for the Community, they answered, Brown 'does not speak for Britain'.[30] The Quai's briefing papers for the visit acknowledged Wilson as a smart tactician 'who has displayed remarkable skill in dodging traps and in making others carry the heaviest responsibilities'. Stewart, though, was unimpressive:

> ... clumsy and self-effacing ... Stewart conceals under a legendary modesty solid administrative abilities ... without preconceived ideas in foreign policy he never risks himself beyond strict orthodoxy and the line decided by the Foreign Office who have found in him their most reliable spokesman.[31]

Brown was described as a son of a lorry driver, number two in party and government, 'a highly coloured personality, courageous and dynamic, renowned for his impulsiveness and imprudent language'.[32] Wilson's biographer did not exaggerate in describing the visit as 'disastrous'.[33] Wilson himself conceded that Pompidou was 'annoyed, and understandably so', when he cancelled one meeting because of a Commons debate on Vietnam and later missed a dinner in Pompidou's honour.[34] *Daily Mirror* editor Cecil King records Edward Heath's remarks:

> Pompidou had come over here with an invitation in his pocket for a state visit of the Queen. But he was so disgusted with his reception by Wilson that the invitation was never extended. He and Couve de Murville returned to France convinced that Wilson does not mean business over joining the Common Market.[35]

Paradoxically, however, the visit's main significance was to convince the French that Wilson *did* 'mean business'. From the record alone it is clear that Wilson was in earnest, but what vexed French ministers was the Prime Minister's adversarial style. Pompidou and Couve were sharply interrogated. Wilson also demanded assurances that after complex and lengthy negotiations France would not spring a veto because of the Anglo-American connection: 'at the end of the day would we have to choose between the US and Europe?' In vain the French wriggled, but the Prime Minister, like a Yorkshire terrier, harried them relentlessly. The irony of the cross-examination cannot have escaped either side; France's blocking tactics, as the discussions demonstrated, had now shifted to Britain's economic and financial unpreparedness. The question of membership, declared Couve, was 'essentially economic'; both he and Pompidou described the tough fiscal measures introduced in 1958 to prepare France for Common Market entry. The point was rammed home by a press briefing that a clean bill of financial and economic health would be a prerequisite for British entry. Pompidou was also quoted as saying that devaluation would be necessary before Britain could join. This briefing accelerated, perhaps intentionally, the run on the pound that peaked in the mid-July crisis.[36]

FROM PROBE TO VETO

Given the state of Anglo-French relations in 1965–66 the central question remains: why did Wilson persist with a second application when he and most of Whitehall knew 'that it is improbable that de Gaulle will let us in'?[37] Pompidou and Couve had left no doubt that France would use Britain's economic troubles to block entry. From Paris, Ambassador Sir Patrick Reilly advised that 'it is very unlikely that the French would be willing to start serious negotiations with us for a year at least'.[38] In his Bristol speech of March 1966 the Prime Minister had promised that entry talks would take place only 'if ... we are able to enter … from a situation of industrial strength'.[39] Vanity surely had a role. Wilson, like Macmillan before him, possessed an inflated opinion of his charm and persuasive powers. Once engaged, it was hard to retreat without serious loss of face. But the critical consideration was the lack of credible alternatives. Constructing a strong European role seemed the only viable option and to have put negotiations on hold for another year or so would have been a major political blunder, sending the wrong signal to the 'friendly five' (Belgium, Germany, Italy, Luxembourg and the Netherlands) and, more importantly, handing the initiative to de Gaulle and the Conservative Opposition. Although the prerequisite of a strong economy had not been fulfilled, the Chancellor declared that 'an attempt to enter Europe would give a boost to economic morale'.[40] Another reason for 'staying in the game' was the timing of devaluation. The domestic political fallout of devaluation would be better absorbed if it could be delayed until Britain's admission, or at least presented as a necessary part of ongoing entry talks. So Wilson forged ahead, partly *faute de mieux*, partly to keep France on the defensive.

The lack of attractive alternatives and awareness of slipping power became painfully apparent at the weekend meeting of ministers and officials at Chequers on 22 October 1966. This was the Cabinet's first opportunity for a full discussion of EEC membership. Of the three choices presented ('Going It Alone' (GITA), an Atlantic free trade area or the EEC) Community membership had the edge. But rather than deepen Cabinet divisions Wilson did not press for a straightforward decision to apply, suggesting instead that he and the new Foreign Secretary, Brown, should conduct a probe of the six capitals. The Paris embassy offered no hope. De Gaulle was currently focused on East–West rapprochement and would not welcome a new British initiative. Moreover, his remarks at his 28 October press conference had been cool. French officials displayed a 'marked reticence' on hearing of the probe. Reilly summed up: 'We can expect no helping hand from the General. On the contrary, the French are likely to do all they can to spread amongst the Five doubts and suspicions about our "real intentions".'[41] There were other soundings. In early December the Conservative Christopher Soames, Churchill's grandson, spoke to Couve and the now Housing Minister, Pisani, and concluded:

> French government's desire to see Britain in the Common Market was no greater today than it was in 1963. Should Britain accept the Rome Treaty asking only for reasonable transitional arrangements for New Zealand their next line of defence would be the

problems that flow from sterling ... you will find them arguing about our presence ... in Singapore and the Persian Gulf in regard to the load on our balance of payments.

'Much of what you say coincides with our own impressions', Wilson acknowledged.[42]

Despite the thumbs down from Paris, and prior to the official probe, Brown launched his own personal probe, meeting Couve on 14 December and de Gaulle two days later. For sheer banality, Brown's Paris talks would score highly on any list. Conversation opened with a children's game of 'first tell me what you want, then I'll tell you what I'll do':

> Couve: first you must tell us what you want
> Brown: you must tell us how you are going to respond when we come in January
> De Gaulle: you say you want to join – what do you want to do?
> Brown: I ask you in return what you want us to do.[43]

Then Brown, probably over-lubricated, confessed Britain's desperation to enter the Community: 'If we fail we'll have to rethink all our world position. So we must get in first with a minimum of conditions.' But since he could not describe Britain's current economic weakness as a plus, he clumsily talked of future benefits: 'entering the Common Market we will bring it a great advantage for we are the centre of the sterling zone; I mean, if we enter with a strong pound and a stable economy'. De Gaulle summed up: 'there is the Common Market and for us there is no problem, for you there is one; you want to get in and that's your problem'. In his memoirs Brown draws the inescapable conclusion that 'it was very clear that de Gaulle was adamantly against us'. But Brown did not circulate a record of the talks and speaking to Cabinet colleagues he prevaricated: 'It was difficult to form any conclusion about his [de Gaulle's] attitude towards our entry into the EEC ... we need not ... take it for granted that there would be French objection to our entry.'[44]

Paradoxically, the more the negatives, the more Wilson and Brown seemed energised. The probe went ahead, starting with Rome, then Paris and the other capitals. The embassy had advised leaving Paris until last, but it was placed second in order to avoid giving further substance to French criticism that Britain was intent on dividing France from the other member states. One reason for the probe was to discover whether the Five would be prepared to oppose de Gaulle in the event of a French veto. While the Italians were welcoming, Wilson confessed that it would be unrealistic to expect them 'to stand up to de Gaulle in the event of his deciding to veto our application', confirming what Whitehall should already have known: 'the Five would not be prepared to disrupt the EEC in order to force the French government to agree to our admittance'. Wilson put a good face on the predictably negative result of the Paris probe, telling the Cabinet that in terms of 'personal relationships' the visit had gone 'well'. However, their best efforts 'did not in any way appear to have changed the view of de Gaulle that he would prefer that we should not join the EEC at present'.[45]

De Gaulle's two vetoes torpedoing the British bid were therefore no surprise. From the summer of 1966 France's overall response had been a virtual veto. Why, then, were the vetoes of May and November necessary? The Cabinet's decision on 2 May to proceed with an application created a new situation to which de Gaulle wasted no time in responding. At his press conference on 16 May he applied what the British press called a 'velvet veto'. Optimists pointed out that it was not a rejection, since the President suggested that some form of association with the EEC might be more appropriate for Britain. But Hervé Alphand, Secretary-General at the Quai d'Orsay, confirmed that the General intended a veto and the reference to association was for cosmetic reasons only.[46] And Wilson treated it as a veto, declaring that he would not take no for an answer. This determination to keep knocking on the door, together with moves to isolate France, triggered the unambiguous veto of 27 November. Thus, French tactics were quite different from 1961–63, when de Gaulle had allowed negotiations with the Six to drag on for over 15 months before applying a veto. The change in tactics may have owed something to Wormser, Ambassador in Moscow since late 1966. Writing to Couve on 14 April, the former Director of Economic and Financial Affairs offered counsel on 'the English affair'. The choice, he wrote, was between nipping matters in the bud or risking a repeat of lengthy and potentially damaging negotiations ending in an impasse. He urged swift action.[47]

Wilson had one last try, flying to Paris on 18 June, anniversary of the battle of Waterloo, for two days of meetings at the Grand Trianon, Versailles. The talks were, however, a Waterloo for the Prime Minister: after three meetings with de Gaulle since January 1967 his diplomacy had failed.[48] '*Le président soleil*' lodged his guest in the newly refurbished Petit Trianon, professing friendship and goodwill but would not budge on British membership. Dinner was followed by a drive in the park in a fairly small car, Prime Minister and President in the back, interpreter in the front with the driver. It was a tight squeeze and the nearest they got to a rapprochement. In Cabinet, Wilson tried to put a positive spin on failure, although at least two colleagues, Healey and Richard Crossman, were unconvinced.[49] De Gaulle 'was now reviewing his whole position ... we should continue to press our application ... it seemed probable that he was now prepared to recognise the inevitability of our membership. If ... we maintained our pressure ... he felt ... there was a reasonable prospect of our succeeding.'[50] But privately the Premier admitted to Brown: 'He does not want us in and he will use all the delaying tactics he can ... I am not sure that he any longer has the strength to keep us out – a dangerous prophecy, as prophecy always is with the General.'[51] Dangerous indeed. Wilson, having exaggerated his powers of persuasion, now underestimated his opponent's skill and acumen. The purpose of the 27 November veto was precisely to avoid being ensnared in the quicksand of prolonged and tricky negotiations *à la* 1961–63.

Labour leaders were now between a rock and hard place. To withdraw the application and go it alone would be a humiliating admission of failure. Yet the application was clearly going nowhere fast. Mounting pressure on the pound, leading to devaluation in mid-November appeared to confirm the main French argument that Britain was not ready for entry. There was one curious coincidence. At the eleventh hour in January 1963, Couve had spoken to both Heath and American Under-Secretary of State for Economic Affairs George Ball in reassuring and upbeat terms. In September 1967 he told Brown that Britain was bound to enter the EEC. When asked when talks could begin he answered, 'certainly before the end of the year'.[52] Was it deliberate deception or was de Gaulle keeping him in the dark?

CONCLUSION

By the end of 1967 the two leading West European democracies had boxed themselves into a corner. De Gaulle managed to exclude Britain from the EEC for over a decade, but it was a hollow and temporary victory. The General's retirement in April 1969 cleared the way for the negotiations that led to entry in 1973. More to the point, the General's vision of a French-led 'European Europe' went unrealised. West Germany's growing political and economic power threatened French leadership. Moreover, after the Franco-German treaty of 1963, Bonn had reasserted ties with Washington, while events in Paris and Prague in 1968 exposed the weakness of Gaullism and the hollowness of de Gaulle's search for East–West *détente*. Nevertheless, de Gaulle had earned worldwide respect and prestige. For Britain there was no grandeur, only misery. The 1960s witnessed the sharpest contraction of power and influence since 1945.

Might the story have had a happier ending? 'The best way to organise Europe was around an Anglo-French entente', US Under-Secretary of State for Political Affairs Eugene Rostow advised Wilson.[53] A firm partnership at the heart of the EEC might have reinvigorated both countries, but de Gaulle overestimated France's ability to play an independent international role and Wilson knew that there was no mileage for Britain in such a course. Yet neither leader envisaged pooling resources in an entente. As bait for Britain's application Wilson offered only a handful of technological projects and vague talk of a 'technological community'. Shaken by the upheavals of 1968 and anxious about German strength, de Gaulle in February 1969 offered political partnership. It was two years too late: unsurprisingly, after so many rebuttals Wilson rejected it as a trap.

Why did London and Paris, given common interests in the containment of Germany and opposition to a supranational federal Europe, neglect an *entente*? Both leaderships were blinkered by *folie de grandeur*, preoccupied with independent great power roles. As a result, there was no radical questioning of policy choices. 'No prospect whatever of de Gaulle letting us in the Common Market', Palliser considered, 'unless we are prepared to make changes in our foreign policy and defence policy of such a substantial nature as to be, I believe, out of the question for any foreseeable British government.'[54] But no policy studies were initiated on what changes might have to be made. The 'special relationship' was taken as a given, and one important reason for joining the EEC was to safeguard the alliance by becoming the gateway to Europe. What was more, Germany, not France, was perceived as the real threat to British power. Brown warned colleagues on 30 April 1967 that 'the US was paying increasing regard to West Germany', and without British entry 'West Germany's influence on the US would more or less replace our own.'[55] Downing Street and Whitehall too readily assumed that de Gaulle shared British apprehensions and would be glad to admit Britain as a counterpoise. Cameron Cobbold, Governor of the Bank of England, reported to Wilson on a meeting with his French counterpart Wilfrid Baumgartner:

> Baumgartner personally takes the same view that I (and I believe you) do – that internationally speaking it would be political suicide for the French to keep us out and allow the Germans to boss

Europe in the difficult years following de Gaulle's disappearance.[56]

Thirty-five years on, the sheer sterility of British foreign policy towards the EEC remains striking. While de Gaulle lasted, Palliser opined, 'we ought to spend the intervening period in making life thoroughly difficult for the General by explaining to all and sundry how thoroughly willing we are to go in and thereby forcing de Gaulle to find much more explicit reasons for keeping us out'.[57] True, the negativity of British policy was in part the consequence of de Gaulle's attitude as well as of Britain's deteriorating international and domestic position. But it also reflected the quality of the Labour leadership and of Whitehall generally. When Wilson and de Gaulle compared their use of leisure, the Prime Minister's response suggested that he was intent on minimising or eliminating any time for reflection. After moving to Number Ten he was asleep 'within seconds of putting out the light'.[58] Brown, habitually drunk, was more liability than asset, surely one of the worst Foreign Secretaries of the century. During their six-capital probe Wilson and Brown overtly criticised each other. Of the many Brown stories, one will perhaps suffice. Meeting a distinguished French leader Brown summoned to his side junior minister Alun Chalfont, saying loudly: 'Here Chalfont, you speak this man's silly language. What's he on about?' The fact, noted Chalfont, 'that "this man" also spoke almost perfect English had evidently escaped his notice'.[59] Sceptics might say that even if the British had got their act together and offered an *entente*, de Gaulle would not have been interested. Frankly, one cannot say what would have happened, but at least it would have been worth a try.

NOTES

1. In particular, the personality and politics of the Prime Minister, whose long-term ambiguity on the European question is subject to intense scrutiny. See Chapter 1 in this book for analysis of the writing of Harold Wilson's European policy.
2. Press conference, 4 February 1965, quoted in M. Vaïsse, *La Grandeur: Politique Etrangère du General de Gaulle 1958–1969* (Paris: Fayard, 1998), p. 592.
3. C. de Gaulle, *Memoires d'Espoir: Vol. I, Le Renouveau, Vol. II, l'Effort* (Paris: Plon, 1970). For more on the making of French foreign policy, see L. Badel, 'Le Quai d'Orsay, la Grande-Bretagne et l'Élargissement de la Communauté (1963–1969): Aspects Fonctionnel et Culturel', in *50 Ans Après la Déclaration Schuman: Bilan de l'Histoire de la Construction Européene – Actes du Colloques de Nantes, 11–13 Mai 2000* (Nantes: CRHMA et Ouest-Editions, 2001), pp. 13–25, and L. Badel, 'Le Rôle tenu par la Poste d'Expansion Économique de Londres dans le Processus D'adhésion du Royaume-Uni au Marché Commun (1966–1971)', in R. Girault and R. Poidevin (eds), *Le Rôle des Ministères des Finances et de l'Economie dans la Construction*

Européene (1957–1978): Actes du Colloque Tenu à Bercy, 26–28 Mai 1999 (Paris: CHEFF, 2001), pp. 28–40.

4. C. de Gaulle, *Lettres, Notes et Carnets, Juillet 1966–Avril 1969* (Paris: Plon, 1987)

5. Vaïsse, *La Grandeur*, pp. 8–10.

6. P. Ziegler, *Wilson: The Authorised Life of Lord Wilson of Rievaulx* (London: Weidenfeld & Nicolson, 1993); T. Benn, *Out of the Wilderness: Diaries 1963–67* (London: Hutchinson, 1987); B. Castle, *The Castle Diaries, 1964–70* (London: Weidenfeld & Nicolson, 1984); R. Crossman, *The Diaries of a Cabinet Minister: Vol. I, Minister of Housing, 1964–66* (London: Hamish Hamilton and Jonathan Cape, 1977); R. Crossman, *The Diaries of a Cabinet Minister: Vol. II, Lord President of the Council and Leader of the House of Commons, 1966–68* (London: Hamish Hamilton and Jonathan Cape, 1976); A. Peyrefitte, *C'Etait de Gaulle, Vol. I, La France Redevient La France, Vol. II, La France Reprend sa Place a la Monde, Vol. III, Tout le Monde a Besoin d'une France qui Marche* (Paris: Fayard-de Fallois, 1994–2000).

7. D. Rusk, *As I Saw It* (New York: W. W. Norton, 1990), p. 271

8. C. E. Bohlen, *Witness to History, 1929–1969* (New York: W. W. Norton, 1973), p. 502

9. Quoted in Benn, *Out of the Wilderness*, p. 481 (2 November 1966).

10. Other major departmental reorganisations included the Ministry of Defence.

11. Public Record Office (PRO): PREM 13/908, 'Longer term economic strategy and our relations with Europe', paper for Chequers meeting, 22 October 1966.

12. PRO: PREM 13/904, 'The danger of a French victory', 7 January 1966.

13. Quoted in J. Girling, *France: Political and Social Change* (London: Routledge, 1998), p. 64.

14. Quoted in H. Macmillan, *At the End of the Day, 1961–1963* (London: Macmillan, 1973), p. 365.

15. PRO: PREM 13/1504, 6 February 1964.

16. For more on the technological dimension of the Wilson bid, see Chapter 5 in this book.

17. Peyrefitte, *C'Etait de Gaulle, Vol. II*, pp. 310–11.

18. H. Wilson, *The Labour Government 1964–70: A Personal Record* (London: Weidenfeld & Nicolson and Michael Joseph, 1971), p. 73.

19. Ministère des Affaires Etrangères (MAE), Série Europe, Grande Bretagne, 214, 263: 'Association éventuelle de la Grande Bretagne au Marché Commun', 19 March 1965; 'La Grande Bretagne et l'Europe', 24 March 1965.

20. PRO: PREM 13/324; MAE: Secretariat General: Entretiens et Messages 1958–1968, 24–5.

21. B. Ledwidge, *De Gaulle* (London: Weidenfeld & Nicolson, 1987), p. 297.

22. Quoted in J. Lacouture, *De Gaulle: The Ruler, 1945–1970*, translated by Alan Sheridan (London: Horvill, 1991), p. 360.

23. PRO: PREM 13/306, valedictory despatch, 3 May 1965.

24. Quoted in J. W. Young, *Britain and European Unity 1945–1999*, 2nd edn (Basingstoke: Macmillan, 2000), p. 91.

25. For more on the public opinion, party political and industry dimensions to the second application see Chapters 2, 3 and 6 in this book.

26. MAE: Cabinet du Ministre, 39, 1958–1966, Note, 23 May 1966.

27. MAE: Cabinet du Ministre, 39, 'Le Royaume Uni et la CEE', 22 June 1966.

28. MAE: Cabinet du Ministre, 39, 'Les États-unis et une eventuelle adhesion du Royaume Uni au Marché Commun', 24 June 1966.

29. Wilson, *The Labour Government*, p. 244.

30. Benn, *Out of the Wilderness*, p. 449 (8 July 1966).

31. MAE: Cabinet du Ministre, 39, 'Notices Biographiques', 20 June 1966.

32. Ibid.

33. Ziegler, *Harold Wilson*, p. 241.

34. Wilson, *The Labour Government*, p. 249.

35. C. King, *The Cecil King Diary, 1965–1970* (London: Jonathan Cape, 1972), p. 82 (2 August, 1966).
36. PRO: PREM 13/907; Archives Nationales (AN): Archives de la présidence de la Republique, Grande Bretagne, 5AG, 1.171; for more on the press briefing, see Wilson, *The Labour Government*, p. 250.
37. PRO: PREM 13/908, Williams to Wilson, 13 September 1966.
38. PRO: PREM 13/892, 3 June 1966.
39. Wilson, *The Labour Government*, p. 218.
40. Castle, *The Castle Diaries*, p. 183 (9 November 1966).
41. PRO: PREM 13/910, 14 November 1966.
42. PRO: PREM 13/922, Soames to Wilson, 14 December 1966; Wilson to Soames, 21 December 1966.
43. AN, 5AG, 1.171.
44. PRO: CAB 128/ 41, 20 December 1966; G. Brown, *In My Way: The Political Memoirs of Lord George-Brown* (London: Victor Gollancz, 1971), p. 220; Castle, *The Castle Diaries*, p. 100 (20 December 1966).
45. PRO: CAB 128/42.
46. PRO: PREM 13/1482, O'Neill to Secretary of State for Prime Minister, 18 May 1967.
47. Archives de la Fondation Nationale des Sciences Politiques, Fonds Maurice Couve de Murville, CM8, letter from Wormser to Couve, 14 April 1967.
48. Wilson met de Gaulle in Paris on 24 January 1967 and in Bonn on 25 April 1967.
49. Ziegler, *Wilson*, p. 336.
50. PRO: CAB 128/42.
51. Quoted in Ziegler, *Wilson*, p. 335.
52. PRO: PREM 13/1484, Brown–Couve meeting at UN, 23 September 1967.
53. PRO: PREM 13/910, Rostow meeting with Wilson and Callaghan, 21 November 1966.
54. PRO: PREM 13/897, Palliser to Wright, 21 October 1966.
55. PRO: CAB 128/42.
56. PRO: PREM 13/1496, Cobbold to Wilson, 5 May 1967.
57. PRO: PREM 13/897, Palliser to Wright, 21 October 1966.
58. Wilson, *The Labour Government*, p. 406.
59. A. Chalfont, *The Shadow of My Hand: A Memoir* (London: Weidenfeld & Nicolson, 2000), p. 118.

9

Dealing with de Gaulle: Anglo-American Relations, NATO and the Second Application

JAMES ELLISON

In a meeting of the National Security Council (NSC) on 3 May 1967, Henry Fowler, Secretary of the US Treasury, characterised American views of France and Europe:

> The French have been trying to use the Common Market structure for the past five years in an effort to diminish our economic, political, and military influences. This French effort in Europe affects our ability to be effective in other parts of the world.[1]

President Lyndon Johnson resented the complications posed by Europe, and particularly by French President Charles de Gaulle, to the war his country was fighting in Vietnam: 'What we need to do is find a solution. We must find a way of getting [the Europeans] to make a larger contribution to the cost of NATO [North Atlantic Treaty Organisation] defense.'[2] De Gaulle's actions towards the European Economic Community (EEC) and NATO during Johnson's presidency heightened American concerns about the future of European unity and European defence. From 1958, de Gaulle had sought to create a French-dominated EEC independent of American influence. This led him to veto Britain's first application for EEC membership in January 1963 and to attempt to impose a Gaullist blueprint on the Community during the 'empty chair' crisis from June 1965 to January 1966. Outside the EEC, by withdrawing France from NATO's integrated military structure in March 1966 and seeking to strengthen Franco-German friendship, he undermined NATO's solidarity and threatened the fundamental US foreign policy goal of tying Germany to the Atlantic Alliance. These events led Johnson to warn the British Prime Minister, Harold Wilson, that 'A growing sense of uncertainty and insecurity on [Germany's] part could lead to a fragmentation of European and Atlantic relations which would be tragic for all of us.'[3] Britain, and its second application for EEC membership, were to play an important role in avoiding this eventuality.

The Johnson administration did not expect the Wilson government to make an early application for EEC membership, given the political situation in Britain and in Europe. Nevertheless, in July 1966 the State Department concluded that 'an unequivocal British willingness to join the Communities would significantly strengthen the Five [Belgium, Germany, Italy, Luxembourg and the Netherlands] in dealing with Gaullist France and indirectly help the Fourteen hold NATO together, whatever the French do'.[4] Expectations of the success of any application were not high, but to a certain extent that was unimportant. It was the demonstration of British intent and the diplomatic effect that it would have on the crises created by de Gaulle in the EEC and NATO that mattered. Thus, when in November 1966 Wilson announced that he would undertake a 'probe' of EEC capitals, Johnson was 'immensely heartened'.[5] While the second application eventually failed at de Gaulle's hands in November 1967, it helped prevent the General from achieving his policy goals in either the EEC or NATO. It also served British foreign policy objectives by paving the way for future British membership of the EEC and providing the opportunity to strengthen Britain's position within NATO. Although not driven by these motives, when the decision to make the second application came in London, it also served to improve Britain's position in Europe, in the Atlantic Alliance and in Washington. It is on these diplomatic factors that this chapter will concentrate and, through doing so, conclude that while de Gaulle's veto rendered the second application a short-term defeat for the Wilson government, it is possible to suggest that it was a medium-term success for British foreign policy.[6]

THE STATE OF ANGLO-AMERICAN RELATIONS IN DECEMBER 1964

On the night of 7 December 1964, Johnson, held a dinner at the White House in honour of the new British Prime Minister, Wilson. In his after dinner speech, Wilson made a proclamation on Anglo-American relations:

We hear arguments, I've heard this often enough, about whether there is a special relationship between the United States and Great Britain. Some of those who talk about the special relationship, I think, are looking backwards and not looking forward ... We regard our relationship with you not as a *special* relationship but as a *close* relationship, governed by the only things that matter, unity of purpose, and unity in our objectives.[7]

General de Gaulle enhanced the closeness that Wilson talked about. The Johnson administration remained a proponent of British membership of the EEC to counteract French influence, even though this was not a reality in the short term at least.[8] There was also Anglo-American agreement on negotiating the 50 per cent linear tariff cut through the Kennedy Round in order to influence future EEC trade policy.[9] On NATO, the British and the US governments were at one on the need to refashion the Alliance to resist de Gaulle's attempts to undermine it; in 1959 France had withdrawn its Mediterranean fleet from NATO control and in 1963 did the same with its Atlantic fleet.[10] These areas of 'unity of purpose', as Wilson put it, contributed to what is generally accepted to be the moderate success of the Johnson–Wilson meetings of December 1964.[11] This was much to do with the Wilson government's attachment to its predecessor's attitude towards the United States which rejected a policy akin to French-style independence and embraced the Anglo-American relationship as a foundation of British national interests.[12] But Harold Macmillan had brought the vital ingredient to relations with Washington – personal rapport – and this was something that the Johnson–Wilson relationship clearly lacked.[13] Under the Labour government, transatlantic friendships at the highest level did not cushion American responses to a period of stark decline in Britain's power. This was most visibly exposed over Wilson's unsupportive attitude towards Johnson's Vietnam War over the long term, a thorn in the side of Anglo-American relations that affected all other aspects of foreign policy interchange.

Although the December 1964 meetings went off well, this is not to say that Johnson and Wilson were in unison on all issues. Significantly, in terms of policy towards Europe and the Atlantic Alliance, there was real difference over the question of nuclear sharing in NATO. Johnson had inherited from Kennedy the American proposal for a Multilateral Force (MLF), an initiative to provide a NATO mixed-manned surface fleet of ships armed with Polaris missiles.[14] The American rationale for the MLF was to strengthen the Atlantic Alliance by giving the Germans a legitimate role in NATO nuclear policy and by avoiding their gravitation towards a Gaullist political and defence union or neutrality. As Johnson told Wilson, 'the object was to keep the Germans with us and keep their hands off the trigger'.[15] What Johnson did not say to Wilson, but what was clarified in the President's National Security Action Memorandum of 17 December 1964, was that via the MLF, Britain would be led 'out of the field of strategic deterrence ... [thus reducing] by one the number of powers aiming at this kind of nuclear strength'.[16]

Fully aware of this, the British government was determined to resist it and the reduction in status within the Atlantic Alliance that it implied. Consequently, during the December meeting with Johnson, Wilson presented Britain's own proposal for NATO nuclear sharing, the Atlantic Nuclear Force (ANF).[17] The essential difference between the MLF and the ANF was that the British plan would retain Anglo-American nuclear cooperation at the heart of the Alliance, while allowing other NATO allies, principally Germany, some control via a mixed-manned element.[18] Although Johnson responded constructively to Wilson's ANF proposal, in private it led him to doubt the value of the Prime Minister's visit to Washington.[19] By obstructing the MLF, Wilson also obstructed the American objectives of finally tying Germany to the Atlantic Alliance and preventing an independent German nuclear policy or, worse, a Franco-German nuclear policy designed by de Gaulle. Thus, prior to the activation of the General's policies in the EEC in 1965 and NATO in 1966, although there was Anglo-American agreement on the necessity of dealing with de Gaulle, there was no prospect of British membership of the EEC and there was disagreement on the future of NATO in particular on the respective roles of Britain and Germany.

DE GAULLE'S CHALLENGE AND ANGLO-AMERICAN RESPONSES

De Gaulle's instigation of the 'empty chair' crisis within the EEC from June 1965, and his consistent criticism of US domination of the Atlantic Alliance and what he saw as a dangerous nuclear policy of massive retaliation, which culminated in French withdrawal from NATO's integrated military structure in March 1966, presented a challenge to the interests of the American and British governments. In his attempt to build a new world role for France, 'de Gaulle pursued policies that would have seemed challenging if practiced by an avowed enemy, but appeared intolerable in an ally'.[20] In the USA, his diplomacy brought great public hostility, leading one Congressman to propose 'disinterring the thousands of American war-dead in France, transporting the bodies across the Atlantic Ocean, and burying them at home'.[21] Within the American government, there was pressure on the President to allow his true Texan self to dictate his response to de Gaulle's attack on US policy. Johnson's decision, however, was to treat the General courteously and not worsen Franco-American relations. Yet his true Texan self was clear in the motives for this approach, when he 'told George Ball, [that] he refused to get into a "pissing match" with [de Gaulle]'.[22]

In less colourful terms, this also described the British reaction to de Gaulle's EEC and NATO offensives. In January 1966, Foreign Secretary Michael Stewart advised the Cabinet that, 'If we cannot deter de Gaulle, we must minimise the damage'.[23] Believing that de Gaulle was an awkward fact of life, there was Anglo-American agreement that the best way to deal with him was to work around him. On 2 March 1966 the Johnson administration instructed its embassies that 'we should lean over backward to be polite and friendly to France ...'.[24] Anglo-American conformity also extended to isolating the crises de Gaulle had created in the EEC and NATO. The Americans estimated that, unless the two matters were kept separate, the General would use the interplay between them by accepting a resolution to the 'empty chair' crisis if the Germans agreed to decline any participation in NATO nuclear sharing.[25] The British were more concerned that, should they decide to make a fresh approach to the EEC, de Gaulle would play one crisis off against the other to drive a wedge between Britain and America and split the Atlantic Alliance.[26]

Nevertheless, such agreement between London and Washington was limited. The Wilson government attempted to entice the Johnson administration into cooperation on Europe's problems, particularly over NATO, by proposing a joint approach to the Germans, Dutch and Italians in June 1965 and bilateral contingency planning in January 1966.[27] Yet while the Americans were happy that the British agreed with the 'softly softly' line towards de Gaulle, there was enough difference between them to stop short of combined action. Reluctance to present an Anglo-American NATO cabal underpinned Washington's attitude, but so too did continued discord over the MLF/ANF question. Achieving German involvement in nuclear sharing remained a key American goal to contain German ambitions and strengthen the Atlantic Alliance.[28] British hesitancy, matched with Secretary of State for Defence Denis Healey's announcement in January 1966 that, for financial reasons, Britain might be forced to make cuts in the British Army of the Rhine (BAOR), were unwelcome complications.[29] The Johnson administration's solution was to propose tripartite talks with the British

and the Germans both to resolve the issue of Atlantic nuclear cooperation and to offset payments for British and US forces stationed in
Germany.[30] The crisis in NATO only intensified the need to solve these
problems, lest they cause German concerns about the Alliance.[31] On 3
June 1966, the US Ambassador to France, Charles Bohlen, produced a
'stark outline' of what he considered to be de Gaulle's aims: 'the real
ultimate danger of [de Gaulle's] policy, if consistently pursued, would
lie theoretically in the possibility of provoking another Soviet–German
deal'.[32] Bohlen's concerns epitomised those held throughout the US
government. If de Gaulle weakened NATO and also sought improved
Franco-Soviet relations, and if no solution was found to the problem of
nuclear sharing by Washington, Germany might be led away from the
West and towards the East.[33] This chilling scenario made it all the more
necessary to embed the Germans within Atlantic institutions.

The Wilson government was also eager to cooperate fully with
Germany and the United States in NATO to strengthen the Alliance
and improve Anglo-German relations. This reflected Cold War policy,
but also the fact that the British had an eye on a future advance
towards the EEC. At the same time, the government maintained the
long-held British scepticism of German power and worked to ensure
that Germany did not 'seek a special American–German relationship
within NATO, from which Britain would be excluded'.[34] The ANF was
the chosen instrument for this purpose as a means of promoting
Germany but not demoting Britain within the Atlantic partnership.
De Gaulle's NATO policy had made such a strategy all the more
necessary, as one Foreign Office official minuted in April 1966: 'It is
the sheer fact that if France is taken out of the pool the German fish
looms proportionately larger.'[35] There was also growing anxiety that
the USA was becoming increasingly disenchanted with NATO, which
had 'proved almost entirely useless' over the its struggle in Vietnam,
and that the Johnson administration prioritised European unity over
Atlantic relationships.[36] These foreign policy concerns – the problem
of Germany and the strains on American views of NATO, worsened
by de Gaulle's actions – encouraged Wilson to consider making a second application for EEC membership and taking a lead in NATO
reform.

THE SECOND APPLICATION AND NATO

'Britain's membership in the EEC had been seen as the single most
important element in strengthening the Atlantic framework' by John
Kennedy's administration, observes Geir Lundestad.[37] De Gaulle's

veto in January 1963 rendered this infeasible, and the Johnson administration therefore concentrated its policy on containing de Gaulle and
buttressing its position in Europe. In July 1966, however, the State
Department prepared a memorandum analysing 'A Presidential Push
on Wilson toward UK Membership in the Common Market'. There
was little expectation that Wilson would make such a move or that de
Gaulle would permit British entry. Nevertheless, it was felt that there
were short-run and long-run 'political gains' to be achieved from
Britain's entry to the EEC, because the British would offer strength to
the Five in their struggle with de Gaulle's France and solidarity to the
Fourteen NATO powers.[38] The announcement of the British probe of
EEC capitals in November 1966 thus brought commendation from
Johnson, who wrote to Wilson that 'I am immensely heartened by
your courageous announcement about joining the EEC'.[39] This was
the limit of Johnson's praise, however, as in the same message he
focused on NATO affairs.

In late 1966, the priority for the Americans was the successful for-
tification of the Atlantic Alliance in the face of de Gaulle's challenge.
The prospects for this were considered to be poor, as revealed by a
State Department Scope Paper of 7 December which stated that: 'The
traditional European leaders (a neutralist France, a weak, self-centred
Britain and a Germany governed by an untested coalition) are unable
to provide reassurance to the other Alliance members.'[40] While
Wilson's probe of EEC capitals gave Johnson heart in one arena of his
European policy, continued British economic fragility was of great
concern in another. In pursuit of strengthening NATO, and assuring
Germany's part within it, the American government prioritised the
successful conclusion of the German–British–American tripartite talks
launched in October 1966.[41] The Americans hoped to see the long running MLF/ANF dispute, and thus the NATO nuclear question,
resolved via these talks.[42] However, this goal was complicated by the
other main item on the agenda: payments from the German government to Britain and USA to offset the costs of stationing their troops
in its country. British warnings of reductions in the BAOR due to economic difficulties threatened the progress of the tripartite talks and
therefore Johnson's policy for European and Atlantic security. In the
light of this, on 26 August, the President had warned the Prime
Minister 'about the dangers of an unravelling in NATO':

> With your urgent need to save foreign exchange in Germany,
> Erhard's budgetary and political difficulties …, my problems with
> our German offset and with the Congress on troops in Europe –

all against the background of the General's antics – there is danger of serious damage to the security arrangements we have worked so hard to construct during the last 20 years. To you, I don't have to spell out the possible political consequences, especially in Germany. And while I would not think it likely that our Russian friends will develop itchy fingers, one cannot rule it out.[43]

Johnson's letter to Wilson of 15 November 1966 on the announcement of the EEC probe spent only one paragraph commending this move and then eight on the tripartite talks. The President's priority was to avert imminent cuts in the BAOR, because of the ramifications this would have for the talks with the Germans, Johnson's domestic political position and America's NATO policy. To encourage postponement of such cuts in November 1966, Johnson placed an additional $35 million (£12.5 million) in defence procurement orders with Britain, which Wilson happily accepted.[44] While this subsidy was designed to help the British, it actually helped Johnson, whose battle with Congressional pressure to avoid redeploying US forces stationed in Germany would have been worsened had the BAOR been downsized. Moreover, in 1966–67, troop reductions would have also possibly weakened German resolve towards de Gaulle's criticism of the Americans and the British. For Johnson, Britain's EEC policy was helpful in the contest with the General, but its continued economic weakness was not in relation to NATO. For Wilson, this American concern gave Britain bargaining power in Washington and the announcement of the probe, together with a compliant attitude on the offset problem, brought a welcome response from Johnson: American dollars.

In 1967, Anglo-American relations were dominated by disagreement over Vietnam and worsened by Wilson's failed attempts to broker a peace with the Soviet Premier, Alexei Kosygin. Britain's declining international influence in American minds was fundamentally underlined by Wilson's decision to withdraw militarily from east of Suez, and the disastrous British economic performance leading to the November devaluation of sterling. These events greatly harmed Anglo-American relations by convincing the Johnson administration that Britain could not be distinguished from the other problem Europeans: France and Germany.[45] Notwithstanding this, however, the British played a successful game in 1967. In Washington, hopes for a second application were always low owing to de Gaulle's implacability, and while it was accepted that the British were knocking on a closed door, it was also felt that at least they were knocking and doing it well. When Wilson's announcement of the application eventually came in the House of Commons on 2 May 1967, it was described by the State Department as having 'placed new stress upon UK political goals in a united Europe. This recognition of [the] basic political nature and objective of European integration seems to us [an] important and constructive new element in [the] UK position.'[46] The US government's overriding view was that the second application was 'simple and clean', 'harder to resist than the first', and that 'British strategy and tactics ... have been both intelligent and effective'.[47] To an administration convinced that de Gaulle was trying to use the EEC to diminish American influence in Europe, Britain's second application, even in failure, was a partial success as it crystallised the Five, further isolated de Gaulle and – of paramount importance – helped keep the EEC intact.[48] It also served America's NATO policy, as the French were reluctant to add a dispute over the Atlantic Alliance to existing problems just as the Fourteen took important decisions on the future of NATO.[49]

December 1967 saw the culmination of a review of the Atlantic Alliance, in light of French withdrawal, initiated by the Belgian Foreign Minister, Pierre Harmel. The year had begun well in American and British eyes after the establishment of NATO's Nuclear Planning Group (NPG) and the continued negotiations for a Non-Proliferation Treaty (NPT), helping to end the unanswered debate over the MLF/ANF question by giving Germany consultative arrangements on NATO nuclear policy, particularly in terms of European conflict.[50] The conclusion of the tripartite talks in April, with German agreement to offset British and American costs in stationing troops in the Federal Republic, further strengthened NATO.[51] Dramatic force reductions were avoided, even though the Wilson government withdrew one brigade and a squadron as the economy worsened.[52] Nevertheless, Britain's policy of riding 'the Atlantic and European horses in double harness', balanced on one side by the second application, was balanced on the other by its diplomatic effort to make the Harmel exercise on NATO's future a success.[53] In Washington, it was felt that the British had been significant in securing agreement amongst the Fourteen on *détente* and on the need for Europe to accept larger responsibilities in NATO. No doubt the French had decided to accept the embarrassment of compromises in NATO in December 1967, rather than risk rejection of the Harmel exercise, for their own reasons. But in a direct way – Minister of State Fred Mulley's pressure on the French NATO delegate – and in an indirect way – deflecting French action away from NATO and towards the second application – the British had assisted American policy.[54] They had, of course, served their own as well and improved their troubled position in Washington along the way.

WAITING FOR DE GAULLE TO GO

In a Cabinet memorandum dated 23 February 1968, the Foreign Secretary, George Brown, urged a 're-think' in British foreign policy given 'the changing pattern of world events', Britain's economic situation and the government's decision to withdraw militarily from east of Suez.[55] The rethink did not amount to a revision, as the Wilson government sustained the thrust of its foreign policies, including those towards NATO and the EEC. If anything, these policies were reinforced by de Gaulle's veto of the second application in November 1967. Brown argued that: 'If we are to have some significant degree of control over the circumstances in which we live we need to be able to operate on a wider regional power basis than this country alone affords.'[56] Essential to this was membership of the Communities 'at the earliest possible moment' and to ensure that de Gaulle's vision of Europe did not prevail. Yet as long as the General remained in the Elysée Palace, Britain's signature of the Treaty of Rome was impossible. Pressure could be kept on the Six to respond constructively to the application that Wilson left on the table in Brussels, but this policy would not produce early fruit. The tactical solution agreed on in London was for Britain to seek cooperation with the Five in areas not covered by the Treaty's jurisdiction, including defence. Such a strategy would complement Britain's policy towards Germany, as Brown warned that: 'To a large extent the French and ourselves are in competition for Germany.'[57] Enhanced Anglo-European cooperation was thus designed to advance the Wilson government's policy of paving the way for EEC membership. It was also designed to ensure that de Gaulle did not win the battle for Germany, especially as *détente* became a more pressing political issue under Willy Brandt. As the Foreign Office had argued for some time, a British initiative in European defence would meet all of these aims, as well as potentially improving Anglo-American relations.[58]

After de Gaulle's veto, the Johnson administration had also concluded that British membership of the EEC was an impossibility in the short-term and announced its opposition to any interim commercial solutions that would be harmful to American trade with Europe. In fact, American priorities in early 1968 were to improve their own trade balance with the EEC and continue the efforts made in the Kennedy Round to break down tariff barriers.[59] On the issue of Britain's relations with the Community, it was felt that the water-treading period imposed by de Gaulle's presence could be used to pursue American goals for NATO. Throughout his administration, Johnson and his closest allies had constantly referred to the selfishness of the Europeans in their reluctance to assume greater responsibility for their own defence in NATO. This view was influenced by Congressional pressure for US troop withdrawals, but also by the stranglehold that the Vietnam War had on the President. Dean Rusk's comment to Belgian Foreign Minister Harmel in December 1967 epitomised this:

> many of the European allies of the United States do not realise that the present position of the United States amounts to a near miracle. More than half a million Americans are involved in Southeast Asia, most of them in combat. In spite of that, the United States is maintaining its forces in Europe. The willingness of the American people to bear the cost, both financial and moral, of such burdens is perhaps taken too much for granted.[60]

It was for this reason – and a desire to see improvement in Anglo-EEC relations – that from spring 1968 the US government encouraged the British to think in terms of a European defence arrangement as a method of enhancing prospects of membership of the EEC and of reinforcing NATO. On 28 March, John Leddy, the influential Assistant Secretary of State for European Affairs in the State Department, 'spoke strongly' to the British embassy in Washington 'about the desirability of [Britain] taking the lead in the formation of a *European defence caucus*'.[61] At the same time, the US Mission to NATO was instructed to announce the administration's intent 'to examine sympathetically and on merits any European ideas or initiatives looking toward improved balance as between Europe and North America within the Alliance'.[62]

The result of these developments was greater congruence in Anglo-American relations. From spring 1968 the Wilson government elaborated its policy towards European defence cooperation, under the guidance of Stewart and Healey. The British were ready to discuss far-reaching proposals with their European NATO partners. On 22 March Stewart wrote to Healey:

> we should make it quite clear that we are putting [proposals] forward as moves towards a new European defence identity within the Atlantic Alliance and that we are ready to discuss all ways of

giving effect to this. Thus, while we should not be putting forward a comprehensive blue-print for a European Defence Community at this stage, it would be clear that we are ready to work for community-type arrangements.[63]

In this the British were spurred on by the United States, particularly in May when the President's National Security Adviser, Walt Rostow, announced that the Johnson administration was ready to give up its dominant position in NATO, and when the American Defense Secretary, Clark Clifford, told Healey that it should not be assumed that American forces in Europe would be maintained at their current level indefinitely.[64] The solution in both instances was for the Europeans to shoulder a greater part of their own defence burden within NATO. Britain's initiatives in late 1968 were thus welcomed in Washington.[65] On 12 November, the Cabinet agreed to Healey convening meetings with the Defence Ministers of the Five, Denmark and Norway to reach agreement on European defence cooperation within NATO. It also invited Stewart to meet with the Five ahead of the January Western European Union (WEU) meeting to consider collaboration in arenas not within the jurisdiction of the Treaty of Rome.[66] By serving the 'unity of purpose' that was at the heart of close Anglo-American relations, the Wilson government had not only met its own objectives, but also those of the Johnson administration.

CONCLUSION

The failure of Britain's second application for EEC membership in 1967 was certainly a defeat for the Wilson government. Yet it was only a limited defeat, as the application achieved much as a demonstration of British intent and as a diplomatic manoeuvre. Although de Gaulle had proved to be an immovable obstacle for a second time in the 1960s, few had expected anything different. After the first veto in 1963 there had been criticism of British policy and diplomacy, but in 1967 it was felt that Britain had done a good job and, in so doing, had paved the way for future entry.[67] This view was held not only in Europe, but also in the United States. The Johnson administration, like its predecessor, wished to see Britain in the EEC and, while it held no illusions about the likelihood of this as long as de Gaulle maintained power, a British move was welcome if only to give the Five strength against de Gaulle. It was also welcome in wider diplomatic terms. The State Department had predicted that a British application would 'indirectly help the Fourteen hold NATO together, whatever the French do' and it had fulfilled such predictions.[68] By frustrating de Gaulle's power play in the EEC and in NATO, Britain had also helped to keep Germany firmly tied to Atlantic institutions. Thus, when looked at from a perspective apart from the immediate impact of de Gaulle's veto, the second application achieved some measure of success.

This success had broader significance for British foreign policy. The second application came amid a period of painful economic crisis and unprecedented international withdrawal for Britain. While the application was not simply designed as a strategy to counteract this, it did provide Britain with opportunity and power to influence events in spite of it. At a time when Britain's global status was at its lowest point in the post-war period, and when the Americans regarded their previously foremost ally as little different from other problem European states, Britain's importance in EEC and NATO affairs grew. This was due in no small part to de Gaulle. In an era of Anglo-American relations characterised by loosening ties because of the problems of sterling, the east of Suez decision, and differences over Vietnam, de Gaulle brought the Americans and the British closer together. The Anglo-American relationship was never stronger than when common bonds were born from a common opponent. De Gaulle was such an opponent, and enabled the British to play a greater role in Atlantic and European events than its strength strictly warranted.[69] Thus, at the close of the 1960s, Britain's reputation in the EEC and its status in NATO had improved as a result of actions taken in response to de Gaulle's challenge. Even after the veto, this effect was sustained by British initiatives to enhance European defence cooperation within the Atlantic Alliance, improving Anglo-EEC relations and bringing American encouragement of British leadership in this area of European cooperation. Now that a British Cabinet had finally accepted that Europe was the foundation of Britain's international position, these were important steps towards membership of the EEC. To achieve that, all Britain could do – all it perhaps could ever do – was wait, along with the Americans and the Five, for de Gaulle's 'departure for another world'.[70]

NOTES

1. *Foreign Relations of the United States, 1964–1968* (*FRUS, 1964–1968*), 13, Western Europe Region (Washington DC: United States Government Printing Office, 1995), document 251, Summary Notes on the 569th Meeting of the National Security Council, 3 May 1967.
2. Ibid.
3. *FRUS, 1964–1968*, 13, document 168, Johnson to Wilson, 21 May 1966.
4. *FRUS, 1964–1968*, 13, document 188, Solomon and Stoessel to Ball, 'A Presidential

Push on Wilson toward UK Membership in the Common Market-Information Memorandum', 19 July 1966.

5. *FRUS, 1964–1968*, 13, document 216, Johnson to Wilson, 15 November 1966.
6. The foreign policy consequences of the second application have not received great attention in existing studies; see, for example, J. W. Young, *Britain and European Unity 1945–1999* (London: Macmillan, 2000), pp. 82–100. Also, from a Cold War perspective, see Sean Greenwood, *Britain and the Cold War 1945–91* (London: Macmillan, 2000), pp. 167–75. American policy towards de Gaulle and Europe has received more detailed treatment: see H. W. Brands, *The Wages of Globalism: Lyndon Johnson and the Limits of American Power* (Oxford: Oxford University Press, 1995), pp. 85-122; F. Costigliola, 'Lyndon B. Johnson, Germany, and "the End of the Cold War"' in W. I. Cohen and N. B. Tucker (eds), *Lyndon Johnson Confronts the World: American Foreign Policy 1963–1968* (Cambridge: Cambridge University Press, 1994), pp. 173–211; and L. Gardner, 'Lyndon Johnson and De Gaulle' in R. O. Paxton and N. Wahl (eds), *De Gaulle and the United States: A Centennial Reappraisal* (Oxford: Berg, 1994), pp. 257–79.
7. H. Wilson, *The Labour Government, 1964–70: A Personal Record* (London: Weidenfeld & Nicolson/Michael Joseph, 1971), p. 50.
8. *FRUS, 1964–1968*, 13, document 5, Department of State to Certain Posts in Europe, 25 January 1964.
9. *FRUS, 1964–1968*, 13, document 9, Memorandum of Conversation, 12 February 1964.
10. G. Lundestad, *'Empire' by Integration: The United States and European Integration, 1945–1997* (Oxford: Oxford University Press, 1998), p. 80.
11. D. Dimbleby and D. Reynolds, *An Ocean Apart: The Relationship between Britain and America in the Twentieth Century* (London: Hodder & Stoughton, 1988), p. 246; J. W. Young, *Britain and the World in the Twentieth Century* (London: Arnold, 1997), p. 177.
12. Public Record Office (PRO): CAB 129/118, CP(64)164, 2 September 1964.
13. Dimbleby and Reynolds, *An Ocean Apart*, p. 247.
14. P. Winand, *Eisenhower, Kennedy, and the United States of Europe* (New York: St Martin's Press, 1996), Chapter 8. See also A. Buchan, 'The Multilateral Force: A Study in Alliance Politics', *International Affairs*, 40, 4 (1964), pp. 619–37, and M. Camps, *European Unification in the Sixties: From the Veto to the Crisis* (London: Oxford University Press, 1967), pp. 144–56.
15. *FRUS, 1964–1968*, 13, document 58, Memorandum for the Record, 7 December 1964.
16. *FRUS, 1964–1968*, 13, document 65, National Security Action Memorandum Number 332, 17 December 1964.
17. *FRUS, 1964–1968*, 13, document 60, Memorandum of Conversation, 7 December 1964.
18. G. Wyn Rees, 'British Strategic Thinking and Europe, 1964–1970', *Journal of European Integration History*, 5, 1 (1999), pp. 57–73 (p. 66).
19. *FRUS, 1964–1968*, 13, document 62, Bundy to Bruce, 9 December 1964, and document 63, Bundy to Johnson, 10 December 1964.
20. Brands, *Wages of Globalism*, p. 88.
21. J. Chace and E. Malkin, 'The Mischief-Maker: The American Media and De Gaulle, 1964–68', in Paxton and Wahl (eds), *De Gaulle and the United States: A Centennial Reappraisal* (Oxford: Berg, 1994), pp. 359–77 (p. 361).
22. Quoted in Brands, *Wages of Globalism*, p. 94.
23. PRO: CAB 129/124, C(66)16, 28 January 1966.
24. *FRUS, 1964–1968*, 13, document 135, Department of State to Posts in NATO Capitals, 2 March 1966.
25. *FRUS, 1964–1968*, 13, document 112, Department of State to Mission to the European Communities, 24 November 1965.
26. PRO: PREM 13/909, Trend to Prime Minister, 28 October 1966.

27. *FRUS, 1964–1968*, 13, document 90, Memorandum of Conversation, 16 June 1965 and document 126, Memorandum of Conversation, 27 January 1966.
28. See Costigliola, 'Lyndon B. Johnson'.
29. *FRUS, 1964–1968*, 13, document 78, Memorandum of Conversation, 22 March 1965; document 117, Editorial Note; document 126, Memorandum of Conversation, 27 January 1966; document 133, Johnson to Wilson, undated, sent 20 February 1966.
30. *FRUS*, 1964–1968, 13, document 157, Rostow to Johnson, 17 April 1966; document 159, National Security Action Memorandum Number 345, 22 April 1966.
31. *FRUS, 1964–1968*, 13, document 171, McNamara and Rusk to Johnson, 28 May 1966.
32. *FRUS, 1964–1968*, 13, document 172, Bohlen to Rusk, 3 June 1966.
33. See Costigliola, 'Lyndon B. Johnson', pp. 192–210.
34. PRO: CAB 129/122, C(65)119, 5 August 1965.
35. PRO: FO 371/190534/6/3, Barnes minute, 18 April 1966.
36. PRO: FCO 41/2, Dean to Hood, 16 November 1966.
37. Lundestad, *'Empire' by Integration*, p. 74. Also see, in general, C. A. Pagedas, *Anglo-American Strategic Relations and the French Problem, 1960–1963* (London: Frank Cass, 2000).
38. *FRUS, 1964–1968*, 13, document 188, Solomon and Stoessel to Ball, 'A Presidential Push on Wilson toward U.K. Membership in the Common Market-Information Memorandum', 19 July 1966.
39. *FRUS, 1964–1968*, 13, document 216, Johnson to Wilson, 15 November 1966. On the probe see Young, *Britain and European Unity*, pp. 89–93.
40. *FRUS, 1964–1968*, 13, document 223, Scope Paper, 7 December 1966.
41. *FRUS, 1964–1968*, 13, document 213, Mission to NATO to Department of State, 22 October 1966.
42. *FRUS, 1964–1968*, 13, document 171, McNamara and Rusk to Johnson, 28 May 1966 and document 186, Acheson to Rusk, 14 July 1966.
43. *FRUS, 1964–1968*, 13, document 198, Johnson to Wilson, undated, sent 26 August 1966. There were similar repeated warnings: *FRUS, 1964–1968*, 13, document 200, Johnson to Wilson, undated, sent 1 September 1966 and document 208, Johnson to Wilson, undated, sent 1 October 1966.
44. *FRUS, 1964–1968*, 13, document 216, Johnson to Wilson, 15 November 1966; PRO: CAB 128/41, CC(66)61st Conclusions, 29 November 1966.
45. See, for example, C. J. Bartlett, *'The Special Relationship': A Political History of Anglo-American Relations Since 1945* (London: Longman, 1992), pp. 107–26.
46. *FRUS, 1964–1968*, 13, document 250, Department of State to Certain Posts in Europe, 2 May 1967.
47. *FRUS, 1964–1968*, 13, document 255, Memorandum of Conversation, 2 June 1967 and document 272, Embassy in the UK to Department of State, 25 October 1967.
48. For concern about de Gaulle's aims to diminish US influence in Europe, see *FRUS, 1964–1968*, 13, document 251, Summary Notes of the 569th Meeting of the National Security Council, 3 May 1967.
49. *FRUS, 1964–1968*, 13, document 281, Rusk to Department of State, 14 December 1967.
50. Costigliola, 'Lyndon B. Johnson', pp. 200–1; Wyn Rees, 'British Strategic Thinking', p. 68.
51. *FRUS, 1964–1968*, document 249, Final Report on Trilateral Talks, undated, April–May 1967.
52. Wyn Rees, 'British Strategic Thinking', p. 71.
53. PRO: FCO 41/2, Barnes to Hood, 7 December 1966.
54. *FRUS*, 1964–1968, 13, document 277, Mission to NATO to Department of State, 23 November 1967 and document 281, Rusk to Department of State, 14 December 1967.

55. PRO: CAB 129/136, C(68)42, 23 February 1968.
56. Ibid.
57. Ibid.
58. For example, PRO: FO 371/184288/6/12, Palliser minute 'British Foreign Policy', 9 February 1965; PRO: FO 371/190534/6/9, Thomson minute, 29 November 1966; PRO: FCO 41/2, Hood to Dean, 26 January 1967.
59. *FRUS, 1964–1968*, 13, document 284, Department of State to Embassy in Germany, 16 January 1968; document 288, Department of State to Embassy in Belgium, 16 February 1968; document 329, Department of State to Embassy in UK, 26 September 1968.
60. *FRUS, 1964–1968*, 13, document 279, Memorandum of Conversation, 11 December 1967. See also *FRUS, 1964–1968*, 13, document 297, Rostow to Johnson, 22 March 1968.
61. PRO: FCO 41/2, Tomkins, Washington, to Hood, 28 March 1968 (emphasis in original).
62. *FRUS, 1964–1968*, 13, document 299, Department of State to Mission to NATO, 10 April 1968.
63. PRO: FCO 41/12, Stewart to Healey, 22 March 1968; PRO: FCO 41/12, Healey to Stewart, 9 April 1968; *FRUS, 1964–1968*, 13, document 305, Department of State to NATO Mission, 9 May 1968.
64. PRO: FCO 41/2, Wood, Washington, to Parsons, 8 May 1968; PRO: PREM 13/2264, Healey to Stewart, 13 May 1968.
65. For a restatement of American objectives see *FRUS, 1964–1968*, 13, document 335, Rusk to Johnson (including 'Enclosure'), 7 November 1968.
66. PRO: CAB 129/139, C(68)139, 8 November 1968; PRO: CAB 128/43, CC(68)46th Conclusions, 12 November 1968.
67. For comment on the significance of the 1967 application for Britain's eventual entry, see Sir C. O'Neill, *Britain's Entry into the European Community: Report on the Negotiations of 1970–1972* (London: Frank Cass, 2000).
68. *FRUS, 1964–1968*, 13, document 188, Solomon and Stoessel to Ball, 'A Presidential Push on Wilson toward U.K. Membership in the Common Market-Information Memorandum', 19 July 1966.
69. See also Bartlett, '*The Special Relationship*', p. 118.
70. *FRUS, 1964–1968*, 13, document 278, Memorandum of Conversation, 6 December 1967.

10

From Imperial Power to Regional Powers: Commonwealth Crises and the Second Application

PHILIP ALEXANDER

Existing studies of Britain's second application for membership of the European Economic Community (EEC), written without the benefit of archival material, tend to conclude that the Commonwealth was a far less significant factor in the deliberations that led to Harold Wilson's formal announcement of Britain's candidature on 10 May 1967 than it had been for Harold Macmillan's government in the period 1961–63. In her general study of Britain's relations with the EEC, Elisabeth Barker asserted that Commonwealth links were becoming more attenuated by the mid-1960s, as 'the image of Britain as the mother-country faded rapidly'.[1] Examining the attitudes of the Labour Party to the EEC, Lynton Robbins felt that 'by the time of the second application in 1967, the concept of the "Commonwealth alternative" was dead, but there was still, of course, the "Commonwealth problem"'. He went on to identify just two lingering features of this: New Zealand butter and the Commonwealth Sugar Agreement (CSA).[2] These were indeed the only Commonwealth issues directly referred to by George Brown in the speech to the Council of the Western European Union (WEU) with which he launched Britain's second application on 4 July 1967.[3] It is also widely recognised that the rapid acceleration of decolonisation in the 1960s stemmed in part from the realisation that Britain's influence over the Commonwealth was waning rapidly.[4] However, the centrifugal forces did not stop with colonial independence. Now that an ever increasing number of colonial territories were attaining independence within the Commonwealth, the expanded institution lost something of its coherence. Britain ceased to be the sole centre of power, as the concerns of

Commonwealth countries fragmented into a variety of regional issues.[5] These developments have been used to explain growing British involvement in the EEC: Britain, abandoning its role as an imperial power, focused instead on building relations with its immediate neighbours in Europe.[6]

What has been less well charted is the way in which a number of other Commonwealth countries emerged as regional powers in their own right. This chapter suggests that it might be necessary to modify the conventional understanding of the second application. At the time of the first application, there had been one principal Commonwealth problem, namely, the consequence of the conditions of entry for Commonwealth countries and their reactions to this. By the time of the second application, there were a whole series of Commonwealth crises that interacted with the decision-making process in different ways. On one hand, Commonwealth crises may well have impelled the Wilson government towards making the second application. With Britain's significance in the Commonwealth declining, and Commonwealth policy increasingly troubled, the EEC became the focus of aspirations for success in British foreign and commercial policies. On the other hand, these new Commonwealth crises complicated the course of Wilson's ultimately unsuccessful bid to take Britain into the EEC.

Over a year before the application was announced, Wilson's Private Secretary responsible for foreign affairs, Oliver Wright, had an opportunity to analyse this paradox for the benefit of the Prime Minister. In January 1966, Wilson received the latest in a series of joint memoranda from his Foreign Secretary, Michael Stewart, and First Secretary George Brown, urging government discussion of a possible initiative in Britain's relations with the EEC. Passing it on to Wright, Wilson noted, 'I seem to be getting at odds with the Foreign Secretary and the First Secretary.'[7] In response, Wright composed a far-reaching survey of changes in the pattern of world affairs that he felt had not yet caught up with the Foreign Office. 'Over the past two years', he wrote, 'the real problems of *"haute politique"* and *"crisis management"* have shifted away from Europe and, in a sense, away from the Foreign Office. All the major problems of the past eighteen months or so, for Britain, have been Commonwealth problems.' He identified 'the real problems of the future' as 'the domestication of China, the elimination of poverty in the Third World and drawing the sting out of race relations'.[8] To explore the interaction between Britain's Commonwealth and European policies, this chapter examines three particular regional issues that demonstrate the part played during the 'second try' by Wright's foreign policy priorities: overseas defence policy, the development of sub-Saharan Africa and South African race relations.

DEFENCE POLICY EAST OF SUEZ

The first of these issues was the debate over Britain's defence commitments in what was dubbed 'east of Suez', a vast area encompassing the Arabian peninsula, much of the Indian Ocean and some of the Pacific Rim.[9] The crucial problem which involved the Commonwealth in this region, and which had a particular impact on Australia, was what Wright called 'the domestication of China', embodied in the threat of communist and other Chinese-sponsored insurgency in south-east Asia. In 1963, President Sukarno of Indonesia, encouraged by China, laid claim to the territories of Sabah and Sarawak in North Borneo, which the British had intended to include in the Independent Federation of Malaysia, itself a Commonwealth country. There followed what was known as the *Konfrontasi* (Confrontation) between Indonesia and Malaysia, during which Britain assisted the defence of the Commonwealth states of Malaysia, Singapore and Brunei.[10] Since the time of the first application, the Australian government had worked to reduce its country's economic dependence on Britain, its focus shifting instead to export markets in Asia. Indeed, during the so-called Kennedy Round of world trade talks held under the auspices of the General Agreement on Tariffs and Trade (GATT) from 1963 to 1967, Australia bargained away some of its concessions in the British market in return for greater access to Asian markets.[11] This expanded economic role in Asia did, though, entail a greater military partnership with Britain in the region. Australia contributed forces to the defence of Malaysia, Singapore, Brunei and, significantly, also sent troops to fight alongside the Americans in Vietnam. As Australian Prime Minister Harold Holt explained to Wilson and the then Secretary of State for Commonwealth Relations, Arthur Bottomley, during a visit to London in July 1966, 'Vietnam is in the area Australians have to live and trade with', and for this reason the war in Vietnam appeared more important to Australia than to Britain.[12]

However, the reluctance of the Wilson government to become too deeply involved in the Pacific stemmed from more than geography. When the Labour Party came to power in 1964, it inherited from the Conservative government a balance-of-payments deficit of £800 million. As a result, from a very early stage in the government's life, a growing body of opinion, especially on the left of the party, advocated a substantial withdrawal of forces from east of Suez as the most acceptable way to reverse the deficit. The two members of the Cabinet who initially began to sympathise with this view were Barbara Castle, the Minister of Overseas Development, and Richard Crossman, the Minister of Housing.[13] The financial crisis, which threatened to overwhelm the Labour government in July 1966, broadened and reinforced support for these views and drew them together with discussions on EEC membership. In a series of emergency meetings between 14 and 20 July the Cabinet argued through the available options, and entrusted a hastily convened official committee with the task of finding economies worth £100 million in overseas expenditure.[14] No member of the Cabinet seemed to be wholly satisfied with the outcome of the meetings or the official committee's report. According to Castle, the usually stoic Stewart 'emerged in a more emphatic temper than I have ever seen him in Cabinet' to fight the proposed cuts:

> At one stage I thought he was going to resign! He said such a cut in our defence commitments would undermine our whole foreign relations and ruin our influence. It would mean completely contracting out of our policy in certain areas.[15]

Stewart made clear in his memoirs that his support for EEC membership stemmed from a desire to maintain, not to replace, Britain's world role.[16] By contrast, Brown shifted towards accepting the end of the east of Suez role because he resented the proposal to cut forces in Germany, a move he believed would undermine Britain's efforts at rapprochement with the EEC. Crossman condemned the whole package as a compromise that resolved nothing: 'By continuing to sustain all our commitments but cutting our costs, we shall weaken ourselves and make our foreign policy totally ineffective.'[17] By mid-1966, then, the Cabinet appeared not to have reached agreement over whether to make a strategic choice between European and Commonwealth defence commitments.

In the Parliamentary Labour Party (PLP) as a whole, the package was also unpopular and the pressure for a reduction in overseas defence forces grew. A large group of left-wing MPs from the PLP back benches were sufficiently outraged by the cuts to publish in late July a pamphlet entitled 'Never Again', in which they demanded an end to Britain's international military and financial roles.[18] A number on the right of the party, including Edmund Dell, also opposed the continuation of the east of Suez role. Yet Stewart still clung to Britain's world role, requesting his department to write a critique of the 'Never Again' pamphlet for him. Wilson also adhered to this stance, and admitted in his otherwise unrevealing memoirs that he had made a mistake 'clinging to our east of Suez role when the facts were dictating a recessional. I was ... one of the last to be converted, and it needed a lot of hard facts to convert me.'[19] Both Wilson and Stewart may have been reassured by Con O'Neill, who urged in a paper on 'The politico-military implications of EEC membership' at the end of July 1966 that EEC membership would help to reinforce Britain's international position. In the paper, he set out two possible interpretations of EEC membership:

> It can be seen as a realisation on our part that we must abandon our dreams of a world role, and that, after some three centuries of wandering, we must return to our original moorings ... Alternatively, our desire to join the EEC can be seen as an effort to strengthen the base from which we exert world influence.

With Stewart's opinion perhaps foremost in his mind, he summed up that 'presumably our objective derives more from the second than from the first of these interpretations', and membership was intended to 'reverse the inward-looking and third force tendencies' in the EEC.[20] In fact, it seems possible that his paper was largely for ministerial consumption, as at other times O'Neill showed scepticism about the value of Britain's overseas commitments. In a first draft for a speech at The Hague in January 1966, he had referred to the world role as 'on the whole expensive and unrewarding', only to be warned by his superior, Sir Paul Gore-Booth, 'controversial, omit'.[21] During a heated argument with the Cabinet economic advisers in June 1966, O'Neill was appalled to be told that Britain could not afford to join the EEC on the basis of existing policies. He intemperately retorted that 'the conclusion to be drawn was not that suitable conditions for entry in to the EEC were not likely to be created in the foreseeable future, it was that present policies were in any case wrong'.[22]

By the time of the crucial meeting of ministers at Chequers to discuss policy towards the EEC on 22 October 1966, several members of the Cabinet were moving in the same direction. Brown was the most obvious example, asserting in his memoirs that 'it seems to me that a purely Commonwealth role for Britain is now unthinkable'.[23] Tony Benn and Crossman, though with less enthusiasm, were reaching similar conclusions. Benn's initial view, before his transformation into a bitter opponent of the EEC in the 1970s, was that involvement with the EEC would purge British policy of the last vestiges of the imperial mentality. Crossman similarly offered muted support for a 'probe' of European capitals by Wilson and Brown in the hope that it might bring about a reappraisal of Britain's world role.[24] Denis Healey subsequently acquiesced in this development, and the draft White Paper on Defence in July 1967 asserted that 'the main commitments we shall have in the mid-1970s will be in Europe'. As John Darwin has observed, Healey's calculations were partly based on the assumption that local powers, especially Australia, would begin to shoulder some of the burden of defence in the far eastern region.[25] Finally, Wilson appeared to be seeking a new role for Britain through adherence to the Treaty of Rome, and he asserted that the need to drive through a renewed application played a part in his decision to move Brown to the Foreign Office in September 1966. This enabled the second application to become the heart of the government's foreign policy, '*faute de mieux*' as Wright later described it.[26] Therefore, although no decision had been taken in July 1966 either on EEC membership or on withdrawal from east of Suez, the pressure to act both in Cabinet and in the PLP was mounting.

Once Wilson had made his November 1966 announcement that his tour of European capitals with Brown would take place at the start of 1967, an inherent conflict emerged between the strategies of the EEC application and Commonwealth defence. On one hand, the two main obstacles to EEC membership were Britain's financial weakness and the reluctance of French President Charles de Gaulle to change the decision he had made in January 1963 to veto British entry to the EEC. To tackle both these problems, O'Neill, in particular, wanted the government to publicise the choices made after July 1966. The news of defence cuts would, it was hoped, renew confidence in sterling and undermine the French government's argument that Britain had too many extra-European commitments to be suited to EEC membership. This was to be the line taken by Wilson and Brown during their discussions with de Gaulle in January 1967.[27] On the other hand, the relationship with the Asian Commonwealth countries and with Australia was based on the military partnership against communism. Successful military strategy relies in part upon secrecy, a point made by Holt in some outspoken criticism of Britain's defence cuts. After a tour of east and south-east Asia in March and April 1967, he forcefully told the Australian House of Representatives:

> Our interest in Asia is deep. It must be developed and it must be permanent, for my Government and I believe that Asia is now the

crucial area of the struggle to preserve the values of independence, liberty and social justice for which we have previously fought in two global wars ... I believe that for all the shift and change in the world, none is more important to us in Australia than the shift of international tensions from Europe to Asia.

Holt firmly conveyed this message of a continental switch in the Cold War (which corresponded closely with the views of Wright) during meetings with Wilson in the summers of 1966 and 1967.[28] These ideas seem to have limited his reaction to the EEC, but they also inspired him to offer some not always welcome advice on Britain's defence policy. For this reason, the timing of his visit to London in July 1966, at precisely the time when Wilson faced agitation from the Labour back benches over 'east of Suez' defence and Vietnam, proved somewhat unfortunate. In a press conference at the end of his visit, Holt complained that Britain had become 'almost oblivious' to events in the Pacific.[29]

Holt showed greater circumspection in 1967, both on the subject of east of Suez defence and on the EEC application. On the defence cuts, he limited himself during the visit in March of Herbert Bowden, the Secretary of State for Commonwealth Affairs, to echoing warnings from Singapore and Malaysia about the risks of announcing the planned withdrawals in advance. Bowden also indicated to his Cabinet colleagues that Australia was 'realistic' about Britain's entry to the EEC.[30] Nonetheless, British defence cuts and EEC entry were inextricably linked in the minds of the Australian Cabinet, where ministers agreed to parallel strategies to shape British policy on both issues. In May 1967, ministers concluded that the best way to make Britain reconsider the changes in defence policy would be to 'show, in terms of the British interest, the developing significance of Asia'. Four months later the Australian Trade Minister, Jack McEwen, who had held the post at the time of the first application, advised his colleagues that the government should accept Britain's pledge of 'best endeavours' for the protection of Australia's interests in the EEC negotiations. He explained that 'in order to induce Britain to fight for effective safeguards for Australian interests, it will be necessary to demonstrate that there are ways by which Britain, and probably the EEC also, could enjoy significant continuing advantages in the Australian market'.[31] The Australians had thus accepted that Wilson's government must pursue policies consistent with British interests, but were not reconciled to the idea that those interests would best be served by a strategic focus on Europe instead of Asia.

DEVELOPMENT AND UNITY IN SUB-SAHARAN AFRICA

The same links and choices between the Commonwealth and the EEC were even more apparent in the case of Wright's reference to the 'elimination of poverty in the third world', a need which was most urgent among the African Commonwealth states. The developing regional power that appeared to be a test case of the relationship between Britain and former colonies in sub-Saharan Africa was Nigeria. Its population of 50 million was significantly larger than any other sub-Saharan African state. It also had considerable economic potential, thanks above all to an emerging oil industry.[32] Britain's growing financial difficulties undermined its traditional role as a source of investment and market for exports, both of which would assist Nigerian development. The massive balance-of-payments deficit which greeted Wilson's Cabinet in 1964 obliged the government to violate the principle of free entry for Commonwealth exports by imposing a universal 15 per cent surcharge on imports of manufactured goods. In May 1966, renewed financial difficulties brought a further restrictive measure in the form of limitations on private capital investment in the Commonwealth.[33] Although Nigeria was not directly the target of this measure, the move clearly indicated that Britain could no longer be relied on as a ready source of funds.

Britain's declining importance to Nigeria obliged the government in Lagos to consider alternative economic relations. The central aspect of this search for new export markets and sources of investment was represented by Nigeria's application for association with the EEC under Part Four of the Treaty of Rome. During Britain's first application to the EEC, Nigeria had joined with a group of developing Commonwealth countries, led by Ghana, to condemn the concept of EEC association as a form of 'neo-colonialism' which would perpetuate the political and economic dependence of former colonies upon their erstwhile European masters.[34] The EEC appeared to respond to such criticisms, and when the process of association was formalised under the Yaoundé Convention during 1963 and 1964, the relationship was changed in two ways: first, the Convention guaranteed that developing countries which associated with the EEC would not have to accord preferences to the member states in return for access to the common market; second, a Council of Association was set up in which the Associated Overseas Territories (AOTs) could negotiate with the Six as equal partners, rather than having their interests represented by the European imperial powers. This countered the resentment that Commonwealth countries had felt when Britain had bartered on their behalf during the first application. Combined with the economic imperatives of development, these concessions to African opinion were enough to reverse the decision of the Nigerian government, which began moves to associate with the EEC in the same year as de Gaulle's first veto.[35]

Once this decision was taken, it became clear that Nigeria's size and significance made it the target of French, or more precisely Gaullist, foreign policy. De Gaulle hoped to expand French influence beyond the francophone African states and Nigeria was the obvious choice as a location to begin this process. As in the debates on defence policy previously discussed, O'Neill played a vital role in bringing this development to the attention of ministers in London. He was assisted by Sir James Marjoribanks, his successor as the British Head of Mission to the European Communities in Brussels. In his valedictory dispatch from Brussels in May 1965, O'Neill engaged in a lengthy tirade against the behaviour of the French within the EEC. One of the examples he held up was the French reaction to Nigeria's association bid. In 1964, the French had begun to demand reciprocal preferences from Nigeria in return for association. This would not only entail Nigeria discriminating against British exports in favour of those from the EEC, it would also be contrary to the GATT's 'no new preference' rule which prevented Britain from expanding the Commonwealth preferential trading system. O'Neill advised the Foreign Secretary, Stewart, that 'it is France alone who stands between Nigeria and an agreement with the Community in line with the GATT ... and Nigeria's tradition of non-discrimination'. In addition, the French demands set an alarming precedent for the three east African Commonwealth states, Kenya, Uganda and Tanzania, which were by that time also considering EEC association:

> France insists, and is likely to continue to insist, on terms which the East Africans will at least be very reluctant to grant and which will damage their relations with other countries if they grant them.[36]

This pessimistic analysis made sufficient impression upon Stewart that he sent a copy to Wilson.

The point was reinforced in the months that followed. The impending agreement between Nigeria and the EEC did indeed seem to be undermining faith in existing trade arrangements. In July 1965, the Nigerian Foreign Minister, Pius Okigbo, dismissed Britain's concerns by saying that the British were being 'too doctrinaire' in their adherence to the GATT. This corresponded with the complaints of the President of the Board of Trade, Douglas Jay, who was pressing the government to issue a warning that 'if Nigeria were to grant the preferences against us, pressures must be expected to arise in this country for the withdrawal of preferences from Nigeria: the pressures would have much substance and it is doubtful if the Government would be able to resist them'. Moreover, officials at the Commonwealth Relations Office (CRO) pointed out that the terms of the Nigerian agreement were far less favourable to Nigeria than those which the Yaoundé Convention accorded to the existing AOTs.[37] In this situation, Ghanaian leader Kwame Nkrumah's fears during 1961–63 that EEC association might be used as a European tool for disrupting African unity began to appear less far-fetched. What became clear to Marjoribanks was that officials in the European Commission were prepared to resist the tide of criticism from Britain because, in reality, there was some sympathy with French plans for expanding the EEC's role in Africa into the Commonwealth. In July 1965, the European Commissioner for Development Aid, Henri Rochereau, who was in charge of the association negotiations, told him that the Commission was

> ... quite prepared to admit that the agreement as it stood was not in conformity with ... the GATT. The alternative, however, was to have no agreement, and the Community, for general reasons in its relations with African states was most desirous of concluding an arrangement with an English-speaking country of Nigeria's size and influence.[38]

The implication was that French policy in Africa had received the blessing of the Commission itself.

The need to counter this development had a profound impact on Stewart and seems to have been a significant factor in his growing support for a renewed application to the EEC. Even before O'Neill's return from Brussels, Stewart warned Wilson that 'the Commonwealth will fix up their own arrangements with the Six ... in which case the EEC will inherit our place in a large part of Africa'. In his memoirs, Stewart explained that this formed a crucial element in his own 'conversion' to EEC membership:

> I had feared that membership of the EEC would estrange us from Commonwealth countries, but it became increasingly clear that one Commonwealth country after another was seeking trade

agreements with the EEC; if we stayed out we should in the long run be further removed from the Commonwealth than if we went in.[39]

The CRO discovered the same trend after February 1966, when a circular telegram was sent to delegations in Commonwealth countries to ascertain the likely reaction to a renewed EEC application. The replies revealed that governments in Sierra Leone, Zambia, Malawi, the Gambia and even Ghana (where Nkrumah had been deposed by General Joseph Ankrah in 1965) had all considered applying for EEC association irrespective of British membership.[40] In 1967, this thinking was incorporated into the EEC application itself, with Wilson and Brown emphasising after their return from their probe of EEC capitals that it would be important for Britain to join the EEC before 1969 in order to participate in the renegotiation of the Yaoundé Convention.[41]

Understandably, if the need to protect the Commonwealth against French opportunism encouraged the Foreign Office to consider a new application to the EEC, this attitude was also likely to reinforce de Gaulle's determination to exclude Britain from the Community. Even during the first application, the French had shown themselves reluctant to allow British territories to share in the benefits of association on the same terms as French colonies.[42] In January 1966, Stewart drew the attention of the Cabinet to the marked antipathy of French policy in Africa towards British interests:

> De Gaulle has succeeded through the Yaoundé Convention in extending the preferential trading system which linked France and her former dependent territories to the EEC as a whole, although it works much more in favour of France than of her partners. This system is illiberal, in contrast to the sterling area, and constitutes a serious obstacle to the introduction of a generalised system of preferences for the developing countries at large.

Stewart concluded the paper with the ominous and uncharacteristically forthright comment that 'I am afraid we are for the present dealing with a regime under the control of a man whose attitudes and intentions are in most cases hostile to our own.'[43]

In 1967 a Commonwealth crisis erupted in Nigeria itself, exacerbating the problems the British government faced in developing a coherent stance towards the EEC and sub-Saharan Africa as a result of French and broader European interest in developing the region for their own ends. Following the murder of Prime Minister Abubakar

Tafawa Balewa in January 1966, a series of military coups had taken place, accompanied by intensifying inter-ethnic violence as the Ibo minority fought for greater power and recognition. In May 1967 the predominantly Ibo, oil-rich Eastern province announced its secession from the Nigerian federation and declared independence as the state of Biafra.[44] The outbreak of the Biafran War had broader implications for the future of many African Commonwealth countries with significant ethnic divisions, and these above all impelled the Labour Cabinet to sustain the Nigerian federal government in Lagos. An official brief prepared for the Defence and Overseas Policy (OPD) committee reported that the 'general African attitude' was one of opposition to the secessionist movement, and because of this 'our NATO [North Atlantic Treaty Organisation] and Commonwealth allies are also likely to be reluctant to recognise a secession'. Yet the brief sounded a warning note on French policy: 'It is conceivable that the French will be prepared to face African criticism if they judge that they could obtain substantial commercial benefits in the East at our expense.'[45]

In the event, the Biafran secession occurred at a time when de Gaulle's campaign against 'Anglo-Saxon' influence was reaching a feverish peak. In this context, the French reaction to developments in Nigeria was even more hostile to British interests than had been expected. The state news agency, Agence France Presse, began to distribute, in English, pleas for support from Biafran leader Colonel Odumegwu Ojukwu, and reports on the civil war entirely focused upon the Biafran struggle for independence. This represented a grave embarrassment for Wilson and Stewart, as British backing for the Nigerian federal government provoked moral outrage from a large group on the left of the PLP, among whom the former Secretary of State for Commonwealth Relations, Philip Noel-Baker, was prominent. The lengthy defence of British conduct by Stewart in his memoirs provides an insight into how deeply the criticism was felt.[46] French efforts to generate international sympathy for Biafra intensified beyond Britain's EEC application, and by 1968 the Commonwealth Office was receiving evidence that French mercenaries were being transported from airfields in neighbouring francophone African states to fight in Nigeria alongside the separatists.[47] One official at the Paris embassy noted ruefully that the French were seemingly in a winning position whatever the outcome of the war. If the Ibos were victorious, France would have an oil-rich client state in Biafra. If the federal government triumphed, it could not afford to retaliate by cancelling French oil concessions in Nigeria, as the French government had 'a hostage, in the form of the EEC association agreement with Nigeria'.[48] Hence, Stewart's fears about the expansion of malign French influence in Africa if Britain failed to enter the EEC were justified. Furthermore, while Gaullist rivalry constituted a strong motivation for Britain to attempt EEC entry, it also reaffirmed the obstacle that France presented.

RACE AND DISUNITY IN SOUTHERN AFRICA

French policy was equally a complication for the last of the three Commonwealth issues, which was undoubtedly at the forefront of Wright's mind when he wrote of 'taking the sting out of race relations'. Southern Rhodesia was one of Britain's last colonies in Africa, and Wilson made strenuous but ultimately unsuccessful efforts to overcome the unrelenting opposition of the colony's small but powerful white minority, led by Ian Smith, to the prospect of black majority rule after independence. On 11 November 1965, the Smith regime made a unilateral declaration of independence (UDI), plunging the Commonwealth into prolonged disputes over how to bring Rhodesia back to legality.[49] The major power in the region was not a member of the Commonwealth, and herein lay part of the problem. The power in question was South Africa, which had abandoned the Commonwealth during the Prime Ministers' Meeting of March 1961 in the face of growing odium over its policy of apartheid. After this time, Britain's strategy towards South Africa became one of containment. Since Macmillan's Cape Town speech of February 1960, British policy-makers had consistently made clear their opposition to apartheid, and sought to prevent its influence from spreading beyond South Africa's borders. However, they feared an outright confrontation which could jeopardise the position of neighbouring states. In addition, Britain was reliant upon South African supplies of raw materials such as uranium, diamonds and above all gold.[50] This strategy became even more important after UDI as the prospect of South Africa reaching out to white minorities in other countries appeared increasingly likely. At the same time, the balancing act became far more difficult.

After a special meeting of the Organisation of African Unity (OAU) in December 1965, Tanzania and Ghana suspended diplomatic relations with Britain over Wilson's refusal to launch an armed intervention to remove the Smith regime. At a Commonwealth crisis meeting in Lagos in January 1966, the same demands were made by many African delegates, but were again resisted by Wilson.[51] A military conflict in Rhodesia would have imperilled Britain's precarious

financial position, and there were concerns that it might also precipitate an attack on neighbouring Zambia by pro-Smith forces.[52] It was in
the aftermath of the January 1966 meeting that Wright composed his
memorandum to Wilson on foreign policy. Significantly, he noted that
'if we fail to solve the Rhodesian problem', it would then be appropriate to consider EEC membership, although for largely negative
reasons. He thought that 'public opinion in this country would under-
go a revulsion from responsibilities and would seek refuge in a form
of Euro-chauvinism'. Wilson's own attempt to preserve Commonwealth unity with the assurance that economic sanctions could be
used to bring down Smith 'in a matter of weeks, not months' proved
highly optimistic. His own adviser on security matters, George Wigg,
later commented that it 'defied history as well as reason'.[53] Certainly,
the illegal regime seemed no closer to collapse when Commonwealth
Prime Ministers again assembled in London in September 1966.

As a result of the acrimonious Commonwealth Prime Ministers'
Meeting in September, the Rhodesian and EEC questions became
linked, for it appears that, having undergone a revulsion from his
Commonwealth responsibilities at this time, Wilson became convinced of the need to apply for membership of the EEC. Wilson
described the Commonwealth conference in his memoirs as 'by common consent the worst ever held up to that time', while Wright later
recalled how 'each PM, when he spoke, seemed to feel that he had to
outdo his predecessor in abuse ... It was quite sickening to me; it must
have been far worse for Harold Wilson.' The Zambian Foreign
Minister, Simon Kapwepwe, eventually walked out of the meeting
and held an impromptu press conference at Heathrow airport, in
which he described Wilson as a 'racialist supporting a fascist government' in Rhodesia.[54] Unsurprisingly, when meeting Commonwealth
Secretary-General Arnold Smith in April 1967, Wilson systematically
poured cold water on all of Smith's ideas for rebuilding Commonwealth links. He refused to hold another conference even to discuss
Britain's approach to Europe, for fear that 'the Afro-Asian members.
... might well press for the use of military force or for sanctions
against South Africa. ... Moreover, the Commonwealth showed little
disposition to help Britain.'[55]

The crisis over Rhodesia also affected other members of Wilson's
Cabinet, and the consequences of the stormy Commonwealth conference were still lingering in the air when ministers discussed the EEC
in October and November 1966. In a joint submission to ministers
attending the 22 October Chequers meeting, Brown and Stewart
noted that 'developments in the Commonwealth may in any case

make it more difficult for us to exercise world-wide influence as the central nation in that multi-racial community'.[56] Wilson's agreement at the Commonwealth meeting to step up sanctions against Rhodesia also threatened further economic damage to Britain, and possibly even a rupture in relations with South Africa. In light of this, Chancellor James Callaghan advocated applying to join the EEC at a Cabinet meeting on 9 November 1966, which followed up the Chequers discussions. He indicated that, in the event of an economic war of attrition with Rhodesia, EEC membership might be essential for maintaining Britain's financial position and restoring international confidence in the economy.[57]

However, if Rhodesia helped propel Wilson's Cabinet towards consideration of an EEC membership application, it once again complicated relations with France. In one of his characteristic press conferences in January 1965, de Gaulle launched into a polemic against the hegemony of the dollar over international payments. His solution, drafted mainly by his personal economic advisor Jacques Rueff, was to restore gold as the international currency by doubling its price against the dollar. This was evidently a plan aimed at striking a blow against American financial power, which he attempted to peddle to world opinion by saying that gold was the only currency acceptable to all, as it had 'no nationality'.[58] This may have been the view from Paris, but it did not correspond with the perspective from London. In November 1966, a Cabinet paper considering the risks of deteriorating relations with South Africa estimated that the country supplied 70 per cent of non-communist gold supplies.[59] With this factor in mind, British officials had recommended rejecting the so-called 'Rueff Plan' at an early stage, and the Treasury brief for Wilson's visit to Paris in April 1965 warned that 'an increase in the price of gold ... would increase liquidity arbitrarily, giving advantage also to the gold producing countries, especially South Africa'.[60] The British government, despite its own dollar shortage which the Rueff Plan might have helped resolve, could not for reasons of Commonwealth diplomacy agree to enhance the economic power of South Africa.

Unfortunately, de Gaulle's government took full advantage of Britain's financial weakness to persist in demands for the reform of international liquidity, and increasingly the French hinted that their agreement to Britain joining the EEC might be conditional upon Britain supporting French financial schemes. The message was driven home publicly by Maurice Schumann, Gaullist leader of the Assemblée Nationale, in a press conference on 12 January 1967. Arguing that Britain could not afford the cost of EEC entry due to national indebtedness, he said that 'classical measures would never enable Britain to repay her debts', and instead advocated something more innovative. Inevitably, the measure he suggested was 'doubling the price of gold'.[61] De Gaulle treated the eventual devaluation of sterling in November 1967 as vindication of these claims in the statement with which he vetoed Britain's second application on 27 November. That Wilson and Callaghan turned to US support for sterling at this time, rather than opting for the Rueff Plan, doubtless reinforced his determination to exclude Britain from the EEC.[62]

In the twilight period between de Gaulle's second veto and 19 December, when the Cabinet accepted that it was impossible to start negotiations with the EEC, South Africa re-emerged as a divisive issue. At an informal meeting with members of the PLP, Callaghan raised the possibility of resuming arms sales to South Africa as part of the measures to right the stricken balance of payments. This was contrary to the spirit of the Party's 1964 election manifesto, which had pledged to ban all arms sales to South Africa, as well as to the United Nations (UN) Resolution of June 1964 which had inspired the manifesto pledge. Callaghan's indiscretion produced a fortnight of violent Cabinet disputes during which, as Healey later managed to joke, 'a good time was had by all'.[63] A study by Tim Bale notes from the comments of Cabinet members that most generally felt the controversy was as much about Wilson's style of government as about attitudes to apartheid, but there was one striking point in terms of foreign policy.[64] Brown and Stewart, who had been allies in advocating EEC membership, found themselves on opposite sides in the debate on South African arms sales. Stewart, variously described as the most principled and logical member of the Cabinet during the crisis, felt that the resumption of arms sales would destroy any vestiges of the multiracial Commonwealth. He seems likely to have been the minister at the OPD meeting of 8 December 1967 who warned that 'the moral issue involved in supplying arms to South Africa was so important and our commitment to it so deep that we should not supply them'.[65] He therefore confirmed the continuing importance he attached to the Commonwealth, even after the EEC application.

By contrast, Brown demonstrated that his priorities lay firmly with Europe. At a Cabinet meeting on 18 December, he argued that the confidence of the 'friendly five' (Belgium, Germany, Italy, Luxembourg and the Netherlands) had already been shaken by the devaluation of sterling. He showed particular irritation at one of the measures proposed to cut Britain's costs following devaluation – the removal of one of Britain's brigades in Germany – exactly the measure he had opposed in July 1966. Once again threatening resignation, he expressed the view that the revenues which would be lost by cancelling outstanding arms contracts in South Africa (approximately £300 million) could have allowed the government to keep the brigade in Germany. He may also have been the unidentified minister who warned at an earlier meeting on 15 December that France might seek to embarrass Britain by stepping into the breach as South Africa's principal trading partner and arms supplier.[66] In practice, however, there is evidence that Brown did not consider Commonwealth relations a complete irrelevance. In February 1967, the long-suffering British Special Ambassador in southern Africa, Malcolm Macdonald, suggested that Wilson should make a tour of Africa, in the style of Macmillan's 1960 visit during which he made his celebrated 'wind of change' speech in Cape Town, to mend the fences broken the previous September. Wilson was implacably opposed to the idea, but Brown told Gore-Booth that he regretted the fact that 'the Prime Minister was inclined to put off this necessary encounter rather longer than was expedient'.[67] It thus appears that Brown did not totally disparage the Commonwealth dimension of British foreign policy. To Michael Palliser, Wilson's Private Secretary, the reason that Brown and Stewart disagreed over east of Suez defence in 1966 and over arms sales to South Africa in December 1967 was a difference in the nature of their support for EEC entry. For Stewart, it was a decision made with the head, which could be overruled where it conflicted with other policy. For Brown, it was a decision of the heart, which overrode other policy.[68] So Brown supported any measures, like east of Suez withdrawal, that he thought would facilitate the EEC application, and opposed any measures, even standing up to apartheid, that he believed would impede the application.

CONCLUSION

It seems that the growing significance of Third World politics, and the increasing financial vulnerability of Britain and French efforts to harness both these developments to their advantage, served to undermine Britain's sway over the Commonwealth. The CRO appeared to approve of this process of devolution, with a brief for Holt's visit in July 1966 commenting that 'the Commonwealth is still inevitably largely Anglo-centric. We hope that it will not go on that way indefinitely.' Holt did not take the same view, and the shifting balance of power within the Commonwealth provoked him to take an unhelpful line on Rhodesia. He told Bottomley that if he 'were a

Rhodesian, he would feel that he was committing racial suicide by giving a majority vote to the Africans'. When he visited again a year later, it was conceded that the Commonwealth was no longer 'a major factor in Australian political thinking. They regret that the white Commonwealth no longer dominates, and regard with horror the behaviour of some of the African members. They are not particularly sympathetic to our policy over Rhodesia.'[69] Such attitudes represented an Australian version of the 'Euro-chauvinism' Wright had warned against, and probably propelled Wilson and other members of his Cabinet towards the EEC application at the same time as propelling Holt away from the Commonwealth.

None the less, the conventional wisdom that London was freer to table the second application because of the declining importance of the Commonwealth as a factor in British foreign policy by the later 1960s does not stand up when tested against the official record. The evidence drawn on in this chapter indicates that the Commonwealth context added two crucial impediments to the second application to the EEC. On the external front, this was a region carefully cultivated by de Gaulle as part of his policy to expand French influence into Africa. Britain's approach to this series of Commonwealth crises served to aggravate Anglo-French relations still further at a time when British entry would surely only have been secured on the basis of closer diplomatic ties. On the domestic front, Commonwealth policy deepened tensions in the Labour Party over Europe. In January 1966, Wilson described Wright's submission as 'ahead of the way I had been thinking, and certainly ahead of establishment thinking', yet Wright's view that the developing world would become a priority for Britain in the forthcoming years was shared by a vocal left-wing group in Wilson's own party.[70] Indeed, it should have been clear in Britain, as a founding member of the Commonwealth, that the organisation's rapid expansion signified the growing importance of former colonies in Asia and Africa in international affairs. All aspects of Commonwealth policy that have been analysed, defence policy east of Suez, the development of sub-Saharan Africa and the Rhodesian crisis, resulted in criticism of the government's conduct from the left wing of the PLP. Some of this criticism surfaced in the Cabinet, mostly through Castle. In addition to her complaints about the perpetuation of the east of Suez role, she also conducted what one of Wilson's biographer Ben Pimlott described as a 'one-woman campaign against concessions to the Smith regime'.[71] These left-wing figures were in many cases the same people whom Wilson had led in opposition to the first EEC membership application in 1961–63 and a significant number remained hostile to a renewed application. Castle was one of the few to vote against making an application at the decisive Cabinet meeting of 30 April 1967.[72]

What Castle and others questioned was whether the EEC application was genuinely undertaken as a means of confronting Wright's 'real problems of the future', or merely evading them. The editor of the *Daily Mirror*, Hugh Cudlipp, told his chairman Cecil King that 'Wilson is in trouble in Rhodesia and in a mess at home and this is, in part, a gigantic red herring to distract attention'.[73] This assessment, while according with conventional depictions of Wilson as a skilled tactician using Europe for personal and party ends, was uncharitable. Official papers not available to Cudlipp indicate that Wilson, Stewart and Brown, as well as O'Neill, were all considering whether an enlarged EEC might in the future share the burden of defence and development outside Europe itself. With the benefit of hindsight, such hopes were by no means unrealistic. However, the historical context of the second application was one of Gaullist obduracy, and the judgements made by Wright both at the time and in retrospect appear accurate. The EEC application was indeed *'faute de mieux'*.[74] It was not necessarily an attempt to distract the attention of the public, but neither was it an immediate remedy to the Third World issues within the Commonwealth which de Gaulle, from his lofty vantage point within the EEC, was already considering. As Wright observed at the time, de Gaulle 'has a clearer idea of the way the world is heading'. Given the position and policies of France within the EEC in 1967, it seems fair to conclude with Wright that 'the time for joining Europe and influencing it is past. The time may come again in the future. But certainly the time is not in the present.'[75]

NOTES

The author would like to thank his supervisor, Dr Ronald Hyam, all those who commented on his presentation during the conference at the Institute of Historical Research in January 2000, and Dr David Reynolds and the members of the International History seminar at Cambridge University, where an earlier version of this chapter was presented.

1.   E. Barker, *Britain in a Divided Europe, 1945–1970* (London: Weidenfeld & Nicolson, 1971), p. 185.
2.   L. J. Robins, *The Reluctant Party: Labour and the EEC, 1961–75* (Ormskirk: G. W. Hesketh, 1979), p. 22.
3.   U. Kitzinger, *The Second Try: Labour and the EEC* (Oxford: Pergamon, 1968), document 25, pp. 196–7.

4. See, for example, J. Darwin, *Britain and Decolonisation: The Retreat from Empire in the Post-War World* (London: Macmillan, 1988), especially Chapter 7.

5. J. D. B. Miller, *Survey of Commonwealth Affairs: Problems of Expansion and Attrition, 1953–69* (Oxford: Oxford University Press, 1974), Ch. 16.

6. J. W. Young, *Britain and European Unity, 1945–1999*, 2nd edn (Basingstoke: Macmillan, 2000), pp. 173–4.

7. Public Record Office (PRO): PREM 13/905, Wilson handwritten comment on Stewart to Wilson, 26 January 1966.

8. PRO: PREM 13/905, Wright to Wilson, 28 January 1966.

9. For a recent overview of this topic see J. Pickering, *Britain's Withdrawal from East of Suez: The Politics of Retrenchment* (London: Macmillan, 1998).

10. Miller, *Survey of Commonwealth Affairs*, pp. 83–98; D. Healey, *The Time of My Life* (London: Michael Joseph, 1989), pp. 285–90; D. Reynolds, *One World Divisible: A Global History Since 1945* (London: Allen Lane, 2000), pp. 261–71.

11. PRO: CAB 129/128, C(67)35, memorandum by Jay (Board of Trade) on 'The Kennedy Round', 21 Mar 1967; PRO: CAB 129/130, C(67)91, Jay memorandum on 'The Outcome of the Kennedy Round', 2 June 1967.

12. PRO: CAB 133/329, pp. 14–15, record of meeting between Wilson, Bottomley and Holt, 11 July 1966.

13. B. Castle, *The Castle Diaries, 1964–70* (London: Weidenfeld & Nicolson, 1984), p. 5 (28 January 1965); R. Crossman, *The Diaries of a Cabinet Minister, Vol. I, Minister of Housing 1964–66* (London: Hamish Hamilton/Jonathan Cape, 1977), p. 117 (3 January 1965).

14. PRO: CAB 130/294, minutes and report of meeting of Working Party on Economies in Oversea Expenditure, 15 July 1966.

15. Castle, *The Castle Diaries*, p. 142 (14 July 1966).

16. M. Stewart, *Life and Labour: An Autobiography* (London: Sidgwick & Jackson, 1980), pp. 199–200.

17. Castle, *The Castle Diaries*, p. 148 (18 July 1966); Crossman, *The Diaries of a Cabinet Minister, Vol. I*, p. 578 (20 July 1966). Some had been moving towards this position while in Opposition. See P. Catterall, 'Foreign and Common-wealth Policy Opposition: The Labour Party', in W. Kaiser and G. Staerck (eds), *British Foreign Policy, 1955–64: Contracting Options* (Basingstoke: Macmillan, 2000), pp. 89–110.

18. Churchill Archives Centre (CAC): Michael Stewart papers, STWT 9/6/8, copy of 'Never Again', dated 19 July 1966.

19. Ibid., Forsyth memorandum on 'Never Again', 20 July 1966; H. Wilson, *The Labour Government, 1964–70: A Personal Record* (London: Weidenfeld & Nicolson/Michael Joseph, 1971), p. 243.

20. PRO: CAB 148/69, OPD(O)(66)24, 'The Politico-Military Implications of United Kingdom Entry into the European Communities' (second draft), 29 July 1966.

21. PRO: FO 371/188327, undated draft of speech to be given at The Hague by O'Neill on 14 January 1966 and comments by Gore-Booth.

22. PRO: CAB 134/2757, sub-committee on economic implications, EO(E)(66), first meeting, 3 June 1966.

23. G. Brown, *In My Way: The Political Memoirs of Lord George-Brown* (London: Victor Gollancz, 1971), p. 209.

24. T. Benn, *Out of the Wilderness: Diaries 1963–67* (London: Hutchinson, 1987), p. 496 (30 April 1967); R. Crossman, *The Diaries of a Cabinet Minister, Vol. II, Lord President of the Council and Leader of the House of Commons, 1966–68* (London: Hamish Hamilton/Jonathan Cape, 1976), p. 30 (10 September 1966).

25. PRO: CAB 129/130, C(67)117 draft White Paper on Defence, 4 July 1967; Darwin, *Britain and Decolonisation*, p. 296.

26. Wilson, *The Labour Government*, p. 272; Wright, letter to the author, 14 April 1999.

27. PRO: CAB 134/2812, EUR(O)(66)36, official brief on 'The Attitude of the French', 10 January 1967; Wilson, *The Labour Government*, pp. 335–8.

28. *Australian House of Representatives Debates*, 54, p. 1173, 12 April 1967; PRO: CAB 133/329, pp. 14–15, record of meeting between Wilson, Bottomley and Holt, 11 July 1966; FO brief for visit of Australian Prime Minister, 1 June 1967; FCO 24/1, Commonwealth Office memorandum on 'Defence Policy in the Far East', 8 September 1967.

29. *Sunday Express*, 3 July 1966, p. 1; *The Times*, 15 July 1966, p. 8.

30. PRO: CAB 129/128, C(67)37, Bowden memorandum on tour of Far East and South Pacific, 17 March 1967; PRO: CAB 129/128, C(67)66, Bowden memorandum on 'United Kingdom Entry into the EEC: The Reactions of the Commonwealth', 27 April 1967.

31. National Archives of Australia (NAA): A5842/2, Cabinet submission 283 (Foreign Affairs and Defence Committee), 'Britain and East of Suez Defence' and Decision 357, 25 May 1967; A5839/2, Cabinet submission 466 (J. McEwen), 'United Kingdom–Australia Trade Relations', 14 September 1967.

32. Miller, *Survey of Commonwealth Affairs*, pp. 252–3.

33. PRO: CAB 128/39, CC 2(64)5, Cabinet conclusions, 22 October 1964; *Hansard: House of Commons Debates*, 727, columns 1444–9, 9 May 1966.

34. See, for example, PRO: DO 161/196, text of speech by Ghanaian Finance Minister Goka to Commonwealth Prime Ministers' Meeting, fifth session, 11 September 1962. On the background to EEC association, see D. K. Fieldhouse, *The West and the Third World: Trade, Colonialism, Dependence and Development* (Oxford: Blackwell, 1999), pp. 99–102.

35. CAC: William Gorell Barnes papers, BARN 7/1, 'Africa and the EEC', paper by T. Soper for Royal Institute of International Affairs study group on 'Britain's Interest in Africa's Relationship with the EEC', February 1966; PRO: FO 371/177380, p. 3, O'Neill, 'Commonwealth Association to EEC: Nigerian Case', 23 January 1964.

36. PRO: PREM 13/306, pp. 8–12, O'Neill to Foreign Office Economic Affairs (General) Department, 3 May 1965.

37. PRO: PREM 13/450, p. 23, Marjoribanks to Foreign Office, 28 July 1965; p. 17, Roberts to Moon, 29 July 1965; pp. 30–1, Moon to Nicholl, 26 July 1965.

38. PRO: PREM 13/450, p. 32, Marjoribanks to Foreign Office, 24 July 1965.

39. PRO: PREM 13/306, p. 125, Stewart to Wilson, 3 March 1966; Stewart, *Life and Labour*, p. 162.

40. PRO: EW 5/6, Commonwealth Office circular telegram to various posts, February 1966; replies from Crombie, 7 April 1966 and Bolton, 14 April 1966; CRO background notes for Western European Union meeting (29–30 September 1966), 19 September 1966.

41. PRO: CAB 129/129, C(67)60, Wilson and Brown memorandum on 'Approach to Europe', 24 April 1966.

42. See, for example, PRO: CAB 134/1514, CMN(62)35, Common Market Negotiations Committee memorandum on 'Association of Under-Developed Overseas Countries and Territories', 15 June 1962; PRO: DO 159/29, Robinson to Foreign Office, 21 May 1962.

43. PRO: CAB 129/124, C(66)6, Stewart memorandum on 'de Gaulle's Foreign Policy in the Next Two Years', 28 January 1966.

44. PRO: CAB 128/42, CC 35(67)3, Cabinet conclusions on Nigeria, 1 June 1967.

45. PRO: FCO 25/234, p. 2, brief by Meyer on 'Nigeria: Secession of Eastern Region', 10 May 1967.

46. See correspondence and cuttings in CAC: Philip Noel-Baker papers, NBKR 4/41

and 4/44; Stewart, *Life and Labour*, pp. 225, 238–45.

47. PRO: FCO 25/232, pp. 52–3, Hunt to Commonwealth Office, 11 and 19 January 1968.
48. PRO: FCO 25/234, p. 74, Everson to Commonwealth Office, 5 Aug 1968.
49. Wilson, *The Labour Government*, p. 170; PRO: CAB 128/40, CC 60(65)1 and CC 61(65), Cabinet conclusions on Rhodesia, 11 and 16 November 1965.
50. For the general background to Anglo-South African relations, see R. Hyam, 'The Parting of the Ways: Britain and South Africa's Departure from the Commonwealth, 1951–61', *Journal of Imperial and Commonwealth History*, 26, 2 (1998), pp. 157–75, and J. W. Young, 'The Wilson Government and the Debate over Arms to South Africa in 1964', *Contemporary British History*, 12, 3 (1998), pp. 62–86.
51. Miller, *Survey of Commonwealth Affairs*, p. 215; Wilson, *The Labour Government*, pp. 195–6.
52. Wilson, *The Labour Government*, pp. 180–1; PRO: CAB 128/41/2, CC 41(66)5, Cabinet conclusions on Rhodesia, 2 August 1966.
53. PRO: PREM 13/905, Wright to Wilson, 28 January 1966; G. Wigg, *George Wigg* (London: Michael Joseph, 1972), p. 326.
54. Wilson, *The Labour Government*, p. 277; Wright, letter to the author, 14 April 1999; *The Times*, 14 September 1966, p. 7.
55. PRO: FCO 25/233, p. 6, record of meeting between Prime Minister and Arnold Smith, 5 April 1967.
56. PRO: CAB 134/2705, 'Britain and Europe', memorandum by Brown and Stewart, 19 October 1966.
57. PRO: CAB 128/41/3, CC 55(66)1, Cabinet conclusions, 9 November 1966.
58. C. de Gaulle, *Discours et Messages, Vol. IV* (Evreux: Plon, 1970), p. 333.
59. PRO: CAB 129/127, C(66)172, memorandum by Bowden, 25 November 1966.
60. PRO: T 312/1320, p. 40, 'Brief for Prime Minister's Visit to Paris', 26 March 1965.
61. PRO: PREM 13/826, minutes of a meeting between Debré, Callaghan and Armstrong, 10 December 1966; PRO: FCO 30/168, Reilly to Foreign Office, 12 January 1967.
62. Kitzinger, *The Second Try*, document 32, pp. 311–16; J. Callaghan, *Time and Chance* (London: Collins, 1987), pp. 217–20.
63. Healey, *The Time of My Life*, p. 336.
64. PRO: CAB 128/42/3, CC 71(67) and CC 72(67), 15 and 18 December 1967, entirely on the sale of arms to South Africa; T. Bale, 'A "Deplorable Episode"? South African Arms and the Statecraft of British Social Democracy', *Labour History Review*, 62, 1 (1997), pp. 22–40.
65. Crossman, *The Diaries of a Cabinet Minister: Vol. II*, p. 604 and Healey, *The Time of My Life*, p. 335; PRO: CAB 148/30, OPD 39(67)4, 'South Africa: Maritime Defence Supplies', 8 December 1967.
66. PRO: CAB 128/42/3, CC 71(67) and CC 72(67), 15 and 18 December 1967.
67. PRO: FCO 25/233, p. 3, MacDonald to Commonwealth Office, undated, February 1967; p. 4, Gore-Booth to Rose, 3 March 1967.
68. Palliser, interview with the author, 7 April 1999.
69. PRO: CAB 133/329, p. 86, brief for the visit of the Australian Prime Minister on 'The Future of the Commonwealth', 1 July 1966; p. 7, meeting between Holt and Bottomley, 8 July 1966; PRO: FCO 24/1, Commonwealth Office brief for visit of Australian Prime Minister, June 1967.
70. PRO: PREM 13/905, Wilson marginal comment on Wright to Wilson, 28 January 1966.
71. B. Pimlott, *Harold Wilson* (London: HarperCollins, 1993), p. 337.
72. Castle, *The Castle Diaries*, pp. 250–1 (30 April 1967).

73. C. King, *The Cecil King Diary, 1965–1970* (London: Jonathan Cape, 1972), p. 95 (10 November 1966).
74. Wright, letter to the author, 14 April 1999.
75. PRO: PREM 13/905, Wright to Wilson, 28 January 1966.

11

'We Too Mean Business': Germany and the Second British Application to the EEC, 1966–67

KATHARINA BÖHMER

Prime Minister Harold Wilson's announcement to the House of Commons on 10 November 1966 that his Labour government would embark on a second attempt to join the European Economic Community (EEC) was met benevolently by the German government. German missions abroad were instructed to declare officially:

> We attach great importance to the Wilson announcement, as for the first time the Labour government thus refers to … Great Britain's accession to the European Economic Community as an objective of their foreign policy … We think that it is now the time to encourage the British on their way to Europe and to pave the way for them.[1]

This favourable attitude should not have surprised the British, as Germany's support for Britain's EEC membership was an important prerequisite for the second application.[2] In contrast to, and perhaps as a consequence of, the abortive attempt to join the Community in 1963, the British application strategy in 1967 was much more focused on the capacity of the 'friendly five' (Belgium, Germany, Italy, Luxembourg and the Netherlands), and especially Germany, to influence France's attitude towards Britain. Like his predecessor Harold Macmillan, Wilson knew that the attitude of the French President Charles de Gaulle would be decisive for the outcome of his government's bid. If there was a lesson that had been learned from 1961–63 it was that 'if the French were reluctant about British membership, then the British would have to ensure maximum German leverage upon them'.[3] One of the questions at stake in 1967, therefore, was whether the Labour government would be any more successful in enlisting German support for its cause than the Conservatives had been.

At the end of October 1967, shortly before de Gaulle's second veto on British membership, German Chancellor Kurt Georg Kiesinger reaffirmed to Wilson that 'we too mean business',[4] explicitly echoing the Prime Minister's words a year earlier.[5] He clearly intended to reassure the British of continued German support for their application. But why did such a favourable German attitude not help the British into the Community? This chapter will explore British–German diplomacy over the second British membership bid in three parts. It begins by considering relations between the two states in the aftermath of de Gaulle's first veto in January 1963, up to the efforts made by Britain to secure German backing for the membership bid in the early months of 1967. It goes on to assess German foreign policy priorities after the change of government in 1966 and their effects on the British application strategy. Finally, it explores the difficulties Germany had in framing a foreign policy that supported Britain's application while at the same time maintaining French support for its first steps of *Ostpolitik*.[6] The main contention is that British and German interpretations of each others' European 'business' within the context of the second British application 1966–67 differed considerably. Thus, it raises questions of mutual perception and misperception: how were Germany's European interests perceived across the Channel? In what ways did the British expect to meet these objectives? How far could German support be only conditional in order not to interfere with constraints and limitations of Germany's foreign policy? In 1966–67, both countries might have 'meant business', but unfortunately for Britain, Germany's 'business' was to stabilise relations with France and eastern Europe. Enlargement of the Community was a sorry third on its list.

ANGLO-GERMAN 'BUSINESS', 1963–66

Seen from London, Germany's relative importance for a renewed approach to the EEC had increased considerably since the abortive application in 1961–63. Although de Gaulle's veto had provoked a crisis in Anglo-French as well as Anglo-German relations,[7] the disappointment about Bonn's failure to pressurise Paris into accepting British membership had not lasted for very long. The accession to power of a new Federal government under Ludwig Erhard in the autumn of 1963, followed by Labour's accession to power in Britain one year later, only intensified bilateral attempts to revive the state of British–German relations, which had apparently been rather 'frozen' in the early months of 1963.[8] By 1965, Queen Elizabeth's highly successful state visit to Germany contributed to the impression that relations between the two countries were again healthy.[9] On the British side, the belief in the German will to integrate Britain politically and economically into Europe even at the risk of provoking French resistance, reappeared. Given the strong position that 'Atlanticists' like Foreign Minister Gerhard Schröder held in Erhard's government, Germany seemed again a very useful partner in Europe. Good relations with Bonn were also needed to help combat the economic crises with which the Labour government had to cope. As Foreign Secretary Michael Stewart explained to the Cabinet in 1965: 'The German economy is so strong that the Federal Government has a part to play second only to the US in deciding whether we obtain what we need from the international community.'[10] In political terms, German policy on the questions of *détente* and disarmament were considered to be equally important for the shaping of the British position on these issues.[11] Germany thus played an important role in British European policy considerations.

Although the idea of enlisting German support in the attempt to join the Community was not new at all,[12] the hope seemed justified that it could prove more successful now than in the early 1960s. From the British perspective, the 'empty chair' crisis which had unsettled the Community in 1965 had revealed Germany's role as the 'leader of the Five' against France.[13] Stewart, for one, concluded that the Germans were 'now showing signs of being readier to stand up to the French', recommending that his colleagues 'secure German co-operation' in order to improve the British 'prospects of shaping Western Europe's economic and political future'.[14] Taking into consideration that de Gaulle was no more willing to accept British EEC membership now than he had been three years earlier, the British application strategy developed in the early months of 1966 attributed a crucial role to the German ability to work in support of Britain's aims in Paris. From Bonn, the British Ambassador Sir Frank Roberts, sustained this image of a 'friendly Germany' throughout the years 1965–66, which was consequently floated within the Foreign Office and successfully conveyed to Cabinet members. While still head of the Department of Economic Affairs (DEA), George Brown, for instance, was only too ready to pick up this view of a German ally and to consider British–German political cooperation as a means of 'outflanking' de Gaulle.[15]

In Bonn, the internal British preparations for a new move on the European front did not remain unknown. In January 1966, the German Ambassador in London, Herbert Blankenhorn, had already reported to the Auswärtiges Amt (the German Foreign Office) that, according to official declarations, 'Labour's famous Five Conditions for British entry would be dealt with more pragmatically'.[16] In May 1966, Chancellor Erhard made clear to Wilson that his government would be glad if Britain's attitude towards the EEC would make further progress and informed him that he had been discussing with Schröder the idea of promoting the British cause within the Community. This, he believed, would be met by a positive reaction from the other member states – except, crucially, France.[17] In the course of 1966, the importance Whitehall officials assigned to Germany's enthusiasm for the British application increased steadily. When Brown took office as Foreign Minister in August 1966, he was briefed by his officials about Germany's 'key position in Europe' and the need to establish 'very close Anglo-German relations' because of converging interests in problem areas such as East–West relations, disarmament, economic cooperation within western Europe, 'including our entry into the EEC' and the 'reconstruction of NATO made necessary by recent French moves'.[18]

During the early months of 1966, in what could best be described as the Labour government's 'ground-testing-phase', the issue of British EEC membership became a live issue in Anglo-German diplomacy. Generally, German reactions to British soundings were positive. In May 1966, Roberts reported a conversation with the German Economics Minister, Karl Schmücker, who had made clear that his government had always advocated Britain's accession to the Community. Indeed, the Germans were more than ever convinced that 'it was a vital necessity and should not be too long delayed'.[19] Schmücker's personal conviction was that the 'EEC would probably break up or fade away' if a favourable decision on British membership had not been reached by the end of 1967, owing to the alarming state of Franco-German relations. He nevertheless pointed out that:

> Although resistance had to be made to the French and Germany was the only EEC country strong enough for this purpose it was politically undesirable in the wider sense that Germany should take up such a lead. During last year's EEC crisis she had been able to work through the Belgians, the Italians or the Dutch in turn but this could not go on forever. The EEC needed the United Kingdom as the essential balancing factor.[20]

This was consistent with one of the most important German motives for support of British membership: its possible effects on Community balance. Schmücker's argument corresponded to the conclusion the British themselves had drawn from the 'empty chair' crisis, which in their eyes had revealed the growing discontent among the Five with the French claim to leadership of the Community, thus suggesting growing acceptance of British membership as a potential counterbalance to France.[21]

In Bonn, the distinct signs of Whitehall's evolving European policy after the March election of 1966 – such as the assignment of special responsibilities for British relations with Europe to Brown and the new Chancellor of the Duchy of Lancaster, George Thomson – induced Schröder to arrange a closer examination of the difficulties of Britain's accession to the EEC within the Auswärtiges Amt.[22] Shortly after Wilson's November announcement, preparations for possible enlargement negotiations were institutionalised. Under the chairmanship of the Auswärtiges Amt, representatives of the ministries concerned formed a working group *EWG-Großbritannien*.[23] But the promising prospects of British–German cooperation on the application issue suddenly seemed threatened when internal difficulties within the Erhard government reached their climax, causing the Chancellor to resign and leading to the formation of a coalition government of the CDU (Christian Democratic Party) and the SPD (Social Democratic Party), the so-called Great Coalition, in November 1966.[24] Kiesinger, the CDU premier of Baden-Württemberg, became Chancellor. The appointment of politicians such as Willy Brandt as Foreign Minister and Deputy Chancellor, and the reputed 'Gaullist' Franz-Josef Strauss as Finance Minister, indicated the new government's foreign policy alignment.[25] The reanimation of Franco-German relations and further improvement of those with the East at the expense of the 'Atlantic' policy of their predecessor were to become central issues. However, the *Regierungserklärung* (governmental declaration) issued to parliament on 13 December 1966 stated among other foreign policy objectives the intention to influence the EEC's further development and the conviction that 'the Community of the Six should be open to all those European states who agree with its aims'.[26] The participation, it said, of Britain and other European Free Trade Association (EFTA) countries would be particularly welcomed, as would the development and deepening of Germany's relations with Britain.

Favourable as this seemed for the British, this statement was slightly watered down by the stress the declaration put on the reanimation

of the Franco-German treaty of 1963 and on the confirmation of intensified German interest in *détente*. The British were left to conclude that
the question of EEC enlargement was only one point among several
German foreign policy priorities; nor did it feature high on the list.
Soon after the establishment of the Kiesinger government, Roberts
voiced his concern that the British 'high level exploration of the position of the Six towards British entry' would now 'unfortunately coin-
cide with first attempts of the new German Government to improve
Franco-German relations', adding that it would be unrealistic to
expect 'tough and active support' from the Kiesinger government.
And despite his attempts to convince the Germans that 'we mean
business and that we expect German professions of support to be
translated into practical help', he had to conclude, 'there are some
frankly discouraging trends'.[27]

GREAT COALITION PRIORITIES

These 'discouraging trends' only multiplied in the course of the following months, as the Great Coalition seemed more and more eager
to avoid anything like a showdown with the French. In January 1967,
Roberts was told by the German Minister of Economics, Karl Schiller,
that 'Kiesinger and Brandt would undoubtedly find it difficult to
introduce the necessary degree of firmness over the problem of
British entry into the EEC into this renewed Franco-German
embrace'.[28] At a conference of European Socialist Parties in Rome the
same month, Brown had to cope with this more cautious German attitude and felt 'greatly discouraged by the negative and unhelpful attitude' of his German colleague.[29] Brandt was reported to have implied
that he regarded the Franco-German alliance as of overriding importance for Germany and that he was not disposed to help the British if
this seemed likely to provoke French distrust.[30] In fact, Brandt was far
more willing to support the British cause than Brown's report would
suggest. A few days later, he and the Italian Prime Minister, Aldo
Moro, publicly agreed on a common line according to which 'both
Italy and Germany wanted the United Kingdom in the Common
Market and would work for it', although neither of them would be
prepared to arrange for the substitution of France by Britain or for the
break up of the Community, two scenarios proposed by the Italian
Socialist leader Pietro Nenni.[31] Brandt recalled in his memoirs the misjudgement 'in some places' that it would depend on Bonn to persuade Paris by exercising German authority. He himself could only
warn of the 'temptation to confront France with a united bloc of the

Five', which in his view had by all means to be avoided.[32] In spite of this friction, Brown continued to keep his German colleague informed about the talks in Rome and in Paris, trying to convince him that de Gaulle would in the end acquiesce, 'provided we all show a solid front'.[33]

Back in London, Brown's Rome experience made a profound impression, particularly on the Prime Minister. Wilson pointed out to the US Ambassador David Bruce 'that in the forthcoming exercise [the British] must expect the Germans broadly to toe the French line and could certainly not regard them as an ally'.[34] Just before the Prime Minister and the Foreign Secretary embarked on their 'probe' of the capitals of the Six, his Private Secretary, Michael Palliser, summed up the prevailing impression in Downing Street: 'We have to win over de Gaulle: if we do, the Germans fall with him.'[35] Changing political reality thus appears to have rendered obsolete the initially promising tactic of winning over de Gaulle with German help. To make German support the precondition for any successful outcome of the membership bid no longer seemed a promising strategy. The optimism of the previous months was therefore beginning to wane even before Wilson and Brown returned from their European tour.

Nevertheless, attempts at official and embassy levels continued to be made, especially in order to influence the German position at the first Franco-German summit.[36] In Paris, Kiesinger referred to public opinion and German industry being in favour of Community enlargement and to Britain's role as an important trading partner for Germany. While emphasising German economic interest in British membership, on a pragmatic note he pointed out that it would be hard for his government to reject the British desire in case the applicant were ready to accept 'all the conditions of the Common Market'.[37] At the same time, however, he assured de Gaulle of his understanding for the French position. Indeed, the re-establishment of good personal relations between French and German leaders as a result of the new German government's attempt 'to make the 1963 treaty work' was seen as the main achievement of this meeting, and judged much more important than the issue of British membership.[38] Following the advice of the Auswärtiges Amt, Kiesinger had tried to avoid getting 'drawn at this stage into an argument with General de Gaulle, the only result of which would have been to stiffen the General's opposition'.[39]

Against increasing pressure from British and German officials favouring British entry, the federal government reacted by reiterating their December declaration.[40] At the official level, however, German assistance was more forthcoming. Referring to the fact that 'the

Germans had had so many difficulties themselves with the French that he thought their experience might be useful', State Secretary Ralf Lahr offered his help in suggesting how to present the British case in Paris.[41] Nevertheless, the Elysée meeting between Wilson, Brown and de Gaulle in January 1967 produced no tangible consequences; the Foreign Secretary's conviction that the General had at last accepted that the British 'meant business' was not shared everywhere in Whitehall.[42] The political climate surrounding the British soundings in Bonn on 15 and 16 February was hardly more promising. A few days earlier, Soviet premier Alexei Kosygin, on a visit to London, had stressed that the Germans would have to sign the nuclear Non-Proliferation Treaty (NPT) 'whether they wanted to or not'.[43] His words had not passed unnoticed in Bonn,[44] and only added to existing bilateral difficulties, as throughout 1967 British–German relations were hardly tension-free. Although there existed the principle of disagreement on British accession to the EEC, other issues put a strain on relations between Bonn and London. The most obvious rift was over the British government's decision in the Defence White Paper of February 1966 to pull forces out of the British Army of the Rhine (BAOR) because of the need to reduce overseas military expenditure, even after securing an improved offset agreement.[45]

But neither the British nor the German side was interested in letting these problems have repercussions on the enlargement talks. Kiesinger and Brandt reaffirmed that they were in favour of Britain's Community membership for political and economic reasons, stressed that they would do what they could to facilitate British entry and suggested further bilateral discussions, but no real commitment was pronounced.[46] Arguably, the limits within which German readiness to pressurise de Gaulle over British membership was considered reasonable, were quite narrow. Nevertheless, during the following months, German 'strong and active support' for the British cause was reiterated at every opportunity.[47]

BRITISH 'EUROPEAN BUSINESS' AND GERMAN 'EUROPEAN BUSINESS', 1967

The official British application to the EEC, transmitted to Brussels on 11 May 1967, was publicly welcomed by the German government, who once again assured the British that they could 'rely on their full support both on substance and procedure'.[48] When, a few days later, the, reputedly, most 'Gaullist' German politician, Finance Minister Strauss, came out in favour of opening immediate discussions among the Six on British accession – while simultaneously criticising de Gaulle for 'thinking that an honourable past and tradition could replace the law of numerical superiority' – this only reinforced the illusion still cherished in parts of Whitehall that Bonn would be willing actively to support the British application.[49] German movements on the European scene were therefore closely observed, especially regarding the summit meeting of the Six in Rome in May 1967, held to celebrate the tenth anniversary of the signing of the Treaty of Rome. After an intense diplomatic tug-of-war, even France had acquiesced in participating, albeit only after the Five had agreed on meeting without the Commission and guaranteed that the application issue would not officially feature on the Rome agenda.[50] Nevertheless, soundings on the summit by Roberts were seemingly reassuring: State Secretary Klaus Schütz of the Auswärtiges Amt informed Roberts that the German intention in Rome remained 'to do everything possible to clear the way for an early reply to [the British] application'.[51] But Brandt's frank admission about German ignorance of French intentions made it questionable what form German 'help' in Rome would actually take.[52]

In Germany, the disappointing outcome of the Rome meeting contributed to growing discontent with the government's performance on the European stage in political and industrial circles, and the Cabinet came under increasing internal pressure to stress 'German national interests in this matter rather more forcefully in Paris and in their public statements'.[53] It was possibly this background of mounting internal criticism that made both Kiesinger and Brandt state once again their intention to press the case for British entry on grounds of German 'national interest' in a parliamentary debate in June 1967. Yet, there appears to be another factor in Germany's unwillingness to turn the Rome meeting into a confrontation on the issue of enlargement. The first months of the Great Coalition witnessed the gradual reorientation of German foreign policy towards eastern Europe, symbolised by the resumption of diplomatic relations with Romania in early 1967. Partly resulting from this process, there existed divergent European policy objectives within the government as well as within both ruling parties and among different ministries.[54] At the beginning of 1967, Kiesinger reassured de Gaulle that his government did not intend to pursue a policy which aimed at British EEC membership against French resistance, and that he wished for close relations with France as a partner in *détente*.[55] Likewise, Brandt was fully aware that his political objectives, the easing of tensions in Europe and especially between the two 'Germanys', had no chance of succeeding without French approval.

But, in spite of the German government's efforts to prevent disagreement with the French on enlargement from interfering with warmer Franco-German relations, the situation between the two states deteriorated after de Gaulle's 'velvet veto' in May 1967. And as friction grew between France and Germany, German support for Britain's accession to the EEC became more qualified. By the end of May, Kiesinger explicitly described the need for Britain to accept the 'Rome treaties and the past and future development of the Community' as a precondition for any further German help.[56] Even if this was only an expression of the Chancellor's 'more careful and reserved attitude',[57] in London it was judged as an indication that support for the British was waning in German governmental circles.[58] Still, the majority opinion in Whitehall remained that the key to a successful outcome of the EEC application lay in Bonn, with the corresponding illusion that a careful handling of German interests – or what was perceived as such – would guarantee success in Brussels. German politicians did their best to nourish British hopes that Germany would back the British application against French resistance. Brandt reaffirmed to Alun Chalfont, Minister of State at the Foreign Office, that the Federal government considered its relationship with France to be of great importance, but that 'this did not mean that they [the Germans] should not do or say things which needed to be done or said' and even hinted that in order to avoid a renewed French veto Germany might 'not be prepared just to continue the existing arrangements for agriculture' within the Community.[59]

Slightly more qualified was the encouragement Chalfont was given by Strauss, who explained that Germany wanted British membership 'though not at the cost of starting the Third World war of this century with the French'.[60] But once the British had become distrustful of the German sincerity they were not that easily convinced. By October 1967, they had come to the conclusion that the Germans, and particularly the Chancellor, saw their role as mediator, rather than negotiator, on Britain's behalf and, while keen not to provoke the General, were still concerned with 'bringing the French round'.[61] In view of this assessment it is all the more interesting to see how closely German officials were working together with their British counterparts. Giving advice on how to handle German politicians, Lahr told Chalfont in October 1967 that the British should try to persuade Kiesinger that 'rather than relying on him to bring pressure on the French, [the British] regarded him as the statesman who was best able to bring about a truly European situation'.[62] But despite all these different British attempts at enlisting German support, the federal government held on to its mediatory role by making clear to the French that Britain's accession was an important aim of their European policy, but that it was not prepared to risk a crisis in Franco-German relations on this issue.[63] In the event, the French were able to veto the British application without meeting German resistance at the Council of Ministers meeting on 19 December 1967, a fact which induced an SPD member of parliament to declare: 'Now we are in the EEC crisis.'[64]

In the months May to November 1967, between the official British application and de Gaulle's press conference that confirmed its failure, relations between Britain and Germany on European questions were characterised by what one could probably best describe as denial of the obvious. Politicians on both sides had come to realise that the real game was played on another stage, namely the French. But although the Anglo-German diplomatic performance had been downgraded to a sideshow, the illusion was maintained in London as well as in Bonn that Germany could still re-emerge as a main actor who would contribute decisively to this 'game of European bluff', as Strauss called it.[65] Despite mounting recognition in Whitehall that ultimately the success of the application would depend on de Gaulle, if Germany and the other member states were not willing to risk a new crisis of the Community by translating their verbal statements into political action, intense diplomatic exchanges had to be maintained. But while the slightest development concerning the British application within German political circles was minutely reported to London, British EEC membership, as a short-term foreign policy goal, slipped further down the German agenda, where it had never featured highly in any case.[66] Kiesinger's hope, shared by his Foreign Minister, that his government's advocacy of British entry would not 'involve unnecessary collision with the French' indicates the limits of German support in Brussels.[67]

CONCLUSION

For Germany, Britain's second application to join the EEC meant the reappearance of the well-known dilemma between friendship with France and the enlargement of the Community.[68] The resulting, somewhat double-edged attitude of the Great Coalition had threatened Britain's approach to Europe from the moment it was formed in 1966. By the time Britain launched its application, it was understood in Whitehall that the Germans were either unwilling or unable to use their political leverage in Paris to help the Wilson bid. However, the

British still counted on a firmer German line *vis-à-vis* the French. The shift back to the strategy of the first application, to deal primarily with the French, was eschewed in favour of at least equal attention to manipulating the Germans. The development of Germany's policy towards Britain's second EEC application can only be satisfyingly explained when taking into consideration the changing character of German foreign policy under the Great Coalition. It is true that integration into the Western world still remained a constant of Germany's foreign policy, but in this period of reassessment and reorientation of German foreign policy towards, on the one hand, re-establishing the Franco-German axis and, on the other, undertaking the first steps of *Ostpolitik*, British entry to the EEC was simply not important enough for Germany to provoke a second Community crisis over this issue. Both Kiesinger and Brandt were convinced that their policy corresponded to intrinsic German interests, and the British application caused an almost insoluble dilemma for both of them, as neither could afford a deterioration in Franco-German relations.

This interpretation of the role that relations between London and Bonn played in the second British membership bid confirms the judgement which has been made concerning the first application: that the timing of the British application was wrong.[69] Based as it was very largely on domestic interests – not without reason many British politicians stressed the need of not 'losing momentum' – the Labour government's European timetable did not allow time for the diplomats to smooth the way with key players such as Germany. Arguably, an important role within the British application strategy was assigned to Germany, but in the event the federal government proved unable and unwilling to fulfil British hopes. The obvious misjudgement and misperception of Germany's 'European business' is therefore part of the failure of Britain's second EEC bid. One important reason for this misjudgement might be that the Labour government's view of Europe and their understanding of the politics of European integration was still blurred by the underlying motives of EEC entry, which had not essentially changed between 1961 and 1967. This British 'blindness' to German and European sentiment is obvious from Brown's exhortation to Brandt in December 1967: 'Willy, you must get us in, so we can take the lead.'[70] The Foreign Secretary's somewhat blunt and simplistic idea of inner European power mechanisms betrays one of the main British motives for the second application. In 1966–67, British European 'business' certainly had first of all to do with the question of how to enter the EEC, but equally with defining

Britain's European role as a potential Community member. Besides the fact that Germany was definitely not keen on replacing French supremacy in the EEC with British, its European interests were centred on issues that were incompatible with enlargement. The problem between Bonn and London in the context of the second application was that their respective European 'businesses' turned out to be conflictual rather than complementary.

NOTES

Research for this article was carried out in the Public Record Office, Kew, with financial assistance from Queen's College, Oxford, for which I would like to express my appreciation. Thanks are also due to Helen Langley and Frieda Warman-Brown for permission to consult the Lord George-Brown Papers in the Bodleian Library, Oxford, and to John Davis.

1. Translation of the original: 'Wir messen der Wilson-Erklärung große Bedeutung bei, weil die Labour-Regierung damit erstmals ... den Beitritt Großbritanniens zur EWG offiziell als Ziel ihrer Außenpolitik bezeichnet hat ... Wir meinen, daß es jetzt gilt, die Briten auf ihrem Weg zu Europa zu ermutigen und ihnen diesen Weg zu ebnen.' H. Schwarz (ed.), *Akten zur Auswärtigen Politik der Bundesrepublik Deutschland 1966* (Munich: R. Oldenbourg Verlag, 1997) (*AAPD 1966*), document 371, State Secretary of the Auswärtiges Amt, Lahr, to German embassy in Rome, p. 1529ff.
2. For the purpose of this article, 'Germany' refers to the Federal Republic of Germany or West Germany, unless otherwise stated.
3. A. Deighton, 'British–West German Relations, 1945–1972', in K. Larres (ed.), *Uneasy Allies: British–German Relations and European Integration since 1945* (Oxford: Oxford University Press, 2000), pp. 27–44. For more on Anglo-German relations and the first application see M. P. C. Schaad, *Bullying Bonn: Anglo-German Diplomacy on European Integration, 1955–61* (Basingstoke: Macmillan, 2000), and O. Bange, *The EEC Crisis of 1963: Kennedy, Macmillan, de Gaulle and Adenauer in Conflict* (Basingstoke: Macmillan, 2000), especially pp. 52–69.
4. H. Schwarz (ed.), *Akten zur Auswärtigen Politik der Bundesrepublik Deutschland 1967* (Munich: R. Oldenbourg Verlag, 1998) (*AAPD 1967*), document 362, record of a conversation between Kiesinger and Wilson in London, 23 October 1967, p. 1419 (English in the original).
5. Announcing his tour of the EEC capitals to the House of Commons on 10 November 1966, Wilson said: 'I want the House, the country, and our friends abroad to know that the Government are approaching the discussions I have foreshadowed with the clear intention and determination to enter EEC if, as we hope, our essential British and Commonwealth interests are safeguarded. We mean business.' *Hansard: House of Commons Debates*, 735, column 1540.
6. Deighton defines this policy succinctly: 'Ostpolitik was both about policy content and about policy style, and the way to effect changes in German–German relations, East–West European relations, and relations with the Soviet Union.' See 'British–West German Relations', p. 41.
7. Deighton, 'British–West German Relations', p. 39.
8. F. Roberts, *Dealing with Dictators: The Destruction and Revival of Europe 1930–1970* (London: Weidenfeld & Nicolson, 1991), p. 235.
9. For the Queen's visit of 18 to 28 May 1965, see H. Schwarz (ed.), *Akten zur*

Auswärtigen Politik der Bundesrepublik Deutschland 1965 (Munich: R. Oldenbourg Verlag, 1996) (*AAPD 1965*), document 239; and Lord George-Brown Papers, MS. Eng. c. 5012, fol. 12, List of Briefs for the Secretary of State, 11 August 1966: 'Anglo-German relations have in fact improved very greatly over the last few years and The Queen's very successful state visit to Germany last year symbolised this improvement.'

10. Public Record Office (PRO): CAB 129/122, 5 August 1965.
11. See, for instance, PRO: CAB 129/39, 23 September 1965.
12. For details see S. Lee, 'Germany and the First Enlargement Negotiations, 1961–1963', in A. Deighton and A. S. Milward (eds), *Widening, Deepening and Acceleration: The European Economic Community 1957–1963* (Brussels: Nomos-Verlag, 1999), pp. 211–25.
13. M. Camps, *European Unification in the Sixties: From the Veto to the Crisis* (London: Oxford University Press, 1967), p. 121.
14. PRO: CAB 129/122, 5 August 1965.
15. George-Brown Papers, MS. Eng. c. 5012, fol. 239, 'Correspondence and Papers as Foreign Secretary', Brown to Wilson, 23 June 1966: 'If we could create a situation in which we, with the Germans, were seen to be leading in the construction of a truly European approach to security, defence and foreign policy arrangements, and one which, unlike de Gaulle's, is explicitly based on *partnership* with the United States, it would, I think, be very difficult for de Gaulle to prevent the Five, and no doubt large sections of French opinion too, from rallying to such a position' (emphasis in original).
16. *AAPD 1966*, p. 179 (author's translation).
17. *AAPD 1966*, p. 667.
18. George-Brown Papers, MS. Eng. c. 5012, fol. 12, 'List of Briefs for the Secretary of State', 11 August 1966.
19. PRO: EW 5/8, Roberts to Foreign Office, 2 May 1966.
20. Ibid.
21. See also N. P. Ludlow, 'Constancy and Flirtation: Germany, Britain, and the EEC, 1956–1972', in J. Noakes, P. Wende, J. Wright (eds), *Britain and Germany in Europe 1949–1990* (Oxford: Oxford University Press, forthcoming).
22. PRO: EW 5/8, Galsworthy to Statham, 19 April 1966.
23. PRO: FO 371/188367, letter from Galsworthy to Statham, 14 November 1966 and Statham's reply to Galsworthy, 25 November 1966. See also *AAPD 1966*, p. 1006. The ministries involved were those of Finance, Economics, Research and Agriculture.
24. See A. J. Nicholls, *The Bonn Republic* (London and New York: Longman, 1997), p. 188.
25. See PRO: FO 371/188367, Roberts to Foreign Office, 1 December 1966: 'It is', he wrote, 'in fact a ministry of all the talents in which what hitherto had been the most contradictory views on Europe ... are represented ... The current mood in restoring a better relationship with France ... goes through all parties.'
26. *Verhandlungen des Deutschen Bundestages: Stenographische Berichte* (Bonn: Deutscher Bundestag, 1950 onwards), 63, p. 3656ff.
27. PRO: EW5/8, Roberts to O'Neill, 19 December 1966.
28. PRO: EW5/8, Roberts to Foreign Office, 9 January 1967.
29. PRO: PREM 13/1475, Palliser to MacLehose, 5 January 1967.
30. Ibid.
31. PREM 13/1475, Shuckburgh to O'Neill, 9 January 1967. For a German account, see *AAPD 1966*, p. 36, and C. Masala, 'Die Bundesrepublik Deutschland, Italien und der Beitritt Großbritanniens zur EWG', *Zeitgeschichte*, 25, 1–2 (1998), pp. 46–69.
32. W. Brandt, *Begegnungen und Einsichte: Die Jahre 1960–1975* (Hamburg: Hoffman and Campe, 1976), p. 197 (author's translation).
33. PRO: PREM 13/1476, letter from Brown to Brandt, 16 January 1967.
34. PRO: PREM 13/1475, Palliser to MacLehose, 10 January 1967.

35. PRO: PREM 13/1475, comment by Palliser on press cutting from the *New York Times*, 10 January 1967.
36. See PRO: PREM 13/1475, Brown to Roberts, 11 January 1967.
37. *AAPD 1967*, document 16, record of a meeting between Kiesinger and de Gaulle in Paris, 13 January 1967 (author's translation).
38. PRO: PREM 13/1475, Paris to Foreign Office, 15 January 1967.
39. PRO: PREM 13/1475, Roberts to Foreign Office, 20 January 1967.
40. See, for instance, PRO: PREM 13/1475, Bonn to Foreign Office, 11 January 1967.
41. PRO: PREM 13/1475, Roberts to FO, 20 January 1967.
42. See PRO: PREM 13/1476, Foreign Office to Bonn, telegram no. 296, 26 January 1967: Letter Brown to Brandt.
43. *AAPD 1967*, document 55, p. 274.
44. PRO: PREM 13/1477, Roberts to Foreign Office, 14 February 1967.
45. Since the beginning of the 1960s, and on American precedent, the British had negotiated several agreements with Germany to offset foreign exchange expenditure on the British Army of the Rhine (BAOR), under which Bonn was expected to procure military equipment from Britain. The Labour government renegotiated the existing agreement in June 1965, extending it to March 1967. With the expiry date drawing nearer and German unwillingness to provide a full offset becoming obvious, the offset commitments became a central issue in Anglo-German talks. Nevertheless, trilateral offset negotiations between Britain, Germany and the USA were successfully concluded in May 1967. On the NPT, German views were rather more diverse. However, influential members of the Great Coalition government raised objections against Germany's adherence to the treaty, advocated by the USA and Britain, for fear of being excluded from any further common nuclear development in Europe. Germany finally signed the NPT in 1969. See W. F. Hanrieder, *Deutschland, Europa, Amerika* (Paderborn: Ferdinand Schöningh, 1995), p. 73.
46. For the German account of the British–German talks in Bonn, see *AAPD 1967*, documents 55, pp. 271–82, and 57, pp. 284–91. For the British account, see PRO: CAB 129/128, 'Approach to Europe', memorandum by the Prime Minister and the Foreign Secretary, 16 March 1967, pp. 79–101.
47. PRO: PREM 13/1480, Roberts to Foreign Office, 27 April 1967.
48. PRO: PREM 13/1482, Roberts to Foreign Office, 11 May 1967.
49. PRO: PREM 13/1482, Roberts to Foreign Office, 22 May 1967.
50. See PRO: PREM 13/1479, record of a conversation between Wilson, Brown and Brandt, 13 April 1967.
51. PRO: PREM 13/1482, Roberts to Foreign Office, 24 May 1967.
52. PRO: PREM 13/1479, record of a conversation between Wilson, Brown and Brandt, 13 April 1967.
53. PRO: PREM 13/1483, Roberts to Foreign Office, 9 June 1967.
54. See D. Kroegel, *Einen Anfang Finden! Kurt Georg Kiesinger in der Außen – und Deutschlandpolitik der Großen Koalition* (Munich: R. Oldenbourg Verlag, 1997), p. 172ff, and R. Marcowitz, *Option für Paris? Unionspartien, SPD und Charles de Gaulle 1958 bis 1969* (Munich: R. Oldenbourg Verlag, 1996), p. 277.
55. *AAPD 1967*, document 16, record of a conversation between Kiesinger and de Gaulle in Paris, 13 January 1967, p. 92; PRO: PREM 13/1475, Paris to Foreign Office, 14 January 1967.
56. PRO: PREM 13/1482, Roberts to Foreign Office, 24 May 1967.
57. Ibid.
58. Ibid. This view was confirmed when Strauss told a foreign correspondent that there were 'different degrees of support for the UK within the Cabinet', whereas he and Schiller were strongly in favour, Kiesinger was more reserved.
59. PRO: PREM 13/1484, record of a conversation between Chalfont and Brandt in Bonn, 5 September 1967.

60. Ibid.
61. PRO: PREM 13/1485, Roberts to Foreign Office, 11 October 1967.
62. PRO: PREM 13/1485, Foreign Office to Bonn, 16 October 1967.
63. See K. Hildebrand, *Von Erhard zur Großen Koalition* (Stuttgart: Deutsche Verlags-Anstalt, 1984), p. 317.
64. Marcowitz, *Option für Paris?*, p. 279.
65. PRO: PREM 13/1483, Roberts to O'Neill, 16 June 1967.
66. PRO: PREM 13/1484, Chalfont to Brown, 8 September 1967.
67. PRO: PREM 13/1483, Roberts to Foreign Office, 9 June 1967.
68. R. Lahr, *Zeuge von Fall und Aufstieg. Private Briefe 1934–1981* (Hamburg: Knaus, 1981), p. 472.
69. Deighton, 'British–West German Relations', pp. 37–41.
70. Brandt, *Begegnungen*, p. 202. See also J. Wright, 'The Role of Britain in West German Foreign Policy since 1949', *German Politics*, 5, 1 (April 1996), pp. 26–42 (p. 41).

——12——

Ireland and Britain's Second
Application to Join the EEC

JANE TOOMEY

In an address to the Institute of European Affairs on 21 March 1994, British Foreign Secretary Douglas Hurd clearly illustrated the extent to which joining the European Economic Community (EEC) was a watershed in British and Irish history:

> Britain and Ireland joined the Community together because of a sense of our place in history. For the British it was about finding a new place in the world after two centuries of imperial experience ... For the Irish, membership in 1972 was about Ireland's place in history, confirming Ireland's position in Europe as a modern state ... and it's decisive shift away from the embrace of Britain.[1]

Closer examination of his words reveals one of the subtle, but at the same time crucial, variables in any discussion relating to Britain and Ireland's second applications to join the Community. The word 'together' is indicative of the entire relationship between the two countries when it came to the bid for membership, and is symptomatic of the way in which the Irish application has been eclipsed in the historiography by the British application. While this is inevitable, it is at the same time regrettable, for the Irish case is of significant interest to our understanding of the broader process and dynamics of European integration.

This chapter argues that, in order to understand more fully Harold Wilson's application to the EEC, greater attention needs to be paid to Ireland's approach to European unity in the 1960s, as there was a myriad of exchanges that took place between London and Dublin leading up to the second application bid. The predicament facing both countries in the 1960s was identical: 'they did not want to knock on some doors and had already knocked on others that were not open'.[2] Instead of being seen as a mere appendage to Britain's application, the Irish approach can indeed be incorporated into a framework for comparative analysis. Only then can one begin to answer such key questions as: what were the motivating factors that impelled Ireland to seek membership during the Wilson era? Was Britain's case unique, or did in fact other countries exhibit any similarities in terms of their approach to the EEC? What was the impact of Ireland's policy on Wilson's attempt and exactly how much did Irish concerns impinge on Whitehall thinking when it came to their European policy?

IRELAND'S APPROACH TO EUROPEAN UNITY

The verdict of a member of the Irish delegation on how the negotiations over British and Irish entry to the EEC were proceeding in the early 1970s could easily be applied to the first and second bids for membership: 'We're riding along on the backs of the British.'[3] Had it not been for the British decision to seek entry, it is highly unlikely that the Irish would have contemplated exploring the option at that time. *'Une île derrière une île'*,[4] sheltered behind Britain, it is no wonder that Ireland maintained such an insular attitude until the beginning of the 1960s. Believing that what happened in Europe was largely irrelevant, statements such as 'we are outside the whirlpool of European politics, we are largely untouched by the intrigues of European diplomacy',[5] voiced in 1934 by John Costello, later the Taoiseach,[6] further reinforced this view. The advent of war in 1939 did nothing to alter the consensus, for 'it was as if an entire people had been condemned to live in Plato's cave, with their back to the fire of life'.[7] Ireland, refusing to be drawn into the war, chose instead to remain neutral. In this context, it is not surprising that Ireland exhibited little enthusiasm for the process of European integration that began after the Second World War. Participation in the Marshall Plan, and membership of the Council of Europe and the Organization for European Economic Co-operation (OEEC), was as far as the Irish were willing to enmesh themselves in European integration. They played both the 'neutrality' card and the 'partition' card to explain why Ireland refused to join the North Atlantic Treaty Organization (NATO). 'In essence', observes Gary Murphy, 'the parameters of Irish foreign policy at this time continued to be defined by the relationship with Britain.'[8] Calls for a 'United States of Europe' fell on deaf ears, as Dublin showed no interest in signing the Treaty of Rome.

Thus, 'up to 1957, Ireland had only one foot rather gingerly placed on the path towards European integration'.[9] What would lead to a change of heart whereby Ireland began to turn towards the nascent EEC? The main driver was economics, a growing acknowledgement of the limits and failings of protectionism. With Sean Lemass, often described as a 'mould-breaker' and a 'mould-maker',[10] succeeding Eamon de Valera as Taoiseach in 1959, and with Kenneth Whitaker navigating the economic course as Secretary of the Department of Finance, it is not surprising that the merits of free trade were about to be embraced, shifting Ireland from an inward-looking to an outward-looking economy seeking new markets. In October 1956, a decision was taken by the Secretaries of the Departments of External Affairs, Industry and Commerce, Agriculture, Finance and the Taoiseach to scrutinise the viability of Irish association with other OEEC countries in a free trade area.[11] This was partly a response to the unveiling of Whitaker's report entitled 'Economic Development', which not only drew attention to the multiple weaknesses of the Irish economy' but also pointed the way towards remedying them. Old approaches would fast be abandoned in favour of new innovative measures; there was a growing understanding, he argued, of 'the need to introduce a little stick as well as carrot'.[12] Just as Frank Lee's report provided critical evidence in support of Britain's first application,[13] politicians in Ireland were finally coming to the stark realisation that the Irish could not keep hiding in Plato's cave any longer.

Hand in hand with the proposal to open up the Irish economy went fear of the consequences of Britain joining the EEC without Ireland:

> We have applied for membership of the EEC because it would be economic disaster for us to be outside the Community if Britain is in it. We cannot afford to have our advantageous position in the British market turned into one of exclusion by a tariff wall, particularly as our chief competitors would be inside this wall.[14]

One only has to look at these words from Lemass to ascertain the degree to which Britain's decision to seek membership necessitated similar action on the part of the Irish. It was largely inevitable that if Britain joined, Ireland would quickly follow suit, for in simple terms, to do otherwise would have been akin to economic suicide. It was sheer economic necessity that impelled the Irish to knock on the door of Europe, or instead they might well have been referred to not as 'the island behind the island', but as the 'bankrupt island behind Britain'.

Besides, the question of sovereignty did not pose a serious threat either to summoning or maintaining support for an application to the EEC. Ireland, due to a combination of historical and geographical factors, had not exercised the level of autonomy thought to be at the disposal of British policy-makers; joining the EEC was seen by many as a way of increasing as opposed to diminishing its independence. Thus, when it came to the decision, 'No farmer was going to say no to protected prices of the community, on the grounds of sovereignty, it just did not weigh in the scales.'[15]

It was these factors, the changing domestic economic agenda and the external influence emanating from Britain, that led to the publication in June 1961 of a White Paper on the EEC and the formal application for membership two weeks before Britain, on 31 July 1961. The path from this point on, however, was not so smooth, and as a result Ireland never even reached the negotiating table. Reservations about Irish membership were aired by members of the Six and the Commission on both economic and political grounds. Determined to rid the Six of any doubts about Ireland's capacity to join and her so-called 'special problems', the Taoiseach not only invited European journalists to a detailed session of questions in Dublin, but also set out to visit the capitals of the Six in October 1962.[16] Whitaker recalled Lemass telling him gloomily after his meeting with French President Charles de Gaulle: 'We have to work hard, he thinks association is good enough for us.'[17] 'Work hard' they did, actively advocating their desire to join the EEC at every turn. At the end of the month the Council of Ministers decided to allow Ireland to enter into negotiations but had yet to set a date. However, it was of little consequence because de Gaulle's '*Non*' to Britain on 14 January 1963 derailed all the applicants' hopes of joining the Community.[18] Britain was not the only country to be seen as 'awkward' in the eyes of mainland Europeans, but while Britain might have considered that it had no alternative to joining the EEC, the real meaning of 'no alternative' could only truly be understood by the Irish. Desmond Williams has contended that 'the foreign policy of states is of course determined by a number of factors, by economic interest, geographical location and military power, also by their past history and by present events'.[19] Pragmatic economic re-assessment, the intensity of Ireland's relationship with Britain and the changed international landscape ensured that Ireland had to apply for membership of the EEC at the beginning of the 1960s. Very similar motivations guided the second bid for membership.

'BRITAIN FIRST, THE REST LATER'

When de Gaulle vetoed British membership of the EEC in 1963, the Irish were automatically barred from joining too. As one Whitehall official put it at the time: 'When our negotiations were suspended in January 1963, the Irish did not pursue the matter further.'[20] Both countries had reached an impasse, and it would be another four years before any concrete attempt was made to launch another application process. On 1 May 1967 Wilson met with the Taoiseach, now Jack Lynch, to discuss the prospect of British membership of the EEC. It was confirmed that 'if we decided to negotiate for entry into the community, the Irish would undoubtedly renew their application'.[21] Within a matter of days, both countries had again declared their intent to seek membership of the EEC.

The joint approach appears to have been adopted for two main reasons. First, the signing of the Anglo-Irish Free Trade Agreement (AIFTA) in 1965 necessitated even deeper economic discussions between the two countries.[22] For example, on 8 and 9 November 1967 a meeting of the Anglo-Irish Economic Committee took place. The meeting was regarded as 'the first opportunity, since our applications were made, for officials from both capitals to sit around a table and review progress'.[23] This illustrates the extent to which economics and foreign policy continually overlap and also the way which both countries prioritised economic over political dimensions of integration. Second, both Wilson and Lynch favoured that strategy. Referring to the meeting between the leaders in February 1968, the *Cork Examiner* highlights the significance of personal diplomacy: 'The terse, uninformative terms of the official communiqué must not be allowed to disguise the fact that meetings between Mr Lynch and Britain's Mr Wilson are very important in the context of the bid for membership of the European Community.'[24] Classified as 'a firm believer in eventual Irish entry into the Common Market',[25] it is easy to see how, at times, Lynch's unswerving belief in the inevitability of admission assuaged some of Wilson's despair. Speaking about Ireland's hopes of entry, 'Mr. Lynch asserted that while he would not like to speculate on how long it would take "it will certainly happen in a matter of years". The same feeling inspires and encourages Mr. Wilson.'[26]

Thus, against the high wall de Gaulle had erected around Europe, it was helpful that, in Lynch, Wilson had a firm advocate not only of Irish but also of British entry to the EEC. The British had on their side a staunch ally to defend their economic policies and European credentials. On numerous occasions the Irish were keen to portray the British in the best possible light. After the visit to Paris in November

1967, Hugh McCann, Secretary of the Department of External Affairs, reported the Irish as 'having defended our position on the sterling balance on orthodox lines'.[27] Finally, through the Irish, the British managed to gain further insights into the attitudes of the French and the so-called 'friendly five' (Belgium, Germany, Italy, Luxembourg and the Netherlands). For example, Britain's Ambassador to Ireland, Andrew Gilchrist, left a meeting with Axel Herbst, Director-General for External Relations of the Commission,

> with the distinct impression that, not withstanding Mr. Wilson's determination to bring British negotiations to a successful close, it will be a very, very long drawn-out affair, that there is in fact little hope whilst the General is in the saddle.[28]

Considerable tension was to arise, however, over the tactics used in the application process, especially when it became feared that Britain might join without Ireland. Just as it was automatically assumed that Ireland would apply for membership of the EEC if Britain did, it was taken for granted that the two countries would negotiate at the same time. It was not something that was questioned or debated until the British Foreign Secretary, George Brown, launched Britain's application in a speech to the Western European Union (WEU) on 4 July. The speech was indicative of British thinking at the time: Britain's ultimate goal was to join the EEC as soon as possible. On 7 July 1967, Francis Gallagher (Head of the Western Economic Department 1965–67, and Head of the Common Market Department 1967–68) alerted the Irish to an approach then being mooted in the Council of Ministers: 'Britain first, the rest later.'[29]

> We naturally hoped that the Irish would be able to join the community [sic] at the same time as ourselves. But this might not prove possible in the event and we were certainly not committed to holding back until Ireland or any other country was ready.[30]

Lynch, who consistently held the view that Ireland and Britain should join the EEC at the same time, responded three days later:

> Our purpose in seeking parallel negotiations is to ensure the adoption of procedure which will afford the Irish government an opportunity of representing their views when any issue of direct concern to Ireland arises in the course of the British negotiations and, of course, vice versa. Our anxiety on this score is naturally

greater than that of other countries, since the terms on which Britain joins the community will have a far greater impact on Ireland than on other new entrants.[31]

The growing tension over tactics was captured by one commentator, Wesley Boyd, who, writing in the the *Irish Times* a month later, remarked:

> Mr. Wilson seems determined to get Britain into the Common Market. He will have enough troubles of his own without adding those of other countries to his shoulders. There can be no doubt that he is favourably disposed towards Ireland's application and would like to see us a member of the EEC along with Britain. However, if he sees an opportunity of taking Britain in without Ireland he can hardly be expected to let it pass. He could well argue that British membership is the best guarantee of Irish membership.[32]

His empathetic approach to London's negotiating stance put him in a minority. Elsewhere, Brown's statement led to bafflement and bemusement. In reaction to the speech, headlines such as 'George Brown bombshell shocks Irish EEC hopes' were not uncommon;[33] such cynicism amongst the Irish, ultimately led the Taoiseach to seek clarification from the Prime Minister. The drama that accompanied the speech was largely a result of Brown only applying for British membership, itself a product of the rushed way in which the application had to be made. But, as Wilson emphasised in a letter to Lynch, 'a situation could conceivably arise in which the processes of negotiation and ratification of our entry had been completed but yours had not'.[34] Not content, Lynch reiterated the point when he wrote to Wilson to inform him of the results of his own soundings of EEC capitals.[35] He stated that he had 'received not only a warm welcome and assurances of support for our application for membership, but also acceptance of our view as to the importance of parallel negotiations and simultaneous entry to the Community for both our countries'.[36]

The overriding concern on the part of the Irish was that the two countries would march in unison towards Europe, not one behind the other. Constant reference to 'simultaneous negotiations' and 'simultaneous accession' were heard as a result of Brown's speech. The Irish had been woken from their complacency: no longer able to take a back seat and allow Britain to drive them towards Europe, they now had to forge their own way. Ironically, Brown's speech served as a timely reminder of the need to adopt a more proactive approach to formulating an Irish European policy. As Boyd pointed out in the *Irish Times*,

> As far as simultaneous negotiations and accession is concerned, Mr. Brown has sounded the warning note – Britain cannot be depended upon to support this Irish policy. Ireland must press its own case vigorously. The Taoiseach and Mr [Charles] Haughey have been doing this and the measure of their success is that the governments of the Five and the European Commission do not regard simultaneous negotiation and accession as a problem.[37]

What impact did such concerns have on the Wilson administration? Did it ignore Ireland's fears? The answer to these pertinent questions is a resounding 'No'. The Wilson administration consistently wrestled with the problem of how to assuage Ireland's doubts. This was mainly because the British needed the Irish to form a united front, thus preventing de Gaulle from exploiting differences between the applicant states. It is to closer analysis of the impact of Ireland's policy on Whitehall decision-making that this chapter now turns.

'ASSOCIATION' OR *'UN ARRANGEMENT INTERMEDIARE'*?

'Sympathy but impossibility' is how Whitaker summed up de Gaulle's attitude towards Britain and Ireland's aspiration to full membership when the Irish visited the General in November 1967.[38] With this in mind, it is hardly surprising that the Irish were asked if they had ever contemplated associate membership. The Taoiseach stated that

> the President had then gone on to refer to the fact that some of the difficulties attached to the British application created difficulties for Ireland also. He then said that in the event of British negotiations and ultimate membership being delayed for a considerable period we would have French support and goodwill for securing an interim arrangement which would eventually lead to full membership.[39]

On a similar note, the *Irish Press* pointed out that Lynch was keen to emphasise that any such 'associate' arrangement 'would require long and detailed negotiations within the context of the Treaty of Rome, the Anglo-Irish Free Trade Agreement and the GATT [General Agreement on Tariffs and Trade] countries'.[40] Initially, then, the reaction to de Gaulle's suggestions was generally not favourable. As McCann pointed out, consideration of 'interim' arrangements might weaken the move towards full membership, but 'nevertheless they would have to take a look at it, if only because of the publicity in Paris which would lead to questions in the Dáil'.[41] As for the mention of the need for another Lynch–Wilson meeting, 'McCann thought this would be a natural development but at a later stage when last week's talks had been fully studied; in any case the Irish did not want to appear to be running to mother'.[42]

The idea of association was not, however, taken off the French agenda. When Bernard Ledwidge met with the Irish Ambassador in Paris, Patrick Commins, he reported that 'the French had left the Irish with the impression that as far as France was concerned, association as a stepping-stone to full membership was available, at least to Ireland'.[43] To the British, however, 'Vague French talk about association was a red herring'.[44] Ledwidge, for instance, worried that

> it looks as if the General turned his redoubtable charm on the Irish to some effect. He has sent them away with the idea that their application is not necessarily linked with Britain's in his eyes and might have a different fate, if that prospect interested the Irish Government. Apparently he has also interested them at least a little in the possibilities of association as a sort of delayed membership, if the answer to their present application proves to be negative.[45]

'At least a little' was certainly the operative phrase now, as what was earlier dismissed outright was now attracting an increasing amount of attention. The 'red herring' was brought up at the Anglo-Irish Economic Committee which met in Dublin on 8–9 November 1967. Upon probing from Arthur Snelling, Whitaker said he believed that the term 'association' had been implied for all the applicants. 'A war of nerves' was how Snelling described the confrontation with the French,[46] as the General raised obstacle after obstacle in order to prevent the British making any progress towards membership of the EEC. Anything less than full membership, he pointed out, was insufficient. 'Association, even if it were available to us, would not meet this fundamental requirement.'[47] His sentiments were echoed by Anthony Galsworthy at the British embassy in Paris, who was told that 'the general feeling in the Prime Minister's entourage was that de Gaulle's remarks either amounted to no more than a gesture of goodwill or else represented an attempt "to turn the British flank"'. He

concluded: 'The French, of course, have an obvious interest in popu-
larising at the moment the concept of association as a kind of purga-
tory for applicants.'[48]

De Gaulle's second veto of British entry to the EEC, delivered on
28 November 1967, destabilised Anglo-Irish relations still further.
Gilchrist contended that 'while the Irish had initially dismissed the
General's suggestions, the devaluation of sterling and the second …
Non … to Britain had prompted the Irish to have second thoughts'
and he concluded that 'they are very far from endorsing our own reiteration of "nothing but full membership"'.[49] He went on to cite part of
Lynch's speech to the Annual Conference of Fianna Fáil in November
1967:

> It will be necessary to examine carefully other possibilities open
> to us for entering into an interim arrangement with the
> Community on the clear understanding that any arrangement
> that might be negotiable would be a step towards membership
> and not a substitute for membership.[50]

What exacerbated the picture of an Irish government considering an
alternative entry strategy were statements by the likes of the Minister
of Finance, Haughey, to the effect that 'it would not be impossible for
this country to become a member of the Common Market without
Britain'.[51]

With Irish observers stressing the extent of de Gaulle's determination to deter the British from entering the EEC, it was becoming even
more pertinent that the British did not lose momentum at this stage.
London took seriously the prospect of a possible rupture with Ireland
in the wake of the second veto, indicating that it wanted to know the
extent to which 'the Taoiseach is interested in pursuing the offer of
association or an "interim arrangement" which President de Gaulle
put to Mr. Lynch when they met in Paris earlier this month'.[52] The
problem facing the British was that they could clearly not afford to
probe the matter too deeply with the Irish; to do so would have been
to put them in a more vulnerable position than they were in already.
The French, in particular, might use a watering down of Britain's
demands for full membership as a way of verifying the doubts de
Gaulle had expressed in his continued opposition to British membership. A cautionary warning was sounded by Derek Day, who stated
that while it certainly would be interesting to have an inside view
of Irish intentions with regard to exploring alternatives to full
membership:

it is not suggested that this idea should be put to Mr. Lynch or to the Irish government. As you know, the Prime Minister has come out strongly against association. This is the policy of Her Majesty's Government. We don't want to look as if we were weakening in any degree. If we say anything to the Irish, it might leak.[53]

THE END OF THE 'RED HERRING'

The alarm in London that Ireland might acquire some form of associate membership while Britain remained outside the EEC was relatively short-lived. A consensus began to emerge in official circles at the turn of 1967–68 that, although on the surface the alternatives open to Ireland were certainly present, they were little more than deviations that led nowhere. As Norman Statham put it, 'the fact is that, whatever the French might mean by interim arrangement ... I cannot see the Five going along with anything like this if, as would be evident, it would be unwelcome to us'.[54] Paradoxically, however, while acknowledging that the vague suggestions put forward by the General amounted to nothing more than tactical manoeuvres designed to further confuse and thwart the British, officials in London observed that there was still a tendency on the Irish side 'to flirt with this possibility'.[55] By the end of January 1968, London had less cause for concern because the Irish, upon exploring these alternatives, found little or no substance behind them. McCann, for example, entered into discussions with officials in Paris and Brussels in order to ascertain the seriousness of the French offers. The discussions, it was reported to London, persuaded the Irish government that 'the French hint was not serious, but was probably dropped for tactical reasons', a way of dividing the applicants.[56] Britain was consequently keen to reiterate the importance of the four applicants remaining in unison (Norway and Denmark applied along with Britain and Ireland) and strongly believed that all attempts to hinder the momentum towards full membership should be resisted. The Wilson administration had already begun to entertain thoughts of cooperation with the Benelux countries and was keen to show the Irish that Europe was not just represented by France. Ironically, however, the second veto had for all intents and purposes shown that, while de Gaulle was ensconced in the Elysée, it was.

A meeting between Wilson and Lynch in February 1968 provided just the forum in which to press the Irish 'to encourage the Taoiseach to maintain solidarity with the other applicants for membership by not giving way to pressure'.[57] London was at pains to emphasise the undesirability of anything less than full membership, which 'could only be a second best'. It was also adamant that any such offer amounted to nothing more than 'a red herring whose purpose is to divert attention from our applications for full membership'. It went on to warn that the French would never offer something without expecting something in return. Hence, if the Irish entertained the General's suggestions they would ultimately have to choose between the EEC and the AIFTA.[58] By this stage, though, it is clear that Britain was preaching to the converted. Emerging from the talks, Lynch's comments confirmed that the Irish were in full agreement with their British counterparts on what course of action to take next. When asked about the possibility of meeting with the Five, he volunteered that, while obviously they would prefer French involvement, if this did not prove possible they 'would be willing' to meet in their absence. This was, Whitaker suggested,

> the firmest statement which Mr. Lynch has made about circumventing the French Veto. Up to now, as British officials have suggested more than once to me, Mr. Lynch has been hedging his bets, refusing to say whether or not he was on the side of the angels. Angels, of course, are British.[59]

So why had the Irish briefly toyed with de Gaulle's ambiguous offers? Furthermore, to what extent was it under British pressure that the Irish gave up on these suggestions? The most likely answer to the first question lies in the radical evolution that had taken place in Irish politics over the previous decade. Ireland was not as vulnerable and ignorant as was sometimes made out, and key policy-makers were well aware that de Gaulle probably viewed Dublin as no more than a pawn on his European chessboard. Yet, to immediately dismiss such offers outright would have been detrimental in Ireland's position. Under pressure from party, polity and public, Lynch had to persevere, and be seen to be exploring all possible options. With increasing demands to move away from the smothering embrace of Britain, it is no wonder that Irish officials went through the diplomatic motions. The majority of course knew what the outcome might be, but at the same time had to be seen to try. In answer to the second question, British pressure to adhere to the policy of 'all or nothing' did not instigate but, more likely, reinforced Ireland's ultimate rejection of de Gaulle's proposals. Between the nebulous nature of the alternatives and the stark economic realities, it is no wonder that Ireland soon retreated back to Britain's original tactics. Careful pragmatic thinking permeated Irish opinion to a degree often overlooked, as an editorial in the *Irish Times* at the time demonstrates:

> It would be unworthy to suppose that in his suggestions to the Taoiseach, the General was merely baiting the British, but no man in his position speaks merely for the benefit of his immediate audience. His remarks are meant to ricochet – and will already be bouncing off chambers in London and Washington as well as Brussels ... The French have no word for 'blarney' – no equally expressive word, at any rate. Diplomatic occasions resound with prose about the historic links between the participating countries. Let us, above all, make sure that we do not read too much into the politeness and consideration with which our delegation was received; the General's great-grandmother will not weigh one ounce in the scales when our entry chances come to be evaluated.[60]

Telling, when one considers that this was penned not after careful coaching from anyone, but at the beginning of November 1967.

CONCLUSION

To look at Britain's second application to the EEC in isolation is to ignore the integral interaction and communication that took place between it and the other applicants, and which ultimately shaped the entire process. Having examined the Irish case and the exchanges that took place between London and Dublin, one can draw four conclusions. The first relates to the motivating factors of applicant countries. Britain was not the only country slow to develop any sense of what might be termed 'European spirit'. Unlike the 'founding fathers', Ireland and Britain had little reason before 1960 to display any genuine interest in the formal process of European integration. Psychologically, as well as physically, they were cut off from mainland Europe and had had a different experience in war, so while Jean Monnet and Robert Schuman were drawing a blueprint for the future of Europe, the likes of de Valera, Costello, Winston Churchill and Anthony Eden felt no such enthusiasm for the supranational approach to unity that was the cornerstone of their plans. It was only the lack of viable alternatives that finally led them to seek admittance to the club Monnet and Schuman had created. Having explored other options, notably the European Free Trade Association (EFTA), policy-makers in London came to view the EEC as something of a panacea for Britain's apparent economic ills. The Irish were quick to follow suit. Fundamentally, it was these differences that set the two islands apart from the Six, leading them to be classified as 'different', 'unsuitable' and 'awkward'.

The second conclusion is that the Wilson administration, once decided on membership, adhered rigidly to a policy of 'all or nothing'. 'Full' membership was sought; no half measures or watered-down proposals such as 'association' would be entertained. A careful examination of the Irish application to join the EEC illustrates this. Time and time again, the Irish were cajoled into leaving behind their temptation to explore de Gaulle's alternatives. The British were adamant that 'interim arrangements' would not satiate their requirements and therefore could be dismissed immediately. It is only through looking at Anglo-Irish diplomatic exchanges that one can fully understand their rejection of alternatives to full membership. It was neither a rash nor a regretted decision, but one taken after much deliberation.

Indeed, the third conclusion is that it was this rigid adherence to an 'all or nothing' policy that succeeded in the long term in securing a place for Britain in Europe. While it certainly did not reap any rewards for Wilson, it paved the way for Edward Heath to maintain that Britain was 'fully European' and had only ever been interested in 'full membership'. Had Wilson abandoned that approach and been content to explore alternatives, it might well have been used as ammunition to paint Britain in a less than 'European' light in years to come. In this respect, Wilson's application to join the EEC can be classified a 'successful failure'. The final conclusion is that Britain and Ireland were committed to a policy of entering together, if at all possible. At first one might think this just an Irish plea, but the British were similarly keen on this entry strategy. There were visible signs of apprehension at times over Ireland's flirtation with de Gaulle's offer of 'association' or an 'interim arrangement'. Thus, Whitehall released a steady flow of reasons why the Irish should refrain from entertaining such thoughts. On both sides of the sea, at different times and for sometimes very different reasons, Ireland and Britain feared that one but not the other would gain entry to the EEC. It is this dimension more than any other that defined and shaped Anglo-Irish policy towards Europe during the Wilson era.

NOTES

1. Douglas Hurd, address to the Institute of European Affairs, 21 March 1994, quoted in P. Gillespie (ed.), *Britain's European Question: The Issues For Ireland* (Dublin: Institute of European Affairs, 1996), p. 7.

2. Interview with Kenneth Whitaker (Secretary to the Department of Finance, 1956–69), 19 February 2001.
3. Public Record Office (PRO): FCO 75/1, Sir Con O'Neill's report on the negotiations for entry into the European Community, June 1970–January 1972, sent to Sir Alec Douglas-Home. Now published as C. O'Neill, *Britain's Entry into the European Community: Report on the Negotiations of 1970–1972* (London: Frank Cass, 2000).
4. J. Blanchard quoted in B. Chubb, *The Government and Politics of Ireland* (London: Longman, 1992), p. 6.
5. *Dáil Eireann Parliamentary Debates* (1934), volume 53, column 62.
6. The Taoiseach is the Prime Minister of the Irish Republic.
7. F. S. L. Lyons, *Ireland Since the Famine* (London: Weidenfeld & Nicolson, 1971), pp. 557–8.
8. G. Murphy, 'Ireland's View of Western Europe in the 1950s', in M. Kennedy and J. M. Skelly (eds), *Irish Foreign Policy 1919–66* (Dublin: Four Courts Press, 2000), pp. 247–65 (p. 250).
9. P. Keatinge, 'Ireland and the World, 1957–82', in F. Litton (ed.), *Unequal Achievement* (Dublin: Institute of Public Affairs, 1982), pp. 225–40 (p. 228).
10. *Irish Times*, 12 May 1971.
11. National Archives Ireland (NAI): Department of the Taoiseach (DT), S 15281-D, interim report of the Committee of Secretaries, 18 January 1957.
12. Interview with Whitaker, 19 February 2001.
13. See, for example, N. Beloff, *The General Says No: Britain's Exclusion from Europe* (Harmondsworth: Penguin, 1963).
14. Lemass quoted in D. Keogh, *Ireland and Europe 1919–1989: A Diplomatic and Political History* (Cork: Hibernian University Press, 1990), pp. 232–3.
15. Interview with Whitaker, 19 February 2001.
16. NAI: DT S 16877 / Q / 61.
17. Interview with Whitaker, 19 February 2001.
18. Between July 1961 and April 1962, Ireland, Britain, Denmark and Norway all applied to join the EEC.
19. T. D. Williams, 'Irish Foreign Policy 1949–1969', in J. J. Lee (ed.), *Ireland* (Dublin: Gill/Macmillan, 1979), pp. 136–51 (p. 136).
20. PRO: FCO 30/230, MEK 4/1/4, Part A, background brief sent by Gallagher to Ratford, 27 April 1967.
21. Ibid.
22. Wilson describes the aims of the agreement as being progressively to 'eliminate all restrictions, whether by quota or by tariff, on our two-way trade, and create a total free-trade area between our countries'. See H. Wilson, *The Labour Government 1964–70: A Personal Record* (London: Weidenfeld & Nicolson/Michael Joseph, 1971), p. 185.
23. PRO: FCO 30/230, MEK 4/1/4, Part B, speaking notes for use by Snelling, sent by Smith to Cambridge, 30 October 1967.
24. *Cork Examiner*, 15 February 1968.
25. PRO: FCO 30/231, MEK 4/1/4, Part B, biographical note on Jack Lynch.
26. *Cork Examiner*, 15 February 1968.
27. PRO: FCO 30/230, MEK 4/1/4, Part A, telegram no. 97, Gilchrist to Commonwealth Office, 6 November 1967.
28. PRO: FCO 30/230, MEK 4/1/4, Part A, telegram no. 38, Gilchrist to Commonwealth Office, 18 October 1967.
29. *Irish Times*, 14 August 1967.
30. PRO: FCO 30/230, MEK 4/1/4, Gallagher to Snelling, 7 July 1967.
31. PRO: FCO 30/230, MEK 5/1/4, Part A, Lynch to Wilson, 10 July 1967.
32. *Irish Times*, 14 August 1967.
33. *Sunday Independent*, 9 July 1967.
34. G. Brown, *In My Way: The Political Memoirs of Lord George-Brown* (London: Victor

Gollancz, 1971), pp. 221–2.
35. Wilson had, at the turn of 1967, undertaken a 'probe' of capitals with Brown, to ascertain 'whether or not to activate arrangements for entry'. See Wilson, *The Labour Government*, pp. 327–44 (quote from p. 328).
36. PRO: FCO 30/230, MEK 4/1/4, Part A, Lynch to Wilson, 17 August 1967.
37. *Irish Times*, 14 August 1967.
38. Interview with Whitaker, 19 February 2001.
39. Statement by the Taoiseach to the *Irish Times*, 6 November 1967.
40. *Irish Press*, 6 November 1967.
41. The Dáil is the parliament of the Irish Republic. PRO: FCO 30/230, MEK 4/1/4 Part A, telegram no. 97, Gilchrist to the Commonwealth Office, 6 November 1967.
42. Ibid.
43. PRO: FCO 30/230, MEK 4/1/4, Part A, telegram no. 1107, Ledwidge to Foreign Office, 7 November 1967.
44. Ibid.
45. Ibid.
46. PRO: FCO 30/230, MEK 4/1/4, Part A, speaking notes prepared for Snelling at the meeting of the Anglo-Irish Economic Committee on 9 and 10 November, 1967.
47. Ibid.
48. PRO: FCO 30/230, PMEK 4/1/4, Part A, Galsworthy to Statham, 10 November 1967.
49. PRO: FCO 30/230, MEK 4/1/4, Part A, Gilchrist to Thompson, 12 December 1967.
50. PRO: FCO 30/230, MEK 4/1/4 Part A, Lynch quoted in Gilchrist's letter to Thompson, 12 December 1967.
51. *Irish Times*, 27 July 1967.
52. PRO: FCO 30/230, MEK 4/1/4, Part A, Williams to Andrews, 29 November 1967.
53. PRO: FCO 30/230, MEK 4/1/4, Part A, Day to Williams, 30 November 1967.
54. PRO: FCO 30/231, MEK 4/1/4, Part B, Statham to Audland, 28 December 1967.
55. PRO: FCO 30/231, MEK 4/1/4, Part B, Jordan-Moss to Audland, 8 January 1968.
56. PRO: FCO 30/231, MEK 4/1/4, Part B, Overton to Statham, 31 January 1968.
57. PRO: FCO 30/231, MEK 4/1/4, Part B, background notes to the Wilson and Lynch meeting 14 February 1968, sent by Smith to Cambridge.
58. PRO: FCO 30/231, MEK 4/1/4, Part B, Brief by the Commonwealth Office, Taoiseach's visit, 14 February 1968, Smith to Cambridge.
59. *Irish Times*, 15 February 1968.
60. *Irish Times*, 6 November 1967.

—13—

Conclusion: The Ironies of 'Successful Failure'

PETER CATTERALL

In February 1963, in the immediate aftermath of the failure of the Conservative government of Harold Macmillan to negotiate entry to the European Economic Community (EEC), the third conference of the leaders of European Socialist Parties met in Brussels. Even though the French socialists at this meeting, like Robert Marjolin, seem to have been no more encouraging to the British than their Gaullist head of state, the representatives of the Socialist Parties of what were to come to be called the 'friendly five', were more supportive. Indeed, the Dutch socialist Sicco Mansholt was to presciently observe that 'within three years a Labour government would be forced to reach the same conclusions as Macmillan'.[1] It was not, however, immediately apparent that Harold Wilson, newly anointed party leader after Hugh Gaitskell's untimely death in January 1963, would prove any more willing to fulfil Mansholt's prophecy than his predecessor had been. The dominant characteristic of Wilson's approach towards Europe, and that of his party more generally, over the previous few years had been ambivalence. An internal policy document in 1961 had recognised that 'from a short-run point of view, the difficulties in the way of Britain's joining the European Economic Community have been greatly exaggerated'. Not that there was much enthusiasm. Entry was seen as likely, at best, to promote modest trade expansion. At the same time, however, European harmonisation was still seen as more likely to fetter than enable a future Labour government.[2]

Wilson, meanwhile, in 1960, whilst recognising that the Six were not a major export market, had been able to offer the House of Commons no more powerful argument in favour of British entry than an essentially negative one based on the risk that American investment would henceforth go elsewhere; that 'in a world of rapid scientific advance there is always a real danger that if Britain is out of the mainstream we shall become, relatively speaking, a backwater'.[3] Against such an argument, in a paper for the Shadow Cabinet, he warned of the effect a British application would have on the European Free Trade Association (EFTA), the Commonwealth and on British horticulture. There was also the danger that joining the relatively dynamic economies of the EEC would exacerbate British weaknesses and balance-of-payments difficulties. Finally, not least, and demonstrating that Mansholt was not the only one with a gift for foresight, there was the risk of a humiliating rejection, especially at the hands of the French.[4]

There were other, more ardent spirits in the Shadow Cabinet at the time. Some, the following year, urged that Labour ought to steal a march on the government by coming out in favour of EEC entry. Wilson, however, urged caution.[5] Given the internal party divisions on this issue, of which both he and Wilson were well aware, this was a line Gaitskell was happy to adopt.[6] Although this non-commital line exposed them to Macmillan's ridicule, the party leadership held to it until the autumn of 1962. Just before the party conference, however, Gaitskell told the Shadow Cabinet that he could not accept the government's negotiating position on European entry because it broke all past pledges to the Commonwealth. This solicitude for the interests of the Commonwealth, the *Socialist Commentary* implied, was a recent development.[7] And the decision to emphasise the Commonwealth so much in the aftermath of the failure of Macmillan's bid, undoubtedly reflected tactical manoeuvring on the part of Labour.[8] However it cannot be dismissed, as some commentators would have it, as simply an imperial reflex.[9] The Commonwealth was seen as an exemplary multiracial grouping in a divided world, and as one of the greatest achievements of the 1945–51 Labour governments.[10] Commonwealth objections, especially as voiced by the leaders of sister parties, were therefore taken seriously. The declining economic importance of the Commonwealth to Britain, despite the inclination of some commentators to seize on this, did not necessarily matter, for, as James Callaghan subsequently put it, 'it was more a sense of responsibility',[11] especially towards its poorer members. This view appears to be borne out by the emphasis laid on aid policy at the time of the Macmillan bid.[12] Gaitskell certainly seems to have been particularly affected by Indian opposition to the British entry negotiations. And in October 1962 at the party conference he came out decisively against entry.[13] Wilson, as conference chairman, led the applause.[14]

The following year Wilson, as newly installed party leader, had to respond to and try to capitalise on the destruction of Macmillan's

European ambitions at the start of 1963. His speech in Washington in April, when he suggested that Labour under him would welcome entry to an open Community, but not to the 'inward-looking, autarkic Europe which would sever Britain from our traditional channels of trade in the Commonwealth and the wider trading world' that was currently on offer,[15] should be seen in that context. Nevertheless, it clearly did not suggest a noticeable warming towards Europe on Wilson's part, or much of a departure from the ambivalent position Gaitskell never totally abandoned.[16] The impression garnered during a transatlantic flight that autumn by the Prime Minister's secretary remained that Wilson

> was opposed to any form of supra-nationality although he would not object to closer political links and even some form of European secretariat provided that these were a facade and that the reality of British independence was preserved in the defence, foreign policy and economic fields.[17]

Europe rarely featured on the agenda of the Shadow Cabinet, or the party's International Committee, in the run-up to the 1964 election. Indeed, the manifesto line seemed to follow closely that taken by Gaitskell in autumn 1962. Wilson, after all, was no less enthusiastic about the Commonwealth than his predecessor. The Commonwealth accordingly received much more attention than Europe in the manifesto, while the Conservative terms for entry were denounced on the grounds they would have 'excluded our Commonwealth partners, broken our special trade links with them, and forced us to treat them as third class nations'.[18] This, of course, also makes clear the extent to which both the Commonwealth and European issues were being played for perceived party political advantages. The failures of Conservative European policy were contrasted as starkly as possible with Labour's commitment to the Commonwealth and Commonwealth development. That exaggerated hopes the Commonwealth were followed by bitter disappointment during the ensuing Wilson government is hardly news. Accordingly, if this work offered no more than a conventional explanation of how Wilson and his government then decided to press their suit upon the Six, in order to try and maintain Britain's international influence by other means, tackle economic deficiencies or address some other incubus of the mid-1960s, its contribution would be slight. This, however, has not been the purpose.

The problems this book has sought to address are instead as follows: what was it that allowed Mansholt's prediction to be fulfilled?

What were the circumstances of and attitudes towards the British bid for European entry prepared and launched in 1966–67? And what were the consequences of that bid? Hitherto, the historiography has tended to locate such processes within wider accounts of either British European policy, or of the Labour Party. The bid has been seen as a turning point in the history of both. Accordingly, there is, for instance, a temptation to talk of Wilson's 'conversion' preparing the way for the 'probe' of late 1966.[19] Treating the bid as an event in this way leads to a historiography which emphasises the roots of change. Wilson's 'conversion' is then seen simply as the result of a concatenation of economic and external influences pressing in on the government. And attention in such accounts is accordingly focused on decision-making by government, without reference to wider environmental factors. In particular, domestic political considerations, while emphasised in all accounts of British European policy-making, have been especially highlighted in studies of the Wilson years. Too often, British European policy is treated as if hermetically sealed, with insufficient reference to the attitudes of external factors such as the Americans or the French, let alone the other member states.

The analyses offered here have instead eschewed both a narrow focus on causation and a one-dimensional concentration on the actions of the British Labour government. Just as the European issue cannot be considered in isolation from the various policy areas upon which it impinges, or the other actors involved, nor can the making of policy on this issue be considered in isolation from the various interest groups, such as the newly formed Confederation of British Industry, affected by and seeking to shape such policies, and attracted by the opportunities for economies of scale that it felt Europe offered. What is remarkable about the analysis of the attitudes of such bodies offered here is the extent to which it does not support conventional views, still being parroted by Europhile politicians,[20] of the slow and reluctant drift of the British towards the inevitability of European membership. In the latter, there is rarely any room for choice, despite the fact that Tony Blair and Gordon Brown remain as keen on enjoying their Europe *à la carte* as their predecessors and their continental neighbours. Instead, the course of European integration is simply presented as an ineluctable process, usually to be sold to the British public on the somewhat negative grounds that they cannot afford not to join. This is history with a built-in teleology. Like all teleologies, it acquires the appurtenances of faith. Wilson, thus, must have undergone a damascene conversion from resisting to embracing the inevitable, in order to fit this narrative.

While useful for politicians like Blair who wish to brand their opponents as antediluvian and imply that they alone understand the key to the future, as an approach to the understanding of history this is worse than childish. Teleologies explain nothing; by imposing a positivist framework on the course of history they simply condemn all those who do not fit in with their insistence on where history is going. In the process, human agency is reduced to either recognising or sinning against the inevitable. But Wilson did not have a damascene conversion. He was already aware of the potential benefits of joining the Community, but also that it involved prices he was not necessarily willing to pay, before he became Prime Minister in October 1964. In this his position was not hugely different from that of the Conservatives in 1961–63. His reluctance, as Helen Parr shows here, remained obvious in early 1966.[21] However, he was more prepared, during the ensuing 18 months, to enter into an open-ended search for full membership than the Conservatives had been a few years earlier. It is not so much that economic and Commonwealth travails, not to mention changes in perspectives on foreign policy,[22] had converted Wilson to the virtues of entry, but they had changed the costs that were likely to be payable. The endeavour also, as the chapters here show, was deemed likely to have an attractive range of potential side-effects both domestically and in terms of, for instance, Anglo-American relations, which encouraged the pursuit of this option. If nothing else, it demonstrated that the government had not been totally derailed by the emergency measures to protect sterling in July 1966.[23] Thus there were both long-term and short-term impulses behind the Wilson bid for entry. These short-term circumstances also ensured a high but, as it turned out, evanescent degree of domestic support for the bid.

Wilson's bid, however, was to suffer much the same fate at the hands of the French as Macmillan's. It might seem that if Macmillan, who spoke excellent French and was an old Second World War comrade of Charles de Gaulle, could not persuade the French leader, what chance did Wilson have? Wilson, after all, did not have a huge amount to offer. His vision of a technological community, while superficially attractive to the French, did not necessitate membership, as the fraught example of Concorde made clear. Meanwhile, the recent 'empty chair' crisis with the French meant that the 'friendly five' had little appetite for further confrontation. In the end, perhaps the best that could be made of a bad job was to once again use de Gaulle's obstructiveness as a means of improving Anglo-American relations.[24]

However, the circumstances of the time again need to be taken into account. While short-run circumstances may have made a bid more attractive at this point, they also helped to undermine its chances of succeeding. For Wilson, who had said in March 1966 that he would only attempt entry from a position of economic strength,[25] was in no such position later that year, or throughout 1967. Britain's economic weakness, as well as the difficulties the Wilson government had already run into with the French over Concorde, did not help to add credence to the technological community idea. Furthermore, as Piers Ludlow shows,[26] playing on the economic problems of the British was the one persuasive weapon in the French arsenal in their attempts to dissuade their partners from supporting the British bid.

There are some rich ironies here, not least that consciousness of British industrial weakness was one of the main reasons put forward for launching the bid. This, it should be noted, was not a new perspective. Although he felt that membership would be risky, Thomas Balogh, later to be Wilson's economic adviser in government, had already argued in 1961 that it 'might be the sole means by which British industry and finance can be jolted into a new dynamic mould'.[27] In a dissenting note, however, Nicholas Kaldor not only exposed the negativity of this argument, but also observed that the state of the British economy required the retention of devaluation as a policy option, something that was, however, explicitly ruled out in Article 108 of the Treaty of Rome.[28] So it is ironic that measures taken in 1966 to avoid devaluation were to be so much part of the French case against British entry the following year.

A further irony is the way in which 'imperial Britain' continued to play a part in the articulation of an economic policy which simultaneously both helped to prompt, and stymied, British attempts to join Europe. It would be misleading to suggest that there was not a whole range of reasons behind the decision for deflation as a way of trying to avoid the devaluation Wilson was eventually forced into in November 1967. However, one factor was a sense of obligation to the Commonwealth members of the sterling area. The continuing pull of old economic ties thus played a part, albeit largely unnoticed, by lending credence to French criticisms of the weakness of the British economy, in the defeat of Wilson's bid to replace these ties with a new economic context. For the French, the subsequent devaluation was proof positive of the merits of their criticisms. But devaluation also effectively demolished the sterling area. Edward Heath's government, which was to float the pound in 1972, had no such considerations to bear in mind when it picked up Wilson's bid. Nor, following the post-

devaluation adjustments of the 1968 Defence White Paper, did they
have the global commitments to which Wilson had hitherto clung.[29]
Furthermore, the agreement on stationing costs for the British Army of
the Rhine (BAOR) reached with the Germans in April 1967 subsequently dealt with one of the main sources of the perennial balance-of-
payments problems which had plagued both Macmillan and Wilson in
the 1960s.[30] All these changes helped to clear the way for Heath.

The extent to which devaluation had succeeded, meanwhile, did
its work in undermining the one French argument which had con-
tained real substance in 1967. William Armstrong, Permanent
Secretary to the Treasury, had suggested in 1966 that membership
without prior devaluation might be difficult to achieve.[31] He was
proved right. Devaluation, no less than that other facet of 1967, the
Wilson bid, indeed helped clear the way for eventual entry in 1973.
However, in a final irony, it might be observed that by this means the
British had to sort out their own economy themselves, rather than, as
Balogh had seemed to argue, seeking in entry an external panacea.

Of course, this then begs the question as to what were the arguments in favour of entry, other than the negative ones offered by
Balogh? The timing of the Wilson bid suggests that these were few
and far between. With the significant exception of the technology
community idea, and related hopes that a European scale might
supply the economic growth the National Plan had been unable to
deliver, the economic arguments in favour of membership remained
as negative as those Wilson adumbrated in 1960. They were, by and
large, about the European rescue of the British state and economy. As
Alan Milward has pointed out, there was nothing exceptional in this.[32]
All member states did and still do naturally privilege their own interests. But they also have to be seen at the same time to be seeking to
advance the interests of the whole in what is, above all, a political project. That Wilson appreciated this is hinted at in his Strasbourg speech
in January 1967, in which he stated that 'over the next year, the next
20 years, the unity of Europe is going to be forged, and geography
and history, interest and sentiment alike demand that we play our
part in forging it and working it'.[33] However, whereas Macmillan, as
befitted a founding member of the Council of Europe, had a distinct
vision of Europe, albeit one that was rather different from the reality
that emerged in the course of the 1950s[34] – Wilson does not seem to
have had a clear idea of what he meant by the unity of Europe, or how
Britain would contribute to building it. The one exception, again, is
the technology community idea. This was, as John Young shows here,
certainly sincere, and reflected some long-standing interests of

Wilson's.[35] It is also clear that it played a part in his thinking about European integration at least as early as 1960. However, it focused, once again, on contemporary British economic concerns, rather than the wider political project of building Europe.

Ironically, the need to build a technological dimension to the European Union was to be very much taken up in the late 1990s. This was fed by anxiety about a failure to keep up with the United States, Europe's perennial 'significant other', in productivity or developments in information and communications technology, and received most concrete expression in the articulation of the 'Enterprise Europe' policy following the 2000 Lisbon summit.[36] Such anxieties, however, did not exist in the 1960s to anything like the same extent in a period when productivity growth in the Six was higher than in the USA.

Meanwhile, as this book makes clear, there was only limited British engagement with the politics of European integration in 1966–67. There was the object of a more open Community,[37] along the lines Wilson had already indicated in 1963. Otherwise, however, the political dimension of the British bid, for instance as an alternative to the Commonwealth, was no more positive than the economic one. And the political implications of entry do not seem to have provoked much more thought than the acceptance of the jurisdiction of the European Court of Human Rights in 1965.[38] This was to have long-term implications. If, as Oliver Daddow argues in Chapter 1, the Wilson bid can be deemed a 'successful failure', not least through preparing the way for the later Heath negotiations, it also needs to be acknowledged that it did little to prepare either the British people or state for the political consequences that entry would bring. Such consequences were to be fudged or ignored, at least as late as the 1975 referendum,[39] and left for later governments to deal with as they saw fit. Gaitskell had complained in his conference speech in 1962 about the poor quality of debate about European integration in Britain.[40] In certain important respects, the bid for European entry launched by his successor did little to improve it.

NOTES

1. National Museum of Labour History, Manchester, Labour Party Archives (LPA): International Committee minutes 1962–63, record of 3rd conference of European Socialist Parties, 23–24 February 1963.
2. LPA: International Committee minutes 1961, Finance and Economic Policy subcommittee paper, 'Britain, Europe and the Commonwealth', January 1961.
3. *Hansard: House of Commons Debates*, 5th series, 627, 1114, 25 July 1960.
4. LPA: Parliamentary Committee minutes 21 June 1960, including Wilson's paper, 'Britain's Relations with Europe', 15 June 1960.

5. Ibid., 10 May 1961.
6. Ibid., 21 June 1961.
7. *Socialist Commentary*, January 1962.
8. P. Catterall, 'Foreign and Commonwealth Policy in Opposition: The Labour Party', in W. Kaiser and G. Staerck (eds), *British Foreign Policy 1955–64: Contracting Options* (Basingstoke: Macmillan, 2000), pp. 89–109.
9. B. Brivati, *Hugh Gaitskell* (London: Richard Cohen, 1996), p. 3.
10. P. Catterall, 'Foreign and Commonwealth Policy in Opposition'.
11. Author's interview with Lord Callaghan, 13 November 1996.
12. See, for example, the National Executive Committee statement reproduced in *Britain and the Common Market* (London: Labour Party, 1962), p. 32.
13. LPA: Parliamentary Committee minutes, 25 September 1962; R. Broad, *Labour's European Dilemmas: From Bevin to Blair* (Basingstoke: Palgrave, 2001), pp. 50–2.
14. J. Hollowell, 'The Labour Party, the World Role and the Shift from Commonwealth to EEC 1962–67: The Evolution from Commonwealth to the "Second Application"', unpublished paper in author's possession.
15. Public Record Office, London (PRO): PREM 11/4331, speech by Harold Wilson to the National Press Club, Washington DC, 1 April 1963.
16. As well as fearing that a de Gaulle-led Europe would prove a destabilising force internationally, Gaitskell clearly felt that much of the argument in favour of entry would be diminished were EEC external tariffs reduced. However, he wrote that if, instead, 'it was a question not of a European state but of an Atlantic federation, then certainly many of my misgivings would vanish'. Quoted in John F. Kennedy Presidential Library, Boston MA (JFK): NSF170, folder 33, Bohlen to Rusk, 5 December 1962.
17. PRO: PREM 11/4332, 'Note for the Record', Sir Philip de Zulueta, 24 November 1963.
18. *Let's Go with Labour for the New Britain* (London: Labour Party, 1964), p. 19.
19. H. Young, *This Blessed Plot: Britain and Europe from Churchill to Blair* (London: Macmillan, 1998), p. 187.
20. See, for instance, the speech by Tony Blair to the European Research Institute, Birmingham, 23 November 2001.
21. See Chapter 4 in this book.
22. A preference for neutralising Germany, an option that came to be seen as impossible once Labour was in government, had earlier been the basis of the need to be able to pursue an independent foreign policy that Gaitskell said EEC entry would threaten. See, for instance, the record of Gaitskell's pronouncements presented in JFK: NSF170, folder 22, Hilsman to Rusk, 10 July 1962.
23. K. O. Morgan, *The People's Peace: British History 1945–1989* (Oxford: Oxford University Press, 1990) p. 272.
24. See Chapter 9 in this book. See also Oliver Bange, *The EEC Crisis of 1963: Kennedy, Macmillan, de Gaulle and Adenauer in Conflict* (Basingstoke: Macmillan, 2000).
25. See Chapter 8 in this book.
26. See Chapter 7 in this book.
27. LPA: International Committee minutes, 1961, Thomas Balogh, 'A Note: Britain's Relations to the Common Market', May 1961.
28. Ibid., Nicholas Kaldor, 'Britain and Europe: A Draft Report: Commentary and Dissenting Note', June 1961. Balance-of-payments crises in 1957 and 1961 had required assistance from the Bundesbank.
29. See J. Pickering, *Britain's Withdrawal from East of Suez: The Politics of Retrenchment* (Basingstoke: Macmillan, 1998), Chapter 7.
30. See S. Mawby, *Containing Germany: Britain and the Arming of the Federal Republic* (Basingstoke: Macmillan, 1999), p. 186.
31. See Chapter 4 in this book. Richard Crossman seems to have made similar observations just before the Wilson bid was launched, see R. Pearce (ed), *Patrick Gordon Walker: Political Diaries 1932–1971* (London: The Historians' Press, 1991),

p. 313 (30 April 1967).
32. A. Milward, *The European Rescue of the Nation-State* (London: Routledge, 1992).
33. Quoted in Broad, *Labour's European Dilemmas*, p. 65.
34. See P. Catterall, 'Macmillan and Europe 1950–56: The Cold War, the American Context and the British Approach to European Integration', *Cercles*, 5 (Spring 2002), pp. 93–108.
35. See Chapter 5 in this book.
36. *Enterprise Europe*, September 2000. Background research on this is offered in *European Economy: Supplement A*, no. 12, December 2000, 'The contribution of information and communication technologies to growth in Europe and the US: A macroeconomic analysis'.
37. See Chapter 4 in this book.
38. See Broad, *Labour's European Dilemmas*, p. 60.
39. R. Broad and T. Geiger, 'The 1975 British Referendum on Europe', *Contemporary British History*, 10, 3 (1996), pp. 82–105.
40. *Britain and the Common Market*, p. 3.

Appendix I:
Labour Cabinet Members, October 1964–June 1970

Prime Minister
Harold Wilson

First Secretary of State
George Brown (October 1964 to August 1966)
Michael Stewart (August 1966 to March 1968)
Barbara Castle (March 1968 to June 1970)

Lord President of the Council and Leader of the House of Commons
Herbert Bowden (October 1964 to August 1966)
Richard Crossman (August 1966 to October 1968)
Fred Peart (October 1968 to June 1970)

Lord Chancellor
Lord Gardiner

Secretary of State for Defence
Denis Healey

Secretary of State for Foreign Affairs
Patrick Gordon Walker (October 1964 to January 1965)
Michael Stewart (January 1965 to August 1966)
George Brown (August 1966 to March 1968)
Michael Stewart (March 1968 to June 1970)

Secretary of State for the Colonies
Anthony Greenwood (October 1964 to December 1965)
Lord Longford (December 1965 to April 1966)
Frederick Lee (April 1966 to August 1967)

Secretary of State for Commonwealth Relations[1]
Arthur Bottomley (October 1964 to August 1966)
Herbert Bowden (August 1966 to August 1967)
George Thomson (August 1967 to October 1968)

Chancellor of the Exchequer
James Callaghan (October 1964 to November 1967)
Roy Jenkins (November 1967 to June 1970)

Chief Secretary to the Treasury[2]
John Diamond

Secretary of State for Economic Affairs[3]
George Brown (October 1964 to August 1966)
Michael Stewart (August 1966 to August 1967)
Peter Shore (August 1967 to October 1969)

President of the Board of Trade
Douglas Jay (October 1964 to August 1967)
Anthony Crosland (August 1967 to October 1969)
Roy Mason (October 1969 to June 1970)

Minister of Technology
Frank Cousins (October 1964 to July 1966)
Anthony Wedgwood Benn (July 1966 to June 1970)

Minister of Overseas Development[4]
Barbara Castle (October 1964 to December 1965)
Anthony Greenwood (December 1965 to August 1966)
Arthur Bottomley (August 1966 to August 1967)

Secretary of State for the Home Department
Frank Soskice (October 1964 to December 1965)
Roy Jenkins (December 1965 to November 1967)
James Callaghan (November 1967 to June 1970)

Secretary of State for Education and Science
Michael Stewart (October 1964 to January 1965)
Anthony Crosland (January 1965 to August 1967)
Patrick Gordon Walker (August 1967 to April 1968)
Edward Short (April 1968 to June 1970)

Secretary of State for Health and Social Services[5]
Richard Crossman (October 1968 to June 1970)

Minister of Housing and Local Government[6]
Richard Crossman (October 1964 to August 1966)
Anthony Greenwood (August 1966 to October 1969)

Minister of Labour[7]
Ray Gunter (October 1964 to April 1968)

Minister of Employment and Productivity[8]
Barbara Castle (April 1968 to June 1970)

Minister of Power[9]
Frederick Lee (October 1964 to April 1966)
Richard Marsh (April 1966 to April 1968)
Ray Gunter (April 1968 to July 1968)
Roy Mason (July 1968 to October 1969)

Minister of Transport
Tom Fraser (October 1964 to December 1965)
Barbara Castle (December 1965 to April 1968)
Richard Marsh (April 1968 to October 1969)
Fred Mulley (October 1969 to June 1970)

Chancellor of the Duchy of Lancaster
Douglas Houghton (October 1964 to April 1966)
George Thompson (April 1966 to August 1967)
Frederick Lee (August 1967 to October 1969)
George Thomson (October 1969 to June 1970)

Paymaster-General
George Wigg (October 1964 to October 1968)
Judith Hart (October 1968 to October 1969)
Harold Lever (October 1969 to June 1970)

Minister without Portfolio
Douglas Houghton (October 1964 to January 1967)
Patrick Gordon Walker (January 1967 to August 1967)
George Thomson (October 1968 to October 1969)
Peter Shore (October 1969 to June 1970)

NOTES

1. The Foreign Office and the Commonwealth Relations Office merged to become the Foreign and Commonwealth Office on 17 October 1968.
2. Not a Cabinet post until October 1968.
3. The Department of Economic Affairs was abolished in October 1969.
4. Ceased to be a Cabinet post after 29 August 1967.
5. Created out of the old Health and Social Security ministries.
6. Ceased to be a Cabinet post after 5 October 1969.
7. The Ministry of Labour was reorganised as the Ministry of Employment and Productivity in April 1968.
8. See previous note.
9. The Ministry of Power merged with the Ministry of Technology in October 1969.

Appendix II:
Chronology of European Integration and the British Approach, 1964–70

October 1964
- Labour Party wins General Election with a majority of five seats
- Prime Minister, First Secretary of State and Chancellor of the Exchequer rule out devaluation of the pound
- Creation of the Department of Economic Affairs and the Ministry of Technology
- Britain imposes a 15 per cent surcharge on all imports except food, tobacco and basic raw materials

December 1964
- Wilson visits Washington for talks with Lyndon Johnson
- Labour Party conference in Brighton

January 1965
- Patrick Gordon Walker loses Leyton by-election. Replaced as Foreign Secretary by Michael Stewart
- Wilson meets Charles de Gaulle for first time, at Winston Churchill's funeral

February 1965
- Wilson states it is not possible to join EEC unless conditions change

March 1965
- Wilson visits Berlin Mayor Willy Brandt and West German Chancellor Ludwig Erhard

April 1965
- Wilson meets President Charles de Gaulle and Prime Minister Georges Pompidou in Paris
- Wilson meets Johnson in Washington
- Conference of democratic socialist leaders at Chequers

- Wilson meets with Italian Prime Minister Aldo Moro and Foreign Minister Amintore Fanfani in Rome
- Reduction in British import surcharge to 10 per cent

May 1965
- EFTA heads of government conference in Vienna

June 1965
- Commonwealth Prime Ministers conference in London

July 1965
- Chancellor Callaghan announces severe deflationary package for the British economy
- Edward Heath elected leader of the Conservative Party

August 1965
- Wilson again rules out British application to EEC

September 1965
- Labour Party conference in Blackpool
- Wilson meets Smith in London and Salisbury

November 1965
- Unilateral Declaration of Independence by Rhodesia

December 1965
- Signing of the Anglo-Irish Free Trade Agreement
- Wilson meets Johnson in Washington

January 1966
- Commonwealth conference on Rhodesia in Lagos

February 1966
- Establishment of Industrial Reorganisation Corporation to promote British exports and technological advance
- Fulton inquiry into workings of the civil service begins
- Parliamentary debate on Vietnam
- De Gaulle announces his intention to withdraw France from NATO's integrated military structure
- Publication of Defence White Paper on withdrawal from east of Suez
- Wilson meets Russian President Alexei Kosygin in Moscow

March 1966
- London meeting of the WEU
- Labour Party wins general election with a majority of 96 seats

May 1966
- Strike by Britain's seamen
- Pound falls to lowest level for 15 months
- Erhard makes heads-of-government visit to London

June 1966
- Row breaks out over Britain's decision to pull out of ELDO
- Tony Benn becomes Minister of Technology

July 1966
- Pompidou makes heads-of-government visit to London
- Australian Prime Minister Harold Holt meets Wilson in London
- Wilson meets Kosygin in Moscow
- Wilson meets Johnson in Washington
- Wilson meets Lester Pearson in Ottawa

August 1966
- George Brown and Michael Stewart swap jobs – Brown becomes Foreign Secretary, Stewart Secretary of State for Economic Affairs.

September 1966
- Commonwealth Prime Ministers conference in London
- Labour Party conference in Brighton

October 1966
- Cabinet meeting on EEC at Chequers; support given to Wilson/ Brown probe of EEC capitals
- Britain informs other EFTA countries that it would try to join EEC

November 1966
- Wilson's speech on the probe to Parliament
- Wilson's Guildhall speech on Europe and the 'technological community'
- Wilson/Smith talks on Rhodesia, aboard HMS *Tiger*
- Britain abolishes its import surcharge

December 1966
- EFTA Prime Minsters conference; agrees to British probe
- CBI declares support for British application to EEC
- Brandt makes plea for Britain to join EEC

January 1967
- Wilson/Brown probe of Italy
- Wilson addresses the Assembly of the Council of Europe in Strasbourg, which supports a British application
- Wilson/Brown probe of France

February 1967
- Wilson/Brown probe of Belgium
- Wilson/Brown probe discussions with the European Commission
- Kosygin visits London
- Wilson/Brown probe of Germany
- Wilson/Brown probe of the Netherlands

March 1967
- Wilson/Brown probe of Luxembourg

May 1967
- Wilson announces decision to apply for membership of the EEC, the ECSC and Euratom to Parliament
- House of Commons debate on membership of the Communities; motion carried by 488 votes to 62
- Conclusion of Kennedy Round of GATT negotiations
- De Gaulle issues his 'velvet veto'

June 1967
- 'Six Day War' in the Middle East
- Wilson meets de Gaulle in Bonn

July 1967
- Brown launches Britain's second EEC application at WEU meeting

October 1967
- Labour Party conference in Scarborough
- European Commission reports on possible effects of British accession to EEC

November 1967
- Devaluation of sterling from to $2.80 to $2.40
- Roy Jenkins replaces James Callaghan as Chancellor of the Exchequer
- De Gaulle issues his second veto on British EEC membership

January 1968
- Wilson meets Kosygin in Moscow

February 1968
- Wilson meets Johnson in Washington
- Wilson meets Pearson in Ottawa

March 1968
- Brown resigns and is replaced as Foreign Secretary by Stewart

June 1968
- Publication of Fulton Report on civil service reform

July 1968
- Signature of nuclear Non-Proliferation Treaty by London, Moscow and Washington
- Outbreak of Nigerian civil war

August 1968
- Soviet invasion of Czechoslovakia

September 1968
- Labour Party conference in Blackpool

October 1968
- Wilson/Smith talks on Rhodesia aboard HMS *Fearless*
- Merger of Foreign and Commonwealth Offices to form the Foreign and Commonwealth Office
- Cessation of American bombing in Vietnam

November 1968
- Richard Nixon wins American Presidency
- EFTA ministerial meeting in Vienna

February 1969
- Commonwealth Prime Ministers conference in London
- Signing of Anglo-German declaration on Europe
- Publication of Defence White Paper
- Nixon meets Wilson in London
- 'Soames affair' breaks

March 1969
- Wilson visits Lagos for talks on Nigeria

April 1969
- De Gaulle resigns

May 1969
- Meeting of the committee of ministers of the Council of Europe in London

June 1969
- Wilson meets the Swedish Prime Minister
- Establishment of the Open University
- Wilson's Guildhall speech, focusing on the technological aspects of closer association with Europe

July 1969
- Pompidou succeeds de Gaulle

August 1969
- Nixon visits Britain
- Devaluation of French franc by 11.1 per cent

September 1969
- Labour Party conference in Brighton (into October)

October 1969
- DEA abolished

January 1970
- End of Nigerian civil war
- Wilson visits Canada to see Pearson
- Wilson visits America to see Nixon

February 1970
- Publication of Defence White Paper
- Publication of White Paper on benefits of EEC membership

May 1970
- Edward Heath meets Pompidou in Paris

June 1970
- Conservative Party wins general election with a majority of 30 seats
- EEC opens negotiations with Britain, Denmark, Ireland and Norway

Bibliography

PRIVATE AND OTHER UNPUBLISHED PAPERS

Lord George-Brown papers (Bodleian Library, Oxford)
William Gorell-Barnes papers (Churchill College, Cambridge)
Philip Noel-Baker papers (Churchill College, Cambridge)
Georges Pompidou papers (Archives Nationales, Paris)
Patrick Reilly papers (Bodleian Library, Oxford)
Michael Stewart papers (Churchill College, Cambridge)

STATE PAPERS

Australia: National Archives of Australia (Sydney)
France: Ministère des Affaires Etrangères (Paris); Archives Nationales (Paris); Archives de la Fondation Nationale des Sciences Politiques (Paris)
Germany: Institut für Zeitgeschichte, H. Schwarz (ed.), *Akten zur Auswärtigen Politik der Bundesrepublik Deutschland 1965*; *Akten zur Auswärtigen Politik der Bundesrepublik Deutschland 1966*; *Akten zur Auswärtigen Politik der Bundesrepublik Deutschland 1967* (Munich: R. Oldenbourg Verlag, 1996, 1997, 1998)
Ireland: National Archives
United Kingdom: PRO (Kew): BT (Board of Trade), CAB (Cabinet and its committees), DO (Commonwealth Relations Office; became Commonwealth Office in 1967), EW (Department of Economic Affairs), FCO (Foreign and Commonwealth Office; separate departments until 1968), FO (Foreign Office), HF (Ministry of Technology), PREM (Prime Minister's files), T (Treasury)
United States of America: John F. Kennedy Presidential Library (Boston, MA)

EEC PAPERS

Council of Ministers Archives (Brussels)
European Commission Historical Archives (Brussels)
SGCI Archives (Fontainebleau)

PUBLISHED PARTY AND OTHER OFFICIAL DOCUMENTS

Action Not Words, Conservative Party Election Manifesto (London, 1966)

Annual Abstract of Statistics (London: HMSO)

Britain and the Common Market (London: Labour Party, 1962)

CBI, *Britain and Europe, Vol. I: An Industrial Appraisal* (London, 1966)

CBI, *Britain and Europe, Vol. II: Supporting Papers* (London, 1967)

CBI, *Britain and Europe, Vol. III: A Programme of Action* (London, 1967)

Command Papers (London: HMSO)

Conservative Party Archives (Bodleian Library, Oxford)

Dáil Eireann Parliamentary Debates

FBI, *British Industry and Europe* (London, 1961)

FBI, *Overseas Trade Policy* (London, 1963)

FBI, *Britain's Economic Problems and Policies: The Next Five Years* (London, 1965)

Foreign Relations of the United States, 1964–1968, 13, Western Europe Region (Washington DC: United States Government Printing Office, 1995)

General Election 1966: Daily Notes (London: Conservative Research Department, 1966)

Hansard: House of Commons Debates (London: HMSO)

Hansard: House of Representatives Debates (London: HMSO)

Labour Party, NEC, Archives (National Museum of Labour History (Manchester))

Labour Party Archives (National Museum of Labour History (Manchester))

Labour Party Election Manifesto (London, 1964)

Labour Party Election Manifesto (London, 1966)

Labour Party: Report of the Sixty-Second Annual Conference, 1963 (London: Transport House, 1964)

O'Neill, Sir C., *Britain's Entry into the European Community: Report on the Negotiations of 1970–1972* (London: Whitehall History Publishing in association with Frank Cass, 2000)

Socialist Commentary (January 1962)

Verhandlung des Deutschen Bundestages: Stenographische Berichte (Bonn: Deutscher Bundestag, 1950 onwards)

NEWSPAPERS AND PERIODICALS

Australian, The
Economist, The

Express
Le Monde
Sunday Express
Times, The
Who's Who 2000

AUTOBIOGRAPHY, BIOGRAPHY, DIARIES AND MEMOIRS

Acheson, D. *Present at the Creation: My Years in the State Department* (New York: Signet, 1969)

Benn, A. *Out of the Wilderness: Diaries 1963–67* (London: Hutchinson, 1987)

Bohlen, C. E. *Witness to History, 1929–1969* (New York: W. W. Norton, 1973)

Boothby, L. *My Yesterday, Your Tomorrow* (London: Hutchinson, 1962)

Brandt, W. *Begegnungen und Einsichte: Die Jahre 1960–1975* (Hamburg: Hoffmann and Campe, 1976)

Brinkley, D. and Hackett, C. (eds), *Jean Monnet: The Path to European Unity* (Basingstoke: Macmillan, 1991)

Brivati, B. *Hugh Gaitskell* (London: Richard Cohen, 1997)

Bromberger, M. and Bromberger, S. *Jean Monnet and the United States of Europe*, translated by E. P. Halperin (New York: Coward-McCann, 1968)

Brown, G. *In My Way: The Political Memoirs of Lord George-Brown* (London: Victor Gollancz, 1971)

Bullock, A. *Ernest Bevin: Foreign Secretary* (London: Heinemann, 1983)

Cairncross, A. *The Wilson Years: A Treasury Diary, 1964–1969* (London: Historians' Press, 1997)

Callaghan, J. *Time and Chance* (London: Collins, 1987)

Carlton, D. *Anthony Eden: A Biography* (London: Allen Lane 1981)

Castle, B. *The Castle Diaries, 1964–70* (London: Weidenfeld & Nicolson, 1984)

Chalfont, A. *The Shadow of My Hand: A Memoir* (London: Weidenfeld & Nicolson, 2000)

Cole, J. *As it Seemed to Me: Political Memoirs* (London: Phoenix, 1996)

Couve de Murville, M. *Une Politique Etrangère, 1958–1969* (Paris: Plon, 1971)

Crosland, S. *Tony Crosland* (London: Jonathan Cape, 1982)

Crossman, R. *The Diaries of a Cabinet Minister: Vol. II, Lord President of the Council and Leader of the House of Commons, 1966–68* (London: Hamish Hamilton and Jonathan Cape, 1976)

Crossman, R. *The Diaries of a Cabinet Minister: Vol. I, Minister of Housing,*

1964–66 (London: Hamish Hamilton and Jonathan Cape, 1977)

de Gaulle, C. *Discours et Messages, Vol. IV* (Evreux: Plon, 1970)

de Gaulle, C. *Discours et Messages, Vol. V* (Paris: Plon, 1970)

de Gaulle, C. *Memoires d'Espoir: Vol. I, Le Renouveau, Vol. II. l'Effort* (Paris: Plon, 1970)

de Gaulle, C. *Lettres, Notes et Carnets, Juillet 1966–Avril 1969* (Paris: Plon, 1987)

Duchêne, F. *Jean Monnet: The First Statesman of Interdependence* (London: W. W. Norton, 1991)

Dutton, D. *Anthony Eden: A Life and Reputation* (London: Edward Arnold, 1997)

Gladwyn, *The Memoirs of Lord Gladwyn* (London: Weidenfeld & Nicolson, 1972).

Gore-Booth, P. *With Great Truth and Respect* (London: Constable, 1974)

Haines, J. *The Politics of Power* (London: Jonathan Cape, 1977)

Healey, D. *The Time of My Life* (London: Michael Joseph, 1989)

Heath, E. *The Course of My Life: My Autobiography* (London: Hodder & Stoughton, 1998)

Heffer, S. *Like the Roman: The Life of Enoch Powell* (London: Phoenix Press, 1999)

Jay, D. *Change and Fortune: A Political Record* (London: Hutchinson, 1980)

Jefferys, K. *Anthony Crosland: A New Biography* (London: Richard Cohen, 1999)

Jellicoe, E. 'Lord Edward Arthur Alexander Shackleton', *Biographic Memoirs of Fellows of the Royal Society*, 45 (1999), pp. 485–505

Jenkins, R. *A Life at the Centre* (New York: Random House, 1991)

Kay, E. *Pragmatic Premier: An Intimate Portrait of Harold Wilson* (London: Leslie Frewin, 1967)

Kilmuir, Earl of, *Political Adventure: The Memoirs of the Earl of Kilmuir* (London: Weidenfeld & Nicolson, 1964)

King, C. *The Cecil King Diary, 1965–1970* (London: Jonathan Cape, 1972)

Kipping, N. *Summing Up* (London: Hutchinson, 1972)

Lacouture, J. *De Gaulle: The Ruler, 1945–1970*, translated by Alan Sheridan (London: Horvill, 1991)

Lahr, R. *Zeuge von Fall und Aufstieg: Private Briefe 1934–1981* (Hamburg: Knaus, 1981)

Ledwidge, B. *De Gaulle* (London: Weidenfeld & Nicolson, 1987)

Macmillan, H. *Tides of Fortune, 1945–1955* (London: Macmillan, 1969)

Macmillan, H. *At the End of the Day, 1961–1963* (London: Macmillan, 1973)

Marjolin, R. *Architect of European Unity: Memoirs 1911–1986* (London: Weidenfeld & Nicholson, 1989)

Monnet, J. *Memoirs*, translated by Richard Mayne (London: Collins, 1978)

Morgan, A. *Harold Wilson* (London: Pluto, 1992)

Morgan, K. O. *Callaghan: A Life* (Oxford: Oxford University Press, 1997)

Owen, D. *Time to Declare* (London: Michael Joseph, 1991)

Paterson, P. *Tired and Emotional: The Life of Lord George Brown* (London: Chatto & Windus, 1993)

Pearce, R. (ed.), *Patrick Gordon Walker: Political Diaries 1932–1971* (London: Historian's Press, 1991)

Peyrefitte, A. *C'Etait de Gaulle: Vol. I, La France Redevient La France; Vol. II, La France Reprend sa Place de la Monde; Vol. III, Tout le Monde a Besoin d'une France qui Marche* (Paris: Fayard-de-Fallois, 1994, 1997 and 2000)

Pimlott, B. *Harold Wilson* (London: HarperCollins, 1993)

Prior, J. *A Balance of Power* (London: Hamish Hamilton, 1986)

Rusk, D. *As I Saw It* (New York: W. W. Norton, 1990)

Shepherd, R. *Iain Macleod* (London: Hutchinson, 1994)

Shore, P. *Leading the Left* (London: Jonathan Cape, 1993)

Short, E. *Whip to Wilson: The Crucial Years of Labour Government* (London: Macdonald, 1989)

Smith, D. *Harold Wilson: A Critical Biography* (London: Robert Hale, 1964)

Spaak, P. *The Continuing Battle: Memoirs of a European* (London: Weidenfeld & Nicolson, 1971)

Stewart, M. *Life and Labour: An Autobiography* (London: Sidgwick & Jackson, 1980)

Walker, P. *Staying Power* (London: Bloomsbury, 1996)

Weidenfeld, G. *Remembering My Good Friends: An Autobiography* (London: HarperCollins, 1995)

Wigg, G. *George Wigg* (London: Michael Joseph, 1972)

Williams, M. *Inside Number Ten* (London: Weidenfeld & Nicolson, 1972)

Wilson, H. *The Labour Government, 1964–70: A Personal Record* (London: Weidenfeld & Nicolson/Michael Joseph, 1971)

Wright, P. *Spycatcher* (Australia: Heinemann, 1987)

Ziegler P. *Wilson: The Authorised Life of Lord Wilson of Rievaulx* (London: Weidenfeld & Nicolson, 1993)

Zuckerman, S. *Monkeys, Men and Missiles* (London: Collins, 1988)

SECONDARY SOURCES (BOOKS)

Badsey, S. *Military Operations and the Media* (Camberley: Surrey Strategic and Combat Studies Institute, 1994)

Bange, O. *The EEC Crisis of 1963: Kennedy, Macmillan, de Gaulle and Adenaur in Conflict* (Basingstoke: Macmillan, 2000)

Barker, E. *Britain in a Divided Europe 1945–1970* (London: Weidenfeld & Nicolson, 1971)

Bartlett, C. J. *'The Special Relationship': A Political History of Anglo-American Relations Since 1945* (London: Longman, 1992)

Beloff, Lord, *Britain and European Union: Dialogue of the Deaf* (London: Macmillan, 1996)

Beloff, N. *The General Says No: Britain's Exclusion from Europe* (Harmondsworth: Penguin, 1963)

Bentley, M. *Modern Historiography: An Introduction* (London: Routledge, 1999)

Birch, A. *The British System of Government* (London: Routledge, 1998)

Blank, S. *Industry and Government in Britain* (Farnborough: Saxon House, 1973)

Brands, H. W. *The Wages of Globalism: Lyndon Johnson and the Limits of American Power* (Oxford: Oxford University Press, 1995)

Broad, R. *Labour's European Dilemmas: From Bevin to Blair* (Basingstoke: Palgrave, 2001)

Bullock, A. and Stallybrass, O. (eds), *The Fontana Dictionary of Modern Thought* (London: Collins, 1977)

Burgess, M. *Federalism and European Union: Political Ideas, Influences and Strategies in the European Community, 1972–1987* (London: Routledge, 1989)

Butler, D. and King, A. *The British General Election of 1966* (London: Macmillan, 1966)

Camps, M. *Britain and the European Community 1955–1963* (London: Oxford University Press, 1964)

Camps, M. *What Kind of Europe? The Community since De Gaulle's Veto* (London: Oxford University Press, 1965)

Camps, M. *European Unification in the Sixties: From the Veto to the Crisis* (London: Oxford University Press, 1967)

Carver, M. *Tightrope Walking: British Defence Policy since 1945* (London: Hutchinson, 1992)

Charlton, M. *The Price of Victory* (London: British Broadcasting Corporation, 1983)

Charmley, J. *Churchill's Grand Alliance: The Anglo-American Special Relationship 1940–57* (London: Hodder & Stoughton, 1995)

Chubb, B. *The Government and Politics of Ireland* (London: Longman, 1992)

Clarke, P. *Hope and Glory: Britain and the World 1900–1990* (London: Penguin, 1996)

Crafts, N. *Britain's Relative Economic Decline 1870–1995: A Quantitative Perspective* (London: Social Market Foundation, 1997)

Cromwell, W. C. *The United States and the European Pillar* (Basingstoke: Macmillan, 1992)

Darwin, J. *Britain and Decolonisation: The Retreat from Empire in the Post-War World* (London: Macmillan, 1988)

Dell, E. *The Schuman Plan and the British Abdication of Leadership in Europe* (Oxford: Oxford University Press, 1995)

Dell, E. *The Chancellors: A History of the Chancellors of the Exchequer, 1945–1990* (London: HarperCollins, 1997)

Denman, R. *Missed Chances: Britain and Europe in the Twentieth Century* (London: Cassell, 1996)

Dimbleby, D. and Reynolds, D. *An Ocean Apart: The Relationship between Britain and America in the Twentieth Century* (London: Hodder & Stoughton, 1988)

Dougherty, J. E. and Pfaltzgraff, R. L. *Contending Theories of International Relations: A Comprehensive Survey* (New York: Harper & Row, 1981)

Edmonds, R. *Setting the Mould: The United States and Britain, 1945–1950* (Oxford: Oxford University Press, 1986)

Edwards, R. D. *The Pursuit of Reason: The Economist 1843–1993* (London: Hamish Hamilton, 1993)

Ellison, J. *Threatening Europe: Britain and the Creation of the European Community, 1955–58* (London: Macmillan, 2000)

Fieldhouse, D. K. *The West and the Third World: Trade, Colonialism, Dependence and Development* (Oxford: Blackwell, 1999)

Foot, P. *The Politics of Harold Wilson* (London: Penguin, 1968)

Frankel, J. *British Foreign Policy 1945–1973* (London: Oxford University Press, 1975)

Gallup International Public Opinion Polls: Great Britain, 1937–1975 (New York: Random House, 1976)

Garton Ash, T. *In Europe's Name: Germany and the Divided Continent* (London: Jonathan Cape, 1993)

George, S. *An Awkward Partner: Britain in the European Community* (New York: Oxford University Press, 1990)

Gillespie, P. (ed.), *Britain's European Question: The Issues For Ireland* (Dublin: Institute of European Affairs, 1996)

Girling, J. *France: Political and Social Change* (London: Routledge, 1998)

Gowland, D. and Turner, A. *Reluctant Europeans: Britain and European Integration 1945–1998* (Harlow: Pearson Education, 2000)

Grant, W. and Marsh, D. *The CBI* (London: Hodder & Stoughton, 1977)

Greenwood, S. *Britain and European Co-operation Since 1945* (Oxford: Blackwell, 1992)

Greenwood, S. *Britain and the Cold War 1945–91* (London: Macmillan, 2000)

Grosser, A. *The Western Alliance: European–American Relations Since 1945*, trans. Michael Shaw (New York: Continuum, 1980)

Hanrieder, W. F. *Deutschland, Europa, Amerika* (Paderborn: Ferdinand Schöningh, 1995)

Hattersley, R. *Fifty Years On: A Prejudiced History of Britain Since 1945* (London: Abacus, 1997)

Heath, E. *Old World, New Horizons: Britain, the Common Market and the Atlantic Alliance* (London: Oxford University Press, 1970)

Heclo, H. and Wildavsky, A. *The Private Government of Public Money: Community and Policy Inside British Politics* (Basingstoke: Macmillan, 1974)

Hennessy, P. *The Prime Minister: The Office and its Holders Since 1945* (London: Allen Lane, 2000)

Hildebrand, K. *Von Erhard zur Großen Koalition* (Stuttgart: Deutsche Verlags-Anstalt, 1984)

Hogan, M. J. *The Marshall Plan: America, Britain and the Reconstruction of Western Europe, 1947–1952* (Cambridge: Cambridge University Press, 1987)

Hogan, M. J. *A Cross of Iron: Harry S. Truman and the National Security State, 1945–1954* (Cambridge: Cambridge University Press, 1998)

Hollis, M. and Smith, S. *Explaining and Understanding International Relations* (Oxford: Clarendon Press, 1991)

Holmes M. (ed.), *The Eurosceptical Reader* (Basingstoke: Macmillan, 1996)

Iggers, G. G. *Historiography in the Twentieth Century: From Scientific Objectivity to the Postmodern Challenge* (Hanover: Wesleyan University Press, 1997)

Jay, D. *The European Economic Community* (Manchester: Manchester Statistical Society, 1970)

Jenkins, K. *On 'What is History?' From Carr and Elton to Rorty and White* (London: Routledge, 1995)

Jordanova, L. *History in Practice* (London: Arnold, 2000)

Jowell, R. and Hoinville, G. (eds), *Britain into Europe: Public Opinion and the EEC 1961–75* (London: Croom Helm, 1976)

Kaiser, W. *Using Europe, Abusing the Europeans: Britain and European Integration, 1945–63* (London: Macmillan, 1996)

Kaplan, M. A. *On Historical and Political Knowing* (London: University of Chicago Press, 1971)

Kavanagh, D. and Morris, P. *Consensus Politics From Attlee to Major*, 2nd edn (Oxford: Blackwell, 1994)

Kennedy, M. and Skelly, J. M. (eds), *Irish Foreign Policy 1919–66* (Dublin: Four Courts Press, 2000)

Keogh, D. *Ireland and Europe 1919–1989: A Diplomatic and Political History* (Cork: Hibernian University Press, 1990)

Kitzinger, U. *The Challenge of the Common Market*, 4th edn (Oxford: Blackwell, 1962)

Kitzinger, U. *Britain, Europe and Beyond: Essays in European Politics* (Leyden: Sythoff, 1964)

Kitzinger, U. *The European Common Market and Community* (London: Routledge & Kegan Paul, 1967)

Kitzinger, U. *The Second Try: Labour and the EEC* (Oxford: Pergamon, 1968)

Kitzinger, U. *Diplomacy and Persuasion: How Britain Joined the Common Market* (London: Thames & Hudson, 1973)

Kitzinger, U., W. Pickles, S. Strange, R. Shone, G. McCrone, R. Mayne, K. W. Wedderburn, A. Jones and L. Beaton, *Britain and the Common Market 1967* (London: British Broadcasting Corporation, 1967)

Kroegel, D. *Einen Anfang Finden! Kurt Georg Kiesinger in der Außen – und Deutschlandpolitik der Großen Koalition* (München: R. Oldenbourg Verlag, 1997)

LaFeber, W. *America, Russia, and the Cold War 1945–1992*, 7th edn (New York: McGraw-Hill, 1993)

Lamb, R. *The Failure of the Eden Government* (London: Sidgwick & Jackson, 1987)

Lamb, R. *The Macmillan Years 1957–1963: The Emerging Truth* (London: John Murray, 1995)

Leigh, D. *The Wilson Plot: The Intelligence Services and the Discrediting of a Prime Minister* (London: Heinemann, 1988)

Lieber, R. J. *British Politics and European Unity: Parties, Elites, and Pressure Groups* (Berkeley: University of California Press, 1970)

Ludlow, N. P. *Dealing with Britain: The Six and the First UK Application to the EEC* (Cambridge: Cambridge University Press, 1997)

Lundestad, G. *'Empire' by Integration: The United States and European Integration, 1945–1997* (Oxford: Oxford University Press, 1998)

Lynch, P. *The Politics of Nationhood: Sovereignty, Britishness and Conservative Politics* (London: Macmillan, 1999)

Lyons, F. S. L. *Ireland Since the Famine* (London: Weidenfeld & Nicolson, 1971)

Mandel, E. *Europe Versus America? Contradictions of Imperialism* (London: New Left Books, 1970)

Marcowitz, R. *Option für Paris? Unionspartien, SPD und Charles de Gaulle 1958 bis 1969* (München: R. Oldenbourg Verlag, 1996)

Mawby, S. *Containing Germany: Britain and the Arming of the Federal Republic* (Basingstoke: Macmillan, 1999)

May, A. *Britain and Europe Since 1945* (London: Longman, 1999)

Mayne, R. *The Recovery of Europe: From Devastation to Unity* (London: Weidenfeld & Nicolson, 1970)

Mayne, R. *The Community of Europe* (London: Victor Gollancz, 1982)

Mayne, R. *Postwar: The Dawn of Today's Europe* (London: Thames & Hudson, 1983)

Mayne, R. and Pinder, J. *Federal Union: The Pioneers* (Basingstoke: Macmillan, 1990)

Miller, J. D. B. *Survey of Commonwealth Affairs: Problems of Expansion and Attrition, 1953–69* (Oxford: Oxford University Press, 1974)

Milward, A. *The Reconstruction of Western Europe* (London: Methuen, 1984)

Milward, A. *The European Rescue of the Nation-State* (London: Routledge, 1992)

Moon, J. *European Integration in British Politics 1950–1963: A Study of Issue Change* (Aldershot: Gower, 1985)

Morgan, K. O. *Labour People: Leaders and Lieutenants: Hardie to Kinnock* (Oxford: Oxford University Press, 1989)

Morgan, K. O. *The People's Peace: British History 1945–1989* (Oxford: Oxford University Press, 1990)

Newhouse, J. *Collision in Brussels: The Common Market Crisis of 30 June 1965* (London: Faber & Faber, 1967)

Newhouse, J. *De Gaulle and the Anglo-Saxons* (London: Deutsch, 1970)

Newman, M. *Socialism and European Unity: The Dilemma of the Left in Britain and France* (London: Junction, 1983)

Nicholls, A. J. *The Bonn Republic* (London and New York: Longman, 1997)

Nicolson, F. and East, R. *From the Six to the Twelve: The Enlargement of the European Communities* (London: Longman, 1987)

Northedge, F. S. *British Foreign Policy: The Process of Readjustment 1945–1961* (London: George Allen & Unwin, 1962)

Northedge, F. S. *Descent from Power: British Foreign Policy 1945–1973* (London: George Allen & Unwin, 1974)

Norton, P. *Dissension in the House of Commons: Intra-Party Dissent in the House of Commons Division Lobbies, 1945–1974* (London: Macmillan, 1975)

Nugent, N. *The Government and Politics of the European Union*, 3rd edn (Basingstoke: Macmillan, 1994)

Nutting, A. *Europe Will Not Wait: A Warning and a Way Out* (London: Hollis & Carter, 1960)

Owen, G. *From Empire to Europe: The Decline and Revival of British Industry Since the Second World War* (London: HarperCollins, 1999)

Pagedas, C. A. *Anglo-American Strategic Relations and the French Problem, 1960–1963* (London: Frank Cass, 2000)

Pickering, J. *Britain's Withdrawal from East of Suez: The Politics of Retrenchment* (London: Macmillan, 1998)

Pinder, J. *Europe Against De Gaulle* (London: Pall Mall, 1963)

Pinder, J. *European Community: The Building of a Union* (Oxford: Opus, 1998)

Pinder, J. and Pryce, R. *Europe After De Gaulle: Towards the United States of Europe* (Harmondsworth: Penguin, 1969)

Ponting, C. *Breach of Promise: Labour in Power 1964–1970* (London: Hamish Hamilton, 1989)

Proudfoot, M. *British Politics and Government 1951–1970: A Study of an Affluent Society* (London: Faber & Faber, 1974)

Pryce, R. *The Political Future of the European Community* (London: John Marshbank, 1962)

Pryce, R. *The Dynamics of European Union* (London: Routledge, 1990)

Radice, G. *Offshore: Britain and the European Idea* (London: I. B. Tauris, 1992)

Ramsden, J. *The Making of Conservative Party Policy* (London: Longman, 1980)

Reynolds, D. *Britannia Overruled: British Policy and World Power in the Twentieth Century* (London: Longman, 1991)

Reynolds, D. *One World Divisible: A Global History Since 1945* (London: Allen Lane, 2000)

Roberts, F. *Dealing with Dictators: The Destruction and Revival of Europe 1930–1970* (London: Weidenfeld & Nicholson, 1991)

Robins, L. J. *The Reluctant Party: Labour and the EEC, 1961–75* (Ormskirk: G. W. Hesketh, 1979)

Sanders, D. *Losing an Empire, Finding a Role: British Foreign Policy Since 1945* (Basingstoke: Macmillan, 1990)

Schaad, M. P. C. *Bullying Bonn: Anglo-German Diplomacy on European Integration, 1955–61* (Basingstoke: Macmillan, 2000).

Seldon, A. *Churchill's Indian Summer: The Conservative Government, 1951–55* (London: Hodder & Stoughton, 1981)

Servan-Schreiber, J. *The American Challenge*, trans. R. Steel (London: Hamish Hamilton, 1968)

Shepherd, R. J. *Public Opinion and European Integration* (New York: Saxon House, 1975)

Sked, A. and Cook, C. *Post-War Britain: A Political History*, 4th edn (London: Penguin, 1993)

Southgate, B. *History: What and Why? Ancient, Modern, and Postmodern Perspectives* (London: Routledge, 1996)

Tannen, D. *The Argument Culture: Changing the Way We Argue and Debate* (New York: Virago Press, 1998)

Thorpe, A. *A History of the British Labour Party* (Basingstoke: Macmillan, 1997)

Twitchell, N. H. *The Tribune Group: Factional Conflict in the Labour Party, 1964–1970* (London: Rabbit Press, 1998)

Vaïsse, M. *La Grandeur: Politique Etrangère du General de Gaulle 1958–1969* (Paris: Fayard, 1998)

Watt, D. C. *Succeeding John Bull: America in Britain's Place 1900–1975* (Cambridge: Cambridge University Press, 1984)

White, H. *The Content of the Form: Narrative Discourse and Historical Representation* (London: Johns Hopkins University Press, 1992)

Winand, P. *Eisenhower, Kennedy and the United States of Europe* (New York: St Martin's Press, 1996)

Young, H. *This Blessed Plot: Britain and Europe from Churchill to Blair* (London: Macmillan, 1998)

Young, J. W. *Britain and European Unity, 1945–1999*, 2nd edn (Basingstoke: Macmillan, 2000)

Young, J. W. *Britain and the World in the Twentieth Century* (London: Arnold, 1997)

SECONDARY SOURCES (ARTICLES)

Aldrich, R. J. 'European Integration: An American Intelligence Connection', in A. Deighton (ed.), *Building Post-War Europe: National Decision-Makers and European Institutions, 1948–63* (Basingstoke: Macmillan, 1995), pp. 159–79

Aron, R. 'The Historical Sketch of the Great Debate', in D. Lerner and R. Aron (eds), *France Defeats EDC* (London: Thames & Hudson, 1957), pp. 2–21

Ashford, N. 'The Political Parties', in S. George (ed.), *Britain and the European Community: The Politics of Semi-Detachment* (Oxford: Clarendon Press, 1992), pp. 119–48

Badel, L. 'Le Quai d'Orsay, la Grande-Bretagne et l'Elargissement de la Communauté (1963–1969): Aspects Fonctionnel et Culturel', in *50 Ans Après la Déclaration Schuman: Bilan de l'Histoire de la*

Construction Européene – Actes du Colloques de Nantes, 11–13 Mai 2000 (Nantes: CRHMA et Ouest-Editions, 2001), pp. 13–25

Badel, L. 'Le Rôle Tenu par la Poste d'Expansion Economique de Londres dans le Processus d'Adhésion du Royaume-Uni au Marché Commun (1966–1971)', in R. Girault and R. Poidevin (eds), *Le Rôle des Ministères des Finances et de l'Economie dans la Construction Européene (1957–1978): Actes du Colloque Tenu à Bercy, 26–28 Mai 1999* (Paris: CHEFF, 2001), pp. 28–40

Bale, T. 'A "Deplorable Episode"? South African Arms and the Statecraft of British Social Democracy', *Labour History Review*, 62, 1 (1997), pp. 22–40

Barnes, J. 'From Eden to Macmillan, 1955–59', in P. Hennessy and A. Seldon (eds), *Ruling Performance: British Governments from Attlee to Thatcher* (Oxford: Basil Blackwell, 1987), pp. 98–149

Beloff, N. 'What Happened in Britain after the General Said No', in P. Uri (ed.), *From Commonwealth to Common Market* (London: Penguin, 1968), pp. 50–61

Broad, R. and Geiger, T. (eds), 'The 1975 British Referendum on Europe', *Contemporary British History*, 10, 3 (1996), pp. 83–105

Buchan, A. 'The Multilateral Force: A Study in Alliance Politics', *International Affairs*, 40, 4 (1964), pp. 619–37

Burgess, S. and Edwards, G. 'The Six Plus One: British Policy-Making and the Question of European Economic Integration, 1955', *International Affairs*, 64, 3 (1988), pp. 393–413

Butt, R. 'The Common Market and Conservative Party Politics, 1961–2', *Government and Opposition*, 2 (1967), pp. 372–86

Camps, M. 'Missing the Boat at Messina and Other Times?', in B. Brivati and H. Jones (eds), *From Reconstruction to Integration: Britain and Europe Since 1945* (Leicester: Leicester University Press, 1993), pp. 134–43

Catterall, P. 'Foreign and Commonwealth Policy in Opposition: The Labour Party', in W. Kaiser and G. Staerck (eds), *British Foreign Policy 1955–64: Contracting Options* (Basingstoke: Macmillan, 2000), pp. 89–109.

Catteral, P. 'Macmillan and Europe 1950–56: The Cold War, the American Context and the British Approach to European Integration', *Cercles*, 5 (Spring, 2002), pp. 93–108.

Chace, J. and Malkin, E. 'The Mischief-Maker: The American Media and De Gaulle, 1964–68', in R. O. Paxton and N. Wahl (eds), *De Gaulle and the United States: A Centennial Reappraisal* (Oxford: Berg, 1994), pp. 359–77.

Charlton, M. 'How and Why Britain Lost the Leadership of Europe

(1): "Messina! Messina!" or, the Parting of Ways', *Encounter*, 57, 3 (August 1981), pp. 8–22; 'How (and Why) Britain Lost the Leadership of Europe (2): A Last Step Sideways', *Encounter*, 57, 3 (September 1981), pp. 22–35; 'How (and Why) Britain Lost the Leadership of Europe (3): The Channel Crossing', *Encounter*, 57, 3 (October 1981), pp. 22–33.

Coopey, R., Fielding, S. and Tiratsoo, N. 'Introduction', in R. Coopey, S. Fielding and N. Tiratsoo (eds), *The Wilson Governments 1964–1970* (London: Pinter, 1993), pp. 1–9

Costigliola, F. 'Lyndon B. Johnson, Germany, and "the End of the Cold War"' in W. I. Cohen and N. B. Tucker (eds), *Lyndon Johnson Confronts the World: American Foreign Policy 1963–1968* (Cambridge: Cambridge University Press, 1994), pp. 173–211

Croft, S. 'British Policy towards Western Europe: The Best of Possible Worlds?', *International Affairs*, 64, 4 (1988), pp. 617–29

Crossman, R. 'Britain and Europe: A Personal History', *The Round Table*, October 1971, pp. 585–94.

Deighton, A. 'Missing the Boat: Britain and Europe 1945–61', *Contemporary Record*, 4, 1 (1990), pp. 15–17

Deighton, A. 'British–West German Relations, 1945–1972', in K. Larres (ed.), *Uneasy Allies: British–German Relations and European Integration Since 1945* (Oxford: Oxford University Press, 2000), pp. 27–44

Deighton, A. 'Foreign Policy-Making: The Macmillan Years', in W. Kaiser and G. Staerck (eds), *British Foreign Policy, 1955–64: Contracting Options* (Basingstoke: Macmillan, 2000), pp. 1–18

Deighton A. and Ludlow, P. 'A Conditional Application: British Management of the First Attempt to Seek Membership of the EEC', in A. Deighton (ed.), *Building Post-War Europe: National Decision Makers and European Institutions, 1948–1963* (London: Macmillan, 1995), pp. 107–23

Dingemans, R. and Boekestijn, A. 'The Netherlands and the Enlargement Proposals', in A. Deighton and A. S. Milward (eds), *Widening, Deepening and Acceleration: The European Economic Community 1957–1963* (Brussels: Nomos-Verlag, 1999), pp. 225–41

Dobson, A. 'The Years of Transition: Anglo-American Relations 1961–1967', *Review of International Studies*, 16 (1990), pp. 239–58

Dutton, D. 'Anticipating Maastricht: The Conservative Party and Britain's First Application to Join the European Community', *Contemporary Record*, 7, 3 (1993), pp. 522–40

Edgerton, D. 'The "White Heat" Revisited: The British Government and Technology in the 1960s', *Twentieth Century British History*, 7, 1 (1996)

Frey, C. W. 'Meaning Business: The British Application to Join the Common Market, November 1966–October 1967', *Journal of Common Market Studies*, 6, 3 (1967–68), pp. 197–230

Gardner, L. 'Lyndon Johnson and De Gaulle', in R. O. Paxton and N. Wahl (eds), *De Gaulle and the United States: A Centennial Reappraisal* (Oxford: Berg, 1994), pp. 257–79

Gardner, R. N. 'Sterling–Dollar Diplomacy in Current Perspective', in W. R. Louis and H. D. Bull (eds), *The Special Relationship: Anglo-American Relations Since 1945* (Oxford: Clarendon Press, 1989), pp. 185–200

Gerbert, P. 'The Fouchet Negotiations for Political Union and the British Application', in G. Wilkes (ed.), *Britain's Failure to Enter the European Communities 1961–1963: The Enlargement Negotiations and Crises in European, Atlantic and Commonwealth Relations* (London: Frank Cass, 1997), pp. 135-42

Greenwood, J. and Stanich, L. 'British Business: Managing Complexity', in D. Baker and D. Seawright (eds), *Britain For and Against Europe: British Politics and the Question of European Integration* (Oxford: Clarendon Press, 1998), pp. 148–64

Grigg, J. 'Policies of Impotence', *International Affairs*, 48, 1 (1972), pp. 72–6

Hamilton, R. 'Despite Best Intentions: The Evolution of the British Microcomputer Industry', *Business History*, 38, 2 (1995), pp. 81–104

Heath, E. 'Realism in British Foreign Policy', *Foreign Affairs*, 48, 1 (1969), pp. 39–50

Hill, C. 'Academic International Relations: The Siren Song of Policy Relevance', in C. Hill and P. Beshoff (eds), *Two Worlds of International Relations: Academic, Practitioners and the Trade in Ideas* (London: Routledge, 1994) pp. 3–25

Hill, C. 'The Historical Background', in M. Smith, S. Smith and B. White (eds), *British Foreign Policy: Tradition, Change and Transformation* (London: Hyman, 1988), pp. 24-49

Hitchcock, W. I. 'France, the Western Alliance and the Origins of the Schuman Plan, 1948–1950', *Diplomatic History*, 21, 4 (1997), pp. 603–30

Hollowell, J., 'The Labour Party, the World Role and the Shift from Commonwealth to EEC 1962–67: The Evolution from Commonwealth to "Second Application"', 2001, unpublished paper

Horner, D. 'The Road to Scarborough: Wilson, Labour and the Scientific Revolution', in R. Coopey, S. Fielding and N. Tiratsoo (eds), *The Wilson Governments 1964–1970* (London: Pinter, 1993), pp. 48–71

Hyam, R. 'The Parting of the Ways: Britain and South Africa's Departure from the Commonwealth, 1951–61', *Journal of Imperial and Commonwealth History*, 26, 2 (1998), pp. 157–75

Immerman, R. H. 'In Search of History, and Relevancy: Breaking Through the "Encrustations of Interpretation"', *Diplomatic History*, 12, 2 (1988), pp. 341–56

Jones, P. 'George Brown', in A. Shlaim, P. Jones and K. Sainsbury (eds), *British Foreign Secretaries since 1945* (London: David & Charles, 1977), pp. 205–20

Kane, E. 'The Myth of Sabotage: British Policy Towards European Integration, 1955–6', in E. du Réau (ed.), *Europe des Elites? Europe des Peuples? La Construction de l'Espace Européen 1945–1960* (Paris: Presses de la Sorbonne Nouvelle, 1999), pp. 291–301

Keatinge, P. 'Ireland and the World, 1957–82', in F. Litton (ed.), *Unequal Achievement* (Dublin: Institute of Public Administration, 1982), pp. 225–40

Kent, J. 'Bevin's Imperialism and the Idea of Euro-Africa, 1945–49', in M. Dockrill and J. W. Young (eds), *British Foreign Policy, 1945–56* (Basingstoke: Macmillan, 1989), pp. 47–76

Kent, J. and Young, J. W. 'British Policy Overseas: The "Third Force" and the Origins of NATO – In Search of a New Perspective', in B. Heuser and R. O'Neill (eds), *Securing Peace in Europe, 1945–62: Thoughts for the Post Cold War Era* (Basingstoke: Macmillan, 1989), pp. 41–61

Lee, S. 'Germany and the First Enlargement Negotiations, 1961–1963', in A. Deighton and A. S. Milward (eds), *Widening, Deepening and Acceleration: The European Economic Community 1957–1963* (Brussels: Nomos-Verlag, 1999), pp. 211–25

Ludlow, N. P. 'Challenging French Leadership in Europe: Germany, Italy, the Netherlands and the Outbreak of the Empty Chair Crisis of 1965–1966', *Contemporary European History*, 8, 2 (1999), pp. 231–48

Ludlow, N. P. 'Constancy and Flirtation: Germany, Britain, and the EEC, 1956–1972', in J. Noakes, P. Wende and J. Wright (eds), *Britain and Germany in Europe 1949–1990* (Oxford: Oxford University Press, forthcoming)

Ludlow, N. P. 'Influence and Vulnerability: The Role of the European Commission', in R. Griffiths and S. Ward (eds), *Courting the Common Market: The First Attempt to Enlarge the EEC, 1961–3* (London: Lothian Foundation Press, 1996), pp. 139–55

Masala, C. 'Die Bundesrepublik Deutschland, Italien und der Beitritt Großbritanniens zur EWG', *Zeitgeschichte*, 25, 1–2 (1998), pp. 46–69

McKinlay, A., Mercer, H. and Rollings, N. 'Reluctant Europeans? The

Federation of British Industries and European Integration 1945–63', *Business History,* 42, 4 (2000), pp. 91–116

Melissen, J. and Zeeman, B., 'Britain and Western Europe, 1945–51: Opportunities Lost?', *International Affairs,* 63, 1 (1987), pp. 81–95

Morgan, K. O. 'The Wilson Years: 1964–1970', in N. Tiratsoo (ed.), *From Blitz to Blair: A New History of Britain since 1939* (London: Phoenix, 1998), pp. 132–62

Mottershead, P. 'Industrial Policy', in F. T. Blackaby (ed.), *British Economic Policy 1960–74* (Cambridge: Cambridge University Press, 1978), pp. 418–83

Murphy, G. 'Ireland's View of Western Europe in the 1950s', in M. Kennedy and J. M. Skelly (eds), *Irish Foreign Policy 1919–66* (Dublin: Four Courts Press, 2000), pp. 247–65

Nugent, N. 'British Public Opinion and the European Community', in S. George (ed.), *Britain and the European Community: The Politics of Semi-Detachment* (Oxford: Clarendon Press, 1992), pp. 172–201

Oppenheimer, P. 'Europe and the Common Market', *National Westminster Bank Quarterly Review* (February 1971), pp. 5–21

Perkins, B. 'Unequal Partners: The Truman Administration and Great Britain', in W. R. Louis and H. D. Bull (eds), *The Special Relationship: Anglo-American Relations Since 1945* (Oxford: Clarendon Press, 1989), pp. 43–64

Philip, A. B. 'British Pressure Groups and the European Community', in S. George (ed.), *Britain and the European Community: The Politics of Semi-Detachment* (Oxford: Clarendon Press, 1992), pp. 149–71

Rollings, N. 'British Industry and European Integration 1961–73: From First Application to Final Membership', *Business and Economic History,* 27, 2 (1998), pp. 444–54

Ruano, L. 'Elites, Public Opinion and Pressure Groups: The British Position in Agriculture During Negotiations for Accession to the EC, 1961–1975', *Journal of European Integration History,* 5, 1 (1999), pp. 7–22

Sainsbury, K. 'Selwyn Lloyd', in A. Shlaim, P. Jones and K. Sainsbury (eds), *British Foreign Secretaries Since 1945* (London: David & Charles, 1977), pp. 117–43

Schwarz, J. and Lambert, G. 'The Voting Behaviour of British Conservative Backbenchers', in S. Patterson and J. Walker (eds), *Comparative Legislative Behaviour: Frontiers of Research* (London: Wiley, 1972), pp. 79–80

Shlaim, A. 'The Foreign Secretary and the Making of Foreign Policy', in A. Shlaim, P. Jones and K. Sainsbury (eds), *British Foreign Secretaries Since 1945* (London: David & Charles, 1977), pp. 13–26

Smith, J. 'The 1975 Referendum', *Journal of European Integration History*, 5, 1 (1999), pp. 41–56

Smith, S. and Smith, M. 'The Analytical Background: Approaches to the Study of Foreign Policy', in S. Smith, M. Smith and B. White (eds), *British Foreign Policy: Tradition, Change and Transformation* (London: Hyman, 1988), pp. 3–23

Spence, J. 'Movements in the Public Mood: 1961–75', in R. Jowell and G. Hoinville (eds), *Britain into Europe: Public Opinion and the EEC, 1961–75* (London: Croom Helm, 1976), pp. 18–36

Straw, S. and Young, J. W. 'The Wilson Government and the Demise of TSR-2', *Journal of Strategic Studies*, 20, 4 (1997), pp. 18–44

Varsori, A. 'The Art of Mediation: Italy and Britain's Attempt to Join the EEC, 1960–3', in A. Deighton and A. S. Milward (eds), *Widening, Deepening and Acceleration: The European Economic Community 1957–1963* (Brussels: Nomos-Verlag, 1999), pp. 241–56

Warner, G. 'The Labour Governments and the Unity of Western Europe, 1945–51', in R. Ovendale (ed.), *The Foreign Policy of the British Labour Governments, 1945–1951* (Leicester: Leicester University Press, 1984), pp. 61–82

Watt, D. C. 'Demythologising the Eisenhower Era', in W. R. Louis and H. D. Bull (eds), *The Special Relationship: Anglo-American Relations Since 1945* (Oxford: Clarendon Press, 1989), pp. 65–85

Watt, D. C. 'Introduction: The Anglo-American Relations', in W. R. Louis and H. D. Bull (eds), *The Special Relationship: Anglo-American Relations Since 1945* (Oxford: Clarendon Press, 1989), pp. 1–14

Wilkes, G. 'The First Failure to Steer Britain into the European Communities: An Introduction', in G. Wilkes (ed.), *Britain's Failure to Enter the European Community 1961–63: The Enlargement Negotiations and Crises in European, Atlantic and Commonwealth Relations* (London: Frank Cass, 1997), pp. 1–32

Wilkes, G. and Wring, D. 'The British Press and European Integration: 1948 to 1996', in D. Baker and D. Seawright (eds), *Britain For and Against Europe: British Politics and the Question of European Integration* (Oxford: Clarendon Press, 1998), pp. 185–205

Williams, T. D. 'Irish Foreign Policy 1949–1969', in J. J. Lee (ed.), *Ireland* (Dublin: Gill/Macmillan, 1979), pp. 136–51

Wright, J. 'The Role of Britain in West German Foreign Policy since 1949', *German Politics*, 5, 1 (April 1996), pp. 26–42

Wrigley, C. 'Now You See It, Now You Don't: Harold Wilson and Labour's Foreign Policy 1964–70', in R. Coopey, S. Fielding and N. Tiratsoo (eds), *The Wilson Governments 1964–1970* (London: Pinter, 1993), pp. 123–35

Wyn Rees, G. 'British Strategic Thinking and Europe, 1964–1970',

Journal of European Integration History, 5, 1 (1999), pp. 57–73

Young, J. W. 'The Wilson Government and the Debate over Arms to South Africa in 1964', *Contemporary British History*, 12, 3 (1998), pp. 62–86

Younger, K. 'Public Opinion and British Foreign Policy', *International Affairs* 40, 1 (1964), pp. 22–33

THESES AND DISSERTATIONS

Ashford, N. 'The Conservative Party and European Integration, 1945–75' (PhD thesis, University of Warwick, 1985)

Bange, O. 'Picking Up the Pieces: Schröder's Working Programme for the European Communities and the Solution to the 1963 Crisis' (PhD thesis, University of London, 1997)

Daddow, O. J. 'Rhetoric and Reality: The Historiography of British European Policy, 1945–73' (PhD thesis, University of Nottingham, 2000)

Wallace, H. 'The Domestic Policy Making Implications of the Labour Government's Application to the EEC, 1964–1970' (PhD thesis, Manchester University, 1976)

Index

de Gaulle and, 12, 78–9, 81, 84, 98, 107, 162, 172, 178, 180; Denmark and, 183; Foreign Office and, 81; France withdraws from, 12, 78–9, 81, 84, 98, 172, 174; German–American–British talks, 178; Germany and, 22–3, 80–1, 172, 174, 176–7, 180, 184; Heath and, 64–5; Ireland and, 228; Johnson and, 172–6, 181–2; Labour left and, 43; Norway and, 183; NPG, 180; technological cooperation in, 100–2 *passim*; tensions within, 22; Wilson and, 81; Wormser on, 161
North Borneo, 190
Northedge, Fred, 6
Northern Ireland, 69
Norway: and NATO, 183; applies to join EEC, 137, 237
Nuclear Planning Group (NPG), 180

Odysseus, Wilson compared to, 15
Official Committee on the Approach to Europe (EURO), 83, 104, 108
Ojukwu, Odumegwu, 199
Okigbo, Pius, 196–7
O'Neill, Sir Con, 197; and CBI, 126; and EEC, 86, 206; and EEID, 75, 82, 83, 87, 89; and France, 159; and Nigeria, 196; at Chequers meeting on EEC, 82; EURO Committee, 82–4; on withdrawal from east of Suez, 192, 193
One Nation Group, 67–8
Organisation for European Economic Cooperation (OEEC), 137, 140; France and, 137; Ireland and, 228
Organisation of African Unity (OAU), 200
Ostpolitik: Britain and, 23, 212; Germany and, 212, 222
Overseas Committee (of the CBI), 126–7
Owen, David, founds SDP, 18

P–1154, 97
Pacific Rim, 190
Pakistan, 11
Palliser, Michael: and Wilson's tactics, 84, 87, 100, 105, 106, 168, 169, 204; 217; attitude to Europe, 155; techno-

logical cooperation, 100, 102, 105
Parliamentary Foreign Affairs Committee, 58
Parliamentary Labour Party (PLP), 39, 44, 205; and Nigeria, 199; and South Africa, 203; debates on Europe, 47; on withdrawal from east of Suez, 191–2, 193; Wilson and, 46–7, 52
Parr, Helen, 20, 247
Pears, Gordon: at the CRD, 59, 65, 66–7
Peart, Fred: at Chequers, 44; and second application, 45
Persian Gulf, 165
Petit Trianon, 166
Peyrefitte, Alain, 157
Philips, 96
Pimlott, Ben, 15, 46, 205
Pinder, John: and EIU, 4; and Federal Trust, 5; and Layton, 4; on Camps, 6
Pisani, Edgar, 156, 164
Plato, 228, 229
Plowden Report, 155–6
Polaris, 107, 174
Policy Committee on Foreign Affairs, 58, 65
Pompidou, Georges: and British membership of EEC, 147, 148, 154, 160; and Wilson, 162–3
Ponting, Clive, 11, 12, 15
Poseidon, 107
Powell, Enoch: and Europe, 52, 57, 69, 70
press (British): and technological cooperation, 100; attitude to Europe, 4, 42, 59, 64
'probe': British diplomacy and, 85–7, 89, 151, 198, 217; Brown and, 85, 165–6; Cabinet agrees to, 45, 84, 159, 164; Conservative Party and, 56, 60–7; Crossman and, 193; Foreign Office and, 82, 84; Heath and, 63–4; Johnson and, 173, 178, 179; of Belgium, 105; of France, 105, 166, 193, 218; of Germany, 218; of Italy, 105, 166; Wilson and, 14, 20, 41, 45, 47, 60, 62, 79, 80, 85, 100, 103–4, 105, 151–2, 165–6, 173, 178, 217, 246
public opinion (British): and first British application to EEC, 49;